Political Philosophy

An Introduction

This book by Richard G. Stevens is a comprehensive introduction to the nature of political philosophy. It offers definitions of philosophy and politics, showing the tension between the two and the origin of political philosophy as a means of resolution of that tension. Plato and Aristotle are examined to see the search for the best political order. Inquiry is then made into political philosophy's new tension, brought about by the growth of revealed religion in the Middle Ages. It then examines the changes introduced by modernity and gives an overview of postmodern political thought. The book covers the most influential philosophers and directs readers to the classics of political philosophy, guiding them in studying these key texts. It is an approachable introduction to a complex subject, not just a history of it. It is a point of entry into the subject for students and for others as well.

Since his retirement from National Defense University in 1994, Richard G. Stevens has taught as Adjunct Professor of Government at American University. He previously taught at the University of Washington and at Georgetown University. He is the author, most recently, of *Reason and History in Judicial Judgment* (2008) and *The American Constitution and Its Provenance* (1997) and is the editor of the third edition of *American Political Thought* (2010), as well as the author of numerous journal articles in the fields of political philosophy and constitutional law.

Political Philosophy

An Introduction

RICHARD G. STEVENS
American University

CAMBRIDGE
UNIVERSITY PRESS

CAMBRIDGE UNIVERSITY PRESS
Cambridge, New York, Melbourne, Madrid, Cape Town, Singapore,
São Paulo, Delhi, Dubai, Tokyo, Mexico City

Cambridge University Press
32 Avenue of the Americas, New York, NY 10013-2473, USA

www.cambridge.org
Information on this title: www.cambridge.org/9780521169011

First published 2011

Printed in the United States of America

A catalog record for this publication is available from the British Library.

Library of Congress Cataloging in Publication data

Stevens, Richard G., 1925–
Political philosophy : an introduction / Richard G. Stevens.
p.   cm.
Includes bibliographical references and index.
ISBN 978-1-107-00043-8 (hardback) – ISBN 978-0-521-16901-1 (pbk.)
1. Political science – Philosophy.   I. Title.
JA71.S788   2010
320.01 – dc22   2010024895

ISBN 978-1-107-00043-8 Hardback
ISBN 978-0-521-16901-1 Paperback

in gratitude
this book
is dedicated to the memory of
LEO STRAUSS

Contents

Acknowledgments

A young man whom I encountered in 1978 had enlisted in 1960 in one of the armed services. He had comported himself then in a manner altogether contrary to the norms of the service. He had indulged in certain forbidden chemical substances; he had consorted with certain then-forbidden partners; he had deserted and was apprehended some 420 days later. The grade inflation in academe against which Harvey C. Mansfield, Jr., has protested had already found a home in the armed services by 1960, so, instead of a court-martial resulting in a prison sentence and a Dishonorable Discharge, the young man was given an "Undesirable Discharge," one of an array of administrative separations that had been developed as the changes in the mores of the country took their toll on the armed forces. Then, in the 1970s, a kind of general amnesty came into being that forgave nearly all past military sins, and the services were required to establish discharge review boards. The young man mentioned applied for an "upgrade" to an Honorable Discharge, as though he had done something or other honorable. His application in its entirety was:

The [service] gave me an Undesirable Discharge. It knew I was undesirable when it recruited me. It tried to reform me but failed. Am I to be held responsible for other people's failures?

Either the applicant was clever or quite at the other end of the intelligence scale. I fall somewhere in between those extremes myself, so a word of explanation regarding my dedication of this book to the memory of Leo Strauss is in order. Through seven courses over a three-year period and a generous allotment of office-hour time, Mr. Strauss tried to educate me, but at best, he succeeded in only small measure. Am I to be held responsible for his failure? You bet! It takes two to tango. Although I express my gratitude for having had as my teacher someone who was perhaps the greatest figure in political philosophy since Machiavelli and whose skill in the classroom was without equal, the reader should note my ready admission that all of the errors herein are my own. What I have gotten right is almost wholly a lesson learned from Leo Strauss. One or two boasts may be allowed. I did learn from him that I ought to eschew academic fads, that I ought to read mostly really serious books, and that I ought to read them seriously – and over and over again.

Thanks also are gladly given to Karl Cerny, George Carey, and James V. Schall, who were gracious hosts during my four years as a Visiting Professor in the Government Department at Georgetown University, where I taught repeatedly the course Elements of Political Theory, which led me to want to write this book.

James H. Nichols of Claremont McKenna College, Leon Craig of the University of Alberta, and Peter Schotten of Augustana College in Sioux Falls, critiqued the manuscript, and Thomas K. Lindsay, in his critique, lavished thorough and constructive commentary. Of course, these four scholars are also absolved of blame for remaining errors. This absolution may sound like boilerplate to the reader, but it is genuine and obligatory.

Waveland Press granted permission to excerpt several passages from the fine translation by Leo Paul S. de Alvarez of Machiavelli's *Prince*, and Ralph Lerner granted permission to excerpt from his and the late Muhsin Mahdi's *Medieval Political Philosophy* passages from Fauzi M. Najjar's translation of al Farabi's *The Political Regime* and passages from George F. Hourani's translation of Averroës' *The Decisive Treatise, Determining What the Connection Is between Religion and Philosophy*.

Beatrice Rehl and Emily Spangler of the New York office of Cambridge University Press provided ample encouragement and guidance during the development of this book. Shana Meyer, Senior Project Manager of Aptara, Inc., ushered me through the production phase with patient understanding. Katherine Faydash, proofreader, saved me from a thousand errors. She must not be blamed for my obstinate clinging to a few of them. My great thanks go to all of these generous people.

Finally, my wife, who endured countless slights over the past five years, deserves a couple of words of gratitude. Thanks, Norma.

Prologue

Perhaps the greatest figure in political philosophy since the sixteenth century once remarked that thought could only be understood thinking. Among the things that might be inferred from that remark is that the proper way to study political philosophy is to read primary texts (the works of the primary figures in political philosophy) rather than secondary works (textbooks written by university professors hoping for tenure). The source of that advice said elsewhere that we are compelled to live with books but that life is so short that there is time only for the greatest books. He did not mean that lighter reading was forbidden, but only that mere textbooks should not be mistaken for the genuine texts, the works of only those who deserve to be called philosophers. First, textbooks can mislead readers into thinking that they have read philosophy. Second, textbooks can render readers' minds numb and shut them off from philosophy once and for all. Students need to acquire, no doubt after many mistakes, a discriminating judgment as to which primary texts are to be believed and which not – which, that is to say, pass as genuine philosophic texts but are in fact only pompous obfuscations. This takes patience and perspiration. Nor did he mean that secondary works – commentaries on the primary texts – are not useful. All of us are aided in our reading of the primary texts by seeing how qualified commentators interpret them. Caution and respectful skepticism are the keys.

This book means to be guided by the foregoing advice. Its intent is limited. There are now some six billion people on the planet. There are not nearly so many authors of the "greatest books." Perhaps only a few hundred or only several dozen may properly be called philosophers. Given the corruption of the word "philosophy" during the past two centuries, it may be difficult to credit this assertion, but the beginning student is asked to be patient. The list of authors of the primary works in political philosophy or the best of the commentaries includes Plato, Aristotle, Xenophon, Cicero, al-Farabi, Averroës, Maimonides, Aquinas, Machiavelli, Hobbes, Locke, Montesquieu,

Rousseau, Kant, Hegel, Tocqueville, and Nietzsche. If you multiplied this number by six or eight, it just might be that you would have named all those who deserve the name of "political philosopher." If you multiplied the list by a few hundred, you might include also all the first-rate commentators and those who fall in the gray area between philosopher and commentator. Why, then, can it be said that life is only long enough to read the best books? The answer is that there are easy books and hard books. Genuine works in political philosophy fall into the hard category. They have to be read with sticking care, and they have to be read over and over and over to move the reader's mind sufficiently. They also have to be read with appropriate skepticism, because they disagree with one another. Likely, some of them are closer to and some further from the truth.

Most of us have some sense of our limitations. Most of us know that we will never find our names listed with those mentioned in the preceding paragraph. Why, then, should we bother to study political philosophy? The first answer is that there is no litmus test for the calling of political philosopher. The ranks of philosophy are, like the major leagues of all the high callings, fixed by elimination. A confident prediction cannot be made at the start as to who will finish in the gold class. Furthermore, it might be asked, what good is skepticism to us if, by definition, most of us will fall in the lesser ranks? Will not the mistaken philosophers be so clever that they will fool us lesser folk? There is a passage in Plato's *Republic* that helps to guide us.[1] Plato has Socrates explain to Glaucon and Adeimantus at 473c

---

[1] There are innumerable editions of Plato's *Republic* (about which title more will be said later) in dozens of languages. It would be impossible to cite a passage in that book conveniently except for the fact that there is an accepted, standard pagination. In the sixteenth century, a printer and editor in Geneva named Robert Étienne (or Éstienne; in Latin, Stephanus) published the first complete collection of the works of Plato in Greek. The pages are numbered consecutively straight through the entire body of works, and each page is divided into five parts: a, b, c, d, and e. The Stephanus pagination came to be recognized as the standard. That pagination appears in the margins of all proper editions of any writing of Plato, in whatever language it happens to appear. The assertion by Socrates that until philosophers are kings there will be no rest from political ills appears at page 153 in Allan Bloom's English translation of the *Republic* published by Basic Books in New York in 1968, but that citation will be of no use to a student in Santiago, Chile, who happens to read English but who happens to have no access to any English translation of the *Republic*, let alone that by Bloom. That student might be better served by a citation to page 318 of the *traducción directa del griego* by Antonio Camarero published in 1963 by Editorial Universitaria de Buenos Aires, but consider the burden that would be borne by an author who wanted to alert any reader anywhere to the place to which he refers. The problem is practically insoluble without the standard pagination. The full, standard citation in this instance would be "Plato, *Republic*, 473c," or, because the work itself has been identified in the body of the text, a simple reference to "473c" is sufficient. This means that the passage will be found at, or beginning at, part c of the Stephanus page number 473. An even more precise citation would include the line number, although, because English syntax, for example, differs from classical Greek syntax, even a scrupulously literal translation will make a line citation in English vary from one English translation to

that philosophers must be kings, and, at 487b, after some elaboration of this remark, Adeimantus says, "Socrates, no one could contradict you in this," but, he continues, one can be misled little by little by a wise or a clever speaker, and "the truth is not affected by this." Socrates agrees. Here again, patience, industry, caution, and respectful skepticism must be our armor. Political philosophy is enticing. It appeals to the young because it is iconoclastic and intoxicating. The student is exhilarated by a sense of belonging to a marvelous and clever conspiracy. This has its good side, but it is dangerous – even dangerous to philosophy itself. It is no wonder that Aristotle, with a poker face, treated the arguments of Plato's *Republic* as though they were prescriptions to be acted upon directly. Perhaps he did so to defuse the smirking overconfidence and destructive rashness of some of Plato's followers, including some of us present-day followers. As if in response to the hesitation of Adeimantus when confronted by the shocking proposal of Socrates, Martin Diamond (1919–77), one of the finest commentators on the political thought of the American Founding, once remarked that it was a great satisfaction that by hard work one could come to a sounder conclusion than that reached by someone with greater natural gifts. Thus, those of us of more modest ability can by hard work approach the writings of the finest intellects with caution and modesty, but without fear. For most of us, this approach promises that we might become worthy students of philosophy, and this may well turn out to be all to our good, not to speak of the general good. A few may become professors, and some of those good ones. Once in a blue moon, a philosopher may emerge from among our number. Further reflection on this will best be deferred until we consider first Plato's and then al-Farabi's remarks about the different sorts of people there are.

   The best way to approach philosophy, then, looks to be to take a vow of poverty, to abandon all worldly delights, and to devote oneself to a lifetime of industrious study of the greatest books. Sure! The best way to do *that* would be to read those books in their original languages. That means that before one embarked on a study of philosophy one would first have to learn all the languages of philosophy. To leave aside such languages as Sanskrit, Aramaic, classical Mandarin, Farsi, Hindi, and a few others would mean that one would have to master Latin, Greek, Hebrew, Arabic, French, Italian, and German. Again, sure! Indeed, the best scholars have done precisely that, but

---

another. In addition, because the page width of one edition of the Greek text will vary from that of another edition, the number of lines in a part of a page in one Greek edition will vary. Thus, in the case of Bloom's English translation, a complete citation to the whole of this sentence (which is longer than the fragment of it mentioned earlier) that Socrates speaks to Glaucon would be "473c11–d5." Paul Shorey's English translation in the Loeb Classical Library edition of the *Republic* appears on recto (right-hand) pages opposite the Greek text on the verso (left-hand) pages. A citation of that sentence to the Greek text in that edition (but not to some other edition of the Greek text) would be 473c9–d9.

to suggest this to all is to raise an insurmountable obstacle for most. Whether such obstacles are salutary is one of the questions before us. For the moment, we can put this aside by pointing the student to excellent translations. Even this route, however, requires at least rudimentary inklings of the original languages so as to distinguish the good from the bad translations. A hint of the problem can be derived from an illustration. Niccolò Machiavelli (1469–1527) wrote some plays, some historical works, and some works in political philosophy. Within this last category the two most widely known works are *The Prince*[2] and *The Discourses* (in Italian, *Discorsi sopra la Prima Deca di Tito Livio*, that is, Discourses on the First Ten [Books] of Titus Livius). Titus Livy, as one would call him in English, was the preeminent historian of Rome. Machiavelli's purpose seems to be to take Livy as the authority on Roman history, but surreptitiously he undercuts the authority of Livy. In 1950, a two-volume English translation of the *Discorsi* by Fr. Leslie J. Walker was published by Routledge and Kegan Paul of London. It is a beautiful edition, but there are problems. In the second paragraph of Chapter 4 of Book II, according to Fr. Walker's translation, Machiavelli says of a portion of the Italian peninsula, "this district was occupied by the Gauls." Machiavelli does indeed say that the place from which the occupiers came was called "Gallia" – that is, Gaul – but he does not call those who occupied part of the Italian peninsula "Gauls." He calls them "Franciosi," that is, "the French." Now, of course, there were no French in those earlier days.[3] The translator has thus "corrected" the author. He makes the same "correction" several times in Chapter 8, but shortly after these instances, Machiavelli's Italian text acknowledges that there were no French in the period of the Roman Empire being discussed. In other words, Machiavelli knows that he is incorrectly calling the "Gauls" the "French." When Fr. Walker "corrects" Machiavelli's "errors," he hides from us the fact that Machiavelli is deliberately calling a people by the wrong name. He thus gets between us and Machiavelli. If he translated what Machiavelli wrote rather than what he thinks Machiavelli ought to have written, we would see a problem. We would see that Machiavelli is "up to something." If we are kept from seeing the problem, we cannot begin to search for the answer. Many translations of the great primary texts suffer from this well-intended and unconscious injury. "Translators" who do not translate but who rather

---

[2] We have become so accustomed to calling this book *The Prince* that some Italian editions now give it the Italian title *Il Principe*. In fact, the original title is *De Principatibus*, which is Latin and could be translated into English as *Of Principate* or *Of Princedom*. In other words, the original title points not to an individual but to practices or offices or doings. This may be a trifle, but many trifles add up to a burden.

[3] The Franks were a Germanic people who settled in the Rhine River region in the third century A.D. The Franks then moved westward from the Rhine into what is now France. Clovis (c. 466–511) established late in the fifth century a Frankish kingdom there. "France" is the descendant of that kingdom and "the French" are the heirs of that establishment.

render into English what they are confident the author "meant" to say do the reader a disservice. Philosophy is a business difficult enough as it is without being further darkened by good intentions. One must remember one's parents' admonition that the road to hell is paved with good intentions. For a brief statement of the necessity of the most literal translation possible, one should read the preface to Allan Bloom's translation of Plato's *Republic*.

As for commentary, there is a great deal of it, and much of it is helpful. Al-Farabi (870–950) wrote in Arabic a commentary on Plato. Thomas Aquinas (1225–74) wrote in Latin commentaries on Aristotle. Their writings are of such a high order that we call al-Farabi and Aquinas philosophers, not just commentators. Nonetheless, much of their work is in the form of commentary on the works of others. A good deal of the writings of the period that we call "the Middle Ages" is of this kind. Even commentary, however, has to be approached with the same caution and respectful skepticism that is appropriate in the case of the primary sources. The distinction between primary texts and commentary is confounded by the fact that over the centuries works have been written that are original in nature but have the appearance of commentary on the ancient texts of Plato and Aristotle. This makes sense, because one can hardly write in the field of political philosophy without taking Plato and Aristotle into account. The graduate student of political philosophy and the more serious undergraduate are well served by a compendious collection of commentary. Such a compendium is distinct from an attempt to write "the history" of political philosophy, an attempt that falls too often into the error of treating philosophy as though it were a product of some sort of stream of history. It is not an "era" or an "age" that thinks, however. It is a thinker. Much of that intellectual movement that came to fruition in the nineteenth century and came to maturity in the twentieth tried to cleanse history of generals, heroes, and thinkers. It was not Plato who mounted the great critique of Greece and its thought, so this drift of argument contends. Plato was just a mouthpiece. Greekness wrote the works we attribute to Plato. There may have been philosophy, but there were no philosophers. It is a small step to the denial of philosophy itself. We shall have to deal more thoroughly with this problem later on. For the moment, one can satisfy the need for commentary initially by consulting a collection edited by Leo Strauss and Joseph Cropsey. It is titled, curiously, *History of Political Philosophy*, the third edition of which was published in 1987 by the University of Chicago Press. It is a history only in the sense that the several philosophers dealt with are presented in the chronological order of their lives. It consists of essays on some thirty-eight thinkers written by some thirty-two scholars.

Now then, we turn to the purpose of (and so the apology for or defense of) this book. As the nineteenth century progressed, the American liberal arts college came into full form. It was an improvement on and follow-up to the high school, the latter being not quite high enough. It was reminiscent of the

French *école supérieure* or the German *gymnasium*. It was democracy's answer to the lack of that cultivation provided to the sons of the upper reaches of society in aristocratic regimes, that cultivation often having been tendered by live-in tutors, learned men kept on retainer by great, old families. In due course the American "college" wedged its way in as a postsecondary institution as distinct from a simply improved secondary school. By the latter part of the nineteenth century, and surely by the middle of the twentieth, most of the liberal arts colleges and most of the universities in the United States required every student seeking a bachelor of arts degree to take two courses in philosophy: Logic and Ethics. In many cases, a student majoring (or even minoring) in political science, as that discipline developed at the end of the nineteenth and the beginning of the twentieth century, was required also to take a two-semester sequence in the history of political philosophy – or, as it came to be called, "political theory." Calling the subject political theory turned out to be more than a mere change of language. By the beginning of World War II in 1939, which the United States entered in December of 1941, these practices were pretty well settled in American colleges and universities. In 1934, Cohen and Nagel confidently asserted that, although "formal logic has in recent times been the object of radical and spirited attacks from many and diverse quarters, it continues, and will probably long continue, to be one of the most frequently given courses in colleges and universities here and abroad."[4] By the beginning of the twenty-first century, curricular changes had shown that confidence to be ill-placed.

We cannot blame Cohen and Nagel for not being prescient, although, soon after World War I (1914–18), the character and ambitions of young Americans had been shown no longer to be what they had been before that war. World War I (in the twenties and thirties, we just called it "the World War" or "the Great War") introduced a profound change into American life that was acknowledged by Cole Porter's 1934 song "Anything Goes."

Porter's song indicated that large moral and cultural upheavals had occurred. Another great change was wrought by World War II. Before that war, a rather small portion of Americans attended colleges. Many did not finish high school, and it was not considered a character flaw to leave school after the tenth grade to find work. If there had then been such a characterization as "dropout," it surely was not heard much. That expression has now become a kind of accusation. Since that war, many incentives (both of the carrot and the stick sort) have been introduced, and it has become the general expectation that everyone is entitled to and surely should get a college degree in something or other. Indeed, it has reached the point at which the fact that a portion of society is still without such degrees is

---

[4] Morris R. Cohen (1880–1947) and Ernest Nagel (1901–85), *An Introduction to Logic and Scientific Method*, New York, 1934, Harcourt, Brace, p. iii.

regarded as some sort of scandalous failure of government or, worse, some deliberate denial of a natural, constitutional, or statutory right. Everyone is told that life without a college degree is a dead end. Such a life is doomed to end in economic shambles. The problem with all this is that there are natural limits to how much people can be improved by schooling. It was true before 1940 and it is still true that a great many people have had all the formal schooling they can stomach by the time they are fifteen or sixteen. There are no longer places to "shelve" these people, places such as apprenticeships and trade schools, so most of them go to college (or, as would be said in England or Canada, "go to university"; many secondary schools in Canada, by the way, are still called "collegiate institutes"). Perforce, colleges have become whatever their inmates can and are willing to do, and the number of universities and professors have increased at a lagomorphic rate. It once was the case that a university concerned itself with the whole universe of higher intellectual pursuits and, except for the "learned professions," nothing else. Some, after the fashion of the continental universities, did not even run lodging houses or dining facilities, nor did any of them field thinly disguised professional athletic teams. The university was divided into parts as a kind of division of academic labor. The core of the premodern university, the university of the Middle Ages, had been the pursuit of philosophy, divided into faculties of natural philosophy and moral and political philosophy. Necessarily, these studies were augmented by languages, linguistics, literature, and history, and, in distinct parts of the university, the learned professions – law, medicine, and divinity – were pursued. Even these things, insofar as their practice was concerned, fell outside the universities' reach. Law, for example, was perfected in apprenticeships with journeymen barristers and solicitors. As far as one's immersion in study was concerned, this legal apprenticeship was more like going to sea than like going to school. It was still the case in every state in the United States well into the latter half of the twentieth century that one could be admitted to the bar after "reading law" in an apprenticeship to an established lawyer. Robert H. Jackson (1892–1954), who served as an Associate Justice of the U.S. Supreme Court from 1941 until his death in 1954, was the last person to sit on that Court without having taken a degree from a law school. He had "read law" in a law office. No one would deny to him recognition as one of the most accomplished lawyers of his day.

Before World War II, a common route to the profession of schoolteacher was to go directly from secondary school to what was called a "normal school" to spend a year or two learning something of the practice of pedagogy. After the war, those schools helped to accommodate the great influx of additional college students by undergoing a metamorphosis and coming to be called "junior colleges." Then they came to be called "colleges" and then some of them "universities," but few if any showed a similarity to the institutions that had borne that name in the first half of the century. It is doubtful if any of them has ever become such as to be spoken of in the same breath with Oxford, the Sorbonne, Heidelberg, Harvard, Chicago, Michigan, or California.

Also before the war, there were in many American cities institutions called "secretarial schools." A young woman who did not become a wife and a mother by her early twenties was by the custom of those days largely confined to nursing, teaching, or secretarial work, and many prepared for this last-named occupation after learning grammar, spelling, and arithmetic in primary and secondary schools by attending a secretarial school to learn typewriting, stenography, filing, bookkeeping, and other business practices. (Some public high schools had introduced courses of this kind as electives.) With the help of changes in accreditation and licensing practices, many of these secretarial schools, with minimal augmentations of their curricula or their faculties, came to be known as colleges, and then universities, but anyone who enrolls in one of them with the hope of studying ancient Near Eastern languages, metaphysics, the history of the Christian Church, or nuclear physics would be looked upon as a fool if not as a downright troublemaker.

This institutional inflation and flood of students has been accompanied by a diminution in substance. There are now old-line liberal arts colleges that no longer require Logic or Ethics or even *offer* courses in Latin or Greek. There is at least one noted university in a great American city where one can be awarded a graduate degree in journalism without ever having been required to read a book – any book. It is now possible in some highly regarded universities in America to be granted the degree of doctor of philosophy in political science without taking a single course in political philosophy or passing a doctoral field examination in what is now called "political theory."

Maybe this is in some respects all for the best. Maybe, given the flooding of the colleges and universities with students who have no inclination to study philosophy – some with no inclination to study anything – the consequence would be that those students who are truly interested would find their classes filled up with the disinclined, thereby lowering the quality of discourse. Perhaps, however, it would be wholesome for colleges, given the openness of their admissions practices, to interpose certain hurdles to be jumped on the way to a degree. Perhaps a rigorous obstacle course should be in place. Perhaps earning a degree ought to be almost as difficult intellectually as making the team is difficult physically. Is it not quaint that things are now such that a suggestion like this sounds quaint? In any case, the full resolution of this educational and political problem is the proper business of some other book written for some other readership. Nonetheless, something akin to this problem, and in fact a subspecies of it, is proper to be addressed here.

If, as we believe, political philosophy is a most difficult and a most high calling, and, as a student's tuition-paying father might allege, it is "not good for anything," in that it does not promise the acquisition of a comforting investment portfolio, and if it is a seductive entrance to a pit that is fraught with danger – danger not just in the figurative sense – maybe the most merciful thing would be to hide it in some inaccessible corner of the university. Maybe the academic authorities should never encourage students to find that corner. Maybe the university should not allow those who stumble upon it to enter. Maybe those once there should be forced to undergo harsh and distasteful studies that, unless they are determined and worthy students, will drive them out so that, over refreshments, they advise their fellow students not to go near the place and report to them that the study of political philosophy subjects one to encounters with eccentric, old, dead fellows who prattle a lot of gibberish. Maybe! Maybe while this is only a half-sensible suggestion, it is at least half sensible. I do not pretend to be of such a stature that I may rightly declare it so, however. Let us, therefore, end this prologue on a more open and hopeful note.

Given what has happened to the American academy, and given what American students bring with them to that academy, political philosophy has one foot in the grave unless those properly drawn to it can receive some direction to its point of entry; some encouragement in fact to enter and then to study; some guidance in that study; and, if all that fails, some gentle and generous direction to the exit for those not truly fashioned for the trade. That guidance and that encouragement are the purposes of this book. It is written with the confident knowledge that it cannot be a substitute for the primary texts. One can, of course, get through college reading CliffsNotes, but an intelligently selfish person knows that doing so is about as satisfying as cheating at solitaire. This book cannot even pretend to take the place of first-rate commentaries such as those just suggested. It is animated only by the modest hope that it might provide some guidance and some encouragement to that fairly noticeable minority of students suited to acquire a substantial introduction to the field such as courses in primary texts would offer. To reach the level of useful guidance, it must in some cases offer secondary analyses – that is, commentary on the primary texts – particularly of the sort that will help the beginning student to enter into the field. In other instances, this book will simply be tertiary. It will gather some observations from good secondary authors and pass them along. This will be particularly true when dealing with those primary authors who are called "the pre-Socratics." Because those particular philosophers are so difficult to master that we shall be compelled to initiate some speculation as to why those pre-Socratics are lumped together and called by that name.

This is a book with a modest aim. From the outside, it wants to delineate the nature, origin, and critical changes in political philosophy. It wants to raise constructively the question as to what political philosophy is and what it is not. Against the accepted views of the moment, it wants to reopen for the student the question as to the origins of philosophy and of political philosophy. Indeed, a rigorous examination of the nature of philosophy and of political philosophy is essential to the confrontation of the question of their origin. Political philosophy, it seems, is a subspecies of philosophy. That is, all political philosophy is philosophy, but not all philosophy is political philosophy. This being evidently so, it will be necessary to seek the nature and origin of philosophy, then to seek the nature of politics, and only then to seek the nature and origin of political philosophy, for that which deserves the name "philosophy" asks about a thing, first, what it *is*. To ask this is at once to ask what it is *for* and how it is conducted. What distinguishes this book is that it asks these questions at the outset and suggests answers to them. The shocking truth is that one can look at several books that are titled *Introduction to Political Philosophy* and find that a majority of them are not aware of the necessity of confronting these questions. They remind one of what it would be like to invent a bit without conceiving of a drill.

Some autobiographical words are appropriate here. For millennia only the few were schooled. The New World modified that. Perhaps that was so because the countries that were formed in the New World were formed in the light of the new philosophy – formed, that is, subsequent to the Enlightenment. Since the Enlightenment, the sons of the bourgeoisie the middle class, the merchant class, have been schooled in ever greater numbers. The prelude to this change was the abolition of primogeniture in the English colonies in America well before the American Revolution, and the debut of it was the provision for public schools in the Northwest territories by the Northwest Ordinance that was enacted by the Congress of the states in 1787. This enactment was reaffirmed by the newly established Congress of the United States under the newly adopted Constitution during its first session in the fall of 1789. In the wake of World War II, a tidal wave of young people, many of them veterans of the war, crashed through the floodgates into the colleges. Quite a few of them were the first ones in their families' histories to attend college. Just as the political order founded under the U.S. Constitution meant to establish the first self-moderating yet effective popular government is still being tested, so also, whether the consequence of that flood of students in the schools means a greater realization of distributive justice or a dilution of what schooling is remains to be seen.

The author of this book was one of those carried along by that flood. He quit school just before his sixteenth birthday, worked as an optician until he was seventeen, and joined the Navy during World War II. At the age of twenty-three, while on his second tour of active duty in the Navy, he began to pick up some courses at Los Angeles City College. Except for a course in philosophy taught by a well-meaning lawyer and a course in American history taught by a well-meaning pedant, he concentrated on modern social science – anthropology, sociology, and psychology. He was at first satisfied by those studies. Then, at twenty-six, he entered graduate study in political science with two years of high school and about one and one-half years of college credit behind him. He had never read a political science book and he had never heard of Leo Strauss. In the last two of his five years of graduate study he took seven courses with Strauss. The dedication to him of this book requires what in ancient usage would be called an "apology."

Plato, the great creative genius of antiquity, traveled to Syracuse in Sicily and tried to educate the tyrant Dionysius in the art of ruling. The effort failed, and Plato was compelled to denounce the claim by Dionysius that the latter had learned philosophy from him. For me to dedicate this book to the memory of Mr. Strauss, my teacher, implies that I was a successful student. Clearly, one cannot be a judge in his own cause. What I can say with confidence is that Mr. Strauss was the greatest mind in political philosophy in the twentieth century and was a classroom teacher of unparalleled excellence. The customary acknowledgment by an author that all the errors in his book are his own must be multiplied a thousandfold here. This book, engendered by the author's experience, is meant to give the beginning student a boost.

Wait! Can philosophy be looked at from the outside in? A certain hesitancy is called for here. This is a problem that must be canvassed in the first chapter.

PART I

THE NATURE AND ORIGIN OF POLITICAL PHILOSOPHY

1

What Philosophy Is

Authors who are not frivolous give careful thought to the titles of their books and of the chapters of their books. What is more, even careless authors are likely to give unwitting indications in their book and chapter titles as to the bottom of their thought. Present-day students often look upon study as a computer-assisted, if not a computer-dominated, acquisition of "data." It might not occur to such a student to take careful note of book and chapter titles and to begin immediately to engage the author in argument. The title of this chapter should raise problems for the reader who is serious. Martin Heidegger (1889–1976), regarded by many as the greatest figure in philosophy in the twentieth century, gave a lecture in 1955 that was published shortly thereafter under the title, *Was ist das – die Philosophie? (What Is This – Philosophy?).*[1] Thus, a figure so highly regarded looked upon the nature or the definition of philosophy as a question, a question the confrontation of which required study and argument. Consequently, beginning with the chapter title "What Philosophy Is" rather than "What Is Philosophy?" seems to suggest that I believe I know the answer to the question and can impart it to a beginning student. Given the fact that someone of Heidegger's stature regards what philosophy is as questionable, an author who seems to take an opposite view appears to be as foolish as someone who questions Darwin, Einstein, or Freud; or who wonders whether there is in fact global warming; or who questions whether sexual harassment, cigarette smoking, and failure to recycle are indeed the crimes of the century. We are handling two-edged swords here, however. If sexual harassment is as great a crime as many think, then Heidegger's character comes immediately into question because, in his thirties, and while married, he began a sexual liaison with one of his students who was eighteen and continued that liaison for some time. What

---

[1] The common English translation of Heidegger's German title is *What Is Philosophy?* As one can see, it is not strictly literal. Perhaps in this instance the slight variation is inescapable, translating from idiomatic German into idiomatic English.

is more, he was an open supporter of the Nazis for no small part of his life. Should we not dismiss whatever it is that Heidegger thinks and prefer another's views?

Caution! Caution! Jean-Jacques Rousseau (1712–78), the very font from which a great many of the passions and opinions of twenty-first-century intellectuals flow, fathered five children with his housekeeper and then sent them each in turn off to the Paris Foundling Hospital, where it was understood that they would soon die. More, even Socrates, the most revered figure in the whole history of philosophy, had three sons and is reputed to have given little thought to their economic well-being. He blithely rose above such mundane questions as where their next meal was coming from. We certainly might expect such conduct from a motion picture actress, but can we listen to someone who offers to be our teacher but who behaves in such a blameworthy way? We must not, however, dismiss hastily what any of these three had to say. No less a figure than Alexander Hamilton reminds us not only that bad men may sometimes be right and that "we, upon many occasions, see wise and good men on the wrong as well as on the right side of questions of the first magnitude to society."[2] It is well to keep an open mind, lest we are reduced to reading sermons by preachers known never to have had their hands in the collection basket – or elsewhere. We do not mean to suggest that one should never consider the character of an author, but only that such consideration ought not to be hasty. We have every need to wonder whether the political advice of Socrates might not be utterly impracticable. We surely ought to be on the *qui vive* when reading Rousseau's *Émile*, a novel that offers guidance on the rearing and education of children and that is chock full of the propositions that inform present-day progressive education doctrine. Heidegger was not at all a *political* philosopher, but the effect on political thought of his general philosophy cannot be left unquestioned, and, in fact, even his dalliance with Nazism cannot be overlooked in a serious attempt to understand him.[3] One could, for example, ask whether his philosophy of being perhaps constituted an ulterior justification for his conduct.

As Michael Gillespie asserts, "Martin Heidegger was the first philosopher since Plato and Aristotle seriously to consider the question of Being."[4] In a general way, Gillespie argues, Heidegger calls into question the understanding of Being as Nature that underlay the whole history of philosophy. Even if we had titled this chapter "The Nature of Philosophy," we would have been at odds with the thought of the most notable philosopher of the twentieth

[2] Alexander Hamilton, James Madison, and John Jay, *The Federalist* (1787–88), No. 1, the 4th paragraph.
[3] See Michael Gillespie, "Martin Heidegger," in Leo Strauss and Joseph Cropsey, *History of Political Philosophy*, 3rd ed., Chicago, 1987, University of Chicago Press.
[4] Ibid., p. 888.

century. Heidegger meant to undercut and overthrow the entire history of philosophy, to bring forward a new understanding of Being itself. Trying to understand Heidegger's project is well served by an analogy. The "case method" of teaching law in law schools in the United States was pioneered at Harvard Law School near the end of the nineteenth century. Instead of reading treatises on law, as had been the method theretofore, students were asked to read cases deciding questions of the different subject matters of the law. It soon became sensible to extract from the law reports those cases bearing on a particular subject matter (torts, contracts, civil procedure, or the Constitution, for example); to collect, arrange, and edit them as seemed best to the professor; and to publish the results in a book to be purchased, studied, and kept by the student. One such book is James Bradley Thayer's *Cases on Constitutional Law*, in two volumes, published in Cambridge, Massachusetts, by George H. Kent in 1895. Since that time a great many Constitutional law "casebooks" have been published. Inasmuch as the jurisdiction of the courts of the United States, as distinguished from that of the courts of the several states, is limited by the Constitution, almost the first question the student will ask about a case in a court of the United States is what justification the court has in entertaining the case and what "standing to sue" the litigant has to bring the case there. It seemed sensible to put cases treating those questions first in the Constitutional law casebooks. Virtually all of the Constitutional law casebooks published in the twentieth century therefore begin with the case of Marbury against Madison in 1803. A great many professors and commentators in the field of Constitutional law in the past several decades have said that that case established "the doctrine of judicial review" – and established it as many understand that doctrine now at the beginning of the twenty-first century. A side effect of putting the courts first leads to the strange view that the United States has a "living constitution" and that the courts make the Constitution – this despite the fact that Article III of the Constitution shows clearly that the Constitution makes the courts. If all the professors and all the commentators teach this, and if they are all wrong, how would one go about fixing the problem?[5] In about 1970, Herbert Storing (1928–77), who, along with Martin Diamond, was one of a handful of scholars resurrecting an open-minded study of the American Founding, suggested to a colleague that the right way to teach Constitutional law would be not to start with cases on the judiciary, but to take the Constitution as it presents itself – first the Preamble, then Article I on the Congress, then Article II on the President, and so forth – then arrange the cases and other materials and discuss them in the

---

5 See Robert H. Clinton, *Marbury v. Madison and Judicial Review*, Lawrence, 1989, University Press of Kansas, especially pp. 5, 7, 138, and 212, and Matthew J. Franck, "Union, Constitutionalism, and the Judicial Defense of Rights: John Marshall," in *History of American Political Thought*, Bryan-Paul Frost and Jeffrey Sikkenga, eds., Lanham, MD, 2003, Lexington.

proper order. Before his untimely death at the age of forty-nine, Storing did in fact begin to teach the subject that way. The task that Storing set for himself is not impossible but it is difficult. It would be a dozen times as difficult as it would be for a litigant to try to get the Supreme Court to overrule a case that had been decided many years before and that had been cited as an authority in many subsequent decisions. If one extrapolated from this latter question to the project set out by Storing and then multiplied Storing's difficulties a hundred thousand times, one might catch a glimpse of the difficulty of Heidegger's project to find the whole history of philosophy to be defective; to find Plato and Aristotle and every single one of their successors mistaken; and to reopen the whole question, "What is being?" and so the question "What Is Philosophy?" To make such an attempt might be the epitome of philosophy itself.

The fact that Storing's project and Heidegger's project are in some respects analogous does not mean that they are equally sound. One can readily make a case that Storing's project, difficult as it might be, is both manageable and salutary. Conversely, it may be that Heidegger's project is altogether wrongheaded, brilliant and famous though he be. For the moment let us just note that a fundamental choice is before us. We can suggest that Being is capable of being determined and that one can posit what it in fact is, or we can imagine that all such imaginings are mistaken and that, instead, there is a fundamental indeterminacy to what is – that Being itself changes over time (i.e., that there is no such thing as nature) and that philosophy's primary task is fluid (i.e., that to question what it is *to be* is a fool's errand). If it is a fool's errand, however, then it might be that philosophy is dead. Before we dance on its grave and "move on," we need to think very soberly.

With that hesitancy we suggested earlier in this chapter, we nonetheless (how? unhesitatingly?) follow Plato and Aristotle and so make an argument about Being and so, as becomes apparent, necessarily about nature, and so about the nature of philosophy.

The word "philosophy" is a Greek word. If we break it into its parts, *philos* means love or friendship, or pursuit or attraction, and *sophia* means wisdom or knowing, or understanding. Thus, re-joined, the word *philosophia* means love of wisdom, or desire for wisdom, or pursuit of wisdom. To say that one is trying to acquire wisdom is to admit that one does not possess wisdom, so the trade of philosophy has ingrained in it a certain modesty, a certain hesitancy, a profound open-mindedness. It is not, however, cripplingly open-minded or cripplingly skeptical, which is the same thing. First of all, it is possible to acknowledge a species of lesser wisdom called practical wisdom or prudence. It is evidently possible for a human being to have a portion of that. The prudent individual knows how to manage his life and affairs. No doubt some lack this capacity, but simply trying to imagine a world in which no one had this species of wisdom founders on the first effort. The human species would long ago have passed from existence. Whether anyone ever possessed wisdom in the higher sense, however, may rightly be held in question, so we owe it to ourselves to clarify what that higher wisdom is or what it would be.

The most extreme statement of this proposition (that the philosopher does not possess wisdom) was made by Socrates himself. Those who knew him regarded him as "the best and wisest and most just man of his day,"[6] yet, at his trial on charges of impiety and leading the youth of Athens intellectually and politically astray (a trial that led to the death penalty for him), Socrates himself emphatically denied that he was wise.[7] We now use the word "sophist" as a term of dispraise.[8] Actually, the word is neutral. "Sophists" means (in the strictest sense) wise ones. Just as we can today use the word "wise" to refer reverently at Christmastime to the "three wise men," so we can speak of "wise guys," and everyone knows we do not mean that as praise. The accusation that Socrates was a Sophist tended toward the latter meaning, but it could not avoid suggesting that Socrates was, indeed, wise. If it seems impossible that something can at once be both praise and condemnation, one need only be reminded of the power of envy in human affairs. Socrates explained at length that he was not wise. His denial had a flavor of ambiguity. On the one hand, he insulted the Assembly trying him by showing that he was wiser than all of them because he knew nothing except that he knew that he knew nothing, whereas all those he had questioned (and had, by that questioning, gotten for himself a host of enemies) knew nothing and even knew not that they knew nothing, and it was impossible to doubt that this characterization applied equally to the 501 members of the court that tried him. Think how many enemies a fellow could make today by asserting that all the professors in all the universities were a bunch of pompous frauds, a suggestion that Thomas Hobbes (1588–1679) made in 1651 about the universities of that day. Then entertain for a moment the possibility that Socrates was right or that Hobbes was right. Western civilization is rightly praised for no longer giving to such a fellow as Socrates the death penalty. The worst punishment such a fellow now gets is having his books remaindered before a dozen copies have been sold. The sting of the speech of Socrates at his trial was great. In his outwardly self-deprecatory words he was at bottom engaging in "big talk," as Xenophon said.[9]

---

[6] Plato, *Phaedo*, 118a. Well, at least that is how it is most often translated. The word actually used by Phaedo in recounting to Echecrates the story of the last hours of Socrates was φρονιμωτάτου (phronimotatou) which is better translated "most prudent."

[7] Plato, *Apology of Socrates*, 21a–23b.

[8] See Richard D. McKirahan, Jr., *Philosophy before Socrates*, Indianapolis, 1994, Hackett, ch. 18, especially pp. 363–89.

[9] Xenophon, *Apology of Socrates*, 1 2. Plato's *Apology* appears as though it were a transcript of the defense speech made by Socrates at his trial. Following John Burnet, we regard it as just that. Xenophon's *Apology*, on the contrary, comes to us from Xenophon, who, twice

Homer was the first and the foremost of the poets. He was the "teacher of Greece." The poets as a group were the source of the Greeks' knowledge of the gods, of their understanding of the virtues and the vices, and of their standards of goodness, justice, and nobility. Socrates, Plato after him, and Aristotle after Plato were so far from being mere reflections of "Greek culture" that they were, on the contrary, the greatest critics of Greek culture and the greatest questioners of the poets. Here, then, is the beginning of an understanding of what philosophy is. The most sensible way to proceed is simply to set out an assertion as to the nature of philosophy and then to follow that with arguments that will, it is hoped, support the assertion. We do this in part from the standpoint of a certain cautious skepticism. This skepticism is cautious in that it is skeptical of radical skepticism – that is, it questions whether one can press skepticism to the point of absolute certainty regarding one's starting point. It may be that radical or absolute skepticism amounts to an infinite regression from the questions naturally raised. Perhaps it amounts to philosophy perpetually sharpening its pencils but never writing. Philosophy, as it were, keeps studying what it would do if it ever got around to doing something. This takes the form of regarding as the principal business of philosophy what is today called "epistemology," that is, the study of knowing or of how one can know. It has increasingly become the view of modern man that the primary activity of philosophy is epistemology.[10] The view of the ancients was that the principal object of philosophic pursuits is not a theory of knowledge but a knowledge of being. The primary business of philosophy is not epistemology but ontology, the study of being, the study of what is, not the study of study. Philosophy is the free and radical pursuit of the truth about being, about what is, about nature, and about the natures of things.[11]

---

removed, had heard an account of the trial from Hermogenes. Xenophon is thus able to describe the portion of Socrates' defense that most shocked the jury as "talking big." (The Greek word is *megalegoria*, and Xenophon's usage of that word is properly translated as "talking big.") Xenophon regards others as mistaken in supposing that Socrates unwittingly spoke so tauntingly to his jury. Instead, he argues that Socrates did what he did deliberately because he had concluded that he wanted to bring on the death penalty rather than grow old and lose his bodily health and mental acuity. Minor disservices are rendered to Socrates, and to the explanation offered by Xenophon, by those whose devotion to Plato and to Socrates rises almost to the level of piety. An example is the translation of Xenophon's *Apology* by O. J. Todd in the Loeb Classical Library series. Todd renders *megalegoria* not in the straightforward and literal way as "big talk" but in a deferential way as "lofty utterance." This makes us work harder to understand Xenophon's explanation of Socrates' conduct. Cf. the chapter "Apology of Socrates to the Jury" in Leo Strauss, *Xenophon's Socrates*, Ithaca, NY, 1972, Cornell University Press, pp. 129–40, especially p. 129.

[10] It seems that this elevation of epistemology at the expense of ontology may be no older than René Descartes (1596–1650).

[11] McKirahan, *op. cit.* note 8 this chapter, says at p. 68 that Xenophanes (a poet of the sixth century B.C.) "altered the course of presocratic thought from speculating about nature to

Inquiry that is properly regarded as philosophic inquiry is free inquiry into the natures of things. To speak of inquiry as free inquiry means that it is free from both external restraints and internal encumbrances. It takes only a moment's reflection to grasp the omnipresence and the weight of these restraints and encumbrances. Aristotle asserted that "virtue requires equipment."[12] Liberality is, according to Aristotle, a virtue, but it is clear that one cannot be liberal if his life is one of grinding poverty. Likewise, it seems that one cannot devote himself to study if all one's energy is devoted to the tasks of self-preservation. The presence of plenty is no guarantee of philosophic inquiry, but the presence of some degree of wealth seems to be the necessary, even though not the sufficient, condition of such inquiry. Only one who is free from the necessity of daily toil may be free to inquire. Even this is questionable, however. Socrates is famous for his disdain of material wealth.

A tyrannical regime, like abject poverty, is an apparently certain restraint on thought. If one is deprived of reading materials and cannot with trust talk with his fellows, he cannot philosophize. Well, let us soften that remark. Let us say that the tyrannical denial of the conditions of inquiry is almost certain to prevent inquiry. Perhaps those who are indefatigable and who possess souls of steel can, despite poverty or tyranny, pursue the truth. These exceptions prove the rule, however. Socrates is proof that one can philosophize despite political restraint – at least for a long time.

Tyrannical restraint of inquiry comes from both extremes. The word "tyranny" normally refers to an unrestricted rule of a strong man over an otherwise civilized place, a citified place, a city, but one where questioning the established order or the accepted accounts of the gods entails severe penalties. Such restraints come as well from uncivilized places, savage or barbaric places, where stern rule is enforced by the tribal elders according to merely traditional views and where the stories of the gods are handed down by an oral tradition and watched over by the tribal priests. Saying these things sounds hopelessly old-fashioned. Since the Enlightenment we have come to suppose that there no longer are any restraints on thought, speech, and inquiry. Stop to think for a moment. Perhaps the problematic condition of philosophy has not been erased by the Enlightenment and its political progeny.

Still, there is another side to this. Many of those who say and write the most outrageously meaningless (or at best foolish) things in the great freedom

---

theorizing about the basis for such speculation. In this change of direction we have, in an important sense, the birth of Western philosophy." McKirahan, a classicist, expresses here a common opinion among philosophy professors for at least the past seventy years or so, the opinion that the core of philosophy is epistemology. We have a contrary view, the view that that core is ontology – not the study of how one knows, but the study of what is.

[12] See especially *Nicomachean Ethics*, 1099a30–b8 and the immediate context.

that, precisely because of the Enlightenment, now obtains in America and Europe are the loudest complainants against their alleged "suppression." In fact, those complaints are most likely to be found in the midst of the most vicious, the most troublesome, the most seditious, the most impious, the most iconoclastic, and the most libelous writings, freely published with impunity and often at public expense. Maybe a little suppression is a mixed burden and so, necessarily, a mixed blessing. Leon Craig has recently written:

It should be sobering for us to reflect on the fact that most of the great literature of the world was produced under what today would be regarded as illiberal conditions. And, in contrast, that the contemporary societies which enjoy the broadest base of literacy in human history and which provide the greatest freedom and the most generous material support for an unprecedented number of writers, have generated so few works of comparable quality. The literary *forte* of such regimes seems to be quantity.[13]

So much for a glimpse of external restraints. We must now speak of internal encumbrances.

It may seem needless to say, but the first internal attribute required for philosophy is mental acuity, a keen intelligence. Thus, lack of intelligence is a fatal encumbrance that disallows philosophy. It is another prejudice of our day that any apparent differences in intelligence must be the consequence of some aspect of upbringing, such as the poverty just noted or parents who manifested what, to use an expression coined in the middle of the twentieth century, is called an "authoritarian personality." The child would have proved to be smarter had not the mother harshly imposed toilet training too early. Common sense denies this. It has never been simply accepted that all human beings are of the same native intelligence, yet much public policy is based on obstinate adherence to that view. University admissions are in some degree influenced by that view. Mostly, common sense checks this folly at the far end of the educational pipeline. If you need abdominal surgery, you want to be satisfied that you will get a bright surgeon. The source of the notion that human beings are all naturally equal both in body and mind may well be Thomas Hobbes. To see the argument in its pristine state, read the first two paragraphs of Chapter 13 of Hobbes's *Leviathan* (1651). The end of the second of those two paragraphs poker-facedly argues that the proof that we are all by nature equally wise is that "there is not ordinarily a greater sign of the equal distribution of anything than that every man is contented with his share." Now a moment's thought persuades us that Hobbes had his tongue in his cheek when he wrote that. This may be the only thing you will

---

[13] *The War Lover: A Study of Plato's* Republic, Toronto, 1994, University of Toronto Press, "Prologue," p. xix. Craig had, in a note to what came just before this passage (see the end of note 3 on p. 296), cited Leo Strauss, *Persecution and the Art of Writing*, Glencoe, IL, 1952, The Free Press.

ever read that suggests that Hobbes had a comic flair, but we stand by our suggestion. It must be added, however, that Hobbes was the Milton Berle of his day. He stole his comic "routines" from other comedians, in this case, René Descartes, who had said the same thing fifteen years earlier.[14]

We do not for a moment deny that external forces may greatly affect natural endowments. To do so would be to call for the abolition of all schools, but even here there is need for discussion and, as is so often the case, analogy is a constructive way to meet that need. The Bible tells us that David, as a youth, "was ruddy, and withal of a beautiful countenance, and goodly to look to."[15] We cannot all picture David from this description, but Michelangelo (1475–1564) did just that. From a thirteen-foot-tall block of marble, he fashioned, over a three-year period, a statue of David. Since 1873 the sculpture has been housed in the Accadèmia di Belle Arti in Florence. Thousands upon thousands of tourists and art fanciers have gone there to look at it. It is perfect proof that beauty is irresistible. Viewers are frozen in their tracks at the incomparable achievement of that sculpture, but more at the stunning beauty of David. Michelangelo conceives of David as the most beautiful human being ever to grace the earth, and he imparts that conception in his sculptured representation of the biblical figure. To look upon the David and not be captivated by its beauty is to have some defect of soul. One would have to suppose that few suffer irrecoverably from that particular defect. Few, we guess, are altogether immune to beauty, but we suppose that there are indeed some.

To speak of David's beauty (and so of beauty itself) is to be reminded that, perversely, even an asset can be the seed of a liability. A beautiful young woman may be wined and dined so much by her admirers that she loses the beauty that brought them to her. Also, a beautiful soul can attract its own diminishment. A bright student may be attracted to academic fads or may be courted by admissions officers, professors, law schools, and politics and, yielding to those forces, become shallow and a dilettante, and intellectually lazy. Not only can an internal good attract its own destruction; an external bad thing, or too much of a good thing, can be internalized. Imagine a doctoral student who smokes three packs of cigarettes a day and so cannot stay in the library stacks long enough between smoke breaks to make any progress at all on the problem set out to be solved in a dissertation. No matter how good a job Google does in putting on disk all the great libraries of the world, the time is not yet at hand when people can sit facing their computers while surrounded by an endless supply of cigarettes, cold pizza, warm beer, and other favored delicacies and really get to the bottom of a serious problem. Sitting in silence with a book has not yet been rendered unnecessary by technology. Therefore, we return to the general matter of

[14] *Discourse on Method*, Part I, the first sentence.
[15] 1 Samuel 16:12.

natural intelligence and add one more aspect. All of us want our automobiles to run well. We therefore need good mechanics. Good mechanics are smart. Philosophy, however, beckons an intellect that leaves the best auto mechanic behind. Philosophy requires the very best intellect that has had the very best development. Given the pitfalls put before us it must be said that it is not only a calling for the few. It is a calling that reaches and holds only a very small minority of a small minority. If that sounds "elitist," ask yourself whether you should be deterred by the curses of the wicked and the foolish who shout epithets at those who resist the prejudices of the day. It is precisely such resistance that is the job of the philosopher. In contrast, do not be discouraged by a modest admission that most of us will at best end up as good students. At least we shall learn how to distinguish the very few genuine philosophers from the charlatans and the well-meaning but stumbling pedants. Those charlatans and pedants, to the extent that they are endowed with sufficient charm and activated by sufficient passion, are the ones who are most likely to lead the potentially serious students of philosophy down the garden path of the mind.

The adjective "radical" in our characterization of philosophy would be easy to explain were it not for fashions in speech. A present-day student is inclined at first to understand "radical" as the equivalent of the interjection "Rad!" which, it seems, simply means "Far out, dude!" If pressed, the most such a student can imagine is that "radical" means left wing; however, the word is simply the adjectival form in English of the Latin word *radix*, which means root. As language develops, it may be the case that nouns and verbs come first and refer to some quite concrete thing or doing; then come the adjectives and adverbs; and, over time, all four of these forms are pressed into usage for things analogous to the concrete sources. One abstracts from the primary, concrete thing or doing, that is, pulls from it some attribute of which one is reminded in a less, and then in a far less, concrete thing or doing. To begin with, "root" simply means the root of a plant, but then one recognizes that it is a good way to describe the beginning of, say, some sentiment, and one can say that the "root" of the disturbed behavior of Mr. X is his sense that his advances have been rebuffed by Miss Y. The use of "X" and "Y" here, by the way, makes a convenient bridge to our noticing that "root" is a term used in mathematics such that the quantity 3, taken as a root, when combined with the power ^{2} produces the quantity 9. In philosophical usage one may say that radical inquiry gets to the root of a matter in that it gets to the bottom of something; that is, it gets to a proposition beneath which one need not search. There is nothing "under" it to which one may have recourse. When the American Declaration of Independence says that we hold certain "truths to be self-evident," it speaks of something rather like a mathematical axiom. It means that there need not be because there cannot be some more basic evidence from which the proposition can be derived. To say that "all men are created equal" is to say something on an intellectual level with saying that parallel lines never meet. To speak of parallel lines means to speak of the impossibility of their meeting. To speak of men is at once to speak of equality. Now of course the Declaration was not written by madmen. They knew, and it knows, that all men are not equally beautiful, equally wise, or equally deserving of the goods of this world. It is not a Herculean task to figure out what the Declaration means and therefore to figure out how it can characterize this truth as "self-evident."

"Self-evident" does not mean very, very evident. If it did there would be no need to declare a self-evident truth, whereas, although there is no need to "prove" it, there is an urgent need to declare it, because awareness of a truth that needs no proof can be suppressed for centuries by those defective political conditions mentioned earlier in this chapter.

To speak of the Declaration in this way is by no means to assert that its authors were philosophers. The American Founding broke new political ground, but it did not break new philosophic ground. It rested on philosophic propositions uncovered by others earlier. The proposition that all politics ought to rest on the self-evident truth of human equality depends on that truth having been uncovered by the political philosophy of the Enlightenment. Men like Thomas Hobbes and John Locke (1632–1704) went to the philosophic bottom of things, to the roots, to reject traditional political views. It would be a mistake to attempt to disprove a truth that needs no proof. If the political propositions of the Enlightenment are to be rejected, it will not be by proofs; it can only be by contrasts, by a dialectical process. We must not get ahead of ourselves, however. We will return to these topics. We have touched this much here only to suggest what is meant by free and radical inquiry.

We cannot complete our argument as to what philosophy is without indicating what it is not. We have already indicated that a part of the modern academy dismisses philosophy as either wrongheaded or unnecessary. Our suggestion was that this view grew through the latter part of the twentieth century, but such things do not happen overnight. A part of the cause of this dismissal is the growth of a particular conception of positive science. It is not evidently the case that positive science and philosophy are naturally at odds. It is only a particular view of the former that sees itself at odds with the latter. Although there are still many adherents of the persuasion, one does not now often hear the word "behavioralism" used stridently. That school of social science inquiry may find its origins in the thought of the German sociologist Max Weber (1864–1920), who passed along a distinction between "facts" and "values." From the 1950s through the 1970s it was a thriving doctrine in the universities of the United States and Canada, not to mention those of the several countries of Europe and to a lesser extent elsewhere. In many schools it quite dominated the several departments of social science. Its genesis in America was the Chicago School of Social Science, so named because the several departments of the social sciences of the University of Chicago were pioneers in this "positivistic" endeavor. A story that comes from that seat of learning furthers our effort to distinguish philosophy from other things often confused with it. The story is told of a young scholar, Jerome G. Kerwin (1896–1977), who joined the Political Science Department at Chicago (in 1926, we believe). It appears that his first responsibility was to teach courses in state and local government. Charles E. Merriam (1874–1953), a leading figure in what came to be called "behavioralism," was chairman of the Political Science Department. It is said that, during a department meeting, Merriam remarked that it looked as though some sort of course in political theory would "have to be" offered and he turned to Kerwin and said, "You're Catholic, Jerry, why don't you teach it?" If this story is true – and we have good reason to credit it – the implication is that Merriam regarded "theory" as a synonym of "philosophy," and he may have regarded philosophy as interchangeable with religion. The further implication is that a course in theory would have to be offered only for the sake of appearances because it, like religion, was just so much nonsense, the antithesis of real science. So pervasive is the identification of philosophy with religion, although not necessarily the bemused dismissal of either of them, that a great many colleges in the mid-twentieth century had departments of "Religion and Philosophy." There are historical reasons for this, but we need not justify or reject those reasons here. What is interesting is that now, at the beginning of the twenty-first century, many bookstores have "Philosophy and Religion" sections, and some of these offer no books that would pass muster in either field. Clarity is needed here. Only someone who does not care much for either would confound the two. The essence of philosophy is inquiry – that is, questioning. It seeks to find the truth about being. The essence of religion is obedience to the revealed word of God. Such questioning as is permitted is within limits, and to go beyond those limits is sin. The name given to that quality of character, that acceptance and obedience, is "faith." The name of the counterpart in philosophy is "reason." The philosopher who made the most strenuous effort to reconcile faith and reason was Thomas Aquinas (1225–74), who is revered as Saint Thomas by the Roman Catholic Church and who is regarded by many in the church as having succeeded in that reconciliation or synthesis of faith and reason, or revelation and reason. It is no denigration of faith generally, of religion in general, or of the Christian Church in particular to wonder aloud whether in fact Aquinas could have succeeded. With faith one knows the highest truths. Although that may coexist with philosophic inquiry, and perhaps the two may even appear to be harmonized, the one is not the other. We may here restate the provisional definition of philosophy: **Philosophy is the free and radical employment of unassisted human reason in pursuit of the truth about being, about nature, about the natures of things. Its mode of operation is to question. All of its questions are parts of the central question, What truly is? It presses its questions to the roots of things. It is hard work. It is the work of a tiny**

minority of a small minority. The small minority are those with truly superior endowments. The tiny minority of that small minority are those who have not been turned aside by internal weaknesses or hemmed in by external encumbrances.

Another observation must be made here. Plato presented an example of philosophic inquiry in written works we call "dialogues." The dialogues look remarkably like dramatic works. Plays are a species of poetry. The great poets of ancient Greece were epic poets, lyric poets, or dramatic poets. Some of the great figures were Homer, Hesiod, Aeschylus, Sophocles, Euripides, and Aristophanes. Plato's work is proof that philosophic inquiry can be represented in poetic form. Closer to our own day, William Shakespeare showed that an intellect of philosophic proportions can pursue its ends by poetic means. Philosophy and poetry are not identical or interchangeable, however. Not all poetry is philosophy. Not all philosophy is presented poetically.

Edgar Guest (1881–1959) was a popular American poet. He wrote columns and commonplace poems for newspapers and several books of poems. All of his poetry was pleasing to the ear, and all of it was devoted to wholesome counsel, but no one in his right mind would put his books on the same shelf with the plays and sonnets of Shakespeare unless he had only two books and only one shelf.[16]

The late Ann Landers and her sister Abigail Van Buren wrote advice on largely prosaic matters in newspaper columns. The columns are certainly not poetic, but many of them are wholesome moralizing. Moralizing poetry is not, as such, philosophy. Moralizing is not philosophy. Philosophers, and certainly political philosophers, of necessity touch on moral questions, but their principal purpose is the elucidation of questions and the search for answers, not particularly the moral improvement of their readers. In Aristotle's understanding, this is the task of statesmen. Ann Landers, Abigail Van Buren, and Edgar Guest are not philosophers. Maybe Shakespeare is. The questions that must be asked about others in history and in various countries are these: Are they closer to Guest and Landers or closer to Shakespeare in the serious attention they deserve? Are they philosophers who happen to employ the poetic mode, or are they mere poets or mere moralizers? On the other side of those questions, one often hears it said that Plato was a moralist. He was not. He was a philosopher.

Finally, it must be said that there can be a search for being only where finding being might be expected. Thus, it is clear at the outset that there can be no such thing as a "philosophy of baseball." Baseball is a nice game. It is, in fact, "the American pastime." It is even an important game in that

---

[16] For an entertaining assault on Edgar Guest, see "Lines to a World-Famous Poet Who Failed to Complete a World-Famous Poem; or Come Clean, Mr. Guest!" in Ogden Nash, *Many Long Years Ago*, Boston, 1945, Little, Brown, p. 39.

billions of dollars are involved in it. A single professional baseball player can amass in a few years a fortune that would make an Oriental despot of yore sink into wonder and despair to contemplate it. There is no bottom truth of baseball to be sought, however. Around 1839, Abner Doubleday (1819–93), a graduate of the U.S. Military Academy at West Point, invented, it is said, the game of baseball at Cooperstown, New York. He made up his mind that the core of the playing field would consist of an exact square (which we call a "diamond" because we look at it from the standpoint of one of its corners), and he even named positions to be played. Just as easily, he could have dictated that the core of the field be three-sided and that there be six, or perhaps twelve, players on a team. One needs to come down from the delirium of fandom to acknowledge this. The only way to think that there is a "right" way for baseball to be played is to confuse the customary with the natural. The old is not the good. We hasten to add, however, neither is the new. What everybody now says is not, by virtue of their saying it, true. The good is the good, the true is the true, and the search for them is the business of philosophy. Philosophy has been so denatured that not only do we speak of "the philosophy of" something of which there can be no philosophy, but we also speak of every individual's opinion, prejudice, or sentiment as "his philosophy of" something, usually "his philosophy of life," yet only a tiny minority of us can be said to have a philosophy of anything. A vacuous television interviewer can ask a brain-dead Hollywood starlet what "her philosophy of life" is, and she will answer something of this sort: "Well, I just think that everybody, like, ought to be authentic. You have to, like, be true to yourself. You have to, you know, like, totally grab life by the horns and, like, make it, you know, all yours." The celebrity interviewer will then look at the celebrity dimwit with admiration and wonder, and a large part of the television audience will swoon and say, "Gosh, what a swell philosophy." It ain't.

If philosophy must be about something, because there can be no such thing as a philosophy of no thing, a philosophy of nothing, then we must raise the question, What are the things, the true things? The answer is that there are two subject matters of philosophy: physics and politics. That is why the medieval university had two core faculties, the faculty of natural philosophy and the faculty of moral and political philosophy. With some reflection it can be seen that everything about which there can be a bottom truth falls into one or another of these two great subdivisions. Theology, insofar as it is a part of philosophy rather than an aspect of religion, is the study of the gods. The gods *are*, according to ancient understanding. Human will or preference cannot change that fact. The study of them is therefore a theoretical, not a practical, science. Their study is part of physics. At his trial, Socrates was charged with, among other things, inquiring into the things in the heavens above and in the earth below, that is, with being a physiologist, that is, doing what came to be called "natural philosophy." The poets had already taught us about the gods. To try to study them and to get to the bottom truth about them is the business of one of the two branches of philosophy. Now to do this is to question the answers given by the city – the official answers, the orthodoxies. It is to set oneself against the city. It is at once impious and seditious, inasmuch as service of the gods is the city's concern. The indictment of Socrates that led to his trial developed during that trial into the charge that he was a physicist or physiologist, and therefore seditious. In his response to the charge, Socrates pointed out that it rested on an accusation that had been made against him many years earlier by a "certain comic poet."[17]

Some have said that there are not two but three chief branches of philosophy. Immanuel Kant (1724–1804) tells us that "Greek philosophy was divided into three sciences: physics, ethics, and logic."[18] There is a difficulty with Kant's division, however. Philosophy, as we just suggested, has to be about something. It cannot be about nothing. Logic, however, is about nothing. It is about itself. It might better be regarded as a propaedeutic to philosophy than as a part of philosophy. Just as one cannot cook without fire, one cannot philosophize without logic, but no one ever suggests that fire making is part of the art of cooking. In the third century A.D., Diogenes Laertius tells us that, according to Aristotle, there "are two divisions of philosophy, the practical and the theoretical. The practical part includes ethics and politics, and in the latter not only the doctrine of the state but also that of the household is sketched. The theoretical part includes physics and logic, although logic is not an independent science, but is elaborated as an instrument to the rest of science."[19] Kant is one of the towering figures in the history of philosophy, so it is with reluctance that one presumes to differ with him. It still seems, however, that there are two, not three, parts

---

[17] Plato, *Apology of Socrates*, 18a–19d. See Aristophanes, the *Clouds*. Socrates elsewhere says that he had been interested in physics when he was younger but concluded that one could not get firm answers in that field so he turned to a different inquiry. See *Phaedo*, 96a–99d.

[18] Immanuel Kant, *Foundations of the Metaphysics of Morals* (1785), tr. Lewis White Beck, Library of Liberal Arts, New York, 1959, Bobbs-Merrill, p. 3 (the first sentence of the Preface). It is an interesting matter to be examined elsewhere that Kant chooses the word "ethics" to characterize what the medieval university had called "moral and political philosophy." Although Aristotle had regarded ethics and politics as two parts of the same science, he nowhere argues that one is the mere subcategory of the other. He does, however, implicitly treat politics as the senior partner.

[19] *Lives of the Eminent Philosophers*, Book V, Chapter 28. (In the R. D. Hicks translation, Loeb Classical Library, Cambridge, 1972, Harvard University Press, vol. 1, p. 475.) We have quoted Aristotle here as Hicks translates him. It should be noted that the Greek word for "science" nowhere appears in the original of the text cited at this point. The question of the relation between philosophy and science and the question whether the two terms are interchangeable will be raised later. Also, the word that Hicks translates as "state" is a form of the Greek word *polis*. For a discussion of the fatal error of translating *polis* into the English word "state," see the long quotation of Harry V. Jaffa in Chapter 3.

to philosophy. It is comforting to be supported by the authority of Diogenes Laertius and by his explanation of Aristotle.

Therefore, **philosophy is the free and radical pursuit by means of unassisted human reason of the truth about physics, and politics, and their several parts. That pursuit is conducted through some sort of logic, some sort of logical argument. The English word "argument" is derived from the Latin *arguo*, which means to put in clear light. Argument may be made dialectically, as in the case of Plato, or demonstratively, as in the case of Aristotle (although the element of dialectic cannot be absent and is not absent even in Aristotle). The English word "logic" is derived from the Greek λόγος (logos), which means speech, or reason, or reasoned speech. In fact, speech that is not reasoned is not properly speech. It is babble or rant. Speech, properly speaking, gets somewhere.**

2

The Origin of Philosophy

The motion picture *Casablanca* was made in 1942. The song "As Time Goes By" was a prominent part of the movie. It made the point that the meaning of some events and some words, such as the words "kiss" and "sigh," remain solidly fixed.[1] That is pretty straightforward. One may kiss a hand, and that is still a kiss, but if one pats a hand comfortingly, that is not a kiss. The executioner who beheaded Lady Jane Grey in 1554 may have sighed resignedly as he did so or he may have bellowed with fury, but if he did one, he did not do the other. A sigh is just a sigh, and no one in his right mind would hear someone bellow and call it a sigh. After all, the fundamental things apply as time goes by – or do they?

Having gone *Through the Looking-Glass*, Alice in due course encountered Humpty Dumpty. During their conversation, Humpty Dumpty used the word "glory." Alice asked what he meant, and he replied that he meant a nice, knockdown argument, so Alice objected that that was not what "glory" meant. "'When I use a word,' Humpty Dumpty said, in a rather scornful tone, 'it means just what I choose it to mean – neither more nor less.'"[2] Alice was seven and a half years old when she had this conversation with the mature Humpty Dumpty, but it is clear that she was right. For, if Humpty Dumpty was right, then he was just as much wrong, because right and wrong do not mean anything because nothing means anything. Conversation is impossible. Reading is a waste of time, if indeed there are such things as waste and time.

Our purpose here is to show the frailty of language, or perhaps we should say the contempt for language. Humpty Dumpty is our teacher. We uncover this frailty to aid us in the search for the origin of philosophy. Because

[1] "As Time Goes By," words and music by Herman Hupfeld, ©1931.
[2] Lewis Carroll (pen name of Charles Lutwidge Dodgson [1832–98]), *Alice's Adventures in Wonderland* and *Through the Looking-Glass*, Baltimore, 1962, Penguin Books, p. 274.

science, in its proper meaning, is an essential element of philosophy, will it not hamper us in our search if, when we speak of "science," we, in the most literal sense, do not know what we are talking about? Ask your fellow students. Ask your family. Ask your professors. Ask, "What is the difference between science and art?" Anyone other than a classical scholar is likely to tell you that science is precise and art is not. Art is driven by a kind of sentimentality, by "feeling." It is no accident that, since Rousseau, it has become common for someone who is asked what he thinks to answer, "I feel so-and-so." It is as though thinking and feeling were the same or, more likely, as though feeling had simply supplanted thinking.

One would be likely to hear medicine now described as "more art than science," which is rather frightening if that means that your surgeon is not precise. This confusion is not inevitable, however. Part of the problem out of which this hesitant and unsettled view of science and art originates may be a change in the way science itself is understood. The very definition of "science" has come to be stated as method or process rather than as content, and to speak of science has come to be to speak of "the scientific method," as though there were one method appropriate for any and every science. The Chicago School of Social Sciences, of which we have spoken, was based on the hope that the social sciences could, with sufficient effort (and sufficient funding), measure up to the method of the physical sciences. They cannot do so. They are different sciences. The inevitable failure of the enterprise has led to the opinion that political science is not really science, and those who believe this and yet carry on as political scientists have made possible the transformation of an academic discipline into a political movement. It is as though the Chicago School has been replaced by a school that believes as ardently in the fact–value distinction as the Chicago School had believed but concludes that facts are worth nothing and so opts instead for values that, by definition, cannot be supported by rational argument so need only be posited, asserted, screamed, or declared in no uncertain terms on a bumper sticker. Reason and faith have not been synthesized here. The distinction between reason and faith is obliterated. The classroom becomes a staging ground for passion, and change itself is marketed as the purpose of study. The good intentions of young people are justified as sufficient in themselves, and there comes to be no need for study. To be ardent is to be right. The altruism natural to youth has been hijacked.

Such substitution of good intentions for inquiry destroys the very reason for a university. There is, however, no need for this hesitant and unsettled view of science and art. There is a clear distinction. A thing *is* what it is *for*. A thing is defined by its end or purpose. A knife is to cut. There is no other reason for there being knives. Science is for knowledge. Art is for production. Medicine is not more art than science. It is an art. The art of medicine produces cures. The art of carpentry produces houses, for example. Landscape painting and portrait painting are not arts because they are "artsy," that is, because the painter wears a funny hat and feels ever so creative. Painting is an art because it produces something. The art of painting produces likenesses. Leonardo da Vinci is famous not only for his works of art but also for his study of anatomy. Anatomy is a science. One studies anatomy to know. There is often a practical end in view, such as in the art of medicine or the art of painting, but anatomy qua anatomy is not painting, curing, or any other art. The science of physics does not produce anything. It uncovers certain kinds of truths. If one studies physics because he wants to build something, that want is to be understood as rather an ulterior motive. In any case, it is not by physics that anyone builds anything. It is by skill in some sort of engineering or architecture, which, to be sure, depends on the science of physics but is not, in itself, that science. The art, trade, or craft of civil engineering does not seek the truth about things, but it depends on the sciences of physics and mathematics to build bridges that do not fall down and roads that do not launch automobiles into space. It is well to remember that our word "art" is derived from the Latin word *ars* (the genitive singular of which is *artis*) and that Latin word *ars* is the near equivalent of the Greek word τεχνη (*techne*) whence come the English words "technical" and "technique." Thus, in building a house, the architect is the chief among the craftsmen, technicians, or artists. His is the superior, the inclusive art. Be careful, however. Remember that most people do not use the word "art" with precision. If you are in the market to buy a house and the developer trying to sell you one says, with a happy smile on his face, that "architecture is more art than science," you might be wise to seek out a different developer.

The English word "science" is derived from the Latin word *scientia*, which simply means knowledge. Knowledge about politics is useful. It can be taught. The Greek word that is the parallel of the Latin *scientia* is ἐπιστήμη (*epistéme*), which means acquaintance with or knowledge of something. Thus, when we moderns speak of "epistemology" we mean the study of how we know, which, as we have mentioned, is a step back from the study of some thing. Those who, moved by the modern understanding of science, deny that there can be any such thing as political science must be confronted with the example of Aristotle (384–322), who surely set out at the beginning of Book Four of the *Politics* a quite complete political science that he called straightforwardly *politiké epistéme*. As to the notion that political science ought to mimic physical science because method is method and there is one method that fits all sciences, Aristotle has answered that proposition by his explicit statement near the beginning of the *Nicomachean Ethics* that different kinds and degrees of precision are appropriate to the different sciences. Aristotle's argument is so compellingly persuasive and is at the same time marked by such plainspoken common sense that it must be quoted here at length:

Our discussion will be adequate if it has as much clearness as the subject-matter admits of, for precision is not to be sought for alike in all discussions, any more than in all the products of the crafts. Now [noble] and just actions, which political science investigates, admit of much variety and fluctuation of opinion, so that they may be thought to exist only by convention, and not by nature. And goods also give rise to a similar fluctuation because they bring harm to many people; for before now men have been undone by reason of their wealth, and others by reason of their courage. We must be content, then, in speaking of such subjects and with such premises, to indicate the truth roughly and in outline, and in speaking about things which are only for the most part true, and with premises of the same kind, to reach conclusions that are no better. In the same spirit, therefore, should each type of statement be *received*; for it is the mark of an educated man to look for precision in each class of things just so far as the nature of the subject admits; it is evidently equally foolish to accept probable reasoning from a mathematician and to demand from a rhetorician [apodeictic] proofs.[3]

During the latter half of the twentieth century, a great many "gaps" were discovered. There was a "missile gap"; there was a "credibility gap"; and, most of all, there was a "generation gap." In speaking of the missile gap and the credibility gap, there was a certain disapproval intended, but speaking of the generation gap rested more ambiguously on such disapproval. At the very least, however, it suggested that parents and their children could not "communicate" because they "spoke different languages." Retrospectively, people began to see generation gaps where hitherto they had not been seen. As an example, Shakespeare's play *Romeo and Juliet* was seen not in its fullness as a profound commentary on politics that rested on an Aristotelian perspective. It was not a tragedy. It was just a mushy love story. It was not seen for its tension between two noble families, the resolution of which was engendered by the tragic deaths of the two young lovers, and that resolution being the prelude to civic peace. It was just about the generation gap. If old Montague had just listened to Romeo and if old Capulet had just appreciated how hot Juliet was for Romeo, there could have been a nice,

---

[3] Aristotle, *Nicomachean Ethics*, 1094b12–26. This is from the translation by Sir David Ross, London,1954, Oxford University Press, The World's Classics series. In the case of the two words in square brackets, I have put "noble" where Ross put "fine" – this is a "fielder's choice"– and I have put "apodeictic" where Ross put "scientific." In this instance I have transliterated strictly from the Greek word ἀποδείξεις, substituting only the adjective form for the noun form in the original. (Just as citations to Plato use the standard pagination established in the sixteenth century by Stephanus, so the standard pagination for Aristotle is that of the first edition of his complete works in Greek, produced in the nineteenth century by the German scholar August Bekker [1785–1871]. The pages are divided into two parts, A and B, and each half page runs about thirty to forty lines. Thus, the present citation is to lines 12 to 26 of part B of page 1094 in the Bekker edition. Similar to good editions of Plato, good editions of Aristotle in any language have the standard pagination in the margins. [Of course, different translations vary the word order of sentences, so one might have to look up or down a line or two in a translated work to find the substance to which a citation to the Greek text is given]).

expensive wedding and a honeymoon at Lago di Garda. However much belief in the generation gap may blind us to some aspects of reality, there is a measure of truth in the notion that one generation does not speak the same language as the next. What then is the case between one generation and the letters written by great-great-grandparents? What if we third-millennium folk try even to read Shakespeare? Many of the words Shakespeare wrote are the same as those we speak and write, but do we communicate? Would it not be better if we just stopped reading books altogether? As an extreme case of this obliteration of meaning, imagine a husband coming home from a job interview and happily asserting that he had gotten the job. His wife asks him what the salary is, and he joyously responds that it is "fantastic." The wife bursts into tears as she contemplates going on welfare. The problem is that she is a classical scholar, and the word "fantastic" means to her of or pertaining to a fantasy. Her husband has just answered her question by saying that there is no salary, that he will be working for nothing. The same thing would happen if he replied "fabulous," because "fabulous" means of or pertaining to a fable. Likewise with "incredible," because that would mean that one cannot believe anything at all about salary. Also, if she asked him, "How do I look in this new dress?," he ought not to answer, "Terrific" without first looking the word up in an unabridged dictionary.

The foregoing illustrations have not been just for fun. Think about the words "science," "art," and "fantastic." The same fate has befallen the word "philosophy." A great change has occurred in scholarly opinion about the origin of philosophy. We mean to set out here the outlines of that change and to leave the reader with a question. We have to notice that two hundred years ago nearly everyone in the Western world accepted the proposition that philosophy began in Greece. Gradually, since about the middle of the nineteenth century, it became common for that view to be denied. It is now asserted that philosophy began in India, perhaps China, or maybe Egypt or Persia. Is this because earlier scholars were ethnocentric or ignorant and could not see the truth? Is it because of a well-intended or perhaps foolish urge to bring Western civilization down off its high horse? Is it because in the past century we have so digested the new prejudice that all cultures are equal – that there is no such thing as a better or worse place – that we have concluded that all cultures must have had an indigenous philosophy and all we need is the learning, the attitude, and the enthusiasm for diversity to look at those philosophies and see them for the first time? Is it a clear truth uncovered by the cumulative progress of scientific inquiry? We brush aside such foolish arguments as that Aristotle "stole his philosophy from the library at Alexandria." It does not take a rocket scientist of a historian to notice that Aristotle died in 322 B.C., Alexander of Macedon (sometimes said to have been Aristotle's pupil) renamed a conquered town in Egypt after himself and died in 323 B.C. (a year before Aristotle), the great library at

Alexandria was actually constructed several years after Aristotle's death, and the whole eastern end of the Mediterranean Sea had been Hellenized – that is, enveloped in Greek intellectual hegemony – and a substantial portion of the books in that library were in Greek.[4] (That library, by the way, has just been restored and reopened with the intent of making it one of the great libraries of the world, if not once again the greatest library in the whole world. Western civilization owes a great debt to the original library for it was there that were shelved many of the great works of classical antiquity that were decimated by disdain in Europe. The library itself was destroyed in the seventh century by Muslim Arabs sweeping across the north of Africa, but many of the books had been shipped off to safety in various royal libraries.)

Not only is it the case that problems occur over time within a language, but at a given moment, a problem can occur between languages in the process of translation. Let us consider a really simple illustration. In English-speaking countries, certain natural creatures are present that, when seen, are called "birds." If someone from an English-speaking country visited Italy he would notice that Italians, seeing the things he called "birds," called them *uccelli*. Thus it is clear that the English equivalent of the Italian word *uccelli* is "birds." Any translation that makes a mistake about this should not be read. Even greater precision is evident. *Birds of North America*[5] offers pictures and descriptions of thirty-two varieties of sparrow, and ornithologists can explain why all should be called "sparrows." Someone from an English-speaking country visiting in Italy, seeing certain birds, would conclude that he was seeing some sort of sparrow, and he would discover that Italians called them *passeri*.[6] Without a doubt, the Italian word *passero* is the equivalent of the English word "sparrow." Also, the Italian words *corvo comune* are the perfect equivalent of the English words "common crow," and so on, through a long list of birds. That is easy. The only problem would occur if we were dealing with a bird that is peculiar to one place and not seen in another. There may be birds in China, for example, that cannot be found in North America or Britain. We need to think about this when considering the origin of philosophy, for the very word "philosophy" is a Greek word, and in all the languages of the West – *philosophia* in Latin, *philosophie* in French, *filosofía* in Spanish, *filosofia* in Italian, *philosophie* in German, *filozofia* in Polish – all one can find are mere transliterations of the Greek word φιλοσοφία. The Turks provide a convenient test case for us. The Turks originated in Central Asia and moved in great numbers into Anatolia (Asia Minor). They were, in their travels, converted to Islam, and

---

[4] See Mary Lefkowitz, *Not Out of Africa*, New York, 1996, Basic Books.
[5] Chandler Robbins, Bertel Bruun, Herbert Zim, and Arthur Singer, *Birds of North America*, New York, 1966, Golden Press.
[6] See Richard Perry, *Uccelli*, Milano, 1987, A. Villardi.

their rule spread westward as far as the approaches to Vienna (just as Arabic Muslims moved across North Africa and across the Mediterranean into southern Spain). The Turkic languages seem to be related to Mongolian and perhaps to Korean, and the Turks have always spoken their own language, even though for centuries they borrowed words from Persian and from Arabic. In addition, because of the influence of Islam, the Turks came to write their language in a variant of Arabic script, but modern Turkey came into being just after World War I, and around 1928, as a part of its drive to westernize itself and secularize its government, it adopted Roman script to represent its language. Even in the Turkish language, the word for philosophy is *felsefe*. Just as in the case of French, Italian, German, and English, the Turkish word is a mere adoption of the Greek original. It may have been adopted by way of the Arabic usage used by philosophers within Islam. The readiest conclusion that one comes to is that Turkish had to adopt the word because there was no word in the Turkic languages that was the equivalent of the Greek φιλοσοφία. We are also compelled to ask why it was that the philosophers within Islam used a borrowed Greek word to characterize what they were doing. In addition, we are compelled to raise this question: Just as *uccelli* is the authentic Italian equivalent of the English "birds," is there in Hindi, Persian, Egyptian, or Putonghua (the standard Mandarin, intended to become the common spoken Chinese language) a clear equivalent of the Greek *philosophia*? To qualify as a clear equivalent, the word would have to mean what "philosophy" meant in the West and would have to be a very old word – two thousand or more years old – that meant in its first usages what "philosophy" meant in ancient Greece. In other words, a borrowing from Latin or Greek that occurred some time after regular contact between two peoples had been established would not qualify. Neither would a word qualify that meant one thing but has come to mean another after some centuries. There could be little doubt that a people whose language is Hindi or Chinese, for example, counts among its number some who genuinely fit the description of a philosopher. If we are to say, however, that philosophy began somewhere other than Greece, we must be able to say with confidence either that the Greeks "picked up" the practice of philosophy from contact with Egypt, China, Persia, or India or at least that the philosophic activity that began in Greece about 2,600 years ago in the person of Thales (c. 640 B.C.–c. 546 B.C.) "lost the race" to an activity that occurred somewhere else beginning more than 2,600 years ago, an activity – whatever it may have been named – that fit exactly that activity which began in the seventh or the sixth century B.C. in Greece, the activity that the Greeks called *philosophia*. The Greeks worshiped gods, and they had sages and poets, and there were Greek moralizers and Greeks who practiced divination, and no doubt these practices have in some instances intertwined with philosophy, but nobody ever called those ancient Greek priests, sages, poets, moralizers, or diviners "Greek philosophers." Therefore, if we are not to be charged with not knowing what we are talking about, we must not call Indian, Chinese, or Persian sages, priests, poets, moralizers, or diviners "Indian philosophers," "Chinese philosophers," or "Persian philosophers" unless they combined their poetry, moralizing, service to the gods, or wise counsel with an activity that fits the definition of philosophy that we have offered: free and radical pursuit of the truth by unassisted human reason about being or nature or the natures of the beings.

As to the origin of philosophy, then, let us first reflect on China. A reasonable beginning is with Confucius, who lived from about 551 B.C. to about 479 B.C. as marked by the Western calendar.

The first chapter of Hyun Höchsmann's *On Philosophy in China*[7] is entitled "The Legacy of Confucius." He begins that chapter thus: "With his love of learning Confucius sought to guide all people, from the emperor to the people of the land to live ethically. Confucius, . . . the most renowned of all philosophers in China, was a person of deep intellectual and moral humility. Through the sheer range and clarity of his ideas Confucius was able to bring together the ways of thought and connect the customs of a vast and complex civilization with moral principles acceptable by all." This is surely a praiseworthy accomplishment and a great social achievement, but one may raise what in parliamentary language might be called "the previous question." Is it a philosophical achievement? "Ethical" and "moral" are interchangeable words, one from the Greek and the other from the Latin. Plato and Aristotle easily allowed that every city had its particular ways. The totality of those ways constituted the *ethos* of that city. "Ethic" or "ethical" is an adjective meaning "of or pertaining to" that ethos. The equivalent Latin root, "moral," likewise means of or pertaining to the mores of a country. Thus, in a strict sense, it is impossible for a city to be unethical or immoral, for whatever its ways, they are the essence of the moral stand of the city. Unethical or immoral conduct can only be attributed to an individual who defies the ways of his city. The charge that one is immoral is, strictly speaking, the equivalent of a mother's saying to her wayward child, "That's not the way we behave in this house." The work of philosophy is not to gather such ways and to find their least common denominator but to question them. Likening the philosopher to that child, his proper work is to say, "Why not, Mother? Others elsewhere behave this way. What is the best way?" To speak of the "best way" is, perforce, to suggest a best city, and so to anticipate a searching inquiry into the character of the best city. Aristotle wrote two books that he regarded as two parts of the same enterprise: *Nicomachean Ethics* and *Politics.* One could surmise that giving to a book the title *Ethics* suggests that one means to offer improvement to an existing ethos, to suggest that in the best city the ethos would be of such and such a description, and truly

---

[7] Hyun Höchsmann, *On Philosophy in China*, Toronto, 2004, Wadsworth.

ethical conduct would be in accord with the ethos of the best city, even if all the while one admits that no actual city has ever measured up to the standards of the best city and perhaps even if one admits that no actual city could possibly measure up to such standards. Still, writing a book on ethics might necessarily mean sailing close to the shore of the prudent, not asking too often, "Why not, Mother?" It could perhaps even be said that neither Aristotle's *Ethics* nor his *Politics* rises all the way to the level of what can properly be called philosophy. Apparently he only uses the word "philosopher" once in the *Ethics* and that is to justify his preferring the truth to friendship (friendship for his teacher, Plato, apparently).[8] Similarly, the word "philosophy" appears rarely (only three or four times) in the *Politics*.[9] It may be that Aristotle's rare references to philosophy in the *Ethics* and the *Politics* mean to mark off the limitations of those two works, because, as he clearly states, these are practical sciences and one may not expect the highest degree of precision in such things, whereas philosophy proper aims at the highest degree of precision. Thus one may say that, for the most part, the *Ethics* and the *Politics* are subphilosophic. No how-to book reaches the level of the philosophic. If one applies this standard rigorously, the description offered earlier in the text by Höchsmann does not show that Confucius was a philosopher, but only that he was surely a great and wise man who influenced China for the better.

Continuing his treatment of Confucius, Höchsmann tells us, "At the center of the power of his philosophy and achievement was his great ability to bring to a synthesis the entire learning and art up to his time. Drawing upon his intensive study of the classics, Confucius provided the one universal standard with which philosophers and rulers sought to reconcile conflicting claims and interests."[10] If, however, Confucius was the first philosopher in China or one of the first ones, it follows that the "entire learning and art up to his time" could not be called philosophy. The "synthesis" achieved by Confucius, without question, would have been the product of profound study and would mark Confucius as one of the most learned men of all times and every place. Although he evidently was an excellent scribe, we need argument showing why what he did deserves to be called "philosophy." We must be patient. The widespread attribution of philosophy to the name and person of Confucius certainly might excuse Höchsmann from beginning

---

[8] Aristotle, *Nicomachean Ethics*, 1096a16. A reader can be misled by translators here. At 1094b13 Aristotle uses a form of the word λόγος (*logos*) which means speech, reason, or, to come closest to correct English, reasoned speech (if that is not a redundancy). H. Rackham, however, in his 1926 translation (Loeb Classical Library edition, London, 1962, Heinemann) translates the word as "philosophy." He makes the same error again at 1095a4.

[9] Aristotle, *Politics*, 1055b37, 1279b13, and 1282b19 and b23.

[10] Höchsman, *op. cit.*, pp. 5–6.

with a definition of philosophy and persuasive proof that Confucius fits that definition. After all, we do not demand that someone writing on al-Farabi, Locke, or Hegel begin with such a proof. Still, having raised the question as to the origin of philosophy, we are bound to consider critically those said to deserve the name of originator.

After a brief biographical sketch of Confucius, Höchsmann states that he "was a pioneer in philosophical thought." There was no established tradition of systematic schools of thought when Confucius began his philosophical activity, according to Höchsmann. This is a sensible point for him to make, if we are to recognize Confucius as the originator of philosophy, except one wonders if the requirement that a philosophical endeavor culminate in a "systematic school of thought" already intimates a notion of philosophy as a product of some sort of historical process. Höchsmann says that all Confucius had before him were the *Book of Changes (Yjing)*,[11] the *Book of Odes*, the *Book of History*, and the *Book of Music*. He tells us that for many centuries these four books were the curriculum of Confucian schooling. Then, strangely enough, he tells us that the *Yjing* was the work of several authors over several centuries, from 1,200 to 249 B.C. He says that it "is the earliest book of antiquity; the recorded history of philosophic thought begins with this work." This would seem to answer the question we have proposed. In other words, philosophy does not begin with Confucius. It looks as though it begins six hundred or so years before him, so that the "synthesis" by Confucius would be some sort of systematization of existing philosophic thought.

---

[11] Höchsmann places in parentheses the Chinese name of the work, spelled out here in Pin-yin Romanization. Until fifty years ago, scholars in various Western countries established ways to write out Chinese words in Roman script so that a pronunciation could be given that, it was hoped, approximated that of a speaker of Chinese. These approximations varied. Thus, a reader of English-language texts would likely find the capital of China spelled "Peking" in some works and "Peiping" in others. A great change was undertaken in the 1950s. One has first to remember that, although the Chinese written language serves the whole of the country, nobody in China "speaks Chinese." Those in the capital and in much of the north of China speak the Mandarin dialect (Putonghua), but a greater portion of the population, in Guangzhou (i.e., Canton, as earlier approximations spelled it) and in much of the south of China, speak the Cantonese dialect. One who goes to a Chinese restaurant in America is much more likely to hear Cantonese spoken. One of the strenuous and truly revolutionary efforts of the People's Republic of China has been to standardize the Chinese language throughout the country. The ultimate goal is to make all Chinese speak as well as write the same language. It well might take centuries to succeed in this. Beginning in 1958, China began an eight-year labor establishing an official, Chinese method of rendering in roman script words in the written Chinese language. This method is called "Pin-yin." In Pin-yin, the capital of the country is spelled "Beijing," and all Westerners are getting used to spelling it that way. Höchsmann has put in parentheses as the Chinese name for the *Book of Changes* the Pin-yin word *Yjing*. If you read a book in a European language published before 1980, you will likely find that title spelled *I Ching*.

Höchsmann begins his discussion of the synthesis by Confucius of "the classics," that is, the four books, by dealing with the *Book of Changes* (the *Yjing* or *I Ching*). That work consists of sixty-four "hexagrams." With a view to helping his readers, Höchsmann explains, "Within the sixty-four hexagrams two central themes which run through all philosophical thought in China are developed. One theme is that the universe is a well-ordered state of existence in which all things are correlated and man and nature form a unity. The other is that the universe is in a process of continuous change, as things are combined and intertwined ceaselessly." In addition, he tells us that the "metaphysics of the *Yjing* is an ontology of process, not of substance. . . . The underlying assumption of *Yjing* is that the universe and man's actions are governed by moral purposiveness." This last observation might be dismissed as a non sequitur, but we would have to leave open the possibility of elaboration of it. What is more interesting, however, is that what came just before, the remark about an "ontology of process," grasps our attention. It begins to look as though Höchsmann does not see Confucius on Confucius's own terms. He sees him through the eyes of his own time. This is a kind of intellectual "astigmatism" that will be examined later.

After treating the *Book of Changes*, Höchsmann turns to the *Book of Odes*.[12] The book contains some three hundred odes that Confucius had selected from the some three thousand that had been written from the Shang Dynasty (1600–1100 B.C.) through the time of Confucius himself. We are told that love odes "are abundant in the *Book of Odes*. The themes of the *Book of Odes* address deep and fervent love and longing, the transience of passions, the hope and despair of desire." He offers us a sampling of the odes. They are tender, gentle, and evocative of romantic settings. Plato, in the *Phaedrus*, shows us Socrates and Phaedrus, who take a walk outside the walls of Athens and sit under the shade of a plane tree by the side of the Ilissus River to discuss a love speech written by Lysias. Socrates turns the conversation into an analysis of the nature of erotic rhetoric and thence into an examination of *eros* itself. Thus it is philosophic in that it sees a universal human inclination as a problem to be solved and it makes progress in solving it dialectically. What is the nature, the being of *eros*, love, or desire? How does it fit in the soul? How is it manifested? What is its relation to things outside the soul, to things higher than the soul and the human? As befits the subject matter, the dialogue is soft and the presentation is poetic. The dialogue is not reducible to poetry, however. There is movement in it. It provides a certain progress to the soul's search for truth about being. It does not settle for making the reader (or listener) feel some sentiment or other – such a sentiment, for example, as the sadness that separation in wartime brings, a sentiment attributed by Höchsmann to one of the odes he quotes.

---

[12] Höchsmann, *op. cit.*, p. 8.

There is a poem by Edmund Waller (1606–87) that, speaking to a rose, says:

> Go, lovely Rose!
> Tell her that wastes her time and me,
> That now she knows,
> When I resemble her to thee,
> How sweet and fair she seems to be . . .
> Then die! that she
> The common fate of all things rare
> May read in thee;
> How small a part of time they share
> That are so wondrous sweet and fair!

Waller's poem is lovely and moving. It is surely an example of erotic rhetoric. Like all fine poetry, Waller's "Go, Lovely Rose" reminds one of philosophy or at least of the need for philosophy. Anyone who has fallen in love is touched by the poem with its erotic urgency and its reminder that love is inseparable from beauty, and cannot help but feel a bittersweet recognition of that urgency and that beauty and of their necessary confrontation with mortality. Nonetheless, having touched our heartstrings and having also summoned us to thought, Waller leaves us there.

Plato's *Phaedrus*, in contrast, begins with Socrates encountering Phaedrus in the city and hailing him, "Ho, friend Phaedrus, whither and whence?" It continues by their examining a speech written by Lysias, a love speech, an instance of erotic rhetoric. Because Socrates counters the enthusiasm of Phaedrus, they examine it without being swept away by it. The dialogue asks a series of questions about *eros* and leads us to alternative answers. The chief question is, "What is *eros*?"

Homer's *Iliad* begins by the summoning of the muse. "Sing, Goddess," says the poet. That is, sing, goddess, through my speeches. It is an appeal to the muse, an appeal to inspiration, rather than an appeal to reason. No doubt Waller would explain the origin of "Go, Lovely Rose" as springing from inspiration. Perhaps Lysias would make a similar claim regarding his courtship writing. To subject an example of inspired erotic rhetoric such as the speech by Lysias to rational examination is about as deflating as dissecting a really funny joke, but unexamined inspirations and jokes may, for our own good, require examination in the name of truth. That is the business of philosophy.

I do not believe that commentators have often called Homer, Waller, or Lysias a philosopher, although some may have done so. This is not even to raise the question whether poetry or philosophy is the superior calling. It is only to insist that the two are not one.

Therefore, we press the question whether the *Book of Odes* that Confucius teaches or the manner of his teaching those odes is more like Edmund

Waller's lyric poem or more like Plato's dialogue that insists on taking *eros* apart. The desire that Lysias and Waller feel for their respective beloved ones can instantly be appreciated, but the desire of Lysias is sublimated by Socrates into a desire for the truth. This is the highest, the noblest, human desire. We do not pretend to have answered here the question raised regarding the status of Confucius and the odes, but serious study demands that that question be raised. One's grandmother may remark that, "they say an apple a day keeps the doctor away," but we cannot settle for a "they say." Even if the whole fraternity of philosophy professors were now to assure us that philosophy began in China, it is no disrespect of authority to raise again the question of its origin. We cannot study philosophy without asking whether what "they say" is true. To raise that question is, itself, the proper business of philosophy.

Höchsmann tells us in a prefatory note that Fung Yu-lan's *A History of Chinese Philosophy* is "the most comprehensive study of philosophy in China" and that James Legge's *The Chinese Classics Series* is "one of the standard authoritative translations of the major thinkers."[13] We need, then, to devote some attention to Fung and Legge.

Fung Yu-lan (1895–1990) published his two-volume *History of Chinese Philosophy* in 1937. He wrote in English a shorter version of the work that was published in 1948. He is described on the back cover of the 1967 paperback edition of that shorter version, *A Short History of Chinese Philosophy*[14] as "a Chinese philosopher [who] is the father of Neo-Confucianism, a theory which fuses traditional Confucian ideas with Marxism." Because Fung has some reputation as the very voice of Chinese philosophy, we shall look at a few passages from his *Short History* and make what we can of them. First, however, this admixture of Marx proves what we just guessed. The philosophy that both Fung and Höchsmann discern in Confucius is a philosophy that has been displaced by "history," that is, by a particular conception of history that developed in the nineteenth century. That discerning is not altogether fair to Confucius.

Fung begins thus:

The place which philosophy has occupied in Chinese civilization has been comparable to that of religion in other civilizations. In China, philosophy has been every educated person's concern. In the old days, if a man were educated at all, the first education he received was in philosophy. When children went to school, the *Four Books*, which consist of the *Confucian Analects*, the *Book of Mencius*, the *Great Learning*, and the *Doctrine of the Mean*, were the first ones they were taught to read.[15]

[13] Höchsmann, note on translation and texts, unnumbered page following acknowledgments.
[14] Fung Yu-lan, *A Short History of Chinese Philosophy*, ed. Derek Bodde, New York, 1976, Free Press.
[15] Ibid., p. 1.

A great many problems are presented by this beginning. When Fung says that the place occupied by religion "in other civilizations" is comparable to the place of philosophy in Chinese civilization, does he mean that other civilizations simply lack philosophy, or that, because of philosophy (or of its particular kind of philosophy), China had or has no need of religion? One cannot understand what Fung means by "philosophy" without understanding what he believes to be the "place of religion" in other civilizations. "Religion," by definition, means "The service and adoration of God."[16] To a Roman Catholic, that means the Mass, simply. There are other "side effects" of religion, such as service to one's fellow man, or a code of ethics, but to reduce religion to these is to leave Hamlet out of *Hamlet*. Is it these secondary aspects of religion to which Fung refers when he says that the place of religion in other civilizations is filled by philosophy in China? Does he inadvertently confess that what he calls philosophy in China is really indistinguishable from what is called religion elsewhere, that is, that it is not philosophy at all?

Fung says that "philosophy had been every educated person's concern" and that, if educated at all, a person's "first education" had been "in philosophy." He goes on to say that, when children went to school, the *Four Books* were the first things they studied. What portion of the Chinese population then went to school? If it was a very substantial minority, then the notion that they all studied philosophy right at the beginning is preposterous. We are compelled to be suspicious when we are told that Chinese children are taught to read philosophy from the tenderest age. Imagine an American kindergarten where the children are made to read Aristotle's *Metaphysics*, Plato's *Timaeus*, or John Locke's *Two Treatises of Government*! Even if Fung has in mind only a small minority who, being educated, were truly educated, it cannot be thought that, even among the elite of the population, the children were able to be, or that they ought to be, educated in philosophy properly understood. Here Aristotle can help us. He tells us that education for the many must be civic education.[17] In addition, the whole of the eighth and last book of the *Politics* is devoted to education. He delineates the four chief subjects accepted as the core of schooling: grammar, gymnastic, music, and drawing.[18] Even as to that part of philosophy that, as we suggested earlier, may be regarded as barely within the fold (namely, ethics), Aristotle is emphatic that pupils must be habituated to good conduct before they are invited to discuss ethics and politics and that that habituation takes considerable time.[19] Here also James Madison can help: "[A] nation of philosophers is as little to be expected as the philosophical race of kings

[16] *Webster's New International Dictionary of the English Language*, unabridged, 1958.
[17] *Politics*, 1260b16.
[18] Ibid., 1337b24–5.
[19] *Nicomachean Ethics*, 1094b28–95a12.

wished for by Plato."[20] Without pretending to have answered the question that is here before us, we are compelled to suggest that at least the beginning of Fung's book does not persuade us that when he says "philosophy" he means philosophy. All that this beginning suggests is that some sort of schooling was given to Chinese children at an early age and that it gave to children something analogous to what in a Christian school would be called a "catechism." Thus, and only thus, might it be said as he says that, in China, "philosophy" held the place that in other civilizations is held by religion.

Springing eternal in the breast of the lover, the litigant, or the student of Chinese philosophy, hope springs here and makes us figure that behind and beyond these disconnected things there must be in the accepted Chinese canon some "formal philosophic works." This is not the case, however. What we see is what we get. The formal philosophic work would then appear to be the result in our souls of our having connected the dots sprinkled before us by the philosophers, but even this hope meets disappointment when the next sentences tell us, "According to tradition, the study of philosophy is not a profession. Everyone should study philosophy just as in the West every one should go to church. The purpose of the study of philosophy is to enable a man, *as a man*, to be a man, not some particular kind of man."[21]

There is an air of condescension in this, but, worse, behind that air there apparently is a shell game. For if everyone studies philosophy, then philosophy is what everyone can study. No matter how egalitarian we may be, we are forced to acknowledge that the more difficult a problem is, the fewer there are who will ever be able to grasp it as a problem, not to mention arrive at tentative solutions. The highest problems, therefore, will be grasped by few indeed. Philosophy is not included in what Thomas Babington Macaulay (1800–59) called what "every schoolboy knows." In Fung's formulation the distinction between philosophers and others disappears. The distinction between philosophy and other "thought" or "sayings" disappears, and with that disappearance goes the disappearance of any reason at all to study philosophy or, in fact, to study anything. What is called "philosophy" by Fung and is said to enable a man to be a man sounds like what in the West used to be called "liberal education" (which did, in fact, include a segment of philosophy – but this was for that minority who then attended liberal arts colleges) or perhaps like what well might be called, with Aristotle, "education for citizenship."

James Legge (1815–97), a Scot, was educated at King's College in Aberdeen. He then studied at the Highbury Theological Seminary in London. China was not then open to Europeans, but British traders had managed to set up shop in Canton (as Guangzhou was then called in English). Troubles arose, however, with the Chinese authorities because

[20] *Federalist*, No. 49, the 6th paragraph.
[21] Fung Yu-lan, *op. cit.*, n. 14 this chapter.

the British were dealing in opium. This led to the Sino-British war (i.e., the First Opium War) of 1839–42, and the British packed up and moved from Canton to nearby Hong Kong, colonial occupation and rule of which had been ceded to Britain in 1842. Legge had gone in 1839 as a missionary to the Chinese and had had to settle for a place in Malacca (in the present country of Malaysia). He then moved to Hong Kong in 1842, where he remained for thirty years. Legge translated the Chinese classics (the books that we have seen listed by Fung) into the first English printing of them. Having returned to Britain, Legge was in 1876 installed in the Chair of Chinese Language and Literature established at Oxford University for him. What English-speaking people know of Chinese literature, including the body of work sometimes called Chinese philosophy, was introduced to the West by his compilation and translation of those works. Legge was a scholar of monumental proportions. He is listed briefly in *Webster's Biographical Dictionary*, but no mention is made of him in the *Cambridge Biographical Encyclopedia* published in 1994. A brief but useful biography of Legge is in the eleventh edition of the *Encyclopædia Britannica*,[22] and Legge is himself the author of the entry on Confucius in that edition.

Because there is no alphabet in the Chinese language, rendering a Chinese word into a written word in an alphabetic language such as English requires that someone listen intently to a competent speaker of Chinese and then write out his words in phonetic approximation of them. The Chinese government has of late attempted to provide a standardized method of rendering for English speakers a Romanized or Latinized approximation of Chinese words. This standardization is what is called "Pin-yin." Of course, the next step after transliteration is translation, which does not carry the word phonetically from one script to another but attempts to replicate in one language the meaning of words from another. As we suggested earlier, success in this venture depends on there being a word in the one language that corresponds more or less exactly to the word in the other. This is relatively easy when translating from one European language to another and when translating the words for concrete objects. We showed this in the case of the Italian *uccelli* and the English "birds." When translating more abstract words, and when translating between languages from two quite distinct "cultures" (as would now be said), the task is much more difficult.

In his *Encyclopædia Britannica* article on Confucius, James Legge first renders into Latin script the Chinese name of Confucius and then translates its meaning into English. Names are, of course, words. Often one finds that an English surname is simply the word for a trade or a calling. Such is the case with "Smith" or "Miller," for example. Because Chinese words are often expressed in one character, that is, in one syllable or sound unit, it is often

---

[22] New York, 1911. This is the edition of the *Britannica* apparently favored by connoisseurs of encyclopedias.

the case that a person's name is also a common word or a sequence of a few common words. Take the name *Sī Dí Wén*. The whole name is called the *ming-xing*, that is, the full name or "royal" name. The surname, *Sī* (pronounced "suh"), is, by itself, simply the *xing* ("shing" in English). That same word, *Sī*, if written the same way, and pronounced the same way, is a verb meaning "to manage" or "direct." The second character, *Dí*, is a verb meaning "to enlighten." The third, *Wén* means script or writing. Thus, the *ming-xing* illustrated here and pronounced "suh-dee-wen" means something like master of enlightened literature. Legge tells us that "Confucius" is simply the rendering into Roman script of the name *K'ung Fu-tze*. He tells us that the Chinese name means Philosopher Kung or Master Kung.[23] Maybe! Master Kung is almost surely correct, but to tell us that the English equivalent of the Chinese name of a man who lived 2,500 years ago is "Philosopher Kung" is to take for granted that there is a straightforward Chinese equivalent for the English word "philosopher" (i.e., for a word derived from the Greek). To say that the word for "master" or "teacher" is also the word for "philosopher" is something of a leap in English and, as far as the Chinese language goes, presupposes the answer to the question faced by this chapter. In fact, in present-day Chinese usage, the second and third of the three-character name of Confucius, in the officially sanctioned Pin-yin pronunciation, is *fuzi*. A recent English–Chinese/Chinese–English dictionary published by Oxford University Press gives as the definition of *fuzi* "a Confucian scholar." The more or less official *Pinyin Chinese-English Dictionary* published by the Beijing Foreign Languages Institute in 1985 gives a little more complete definition. It is: "(1) an ancient form of address to a Confucian scholar or to a master by his disciples (2) pedant." Those same two characters preceded by the character *yū*, resulting in the expression *yūfūzì*, are defined somewhat more expansively by that same dictionary as "a pedantic old fogey." Perhaps James Legge was misled by his enthusiasm to translate *K'ung Fu Tze* as "Philosopher Kung," and, contrary to what Fung Yu-lan has told us, we are compelled to ask him to reconsider whether a philosopher is a "particular kind of a person." If a philosopher is not a particular kind of person, then the word "philosopher" is just so much surplus baggage. If a philosopher is a particular kind of person, then Confucius is not, by the sheer force of the meaning of his name, shown to be one.

Relying in some measure on Mencius (372–289 B.C.), who was a follower of Confucius, Legge tells us that the childhood of Confucius was one of modest circumstances and that he therefore had had to learn many practical arts to earn a living. Then, at twenty-one, Confucius began his career as a teacher of "young and inquiring spirits who wished to be instructed

---

[23] "Confucius," *Encyclopædia Britannica*, 11th ed., "Handy Volume Issue," New York, 1911, vol. 6, p. 908 (sc. the 4th paragraph of the article).

in the principles of right conduct and government."[24] He taught for many years, hoping, it appears, to find a ruler who would follow his teachings. This hope was not realized, but the thread of interest in practical moral and political matters and in the connection between what we should call "theory and practice" seemed never to leave him. "A disciple once asked," Legge tells us, "what he would consider the first thing to be done, if intrusted with the government of a state." Confucius answered, "The rectification of names."[25] Perhaps he meant by this something like "calling a spade a spade," the clarification of discourse, or clear statement of universals. This would perhaps suggest the lineaments of philosophy as it has been understood in the West. At least it is clear from Legge's account that Confucius wished to be, to borrow here an expression from Niccolò Machiavelli (1469–1527), "a secretary to a prince." Now it is possible to view this task simply from a moralistic vantage. The political advice of those Chinese called by Westerners "philosophers," that the ruler "must rule justly," does not rise above the level of a wholesome admonition. A "secretary to a prince," in Machiavelli's understanding however, does not caution the prince after the fashion of a doting mother. What we have not seen in accounts of Chinese philosophers is any vestige of an examination of princedom as one rulership among possible alternatives, nor any comparison of the benefits and burdens of the different forms of rulership, nor any penetrating examination of the nature of justice. It is all very well to "tut-tut" a bit and demand that justice be done, but a philosophically necessary accompaniment of such a demand is a deliberate and exhaustive study of justice. What is it? As we shall see, these questions are the hallmarks of political philosophy in the West, beginning with Socrates and Plato. We must wait until we examine "politics" and the "nature and origin of political philosophy" to return to this matter.

If we should go back far enough, we would find that thoughtful people in the West regarded philosophy as the province of the West, having its origin in Greece. It is not clear at what point that view came into question. Possibly that change occurred in the seventeenth or early eighteenth century. Certainly by the middle of the nineteenth century, as witness James Legge, there were those who spoke of a Chinese philosophy of ancient origin. Our argument so far has touched on Höchsmann, Fung, and Legge, and the glimpse of them that we have had indicates the possibility that Legge, for example, went to China, mastered the language, read the old books, and called what he saw "philosophy" without a critical yardstick to justify his calling it that. Others might have done likewise. The older view, that philosophy began in Greece, is still held by many, and in fact it would be difficult to find anyone who is regarded as a philosopher (as distinct from a professor

---

[24] Ibid., the 7th paragraph.
[25] Ibid., p. 909, the 14th paragraph.

of philosophy) who speaks of China, India, Persia, or Egypt as the cradle of philosophy. Perhaps Montesquieu (1689–1755) might be an exception.[26] For a strong view that Greece and only Greece is the cradle of the discipline, we shall turn to the Scottish classicist John Burnet (1863–1928). First, however, having used the word "culture" a few times, we are obliged to explain that word.

We have already spoken of the refusal of words to hold still. So constant is this inconstancy that it sometimes appears that two people of different generations do indeed speak two languages that are each foreign to the other. According to twenty-first-century usage, the word "culture" and the word "ethnicity" are reciprocals. The former, culture, is what the latter, ethnicity, has. A culture, as that word has come to be used, is an attribute of an ethnicity. The political liberal and the political conservative are in agreement that "cultures" and "ethnicities" are sacrosanct. What is strange is that these words in their present usage simply did not exist in your grandfather's day. This means either that the whole human race was hopelessly ignorant a short time ago, or it means, as nice ladies used to say, "fashion dictates." In the first edition – the 1933 edition – of the *Oxford English*

---

[26] Charles de Secondat, Baron de la Brède et de Montesquieu (1689–1755). In his masterwork, *The Spirit of the Laws*, published in 1748 (see the English translation, tr. and ed. Anne M. Cohler, Basia Carolyn Miller, and Harold Samuel Stone, Cambridge, 1989, Cambridge University Press), there are more than fifty instances in which Montesquieu mentions China or the Chinese. In one of these he mentions a "Chinese philosopher," but the reference is to the work of a French priest. It appears that the Chinese individual mentioned is someone much closer to Montesquieu's day than he is to the time of Confucius (Book 24, Ch. 19, p. 473). Furthermore, in another place he mentions "[o]ne of China's classics" and he does not there make any reference to philosophy or to a philosopher (Book 16, Ch. 8, p. 269). Nearly all of the mentions of China refer to the same book by that French priest: Jean Baptiste du Halde, *Description de l'Empire de la Chine*, published in Paris in about 1735. The first European to travel to China and bring back accounts of it was the Italian Marco Polo (1254[?]–1324[?]), but great voyages of discovery occurred in the fifteenth, sixteenth, and seventeenth centuries, and John Locke (1632–1704) was interested in the accounts of them, other travelers' tales, and various descriptive works, as is shown by their presence in his library. In his *Two Treatises of Government* (1690) (Peter Laslett, ed., Cambridge, 1960, Cambridge University Press), Locke cites some of them, including El Inca Garcilaso de la Vega's *Comentarios Reales del Peru*. Locke had read an English translation of a French translation of the Spanish original. Locke mentions China only once, however, and that is to convey a mention of China by Sir Robert Filmer whose *Patriarcha* served as a foil for Locke. See Locke, *Treatises*, I, 141. Therefore, it looks as though more detailed knowledge of China had only penetrated England and France after Locke lived and wrote and, in the case of Father du Halde, just before Montesquieu's great work. Not until Legge's translations of the Chinese classics in the middle of the nineteenth century was there easy access to them for English readers. Thus, nothing can be made of the absence before the eighteenth or probably before the nineteenth century of European mention of Chinese "philosophy," so, if one is to question the characterization of the Chinese classics as "philosophy," it cannot be done simply by noticing the absence of that characterization prior to the eighteenth and nineteenth centuries.

Dictionary, a dictionary that ran to thirteen volumes, a dictionary in which a definition often ran to two, three, or more columns and which, as a rule, included several illustrations of usage over some centuries, the word "ethnicity" has a marvelously brief definition. It is: "Heathendom, heathen superstition." "Culture," in contrast, has as a noun a set of six principal definitions running to about one-third of a page. None of the six defini-tions bears a resemblance to its usage in the twenty-first century, a meaning developed largely after the 1933 publication of the *Oxford English Dictio-nary*. The root of the word seems to be "cult." Thus, the first definition is "cultivation, tending, in Christian authors, worship." The second definition is "the action or practice of cultivating the soil; tillage, husbandry." (The common word "agriculture" illustrates this.) The third definition is: "The cultivating or rearing of a plant or crop." The fourth is: "The cultivating or development (of the mind, faculties, manners, etc.); improvement or refinement by education and training." The fifth is: "The training, devel-opment, and refinement of mind, tastes, and manners; the condition of being thus trained and refined; the intellectual side of civilization." The sixth is: "The prosecution with special attention or study of any subject or pursuit." In other words, culture, in the fourth, fifth, and sixth senses in the 1993 *OED*, is what the cultivated portion of the population acquires. The cultivated are the few. The present notion that everybody in a place has culture just by being there is as absurd as referring to a weed patch as the product of a distinct agriculture. By thus demoting the word, the distinction between one ethnicity and another is abolished. All ethnicities have culture and each is of equal dignity. Curiously, one can state a doctrine of cultural relativism (i.e., equality), and in the same breath demand, as at Gleneagles, Scotland in June of 2005, that some cultures give large sums of money to other cultures to promote their development. If all are equal, how can it be that some require development and ought to be developed at the expense of others? Our purposes here are met by noting that the firm attribution of equality of cultures seems to be the precondition of finding in each culture the counterparts of all the things one finds in any. Let us now turn to John Burnet.

First, a reminder. Michelangelo lived from 1475 to 1564. His art is an example of that movement in Europe in the fifteenth and sixteenth cen-turies that historians call "the Renaissance." The English form of that word is "rebirth." The Renaissance was a self-conscious rebirth or recovery of the high culture of classical antiquity. If one looks at ancient Greek sculpture and then at the Roman continuation and imitation of it, one is struck by the devoted regard for the naked, human body. That fascination takes the beauty of the excellent human body as the standard that art is meant to imi-tate. Every sinew of every muscle that one can observe in every action of the body is studied and then represented in sculpture. Michelangelo's sculpture of David is an example of the Renaissance rebirth and recovery of classical sculpture. What strikes a visitor to museums in the Far East is the absence of that fascination with and faithful representation of the beauty of the naked, human form – the absence, in general, of naturalistic art.[27] There can be no denying the captivating beauty of Oriental art. Except from the stand-point of housecleaning, no sensible person can favorably compare a beige wall-to-wall carpet with an intricately patterned Persian rug. Westerners of means gladly and wisely gather into their houses from China and Japan cloisonné vases, lacquered furniture, and hauntingly affective silk screens of pretty ladies in pretty gowns in pretty gardens, but to the extent that Oriental art is not devotional and stylized (as in sculptures of the Buddha), it is largely decorative and stylized. Noticing this striking difference between Occidental and Oriental sculpture and painting, one is driven to wonder how and how much that difference spreads to matters other than sculpture and painting. It is here that John Burnet helps us.

Burnet was born in 1863. He taught Greek for more than thirty years at St. Andrews University. He died in 1928. Among the products of his labors are annotated editions of the Greek texts of Plato's *Euthyphro, Apology*, and *Crito* and of Plato's *Phaedo*. These editions are indispensable if one wishes to study those Platonic texts carefully. Burnet also set about to do a complete study of Greek philosophy. The first volume of that study is called *Greek Philosophy, Volume I, Thales to Plato* (1914).[28] The Introduction to that volume confronts the assertions already abroad in Burnet's day that philosophy began in Egypt, Babylon, or India, and it does so in part by pursuing the questions that ensue from our observations here about the differences in Eastern and Western sculpture and painting. Burnet says:

In the first place, philosophy is not mythology. It is true that there is plenty of mythology in Plato, and we shall have to consider the meaning of that later. It is also true that we shall have to take account from the first of a mass of cosmogonical and eschatological speculation which influenced philosophy in many ways. These things, however, are not themselves philosophy, and it cannot even be said that they are the germ from which philosophy developed. It is important to be quite clear about this; for in some places cosmogonies are still paraded as the source of Greek philosophy. . . . It is possible, though it has certainly not been proved, that the oldest Greek cosmogonies, or some of them, came from Egypt or Babylon. . . . These things, however, have nothing directly to do with philosophy. From the Platonic point of view, there can be no philosophy where there is no rational science. . . . Now rational

---

[27] See Robert E. Fisher, *Buddhist Art and Architecture*, Singapore, 1993, Thames and Hudson; Michael Sullivan, *The Book of Art*, vol. 9, *Chinese and Japanese Art*, New York, 1965, Grolier; and see the curious afterthought in H. W. Janson, *History of Art*, Englewood Cliffs, NJ, 1974, Prentice-Hall. In an apologetic section entitled "Postscript," Janson devotes the last eight pages of a 578-page book that had been the standard college text in the field for many years to a glancing treatment of Oriental art.

[28] John Burnet, *Greek Philosophy, Volume I, Thales to Plato*, London, 1914, Macmillan.

science is the creation of the Greeks, and we know when it began. We do not count as philosophy anything anterior to that.[29]

Now it is perhaps beyond dispute that political philosophy is a branch of or a kind of philosophy and further that there was philosophy before there was political philosophy. If it were possible to manipulate this plain fact, we might suggest that long before there were chronicles that we might consult there were different groups or gatherings of people – let us for convenience call them "tribes" – and that each tribe, noticing another, noticed first that "they" do not do as "we" do. It is one thing to notice that they do not do as we do; it is another thing to ask "Why do they do as they do and not as we do? Is there a right or a best way?" These questions are the sparks that when fanned ignite what properly may be called philosophy. A long quotation from Burnet discusses science as the foundation of philosophy:

It is true, of course, that science originated at the time when communication with Egypt and Babylon was easiest [but if] the Egyptians had possessed anything that could rightly be called mathematics, it is hard to understand how it was left for Pythagoras and his followers to establish the most elementary propositions in plane geometry; and if the Babylonians had really any conception of the planetary system, it is not easy to see why the Greeks had to discover bit by bit the true shape of the earth[30] and the explanation of eclipses. It is clear that these things were not known at Babylon.... Of course everything depends on what we mean by science. If we are prepared to give that name to an elaborate record of celestial phenomena made for purposes of divination, then the Babylonians had science and the Greeks borrowed it from them. Or, if we are prepared to call rough rules of thumb for measuring fields and pyramids science, then the Egyptians had science and it came from them to Ionia. But if we mean by science what Copernicus and Galileo and Kepler, and Leibniz and Newton meant, there is not the slightest trace of that in Egypt or even in Babylon, while the very earliest Greek ventures are unmistakably its forerunners.... The only remains that have come down to us show that the Egyptians were not without a certain ingenuity in the solution of particular arithmetical and geometric problems, but there is not the slightest trace of anything like general methods. If inconvenient remainders occur they are simply dropped.[31]

Burnet reminds us of a factor that, speaking generally of later developments in China, India, Egypt, and Persia, we mentioned earlier. "In the case of Babylon," he writes, "it is even more important to distinguish the times before and after Alexander the Great."[32] It would be a great mistake to read

---

[29] Ibid., pp. 3–4.

[30] One of the silliest fallacies of commonplace wisdom for the past few centuries is the proposition that everyone believed that the earth was flat until Columbus discovered otherwise.

[31] Burnet, *op. cit.*, pp. 4–5. It is generally known that if one receives a bank statement and reconciles it with his or her check stubs it is either right or wrong. If the check register is off so much as one cent, it is off and that is all there is to it. As the old saying goes, "close only counts in horseshoes and hand grenades."

[32] Ibid., p. 7.

Niccolò Machiavelli's *The Art of War* (1521) and conclude that Italians had some time earlier invented gunpowder. It appears that Europeans figured out how to use gunpowder to propel projectiles, but it is likely that it was the Chinese who invented gunpowder in about the tenth century. Likewise, finding early philosophy in ancient China by reading backward into the sayings of the ancient sages scientific and philosophic exercises that are evident after the spread of the elements of Greek learning would be a mistake.

Then Burnet makes a connection between science and sculpture:

The Greeks achieved what they did, in the first place, because they were born observers. The anatomical accuracy of their sculpture in its best period proves that.... The Egyptians, we may remember, never learnt to draw an eye in profile. But the Greeks did not rest content with mere observation; they went on to make experiments of a quite modern character. That by which Empedokles illustrated the flux and reflux of the blood between the heart and the surface of the body is best known, for we have a description of it in his own words. It also establishes the corporeal nature of atmospheric air....

But, while philosophy is thus intimately bound up with positive science, it is not to be identified with it.... If we look at Greek philosophy as a whole, we shall see that it is dominated from beginning to end by the problem of reality (τὸ ὄν). "What is real?"... [W]here that question is asked, there we have philosophy.[33]

The next seven chapters of Burnet's book – about a hundred pages – deal with philosophy prior to the advent of political philosophy. The individuals with whom Burnet deals are those known collectively as the "pre-Socratics" to virtually all who, accepting the view that philosophy is Greek, have written histories of philosophy. Our knowledge of them ranges from fragmentary to scant. To get some inkling of them we shall skim over the top of them, relying on the treatment of them by Burnet, by Fr. Frederick Copleston, and by Richard D. McKirahan. But first, not to leave John Burnet standing alone, we need to touch briefly on Georg Wilhelm Friedrich Hegel (1770–1831).

Hegel was among Western philosophers an early questioner as to whether some of his contemporaries were mistaken in speaking of the early Chinese as being engaged in philosophy, and he came to the conclusion that they were indeed mistaken. He was born in Stuttgart in 1770, took his doctorate in theology at Tübingen in 1791, and taught at Jena, then Heidelberg, and then Berlin from 1818 until his death in 1831. His writings include *Life of Jesus*, the *Phenomenology of Mind*, the *Philosophy of History*, and the *Philosophy of Right*. Whatever may be said of the difficulties his *Philosophy of History* may

[33] Ibid., pp. 10–11. We must emphasize here that "to be" means "to be always," for whatever was but is no more is an object not for philosophical but for historical study. History is made of proper names. Philosophy uses proper names as illustrations only. This distinction between philosophy and history raises questions about Hegel's *History of Philosophy* just as much as about his *Philosophy of History*.

have presented to those who came after him, something of a counterpart to that work was his series of lectures on the history of philosophy. These were presented several times at Jena, then Heidelberg, and then Berlin, and, of course, each successive presentation was characterized by refinements on those that had preceded it. Students of his compared their lecture notes,[34] and these composite notes were published after Hegel's death as *Vorlesungen über die Geschichte der Philosophie.* An English translation, *Lectures on the History of Philosophy,* from the first volume of which the following comments are drawn, was published in 1995.[35]

The beginning student should not be daunted but cautioned by the fact that Hegel is difficult to read. The blessed exception is the brief chapter "Oriental Philosophy." That chapter begins thus:

The first philosophy in order is the so-called Oriental, which, however, does not enter into the substance or range of our subject as presented here. Its position is preliminary, and we only deal with it at all in order to account for not treating of it at greater length, and in what relation it stands to Thought and to true Philosophy. . . . That which we call Eastern Philosophy is more properly the religious mode of thought and the conception of the world belonging generally to the Orientals and approximates very closely to Philosophy. . . . We do not similarly maintain that the Roman, Greek, and Christian religions constitute philosophy. . . . The first subject of remark with regard to the Chinese respects the teaching of Confucius (500 years before Christ) which made a great sensation in Leibnitz' time; this teaching is a moral philosophy [*sic*]. . . . We have conversations between Confucius and his followers in which there is nothing definite other than a commonplace moral put in the form of good, sound doctrine, which may be found as well expressed and better, in every place and among every people. Cicero gives us *De Officiis,* a book of moral teaching more comprehensive and better than all the books of Confucius. [Confucius] is hence only a man who has a certain amount of practical and worldly wisdom – one with whom there is no speculative philosophy.[36]

The foregoing gives us a sample of Hegel's thirty-one-page chapter "Oriental Philosophy." Now, in the twenty-first century, to say such things is heresy. In the name of "diversity," it is almost a punishable offense. If we are to pursue the truth, however, we have to get over the notion that the whole human race has gotten much smarter than the poor souls who lived two

---

[34] German professors who, as exiles from the Third Reich, taught in America, initially found the experience shocking. In Germany, up to and even after World War II, professors immersed themselves in study and delivered the fruits of that study in a course of lectures. The students sat silently and endeavored to transcribe verbatim what the professor said. Having come to America, the professors were confronted with a new breed of students who interrupted the professor to ask questions and even to disagree. Some of the displaced professors found this troubling – impertinent. Others found it refreshing and intellectually stimulating. For better or for worse, the forms and practices of American university education have spread worldwide during the last half century.

[35] Georg Wilhelm Friedrich Hegel, *Lectures on the History of Philosophy,* 3 vols., vol. 1, *Greek Philosophy to Plato,* tr. L. S. Haldane, Lincoln, 1995, University of Nebraska Press.

[36] Ibid., pp. 117, 120, 121.

hundred years ago. It is the habit of an adolescent to reflect on the hopeless ignorance of his parents. Two hundred years? Does this not mean doubly hopeless ignorance?

Having opened the question of the origin of philosophy, and having settled at least provisionally on the old-fashioned view that its place of origin was Greece, let us turn now briefly to a scanning of those Greeks called the "pre-Socratics."

The Ionians

Boeotia, just north of Attica, seems to have been the home of the poet Hesiod, who flourished in the eighth, or perhaps the seventh, century B.C. McKirahan indicates that Hesiod was something of a precursor of the pre-Socratics in his interests, but he distinguishes the latter from Hesiod by saying that the "philosophers of sixth-century Miletus managed to take the decisive step of abandoning mythological ways of thought."[37] The Greek settlements on the islands of the eastern part of what we today call the Aegean Sea and those along the adjacent coastal areas of Asia Minor constituted what we know historically as Ionia. The ancient city of Miletus lay on the west coast of Asia Minor about eighty miles south of Smyrna (Izmir in present-day Turkey). Why Ionia should have been the site of the beginnings of philosophy is a question that invites speculation. Thales (640[?]–546), a Milesian, was the "first human being who can rightly be called a man of science," according to Burnet. With Thales, "a new thing came into the world."[38] We get some appreciation of his place by noting that Herodotus, the "Father of History," who flourished in the fifth century B.C., tells us in his account of the Persian War (c. 490–479 B.C.) that Thales had correctly predicted an eclipse in 585 B.C.,[39] a great scientific feat. Thales pursued questions of mathematics, cosmology, and physics, and (as Burnet puts it) his greatness is not in his answers but in his asking the questions. He has been regarded in the West as the first person deserving of the name "philosopher." Thales speculated on the bottom cause of physical reality, and Aristotle opined that Thales viewed water as the material cause of all things.[40] McKirahan offers an amendment to the effect that Thales "is a threshold figure, standing at the beginning of the Western scientific and philosophical tradition, but strongly influenced by the past . . . yet his demythologized understanding of the world, whatever its details, is new."[41]

---

[37] Richard D. McKirahan, *Philosophy before Socrates*, Indianapolis, 1994, Hackett, p. 19.

[38] Burnet, *op. cit.*, p. 18.

[39] Herodotus, I.74.

[40] Burnet, p. 21, and see Frederick Copleston, S.J. (1907–94), *A History of Philosophy*, New York, 1993, Doubleday, vol. 1, pp. 22–23, and Diogenes Laertius (third century A.D.), *Lives of Eminent Philosophers*, tr. R. D. Hicks, Cambridge, MA, 1925, Harvard University Press, vol. 1, I.27. (pp. 27–9).

[41] McKirahan, *op. cit.*, p. 31.

Two Milesians following in the footsteps of Thales were Anaximander (died c. 546 B.C.) and Anaximenes (flourished c. 546–525 B.C.). Whereas Thales perhaps did not reduce his thoughts to writing, Anaximander did write a book. "It is probable that it was the first Greek book written in prose."[42] According to Burnet, he "seems to have thought it unnecessary to fix upon 'air,' water, or fire as the original and primary form of body. He preferred to represent that simply as a boundless something . . . from which all things arise and to which they all will return again. . . . [H]e had been struck by [the] fact . . . that the world presents us with a series of opposites, of which the most primary are hot and cold, wet and dry."[43] We need not notice other of his views here. This is enough to enable us to notice that this effort to find satisfactory explanations of physical phenomena and to reduce those explanations to the fewest and most comprehensive is illustrative of the character of natural philosophy.

According to Father Copleston, Anaximenes reverts to the view of Thales that there is one primary substance. (We may call it an "element," but we need to caution ourselves not to equate it with the sense in which we speak now of "elements.") Copleston borrows the German word *urstoff* to explain Anaximenes. There is one *urstoff*, one stuff, of which all of physical nature is an array of manifestations or examples. Whereas Thales had put forth water as that stuff, Anaximenes offers air, and he introduces as an explanation of those manifestations the notions of condensation and rarefaction.[44]

Milesian civilization, and in fact Ionian civilization as a whole, broke down under the pressure of the Persian occupation. (Miletus fell in 494 B.C.) The character of Ionian philosophy had been, as Burnet asserts, altogether secular. That means, of course, that Greek philosophy likely could not have arisen out of the cosmogonies of Egypt or Babylon. Even the word "god" as a label for things or forces or in the case of personifications of natural things or forces did not mean in all cases of Milesian usage the name of an object of worship. The breakdown of Ionian civilization necessitated the movement of the center of philosophic gravity from Ionia to elsewhere in the Greek world. The southern part of the Italian peninsula became that location.

Pythagoras and His Disciples

To learn carpentry, one has to be apprenticed to a carpenter, a journeyman carpenter. When it comes to philosophy, only a handful of men in history have mastered the calling without a teacher. Even vast libraries,

---

42 Burnet, *op. cit.*, p. 22.
43 *Loc. cit.*
44 Frederick Copleston, *A History of Philosophy*, New York, 1993, Image/Doubleday, vol. 1, pp. 26–7. And see Burnet, *op. cit.*, pp. 24–6.

high technology, and what is so self-consciously called "the information explosion" have not changed that. It is not without reason that the various branches of learning that occupy a university are called "disciplines." The word "disciple" means pupil, and the word "pupil" is the correlative of teacher or master, that is, *dominus*.[45] From the master the disciple learns the discipline. Pythagoras flourished a few years after Anaximenes. We do not know who, if anyone, was the teacher of Pythagoras. Perhaps he was one of that handful of people who did not need a teacher.[46] At the beginning of his second chapter, Burnet says that he "must have been one of the world's greatest men." He was from Samos, one of the larger islands off the coast of Asia Minor. In 535 B.C., Polycrates and his two brothers took over the rule of Samos, and within a few years Polycrates assumed tyrannical power. It appears that, because of the single and unrestrained rule of Polycrates, Pythagoras left Samos and settled in Croton in the southern reaches of the Italian peninsula.[47] In the latter part of the sixth century B.C., he and his disciples began a society or "school," which, according to Copleston, had an ascetic and religious side to it, but that certainly had a clearly scientific character as well.[48] Both Burnet and Copleston, among other commentators, remind us of the difficulty in attributing Pythagorean doctrines to Pythagoras himself as distinct from his followers or school. It may be that those doctrines developed over many decades and in fact over a few centuries.

---

[45] Within the tradition of Christianity, the word "disciple" seems to some to have a special meaning associated only with Jesus, but the word "disciple" found in the King James and the Revised Standard versions of the New Testament is simply a translation of a Greek word that is a form of μάθησις (*mathēsis*) which refers to the act of learning, which makes sense in the case of Jesus inasmuch as a rabbi is, first and foremost, a teacher. What is learned is called *mathēma*. From the core of that Greek word comes the English word "mathematics." In Greek, *mathema* meant all learning, not the altogether quantitative science we mean now by the word "mathematics." The Scripture of the Jews was written in Hebrew, but because the homeland of the Jews was in what had come to be the Hellenized part of the world and, so, many Jews spoke Greek, there was developed a Greek Testament (called the *Septuagint* after the seventy scholars who cooperated in its translation from the Hebrew into Greek). The New Testament, of course, was written in Koine Greek. Much of the biblical tradition, insofar as it comes down to Europeans in other than the original languages, comes down through the filter of the Latin language, the spread of Christianity being largely coterminous with the reach of the Roman Empire. The English word "disciple" derives from no Greek word but from the Latin word *discipulos*. If you were to translate the Greek New Testament into Latin, that is the word you would use, and, in fact, the Vulgate Bible (i.e., the Bible in Latin) does exactly that. See, for example, the Greek original and the English translations at Luke 9:43 and John 13:35. There are some slight variations in the Latin translation, so those passages in the Vulgate Bible are at Lucae 9:44 and Joannis 13:35.

[46] Burnet (p. 39) gives credit to the opinion that Pythagoras was a disciple of Anaximander.

[47] If you look at what is called the "boot" of Italy, the Gulf of Táranto sits below what one would have to call the "arch" of the "foot." Croton (now called Crotone) is on the bottom of the "foot," just about where the "arch" meets the "sole."

[48] See Copleston, *op. cit.*, p. 29.

Pythagoras adhered to the doctrine of metempsychosis. He and his school made progress in mathematics (including the perfected doctrine regarding the properties of a right triangle that still bears his name, and the discovery that concordant musical intervals can be expressed in mathematical terms) and made progress as well in medicine and astronomy.[49] Plato, in his *Republic*, has Socrates avouch to Glaucon and Adeimantus a doctrine of metempsychosis, but the careful reader of that text takes that teaching with a grain of salt. Perhaps Glaucon and Adeimantus were less than wholly persuaded by that doctrine. Thales was the first man later generations called a philosopher. Pythagoras was the first to call himself such.

Heraclitus

Ephesus was an Ionian city in Lydia, a region of Asia Minor along the Aegean coast about midway north and south. The Lydians were an Indo-European people (i.e., not Greek) but nonetheless developed as part of Ionian (i.e., Greek) civilization. After the Persian conquest late in the sixth century, Lydia became a satrapy of the Persian empire. Heraclitus was an Ephesian who flourished in about the turn of the sixth to the fifth century B.C. Relying on Plato, Aristotle, and Diogenes Laertius, as well as on fragments from Heraclitus himself, Copleston describes Heraclitus as a crusty sort of fellow who sharply criticized almost every one of his contemporaries and all of his philosophic predecessors. Writers often quote out of context some engaging saying of a notable person and thereby perpetuate a misunderstanding of him. In the case of Heraclitus, the saying is, "All is in flux." By itself, and

---

49 Cf. McKirahan, *op. cit.*, p. 91. One often hears present-day adherents of cultural relativism maintain that the music of other cultures is indeed music and that all musics are of equal rank. Unfamiliar music is simply "their" music, not defective or inferior music. This is a generous and open-minded view, and it has led to the establishment in some American universities departments of ethnomusicality in their schools of music. Western music is not music; it is simply "our" music according to this view. Two things need to be considered in weighing this view. One is that the development of music and of panharmonic instruments, beginning with the Greeks and continuing to the present, involves precise mathematical measurements of the length of strings, for example, and then of the frequency of vibrations. The other thing is that if there are schools that actually teach Westerners, say, African music, recitals by their pupils in Western cities must be rare if not nonexistent, whereas there are schools of music in China, Japan, Korea, and India, for example, that develop virtuosos of the piano and the violin who travel throughout the world and are received not as Chinese, Japanese, Korean, or Indian but simply as accomplished violinists and pianists whom one would stand in line to hear. Also, there are fine symphony orchestras in many Eastern cities. Ravi Shankar is an Indian who plays an instrument called the sitar. It is a string instrument. He is perhaps the greatest virtuoso of that instrument, and he gives concerts in Europe and America. It is no doubt pleasant to attend one of these concerts to hear him play, but an American would be hard pressed to name a second sitar player, and, although an American student might learn the sitar – perhaps for the novelty of doing so – that would not likely be a promising career path. One does not hear of great sitarists named Smith or Jones playing the concert circuit in England, Italy, India, or China.

at face value, this would mean that Heraclitus believed that nothing is, that there is no reality, but then there would be no Heraclitus and no believing, and clearly to philosophize or to teach would be futile. In other words, such a saying meant in such a way would be self-canceling. It would be as though one of us today, attempting to win a war of words with the *Cogito ergo sum* ("I think therefore I am") of René Descartes (1596–1650), should puff himself up and say, "I think that nothing is and so I am not and thus I do not think." Such an argument would spiral itself down into the ultimate philosophical question, Who cares? The only thing one could say about such a line of thinking would be that no one had thought of it before. In a world that treasures novelty – the world of the present – it is regarded as high praise to characterize a writer by saying, "Oh my! Isn't he positively outrageous?"

Fung Yu-lan, the twentieth-century Chinese Marxist scholar discussed earlier in this chapter, explained that Occidentals are put off by the manner of those he calls "Chinese philosophers." They presented their views in brief sayings and in a mode that reminds one of poetry and of religion. That, Fung said, makes them appear less than philosophic to the Occidental student. We are confronted here with the same problem in the case of some ancient Greek thinkers. Of course we cannot say that Heraclitus wrote in fragments. It is rather that fragments of what he wrote are all that remain to us. We must say here that a mode reminiscent of religion does not in itself deny to the thinker the status of philosopher, but if we are to call Heraclitus, for example, a philosopher, we have to see within and behind that mode proof that he met the criteria we laid down at the outset for recognizing philosophy. Both Copleston and Burnet lead our inquiry into this matter. Heraclitus, almost mysteriously, claims that to follow him one must understand his "Word." This seems to add up to the proposition that to understand that all is in flux is to understand that there is, in fact, a unity but there is also a diversity and the never-ending tension between the unity and the diversity is the definition of reality. As far as the kinship between his thought and religion goes, Burnet tells us:

Yet Herakleitos has one thing in common with the religious teachers of his time, and that is his insistence on the idea of Soul (ψυχή, [that is, psyche]). To him, as to them, the soul was no longer a feeble ghost or shade, but the most real thing of all, and its most important attribute was thought (γνώμη) or wisdom (τὸ σοφόν). Now Anaximenes had already illustrated the doctrine of 'air' by the remark that it is breath which keeps us in life.... If we follow up these hints we may perhaps find ourselves on the right track.... [T]he thought of Heraclitus was dominated by the opposition of sleeping and waking, life and death, and that this seemed to him the key to the traditional Milesian problem of the opposites, hot and cold, wet and dry.... Now we see that the soul is only fully alive when it is awake, and that sleep is really a stage between life and death.[50]

50 Burnet, *op. cit.*, pp. 59–60.

Burnet rounds out his summary of Heraclitus with the proposition that he maintained that strife, strife between the opposites, is what makes the world go round. He closes that summary by taking the proposition of Heraclitus that all is in flux, that one never steps into the same river twice, and showing that it follows that we are never the same for two successive instants. He cites the Sicilian comic poet Epicharmus (late sixth through early fifth century), who put the doctrine of Heraclitus into the speech of a character in one of his plays trying to disavow a debt by saying that it was not he who had borrowed the money.[51]

Parmenides

Parmenides was from Elea, a city in the southern part of the Italian peninsula.[52] He must have been born about 515 B.C., because in the dialogue named after him Plato has him conversing with Socrates when Parmenides was about sixty-five and Socrates about nineteen, that is, about 450 B.C. Father Copleston says that, despite some attributions of the honor to another, Parmenides was truly the founder of the Eleatic school.[53] Parmenides began as a Pythagorean but "afterwards abandoned that philosophy in favour of his own."[54] Whatever may be the true historical account of the change in Parmenides from Pythagorean doctrine to a doctrine he himself formulated, it is evidently true, as Burnet tells us, that his writing in poetic rather than prose form was a change from his philosophic predecessors. Burnet says that it was rather too bad that Parmenides wrote in hexameter verse because he was not much of a poet.[55] According to McKirahan, "Parmenides deserves recognition for introducing deductive arguments to philosophy."[56] His predecessors had asserted a principle of

[51] See Burnet, *op. cit.*, pp. 62–3. According to a modern saying, it is love that makes the world go round. The origin of that saying may be lost in the mists of time, but we can find it in Lewis Carroll's *Alice's Adventures in Wonderland* and also in the Gilbert and Sullivan opera *Iolanthe* (see W. S. Gilbert, *The Savoy Operas*, Ware, Hertfordshire, 1994, Wordsworth Ref., p. 247), where, in a song, almost every old saying known to man is repeated. Of course, it might be said that love is itself a manifestation of strife, but we, having recourse to Plato's *Phaedrus*, would adamantly deny this.

[52] Elea was in Lucania, a region on the west coast of the Italian peninsula, the coast fronting what is now called the Tyrrhenian Sea. It was about seventy miles south of Naples. (Naples is the anglicized version of the Italian *Napoli*, which is itself the Italianate version of the Greek *Neapolis*, or New Polis, i.e., New City.)

[53] Copleston, *op. cit.*, p. 49. The other to whom that foundation was ascribed by some in classical antiquity was Xenophanes, q.v. *Oxford Classical Dictionary*, 3rd ed., Simon Hornblower and Antony Spawforth, eds., Oxford, 1996, Oxford University Press., p. 1628.

[54] Ibid., pp. 47–8. Copleston cites Diogenes Laertius, ix, 21 for this, but that section of Diogenes, at least as the Loeb Classical Library edition (see note 59 *infra*, in this volume) presents it, does not declare what Copleston declares.

[55] Burnet, *op. cit.*, p. 64.

[56] McKirahan, *op. cit.*, p. 157.

change or motion, but Parmenides puts forth a contrary view as explaining things. He "argued that the world revealed by our senses is an illusion, that there is only one thing, and it does not change or move."[57]

Zeno

Zeno, another Eleatic, was a follower of Parmenides and supported his views. "Insofar as he deserves the title of father of dialectic," McKirahan asserts, "he sired an offspring with a long and vigorous life in philosophy and other fields."[58] To lay a groundwork for what is to come later in this book, and at the risk of seeming to descend to trivialities, we here note that McKirahan, despite his recognition of the significance of dialectic in philosophic inquiry, fails to take into account the dialectical character, or perhaps we should here say the dialogic character, of Plato's writing, for McKirahan says that Zeno's "book was a series of forty arguments, of which Plato claims to state the first."[59] Plato, it may be reasoned, claimed nothing of the sort. Plato wrote that Cephalus said that Antiphon remembered that Pythodorus had recounted that he heard a conversation among Parmenides, Socrates, and Zeno in which Socrates asked Zeno to repeat "the first argument." We do not doubt that Plato wrote the dialogue, but the account of the "first argument" is buried under five, six, or seven layers of recollection. Such layering is an important part of Plato's style.

Anaxagoras

Anaxagoras (c. 500–c. 428 b.c.) was an Ionian, and, as McKirahan reports, "his philosophy marks a return to the philosophical and scientific interests and style of the Milesians, though he was also keenly aware of and deeply influenced by Eleatic philosophy." He lived in Athens for thirty years and became an associate there of Pericles. He was prosecuted, convicted, and banished from Athens for impiety because "he believed the sun to be not a god but a fiery stone. Anaxagoras thus has the honor of being the first philosopher to be prosecuted at Athens."[60] McKirahan concludes his treatment of Anaxagoras with the observation that he has close connections with his Ionian forebears, as is shown by his interest in cosmogony and cosmology, the absence of any religious or mystical tendency in his writing, and his determination to give a plausible account of the world around us in terms of a rationally comprehensible set of principles."[61] This summation describing

---

[57] Ibid., p. 179.
[58] Ibid., p. 194.
[59] Ibid., p. 181. McKirahan cites Plato's *Parmenides,* 127d.
[60] Ibid., p. 200.
[61] Ibid., p. 231.

Anaxagoras is an illustration of what we have said are the attributes of philosophy – free and radical pursuit by unassisted human reason of the truth about the natures of important things.

Empedocles

Empedocles was from Acragas (Agrigentum) on the southern coast of Sicily. He lived from about 492 B.C. to about 432 B.C. Except for those called the "Sophists," who occupy a problematic place, and the Atomists, Empedocles is the last of the pre-Socratics on our list. He is "one of the most difficult presocratics to understand, and also one of the most interesting." The fragments of his work are "the largest bulk of material surviving from any presocratic."[62] This fact alone makes him of especial consequence in the discussion of the pre-Socratics that we shall open later herein. It is enough here to mention that he was a physiologist of considerable reach and that he introduced the *daimon*, or demon, as the moving force in physical phenomena, as distinguished from the *psyche*, or soul, in the philosophy of the Pythagoreans. In his doctrine of metempsychosis, the *daimon* "preserves its identity through its incarnations." It, and not the body, is the "bearer of personal identity."[63] Overarching these individual actors are the contrary forces of Strife and Love, the latter being the constructive of the two.

Our argument so far is that philosophy is the free and radical pursuit by means of wholly unassisted human reason of the truth about physics and politics, and the evidence points to Greece as the point of origin of this activity in the sixth and fifth centuries before the Common Era. We are compelled to follow Aristotle's view that the end of philosophy or science is not making but knowing. The practices of the productive arts, however, reflect something suggestive of an increasing application in those arts of the practical knowledge that has multiplied a thousandfold since those pre-Socratic beginnings. It would be a great mistake, however, to smile condescendingly at those early beginnings. What, after all, when we turn from making to knowing, is our present explanation of things? Do we not say that all matter is composed of tiny, invisible things? Is there not said to be a likeness between those microscopic things and the big thing, the macrocosm? Is not the essence of either of them the fact that there is a heavier thing in the middle and that there are lighter things on the periphery? Do not the lighter things necessarily "revolve around" the heavier in "orbits?" Why do they do that? Is it not said that they do so because they are "attracted to" the heavier thing in the middle? Does that mean that they lust after the center? Does love really make the world go round? By the way, if they are attracted to the center, why do they not just go there and have

---

[62] Ibid., pp. 255, 256.
[63] Ibid., p. 286.

done with it? Perhaps it is just not true love. Maybe the center is just a tease. Finally, has mere making usurped the place of the search for knowing?

Having now had a glimpse of the nature and origin of philosophy itself, we must next pursue the question of the nature of politics and then put two and two together and further pursue the question of the nature and origin of political philosophy. First, let us turn to politics.

3

The Nature of Politics

If philosophy is the free and radical pursuit of the truth about important things there must be a limited number of things that qualify as "important." Reflection shows, as Chapter 2 has asserted, that there are two such things: physics and politics. Political philosophy is thus a branch, a major branch, of philosophy. Deferring for a bit a fuller statement, we can say here that political philosophy is the free and radical pursuit by unassisted human reason of the truth about the nature of politics. However, just as the word "philosophy" has undergone a denaturing process for the past two centuries, so the word "politics" has come to mean almost nothing that will hold still to be studied. An illustration will help. If a member of One party in the legislature proposes some measure we can be certain that soon thereafter a member of the Other party will charge that the action of the One is "just politics." But of course! Why else would the voters send either of them to the legislature: to sing and dance perhaps? If, in fact, the member of the Other party rightly uses the word "politics" as a term of dispraise, then we ought to send the whole lot of them in both parties packing and shut the legislature down because it would be, by its nature, a den of sin. We do not intend here to deny categorically the proposition that some of what goes on in that legislature is "just" politics, but we reach a difficulty. We cannot study political philosophy without knowing what politics is and it turns out that that is itself a problem that requires clarification and resolution. Happily, the clarification and resolution are pretty easy to make to the student with reasonable intelligence and a reasonably open mind. It just requires the breaking of a few bad habits. But wait! It may be that at the end of the road one returns to the view that politics, all of it, deserves a measure of disapproval. Intelligence and open-mindedness need to be augmented with patience and with a measure of resignation.

Once a useful definition of politics has been reached, the next chapter will put philosophy and politics together and undertake to explain the origin and nature of political philosophy, but we need to jump ahead here just so far as to state that the first political philosopher was Socrates, an Athenian who lived from 469 to 399 B.C. For good and sufficient reasons, he wrote nothing at all. His disciple, Plato, an Athenian who lived from 427 to 348, was the first political philosopher to leave behind a body of writings. He did so for different good and sufficient reasons. His pupil, Aristotle, from Stagira, who lived from 384 to 322, also left a great body of writings. The Jews, Christians, and Muslims who are the principal political philosophers from the fourth to the fifteenth centuries appear chiefly as commentators on Plato and Aristotle and most mention Aristotle's name rather reverently. They call him "*the* Philosopher" and in some cases they sound almost like a tape recording of Aristotle – which I surely do not mean as criticism. Some medieval authors appear heavy and pedantic and that appearance did not end with the arrival of modern authors. So much is this the case that Thomas Hobbes, the English philosopher who lived from 1588 to 1679, spoke of the university professors in his day as not so much teaching philosophy as teaching "Aristotelity."[1] On the other hand, there have been those who have spoken of all philosophy as quite properly nothing more than a footnote to Plato and Aristotle. Those two did, after all, raise and explore every question that could be raised about politics.[2] Indeed, some have even seen Aristotle himself as a mere footnote to Plato.

Some in the past two centuries, after the manner of Thomas Hobbes and Niccolò Machiavelli, but without their wisdom or quickness of mind, have dismissed the political philosophy of Plato and Aristotle as radically defective. Many still believe, however, and with all due respect, the present text rests on the belief, that Plato and Aristotle laid down the language and the arguments that make all political philosophy intelligible. Plato, I believe, takes the mind deeper into the great questions of politics, but his writings are elliptical and poetic and in fact almost mysterious, whereas Aristotle's works look to us as veritable textbooks by contrast. To make the meaning of "politics" clear we shall, therefore, rely almost exclusively on Aristotle.

Aristotle's learning is encyclopedic. He wrote on every matter of consequence, including physics, metaphysics, biology, medicine, ethics, politics, rhetoric, poetry, the soul, education, logic, and economics. If one were to found a liberal arts college and could choose only one author to read, Aristotle might be the natural choice. Diogenes Laertius, from Cilicia, who apparently lived in the third century A.D., lists more than 150 works. He tallies them up as amounting to 445,270 lines. That would add up to more than fifty 300-page books by present-day calculations. Not until the nineteenth century were all of his works that had survived through the centuries

[1] Hobbes, *Leviathan*, the 13th paragraph of Chapter 46.
[2] Throughout his life, every joke the author has heard has seemed to be some variation on one his father told him. As with jokes, so with political philosophers. It is almost possible to say, "Oh, yes. I've heard that one."

published in one comprehensive collection. Those five folio volumes of the Greek texts were published in Berlin between 1831 and 1836, edited by August Immanuel Bekker (1785–1871). The pages of those volumes were numbered consecutively through the five volumes and the halves of the pages were marked "a" and "b" and the lines in each half page were numbered, there being some thirty to forty lines per half page. Any good edition of Aristotle, whether in the Greek or in translation into English, or Latin, or French, or any other language, shows the Bekker pagination in the margins. Thus, after the title page and some other "front matter," and then the Introduction, the first page of the text of Carnes Lord's 1984 English translation of Aristotle's *Politics*, published by the University of Chicago Press, is page 35, but the first line of text on that page is marked "1252a1," that is, line 1 of part a of page 1252, and every fifth line is numbered until one reaches, on Lord's page 36, the 34th line of 1252a followed by "1252b1" and goes on until getting to page and line 1342b35 on the last page of text in Lord's translation, page 241. Without this standard system of pagination, a citation would have to be to a page number in a particular edition and a reader of English trying to follow up citations from several works of secondary literature would have to have in his possession translations by Benjamin Jowett, Ernest Barker, H. Rackham, Carnes Lord, and many others to find his way.

In a 1946 essay titled "Politics and the English Language," George Orwell (1903–1950), the British journalist and social commentator, offered six rules for sound writing, one of which was a warning against jargon. In our day, despite Orwell's guidance, jargon is everywhere. Some of it is fun and harmless, and measured imitation of it can even be useful. It is said that high school girls in the San Fernando Valley northwest of Los Angeles developed something called "Valleyspeak," but that was altogether a lark. Unfortunately, government officials, and especially people in or associated with the armed forces, make up important sounding neologisms and acronyms in earnest. There are words in "eduspeak" (words coined by faculties of university departments of education) and monstrous locutions fashioned by "consultants" who offer "motivational courses" to businesses that the rest of us cannot fathom. Worst of all, some academic social scientists write things that they themselves cannot decipher the next day.

It never occurs to Aristotle to make up a clever, new, academic language intelligible, if at all, only to people schooled in that artificial language. Using the ordinary language of citizens and politicians, he opens the *Politics* in straightforward Greek that *could be* translated somewhat as follows:

Since every city is, as we see, a kind of community and every community is made up with a view to some good (for all do all that they do for what seems to them good), it is therefore evident that, all communities aiming at some good, the one which is highest and includes all the others most of all aims at some good and aims at the highest good; this one is called the city, or the civic community.

Now this translation introduces a problem that is almost insoluble. The words "city" and "civic" derive from the Latin. If the whole paragraph were in Latin, it could be formed so as to make sense. The Latin source of the English word "city" is *civitas*, but *civitas* does not mean the same thing that the English word "city" means. We would be better off if we did not translate the Greek into English at all in the case of this word but instead simply put the Greek word, transliterated into Roman script, in our English sentence. Then we would start by saying, "Since every *polis* is, as we see, a kind of community," and we would end by saying, "This one is called the *polis*, or the political community." Now it is clear to the naked eye that "political" is an adjectival reference to *polis*. A sensible dictionary definition of "political" would be "of or pertaining to the *polis*." But is it not strange? We have in English the word "political" but we *don't* have the word "polis." This is because Greek is pretty much Greek and Latin is pretty much Latin and each of them has roots in earlier languages, but the descent is straightforward and complete. Things make sense in Latin or in Greek. But the English language is derived from Greek and Latin and French and Anglo-Saxon and in lesser measure from other ancient languages, and is augmented by adaptations of loanwords from other languages. The reader of English who is not patient or inquiring is at a disadvantage.

The most useful clarification of these opening lines of Aristotle has been made by Harry V. Jaffa, who writes:

There is no single English word that will translate *polis*, and to understand why is indispensable to any introduction to Aristotle's political philosophy. The *Politics* begins with a definition of the *polis*, and the student who reads that as a definition of the "state," with all the connotations alien to Aristotle in that expression, is apt to be estranged forever from his thought. Our word "politics," although a noun, is the plural form of the adjective "politic." A parallel instance is the word "athletics," formed from the adjective "athletic." Now athletics is what athletes do. The Greek noun *athlētēs* – from which athletic and athletics are derived – survives virtually unaltered in our language. We know what athletics is because we know what an athlete is. The latter is a concrete subject of observation while the former is an abstract general characterization of his activities. But the Greek noun *polis*, which does not survive in our language, is to politics what athlete is to athletics. Politics, the abstract general characterization derived from the Greek survives, but *polis*, the concrete subject, does not.[3]

[3] This quotation is drawn from Jaffa's essay "Aristotle" which may be found in the first and in the second edition of Leo Strauss and Joseph Cropsey, *History of Political Philosophy*, Chicago, 1963 and 1972, Rand McNally, p. 65. The third edition of the book, published in 1987 by the University of Chicago Press, substitutes an essay by Carnes Lord. The University of Chicago Press had, in 1984, published Lord's translation of the *Politics*. The present author recommends both the Jaffa and the Carnes essays as excellent. Beyond reliance on rumors, he cannot offer an explanation for the substitution of one for the other. No doubt it would be profitable for the student to read both. The passage here quoted from the Jaffa essay seems absolutely essential to understanding Aristotle.

Jaffa's explanation is an analogy, or a proportion. A proportion in algebra is the comparison or likeness of two ratios. The gist of Jaffa's formulation may be grasped by setting up the proportion in mathematical form: politics:X = athletics:athlete; that is, politics is to X as athletics is to athlete. Put this way, after the manner of a mathematical formula, one can only make sense of it by solving the term "X." In a sheer arithmetic example, 2:X = 4:8, one can solve the problem by simple calculation without looking abroad for other information. Clearly, X is 4. In the problem before us here, the value of X cannot be solved by straightforward mathematical calculation. We have to "study Greek" a little. Jaffa has already done that for us. Without doubt, X is πόλις, that is, *polis*. Since, as we see, *polis* is not the equivalent of "state," or even of that made-up expression "city-state," or of "city" as we now use that word (although we shall come back to that word in due course), our only sensible recourse is to use the Greek word itself, but let us make things easier by adopting the word as a loanword into English. We shall just say "polis" without the italics. Now we can sensibly render the first eight lines of Aristotle's *Politics* thus:

> Since every polis is, as we see, a kind of community, and every community is made up with a view to some good (for all do all that they do for what seems to them good) it is therefore evident that, all communities aiming at some good, the one which is highest and includes all the others most of all aims at some good and aims at the highest good; this one is called the polis, or the political community.

Notice the common sense of this. Except for the last ten words of the quotation, every bit of it is plain observation. There is no resemblance to fancy, abstract, twenty-first-century political science. "Look!" Aristotle says. We *see* this. It is an undeniable starting point. The last ten words, however, constitute a bold assertion by Aristotle, one that present-day "value-free" social science, or sociology, or "interest-group politics" political science might deny. The student, if he is sensibly selfish, will not be swept off his feet by "cutting edge" social science on the grounds that the newest is always better than what came before. If the constant ringing of the changes on Aristotle by centuries of commentators seems pedantic and boring, we are justified in reminding ourselves that neither is the old the good or the true because it is old. The good is the good and the true is the true. The individual whose, forgive us, "philosophy of life" simply accepts the notion that the latest view must be the right one will want to close this book here and now. We wish him wealth and pleasure. But those who are, as we just said, sensibly selfish will want to weigh for themselves the relative merits of the various answers to the questions implicit in the opening sentences of the *Politics*.

A thorough grasp of these first eight lines of Aristotle's book will almost amount to a grasp of the whole book and so almost to a grasp of politics itself. If the last ten words of the translated passage are true, enormously consequential judgments follow, even with respect to current politics. *Is the* polis the comprehensive community? Is everything else subordinate to it? *Does* it aim at the "highest good?" What *is* that good? Having adopted the word "polis" into our English usage, we are off to a good start. But wait. On reflection, we realize that we "don't know what we're talking about" because we don't know what the polis *is*. We are in good company. Aristotle asks at the very beginning of Book III of the *Politics*, "Whatever is the polis?" For he says, there is some confusion about that matter. The first thing we notice in the text is that "the polis is a kind of community." Thus, to know what the polis is we have to know what a community is. More, we have to know what *kind* of a community the polis is. Each of these two questions must be asked.[4]

A community is not simply a contractual arrangement that issues from the individualistic appetites or wills or interests of the "parties" to it. A community is a kind of communism, or sharing, or having in common. Aristotle helpfully raises the question whether the political community is a sharing of everything, or of some things, or of nothing. Clearly, sharing nothing is not a sharing, so the choices are reduced from three to two. In the present-day United States, several of the states have what are called "community property laws." The laws were conceived at a time when most wives in America stayed at home to bear and rear children and to keep house for the husband and children (and often some grandparents, too). The husband earned all the income and often had most of the property, such as the house or the farm. The community property laws generally provided, among other things, that if a husband and wife parted in divorce, the contributions of the two to the accumulation of wealth would be acknowledged, and the divorce court would divide the property between them in more or less equal shares. To understand the polis as a community, we need to understand that it is a sharing that, on dissolution, *cannot* be divided up and parceled out. The best way to understand community is to think of that husband and wife in happier times. They kiss. When they do, each has all of the kiss. When the kiss ends, neither has any of it. They do not part, each taking away a half kiss. To understand politics, one must understand the polis. To understand the polis one, must understand community. To understand community is

---

[4] The Greek word here translated as "community" is κοινωνία, (*koinonia*). Ernest Barker translates that word as "association." H. Rackham and Carnes Lord both translate it as "partnership." No doubt other translations can be found. Having but a smattering of Greek, we do not mean to be presumptuous in preferring our own translation to those of Barker or Rackham or Lord, but we respectfully recommend our choice and hope that the analysis of the word in the text will justify that choice. Benjamin Jowett, Regius Professor of Greek at Oxford University, produced in 1885 a two-volume translation of and commentary on the *Politics*, and he translates *koinonian* into the English word "community," but this is not enough to recommend the rest of the translation, much of which falls into the error mentioned earlier of not so much translating as rendering into English what he believes Aristotle surely must have meant by what he wrote.

to understand that it is a sharing. To understand what kind of a community the polis is, we need first of all to see that it is not simply the sharing of tax revenue, or the sharing of a certain extent of territory, or the sharing of an armed force. It is a sharing like the sharing of a kiss. The distinguishing attribute of a polis is that it is a community that, when it dissolves, has nothing. The dissolution of the community means that the shared thing that is its very essence goes up in smoke.

Before understanding the vital question as to what *kind* of a community the polis is, we would do well to conjure up some sort of imagined view of the ancient polis. If we could do that directly, however, and see a polis before our very eyes, we would not truly see it. Seeing it with *our* eyes, we would see what is not there and not see what is. We need a bridge from here to there. That takes work, and it will seem to insult the intelligence of the reader to lead him into that labor. But we shall do our best to be clear and brief. We suggest as a bridge a town in the American West of the nineteenth century. That itself is a long way off and alienated from us by the sea of technology in which we struggle to keep our minds afloat, but it is a great deal closer than the Athens of 2,400 years ago. I remember visiting in my childhood small towns in the rural Midwest where paved roads did not exist and where many homes were without inside plumbing or electric (or even gas) lights. There was a pump, a hand-powered pump, outside the door, and another, rather unmentionable, alternative to inside plumbing, also outside, and this led to other rather unmentionable appliances, because in the winter it was often awfully cold at night. It was also dark. There were no streetlights and, inside the house, since light was supplied by kerosene lanterns, one generally just went to bed when it got dark and got up when it got light, or a little before. Even I, however, was a good deal more than a country mile away from the Western town of the nineteenth century. I spent the bulk of my childhood in Chicago and took for granted telephones, electricity, automobiles, radios, and motion pictures. (The "talkies" arrived when I was about four years old. For a few years thereafter I sometimes went to a theater that still showed "silents.")

Ah! Perhaps the movies are our route to the Old West, and thence to Athens. Those who made the movies included some "old timers" who had personal recollections of that Old West. Additionally, there were photographs going back to the 1860s and a wealth of records and memoirs. (We shall largely leave aside here the troubling fact that Hollywood has been lying to us for about a hundred years, first one way and then another.) The lineal descendants of the motion picture "western" were the westerns that were made for television, beginning in the 1950s. One memorable television western was *Gunsmoke*, which screened weekly for twenty years from 1955 to 1975. If a studio today wanted to start a new series reminiscent of *Gunsmoke*, the first order of business would be to build a "set." That is, a whole town would have to be constructed (or at least the facades of such a town) in which to play out the action of the episodes. Think of what would have to be on that set: a jail, a saloon, a general store, a livery stable, a few houses, and so forth. These places would have to be peopled by a sheriff, a barkeep, a clerk, a blacksmith, and so forth. For us to imagine such a town, we presuppose a *division of labor*, and thoroughly understanding such a division is a step in the direction of visualizing the ancient polis, and so of understanding politics.

Our television western is a "drama." Drama requires conflict and an eventual dénouement in conflict resolution. The internal conflict in our town comes from the fact that some of the cowboys are "good guys" and some are "bad guys." But there are also external sources of conflict. In the lies of the earlier Hollywood, the external bad guys were always Indians. In our new television western, no doubt we would tell different lies. Even in those earlier westerns, however, there is an element that keeps the ancient polis at arm's length. When the Indians came storming over a hill bent on scalping everyone in town, things looked very bad for a while, until the cavalry came storming over another hill to the stirring music of the bugle. As for the internal threats, a bad cowboy shoots a good cowboy. We are terribly concerned until the sheriff shoots the bad guy and townspeople carry the injured good guy up the stairs to the doctor's office where he is saved so that he can recover and marry the pretty girl who works in the general store. However false a picture the television western may give us of the West it portrays, two things here are clearly imaginable, and those two things make that nineteenth-century American town a galaxy away from the ancient polis. In our western town, whence came that cavalry and where did that doctor learn medicine? While it is true that someone who learned medicine in one ancient polis might move to another and set up practice there, and it is true that the armed force of one polis might come to the aid of another polis, there are some distinguishing things. One thing is clear: That armed force from the other polis was not a separate entity in that polis. Its armed force, like that of the polis to whose aid it came, was simply the citizenry armed. Further, while a physician may learn his art in one place and then practice it in another, the truly complete polis of antiquity included not only its own armed citizenry and a division of labor. It also included a sufficient number of people so that the division of labor that characterized it was comprehensive enough to ensure that everything that was needed to be fully human was supplied for the polis by the polis itself. The polis was *complete*. It was not simply a piece of something larger. That means it was composed of some thousands of people, not just a few dozen.

But if a polis is a community, then it cannot have too large a population, because too many people would mean that the sharing that puts the unity in community would not be possible. It would be a polyglot place with a cafeteria selection of discordant gods. It would not have a shared history, or shared poets, or shared struggles, or shared views of justice, or even a shared language. It would be a place struggling with itself. Aristotle makes this plain when he shows that Babylon was so large that it was a defective polis, because when it fell in battle it was said that "its capture was not noticed in a certain part of the city for three days."[5] The last serious argument over the proper *size* of a political community occurred at the American Constitutional Convention in 1787. In recommending the ratification of the Constitution formed at that convention, James Madison, writing as "Publius" in the *Federalist Papers*, asserted that the problem of size was solved by "a judicious modification and mixture of the *federal principle*."[6]

One last thing needs to be said about our imagined western town. Every child knows that milk does not come from stores. It comes from cows. As far as our western town is concerned, the cows are on farms or ranches and these are "down the road a piece" from the town, some in this direction, some in that. The modern American city, on the other hand, is a creature of the state in which it sits, with its city limits and its powers of governance set by the legislature of that state. The state itself is one of many and those states and the union of them are subordinate to a written Constitution adopted by the people of the United States and amended from time to time by them. Thus there is artifice and there is convention in the coming into being of the modern city. In a diluted way, something of the same is true of our imagined western town. But if we had asked where the "city limits" of that town were, we would have confronted a puzzle. Think of the farms and ranches where we found the cows that provided the milk consumed in the town. If we go down one of those roads, we come, let us say, to farm A and then to farm B and then to farm C, and so on. Perhaps the milk comes from farms A and B, but the farmer at farm C finds it too far and too inconvenient to bring the milk to our town. That farmer takes his milk to, and finds the commodities he needs and his friends in, and consults the sheriff and the physician of, another town. In a certain sense, the natural city limit is somewhere between farm B and farm C. Perhaps it would be better to say that the natural limit of the geographic area in which our town sits is there at that point, indistinctly, between farm B and farm C. In this respect, our western town does lead us the better to see the ancient polis. The "limits" in each case are simply natural. Our Western town comes to

---

[5] *Politics*, 1276a30. The English here is that of the Carnes Lord translation.

[6] *Federalist*, No. 51, the very last line. It is worth our baldly asserting here that the expression "federal government" is a contradiction in terms. One should note that the word "federal" nowhere appears in the U.S. Constitution. A form of the word occurs in Article VI, but a little study of the problem shows that this usage rather affirms than denies this fact. We believe that in 1787 and 1788 James Madison fully understood this. Notice that he does not recommend the "federal principle" but only a "judicious modification and mixture" of it. Politicians, like philosophers, are forced to toe-dance on a greased stage. The present facile use of the expression "the federal government" ignores rather than disproves this fact. All this, however, must be treated elsewhere.

sight first as a *center*, a center of commerce and communication, and this is what characterizes the ancient polis.

To summarize what we have considered up to this point, the ancient polis, while small enough to retain its oneness was large enough to make possible a sufficient division of labor to assure everything needed for its people fully to achieve the humanity potentially possessed by them. We shall surely have to return to this matter of achievement to understand it better. In a word, the ancient polis had a certain completeness about it. There was no cavalry coming over the hill to its rescue. As far as its unity was concerned, that consisted in a shared language, shared gods, and shared views of good and bad, noble and base, and just and unjust, as well as an appreciation of a body of poetic works – stories, plays, and poems. In other words, what was shared was what has recently come to be called "a culture," and it was natural. To speak more precisely and in keeping with Aristotle's teaching, its being was by nature, but its coming into being was the product of artifice and convention wrought by a founder, a lawgiver. That is, its human completion is the completion or perfection of what is there by nature, but the actualization of that completion depends on the positive action of some human or humans, some artifice and convention. It comes to be without its end being visible, but its end is what ultimately forms it. Its coming into being is for the sake of mere life – defense and commerce – but its being, that which defines it, is its perfection, which is the good life or the noble life, not mere life or mere self-preservation.

A moment's reflection shows that not all aggregations of people fit this picture. Some places may fail to meet the description of a polis. Some peoples live political lives; others do not. Since the social science fiat a few decades ago that "all cultures are equal," it has become academically and socially impermissible to draw the common sense conclusions that follow from the acknowledgment of these differences between peoples. To see the problem, we are helped by again having recourse to the Latin equivalent of the Greek word *polis* and to its English descendants. The Latin word is *civitas*. From this are derived the English words "city" and "civil." As Aristotle teaches (and as common Greek usage held), each individual *polis* is formed up or constituted in its own way. The form is known as its *politeia*. That word is translated into English as "regime" or "constitution." Once again, the translation loses the trace. We do not know what we are talking about. If we approach the problem in English, it will be useful to make up a new word to follow the track. We shall use that new word just long enough to make our point and then abandon it. The new word is "citification." What that new word enables us to say is that every city has its particular citification. Now we encounter difficulties if instead of Greek or English we start with Latin and then use a clearly related English word with a meaning different from present, customary, English usage. Every *civitas* has its particular civilization. Each is civilized in its particular way.

One city is "citied up" this way and another is "citied up" another way. If we use these neologisms and barbarisms, we can make some sense of this problem in broken English. Every city is constituted in its own particular way. Every city or polis has its own constitution, or citification, or civilization, or *politeia*.

Some aggregations of people, however, do not fit this template. An aggregation may not dwell in a city, in a *polis*, in a *civitas*. Now, of course an individual may be away from cities and may be reared by parents whose upbringing was in a city, and that individual may perhaps be regarded as citified, but if a whole nation, a whole people, is without cities, they are not politicized, not citified, not civilized. This distinction could in a particular instance be, but need not be, based on race or genetics. The critical thing here is to understand the traditional distinction between civilized and uncivilized peoples, between those who are citified and those who are not.

Some literary works can help us to grasp the distinction between the civilized and the uncivilized. Daniel Defoe (1659–1731), an Englishman, began his adult life as a journalist, then worked for many years writing official papers and reports as a civil servant, and even did a little espionage work for the Crown. At the age of sixty he turned his pen to fiction. Resting his narrative on the real-life adventures of a Scot named Alexander Selkirk, he wrote *Robinson Crusoe*, which some literary commentators have regarded as the first English novel. The story is told in the first person. Crusoe opens the account by telling us, "I was born in the year 1632, in the city of York, of a good family." When he is shipwrecked, he lands alone on what seems a deserted island. When the weather clears, he manages to get back to the ship, it being grounded somewhat off shore. He finds provisions, liquor, arms, and tools and brings them ashore with him. With these and the art he possesses, he survives and makes a life for himself on the island. In due course the story brings an indigenous person to him, whom he names "Friday." The story then turns for a long time on the relationship between Crusoe and Friday. What is clear is that his tools and arms and his successful use of them are the product of a highly developed civilization, whereas Friday lacks both tools and art. Two souls like Friday – let us call them Thursday and Friday – might have remained naked, unskilled, unequipped, and defenseless. Their condition would not have been due to inherent defects as is shown by Crusoe's eventual success in developing a degree of civilization in Friday. Civilization is good. Its absence is a fault, a defect. Of course, in its fullest meaning, civilization is a great deal more than gunpowder, rum, a saw, a hammer, and the art to use them. That Crusoe is what he is is the consequence of his coming to us from a city and a good family. Aristotle will teach us.

The first line of Aristotle's *Politics*, stating that the polis is a kind of community, compels us to confront the question, What kind? The short answer to this question comes to us from within the boundaries of the first eight lines of the book. The polis is the highest, most comprehensive, most complete, most commanding community, and it aims at the highest good. Elaboration is necessary, however, if the meaning of that is to be grasped. To develop that meaning, Aristotle explains the other communities in their relation to the *polis*, and behind that explanation there is always the distinction between being and coming into being. The lesser communities are that between man and woman, that between master and slave, and that which is the combination of and a certain intermediate completion of those two communities, namely the community of the household. The household, the *oikon*, is composed of freemen and slaves and may contain three or more generations of kin. The number of the whole may run to a few dozen human beings. The household masters several arts. It can weave fabric, cut and sew clothes, cobble shoes, grow and harvest foods, cook those foods, cut hair, perform fairly sophisticated first aid, tend the sick, bury the dead, and perform services to the gods. It is, that is to say, able to satisfy the ephemeral (daily recurring) needs of the human beings. As the household grows, it becomes so large that the house cannot contain it. Members of younger generations marry and "spin off," forming new households. These are, for a time, dependent on the first household, and they are surely near to it. When there is a whole cluster of households, they appear as a village. A mutual dependence and a division of labor allow a more satisfactory meeting of the daily recurring needs, but the village still satisfies only those daily recurring needs, and, because of the kinship and the proximity, a degree of sharing of material well-being continues, without clear demarcations between households. In the village, wherein the several households share the same ancestors, the several households therefore have the same gods, inasmuch as the gods are "our oldest ancestors."

At some point the need for military defense and the conveniences of commerce may lead several nearby villages to join together, forming a *polis*. The "efficient cause," to use Aristotle's language, is the desire for safety and comfort – for a citizenry large and strong enough to be able to form up as a defense force, and for a high degree of division of labor between (as distinct from within) households that guarantees a supply of well-constructed goods and the provision of excellently performed services. This newly established good is called commerce. A new possibility arises and circumstances make its actualization possible, namely, such a high degree of division of labor that new needs, not hitherto acknowledged, are understood and are able to be satisfied. Where previously household slaves had tutored the young of the freemen, now schools develop and, with their own internal divisions of labor, do a better job of educating. A bit more etymology is useful here. From the root word for boy or child, the Greek word for what a child undergoes is παιδεία (*paideia*), that is, rearing, training, or education. From this we get the English words "pedagogue" and "pedagogy," that is, teacher and the art of teaching.[7] Ultimately, a higher-class school, where the greatest questions can be studied and taught, may develop. The proper word for what goes on there is "philosophy," and it takes "leisure" (*scholé* in the Greek, whence English derives the word "school") for someone to devote himself determinedly to philosophy. We do not mean to suggest here that the pursuit of the truth can be routinized and reduced to a set of lesson plans. Perhaps it would be incorrect to suggest that philosophy can be taught in a school. At the least, philosophy can be pursued only by an exceptional and independent mind. The philosopher himself must, by trial and error, identify an apt pupil, or apprentice, or disciple, and he approaches the task of developing that apt pupil by a method fashioned exactly for the characteristics of that pupil. There can be no curriculum. No doubt we shall have to soften this forbidding statement in due course.

Finally we have a fully developed polis. Everything that is needed for the full development of what it is to be human is in the polis. Surpassing the household, it supplies not just the daily recurring needs (e.g., food, clothing, shelter, haircuts) but all the human needs. High needs, the need to inquire as to the systems of the body that the true physician needs, the need to inquire systematically as to the questions of the earth and its seasons, the need to turn one's back on the poets to ask what truly are the natures of the gods, the need in the first instances for those poets, the need to ask what is truly just and unjust, and so on, and the development of all the productive and mimetic arts. This kind of division of labor and variegated devotion to arts and sciences requires that somebody else do all the hard work of providing food, clothing, and shelter so that teachers, philosophers, and physicians may be free to pursue their callings excellently. This requires not only a division of labor in the primary, or simple, sense. It requires, it turns out, some sort of class division, between gentlemen and others, and perhaps even the existence of slaves. Aristotle however, shows that slavery is appropriate only for those who are fit by nature only to be slaves and nothing more. This, by the way, to anticipate questions that might now be raised, does not rest on distinctions of race or color. Slavery is suitable only for those who "differ from other men as the body differs from the soul," and such men come in all races and all colors. Of course we are not through with this subject, but we must lay it aside for the moment.

This high division of labor rests on acknowledgment of the fact that people are radically unequal. It is vital at this point to appreciate the fact that

---

[7] We also get "pediatrics," doctoring for children, from the word for child to which the suffix *iatros*, the word for physician, is added, and also the word "orthopedics," which applies to people of all ages but is rooted in the word for child to which is added as a prefix *orthos* (the word for straight, true, or correct). Hence, "orthopedics" means a straight or correct growth in childhood, or, by extension, the keeping or making straight of chiefly the bone structure in a person of any age.

modern political philosophy did not discover equality, a thing of which the poor, benighted ancients were ignorant. Both ancients and moderns see that men are equal in some respects and unequal in others. The difference is that the ancients regarded the inequalities in such things as virtue and wisdom as the politically crucial factors, whereas we moderns regard the equalities as the politically crucial factors. The U.S. Declaration of Independence in 1776 saying that "all men are created equal" does not mean the patently false notion that all men are equally wise, equally beautiful, or equally swift, and it *surely* does not mean that all men are entitled by nature to equal shares of good things. It means, as it well says, that "all men are created equal" [in that] "they are endowed by their creator with certain unalienable rights," among which are the rights to "life, liberty, and the pursuit of happiness." Radically different political orders are dictated by the ancient and the modern emphases on inequalities and equalities, respectively. That we not get hopelessly distanced from our immediate subject, we must defer further discussion of this to a later chapter.

Our immediate subject is the nature of politics, as we learn that from Aristotle. The completed *polis* provides for the full development of human potential, but because men are unequal in critical respects, it follows that only some men are capable of the full actualization of the highest human potential. That highest human development makes one fit for the highest human callings, politics and philosophy. Politics, properly speaking, is taking part in conducting the affairs of the *polis* that makes possible that high development. Philosophy is, as we have argued, freely and radically pursuing the truth about the highest things. Political philosophy pursues the truth about the nature of the *polis* and the nature of the best *politeia*.

In Book One of the *Politics*, Aristotle teaches that the *polis* is by nature, because man is by nature a political animal. He is certainly an animal. The Latin word *anima* means in English both breath and soul. Animals are called animals because they are animated. They breathe. They are besouled. They are composed of both body and soul. The souls of the lesser animals develop quickly. It is touching to watch a red fox and his vixen, with which he mates for life, or a pair of mated Canada geese take care of their young. They obviously care deeply for their offspring and they watch over them jealously and train them in certain skills of self-preservation – and then they bid them good-bye. This love, care, nurturing, and teaching take a few weeks, and, what is more, it is almost impossible to imagine a gosling that (if it lives a few months) fails to develop fully into a goose or a red fox kit that (if it lives several months) fails to develop fully its vulpine nature. It seems that it just happens. People are not like that. The nature of humans is not defined simply by survival skills. Humans are not fully human instantly, or even in several months of learning to forage. By becoming habituated to all the moral virtues and developing the intellectual virtues, some men fully realize their potential. Not all are destined to be perfected.

Here our modern presuppositions are so determinative of our thoughts that we have to shake ourselves vigorously and splash cold water in our faces to appreciate the vast distance between the ancient and the modern views. The very definition of an acorn is an oak that has not yet fully developed. An acorn is not yet an oak, although understanding its nature means understanding what an oak is and understanding that, given some beneficial circumstances, the acorn will, quite without the care and supervision of a mature oak, become an oak, an oak just as much an oak as the oak whence it fell. Just as the human being differs from the other animals so he differs from an oak. Full human development does not just happen. The human child develops his human potential not only under the loving supervision of his parents but after a considerable schooling. He won't grow straight and well unless both his body and his soul are properly nurtured, and the nurture of the soul in particular requires *paideia*, schooling.

Now, as we see in the present, it happens that some young humans have had all the schooling they can stomach by the time they are twelve or fourteen. Forcing such young people to stay in school for twelve years and to finish high school is less an educational project than a custodial one, and, worse, high school becomes merely subsequent school, requiring not high learning but only that learning that everyone, including those whose souls "checked out of" school a while back, can digest. This is to the detriment of those for whom higher schooling is genuinely suited. This problem did not plague the ancients. Genuine schooling, the kind that develops "gentlemen" who can take a sound and productive part in the affairs of their *polis*, may well take ten or twelve years. In addition, the peak of human potential – the free and radical pursuit by unassisted human reason of the truth about the *polis* and about other great things – requires a longer term and just the right circumstances and surroundings. A complete city and only a complete city can provide those circumstances and surroundings, and that higher schooling will only "take" with a minority of the human beings in the *polis*.

Man is by nature a political animal because he is the animal who can only develop fully his natural potential in and through the polis, the political community, and then only in a polis that has a good *politeia*, a good constitution. By nature, political life is both the necessary and the sufficient condition for man to become fully man. Unlike the case of geese, or that of foxes, the development of men does not "just happen." Man is the animal he is because he is the only animal endowed with the faculty of speech. The Greek word is *logos*, which means speech, or reason. In fact, it means reasoned speech, because an array of sounds that do not reason is not speech. It is merely the expression of appetites and fears through grunts or whines. *Logos*, reasoned speech, is capable of argument about and search for the truth about nature and about the just and the unjust, the good and the bad, the noble and the base. Only men argue about and try to understand such things. Only men are intellectually reflexive. Only men look inward and ask what is the right life for man. A red fox kit becomes a red fox without ever asking himself what it is to be a fox. If he lives to be twelve, which sometimes happens in the protective surroundings of a zoo, he knows he is not the same as the men who look at him nor the same as the mice he eats, but in all that time he never asks himself, "What makes me not a man or a mouse but a fox? What is the right life for fox?" There is no such place as Vulpine University where foxes pursue the truth about this or dispute with each other about it. Foxes do not ponder different lifestyles. They do what foxes do. That is all. It is possible for a human being to pervert a dog by, say, teaching it to stand on its hind legs for long periods, to wear clothing or spectacles, or to hold a pipe in its mouth, but no dog, fox, or goose can pervert itself.

So much is it true that man is the sole animal that becomes what he truly is only in and through the city that one can say that man is the only animal that can go wrong.

Research has taught us that primates and dolphins are clever, and, like dogs, primates, dolphins, and some birds can learn a lot of things taught by humans. Research shows that primates and dolphins communicate with each other, and even with other species, including the human species. Anyone who has ever had a dog knows something of this without funded research. A dog owner knows that a dog can tell his master when it wants to go out, or that it is happy, that it is hungry, or that it is ashamed of some wrongdoing, of which it is aware, but it will not ask why the wrongdoing is wrong. It may, in a way, communicate that it wants to know just what it is that is demanded of it, but there is no such place as Canine University where dogs matriculate to dispute what makes dogs dogs, to study what is the nature of dog as distinct from the nature of humans. At some point in the middle of the twentieth century, some innovative professor thought of speech as a subspecies of or as the same as communication. Before long, after some research on primates and dolphins, and the discovery that they communicated, it became possible for someone who had not really thought well about it to say that Aristotle was mistaken. But Aristotle knew that other animals communicated. He did not say that man was the only animal endowed with communication skills. He said man was the only animal endowed with *logos*. This made man the only truly *political* animal, though surely many species of animal are *social*. Aristotle at first draws a merely quantitative distinction, saying that "man is much more a political animal than any kind of bee or any herd animal," but in the next breath he states the matter qualitatively. The other animals have voices that enable them to express pain or pleasure, but man is the only animal endowed with *logos*. Man is the only animal who argues about the good and the bad, the noble and the base, and other such things.[8] Trillions of dollars of endowed

---

[8] *Politics*, 1253a8ff. The English here is that of the Carnes Lord translation.

funding and hundreds of years of funded research are not likely to change this. Aristotle's conclusion is a sound one on which to rest one's inquiry as to the nature of the *polis*.

Aristotle clarifies for us the distinction between being and coming into being. This clarification, too, encounters and may founder on present presuppositions. To present thinking, nature is something "back there." The nature of a thing is its earliest state. According to the modern view, to understand the nature of an oak requires that we dissect an acorn. Aristotle understands the true aspect of things. If we learned our lessons from Aristotle, we would not lose the ability to understand that an oak is what comes to be from its beginnings in an acorn, but, following Aristotle, we see that an acorn that does not become an oak is a failed acorn. It has not come to be what is immanent in it to come to be. Its nature, its being, is not its rudest beginnings but its most perfect completion. As for man and the city, Aristotle teaches that, although the individual man is in the order of time first, or primary, it is essential to recognize that in the order of nature the city is primary, because the nature of man is latent until the city brings it to fruition. The city, that is, the polis, is the whole and men the parts. One cannot understand an arm simply as an arm. It is an unintelligible entity unless we understand it as an arm of a man. It is the man as a whole that makes intelligible the nature of an arm. And it is the polis that makes intelligible what a man is, what man is. A profound misunderstanding of Aristotle is possible at this point. If we start with freedom as the first and only good without asking what freedom is for, we are likely to see Plato and Aristotle as statists or collectivists. One hears it said that Aristotle wrongly thinks that the individual was made for the state, whereas we wiser and better moderns see the state as serving the individual. This presupposes that Aristotle starts as we do with radical individualism and then collects the individuals into a state. This is a sensible charge to make against Karl Marx. Unlike Marx, however, Aristotle did not study political science in the shadow of Thomas Hobbes. Following Hobbesian individualism, civil society is seen as a necessary evil, a departure from nature. In the condition of mere nature, Hobbes teaches, the condition of man is one of war of every man against every man where "life is solitary, poor, nasty, brutish, and short." In that condition, "everyone has a right to everything, even to one another's bodies." Of course neither Hobbes nor any other observer has or can have empirical knowledge of such a condition. Hobbes knows this. He knows that no one who is alive and so available to testify has ever seen man in such a state. But the whole argument of Hobbes rests on the necessity of positing such a condition, such a "beginning." The way out of that condition is for everyone to give up his rights – all of them except for the few that it would be self-contradictory to give up inasmuch as it is to secure those few that we give up the others. Those few turn out to be the same three that one finds in one or another guise in the American Declaration of Independence and Constitution – life, liberty, and property. We give up all the other rights to a governance that repays us by securing the unalienable ones. One may contrast Aristotle with us moderns by saying that for us to find the nature of an oak we must dissect under the microscope the acorn, whereas Aristotle would say that to understand the acorn one must stand back and contemplate the oak. The nature of a thing is not its rude beginnings but its most perfect completion, and the nature of man cannot be seen by regarding him as a solitary warrior in a war without form or character or limit. For Hobbes and us moderns the nature of man is "back there" but the condition back there is so terrible that we depart from nature as quickly as we can. Civil society is for us, as for Hobbes, natural, but only in the sense that it is natural for men to flee from nature to form that society. For Aristotle, the nature of man is completed by and made intelligible in the context of the polis. What man *is*, is a *member* of the highest and most comprehensive and most commanding community, the political community. Without the polis man would be an aimless wanderer. He would not *become* in actuality what by nature he *is*. If one starts with Hobbes rather than with Aristotle, humans become nothing more than consumers, and, after they consume all that they need, they need more. Being human is rather like an itch.

Aristotle's observation that the polis *is* by nature is to say that the being of the polis is natural, a natural completion, a completion of the nature of man. Its coming into being is, however, to be viewed differently. Somebody had to say, "let us form up." Someone had to found the first polis. Some human action was the agent of the completion of that which was immanent in the nature of man. That first founder was, Aristotle teaches, a "great benefactor." The actual founder has in mind immediately, as we said earlier, only defense and commerce, but once launched, the polis has a life of its own. It becomes what its nature makes it, the completion of what it is to be human.

What is it to be human? It turns out that human perfection is the perfection of the virtues. Uh-oh! Nobody likes to talk now about virtues. It sounds preachy and "judgmental." We cannot avoid the subject, however, but we must defer it until we have taken care of some loose ends regarding the hierarchy of the communities.

Aristotle teaches us that the household is a community which is subsumed by and under the polis. What that means requires us again to dabble in the Greek language. We noted earlier that the Greek word for household is *oikon*. Now it happens that the Greek word *nomos* means law or custom or way or management. The Platonic dialogue that we call the *Laws* is, in Plato's language, *oi nomoi*, the plural of *nomos*, and so *The Laws* is a literal translation of Plato's title. If we attach the two words *oikon* and *nomos*, using the adjectival form of *nomos*, namely *nomiké*, we get *oikonnomiké*. If we follow Jaffa, who showed that the noun "politics" is nothing more than the plural of the adjective "politic," we see that we have in the plural of the combined noun *oikon* and adjective *nomiké* the adjective economic, which, pluralized, renders the noun "economics." Thus, the exact meaning of the word "economics" is household management. This seems strange to us. That is not at all what the word means to us now. How did that happen? We can best get to the answer indirectly.

As the space age loomed after World War II, a book appeared with the title *Lunar Geography*. That is, of course, ridiculous. "Geo" means earth, and the suffix "graphy" means a writing up, description, or display. These two parts of the word are Greek. *Luna* is the Latin word for moon. Leaving altogether aside the correctness or error of the mixture of the two languages, is it not still ridiculous to speak of the "writing up of the earth of the moon?" Well, who cares? We know what the author of such a book intended and we forgive him his loose use of language. We pay no price for the mix-up unless we try to land on the moon without an oxygen supply. The confusion about economics is likelier to make us fall into an intellectual hole than is the confusion intrinsic in the expression "lunar geography." We cannot understand Aristotle without straightening out this matter. We need to see how we got from Athens to here. Aristotle had explained that wealth was best held in private hands, although it was best that it be used for public purposes. Thus, the distinction between the *polis* and the household was the distinction between the public and the private, between politics and economics. Wealth, was, by its nature, the wealth of households, but households were, by their nature, parts of, and subordinate to, the polis. Economics (or household management), or the use of wealth, was a subordinate part of politics. The completion of the nature of man is not made fully possible by the household but only by the *polis*. One could imagine a book on economics being called *The Wealth of Households*. A considerable discussion of that very topic takes up the latter half of Book One of Aristotle's *Politics*. In 1776, Adam Smith (Scotland, 1723–90) wrote a book called *An Inquiry into the Nature and Causes of the Wealth of Nations*. This book might well be regarded as the very foundation of the modern science of economics. Edwin Cannan, in his "Editor's Introduction" to the Modern Library edition of the *Wealth of Nations*, says that there is no doubt that Smith regarded the phrase "political economy" as identical in meaning to the title of his book, but there were reasons why he chose not to give the book the title *Political Economy*.[9] If we think of the book as having had the longer title, *Political Economy: An Inquiry into the Nature and Causes of the Wealth of Nations*, we are justified in thinking of that title as being as ridiculous as the title *Lunar Geography*, but the great genius of Adam Smith is shown by appreciating that he is elbowing his reader in the ribs to awaken him to understand that there is not only a wealth of households; there is also a wealth of nations, and the latter needs as much as the former to be considered and managed. Although

[9] Adam Smith, *An Inquiry into the Nature and Causes of the Wealth of Nations*, Edwin Cannan, ed., New York, c.1937, Modern Library, pp. xxvii–xxviii.

we would easily accept the title *Political Economy*, we would, on reflection, see that the literal meaning would be the management of the household of the polis.[10] In present-day university departments of economics, their courses in microeconomics and macroeconomics might be sorted out by thinking of Aristotle's household management and Smith's *Wealth of Nations*.

Aristotle's extensive discussion of household management in the latter half of Book One covers three sorts of relationship or management and raises some questions about a possible fourth sort. He speaks of the relationship between husband and wife, that between father and child, and that between master and slave. Putting these three – husbandship, fathership, and mastership – together, we have household management. Aristotle, however, raises the question whether the getting of wealth is also a part, a fourth part, of household management. After all, wealth is essential to the household. Obviously the use of wealth is an aspect of the management of the household. What about the getting of it? Aristotle shows that some kind of wealth getting is part of economics, that is, part of household management. That kind of wealth getting is natural and it is limited – limited to the needs of the household. That is, wealth is by nature for use, not for accumulation. Speaking in easily understood terms, we might say that every household needs a plow, probably a second plow, and a spare plowshare, but no householder in his right mind would set himself to acquiring as many plows as he could lay hands on.

There is another kind of wealth getting, however, that is not part of household management, not natural, and not limited. That is the sort that is involved in trade or commerce. There are people engaged in that activity, and their end is precisely accumulation – not of plows, obviously, but of coin. Aristotle immediately turns away from this subject for to speak of it at length would be distasteful to gentlemen.

In 1690, in his *Two Treatises of Government*, specifically in Chapter Five of the *Second Treatise*, John Locke (England, 1632–1704) confronts the seventeen centuries of Christian disapproval of acquisitiveness, a disapproval that seems in part to echo that of Aristotle. Locke makes the argument that, although it is true that God gave the earth to man in common, the goods of the earth – apples, say – are no good to anyone unless someone takes them to himself, to his own proper self, that is, makes them proper to himself, makes a property in them, a private property. (This is what economists came to call "primitive acquisition.") In that finely crafted chapter of his finely crafted book, Locke liberates acquisitiveness from the traditional, Christian disapproval. He argues that ensuring rights to property frees men to accumulate wealth and, in so doing, makes everyone better

---

[10] Some present-day universities offer courses titled Political Economy, but there is reason to believe that the meaning and intention of their usage of that phrase differs from Smith's.

off. Man left to the fruits of nature is confined to an acorn, an apple, a sip of water. With property rights, men will cultivate the earth, which they would not do if the fruits of their labor were not secure in their hands. That cultivation of the earth leads to plenty – plenty for everyone. Man's labor is worth ten times – no, a hundred times – actually, as many times more as five pounds is more than a penny, namely, twelve hundred times. Well, would you believe at least a thousand times? Think of it! Human labor is worth a thousand times the worth of what God provides. Where God's providence gives us an acorn, an apple, and a sip of water, the labor of man provides a martini cocktail with a twist of lemon, a sizzling New York strip steak, and a strawberry shortcake. (Oh, all right, Locke does not say that, but what he does say adds up to that.) Reflecting on the paragraph just before this one, two things become clear. First, in the fourth century B.C. Aristotle knew everything John Locke taught in the seventeenth century A.D., but he refuses to talk about it. Why?[11] The second thing that becomes clear may answer the question: The content of the *Politics* is not addressed solely to philosophers. It is meant to be intelligible to and formative of a class of subphilosophic people, the gentlemen; so, too, is Locke's book addressed to gentlemen. Aristotle wished not to disturb the predispositions of the class of gentlemen. Locke emphatically wished to overthrow these predispositions.

Like the word "philosophy" and the word "politics," the word "gentle-man" has lost its meaning for us. It is a word left over from aristocratic regimes, a word that we have democratized. The word is a translation of the Greek phrase *kalós kai agathos*, which translates to noble and good. The Greeks contracted the phrase into a word, the word *kaloskagathos*. As a consequence of democratization, everyone who is not a lady in our democratic speech is a gentleman, so we have to push our thoughts back a bit. In aristocratic Europe one who was called a gentleman – one of a distinct class, a distinct minority – was in ancient Athens called a "nobleandgood." Aristotle's predecessor, Plato, and a ninth- and tenth-century-A.D. philosopher al-Farabi, will have to help us to an understanding here. We shall give a condensed statement now of something that will shortly occupy a whole chapter. In his dialogue the *Republic,* Plato has Socrates answer a difficult question put to him by Glaucon and Adeimantus by imagining a city that has never been. He talks the city up. That is all it is, a talked-of city, a city in speech. In it, a small element, namely, one person only or perhaps a few, who is or are philosophers and who have gold in their souls, with the unquestioning support of a military class, a minority of perhaps a thousand

---

[11] I am indebted for this explanation to Dr. Ann Colmo, who had taken a class from me as an undergraduate and who, as a graduate student, had learned this connection between Aristotle and Locke from Professor Joseph Cropsey. She then pointed it out to me.

men and women who have ample spiritedness and who have silver in their souls, rules absolutely over everyone else, the great majority of the people, who have bronze and iron in their souls. It becomes clear, especially from the last page of Book Seven, that such a city will never come into being in actuality. Aristotle seems to have in mind a watered-down, rather prosaic, but quite practicable version of Plato's threefold division of the population in the imaginary city in speech talked up by Plato's Socrates. Aristotle's gentlemen correspond to the silver class in that city in speech. (By the way, whatever you may find in some translations, neither Plato nor Aristotle ever uses such an expression as "ideal city" and most emphatically, never says "ideal state.") Al-Farabi tells us that in a city there are "three kinds of brains." The best of the three, who sounds like a philosopher to us, is capable of understanding the beings of nature and explaining them by demonstrative reasoning. The members of the second class, a larger minority, cannot reach such an understanding on their own, but can be led to understand it by excellent teaching. The third class, the majority, cannot understand demonstrative proofs at all, and so must be led by similitudes. That is, the best they can do is to live by stories, that is, live in accord with wholesome prejudices. The second class, the gentlemen, start with certain natural proclivities and capacities and become what they become by way of what just a few decades ago was called "liberal education." That education consists (in present terms) of language and literature, history, geography, physics, chemistry and biology, as well as ethics, politics, logic, and, certainly, religion.

"Culture" is another word denatured in our day. Its original meaning was what cultivated people had. To speak of popular culture or to say that all cultures are equal is to render us incapable of understanding anything that antedates the Internet gossip about which actress is sleeping with which football player this week. Culture becomes keeping up with the "celebs" and their "fave" things. Culture, speaking exactly, is the possession of a class of people who have had a sound, liberal education, well-taught and well-understood, and it is carried on from generation to generation. It is somehow the possession of old families. Consequently, *those* young and *those* old can understand each other. For this reason, Aristotle devotes the last two books of the *Politics* to the subject of education.

We have been sketching a definition of the *polis*. Aristotle holds that it is the most comprehensive and the highest community and that its aim is the highest good. There are three possible senses to be drawn from this assertion. First, Aristotle may mean that the *polis*, and so politics (and its ends) is the highest good imaginable, even the highest good of the gods. This is well-nigh unimaginable. Such a view would cancel out the whole remainder of Aristotle's political thought. The second possibility is that he means that the end of the *polis* is the highest end for man. The possibility of this must be entertained, but if this is what he meant then his view would be indistinguishable from the view later held by Machiavelli. I believe that this possibility, too, must be dismissed, for it too would cancel out the remainder of his political thought. I believe that he means only that the political good, the good sought by the *polis*, is the highest good that can be pursued in community. The good in the most supreme sense can truly be sought only by the philosophic pursuit, and that pursuit is an enterprise for a few individual human beings who, in the course of that pursuit, transcend the *polis*. Man is by nature a political animal – the only animal endowed with the faculty of speech – so he is able to be a part of a *polis*. He must be, because his achieving his potential humanity depends on the *polis*. Man falls short of being man in the fullest sense without the *polis*. The nature of a thing is defined by its purpose, its function, what it does. The *polis* is that which makes possible the completion of man, which is the good life or the noble life. The purpose or function, the end, of the *polis* is the good life, the noble life. The good life in the fullest sense is the noble life, a life that possesses and exercises the best qualities, the virtues. Aristotle sometimes speaks of the good life and sometimes of the noble life, and it appears that the terms are nearly, but only nearly, interchangeable. A problem insinuates itself, however. Perhaps the good is higher than the noble. Maybe "the good life" is an ambiguous term. Maybe there is a merely good political life and that is the thing that Aristotle speaks of in this book that we have described as a subphilosophic book. Maybe there is a good that is beyond the political good, beyond the end of the *polis*. It is this very self-awareness of the philosopher as a superior being, a being who, like a shooting star, streaks away and leaves the political behind, that makes the city fear and suspect the philosopher.

This is a good moment for a strong caution to university students who are vulnerable to all sorts of political silliness. In the silly season of a presidential election year, a dozen would-be presidents, divided evenly between the parties, prattle about change. To call for change is to presuppose that something is enormously wrong and needs fixing. A candidate can strike a mock-heroic pose and fancy himself the true agent of change without bothering to identify the thing to be changed and the change from what to what that is being proposed. The philosopher is not just one more politician. His aim is not to alter the political order. He is not an activist, that is, a busybody. To borrow a phrase from Plato's *Republic*, the philosopher despises politics. The philosopher is transcendent not because he wants to overthrow the political order but because he levitates above it. The definitive lesson is the case of Socrates. We must point out that Socrates accepted the unjust sentence of death. He refused to break the law. To put this succinctly, the philosophers goal, insofar as it can at all be thought to be the consequence of action, is a thousand times grander than replacing the party of Tweedledee with the party of Tweedledum. The philosopher is not a politician. The philosopher is above politics. This is not to denigrate politics. It is, as Aristotle makes plain, the second-highest calling. We must wait until Chapter Five to contemplate those circumstances that might force the philosopher to descend to the political level.

To return to the more prosaic subject of the virtues – the virtues developed by proper upbringing, the moral virtues, the virtues which in their fullness mark the noble life – we need here to confront a strange unwillingness even to talk about such things, as though virtues were simply the stuff of dull sermons. A homely analogy helps. The human virtues are, in some respects, similar to the virtues of any useful appliance. For example, the virtue of a knife is sharpness. The definition of a knife is that it cuts. A knife is to cut. Its end or purpose is cutting. A dull knife is a poor knife. A knife so dull that it can no longer cut at all may make a good doorstop, but rightly speaking it is no longer a knife because it can no longer do what knives do. If we speak of "that knife that holds the door open," it is only by a kind of recollection that we call it a knife at all after it has ceased to be one. The human being is a great deal more complicated. The human being is composed of both body and soul. The obvious virtues of the body are health, beauty, and strength. It does not dehumanize someone to speak of him as "crippled." We may esteem or love a crippled human being, but to be crippled is to be defective in some way. The proof of this is that no one would wish to be crippled. No one who is mentally well wants to be physically ill, or ugly, or weak. In the same way, the virtues of the soul are the wanted things. The traditional list of the cardinal virtues – the four crucial ones – enumerates wisdom, courage, moderation, and justice. Again, no one desires to be stupid, or cowardly, or gluttonous, or unjust. This is easy to see in the case of the first two, a bit difficult in the case of the third, and even more difficult to see in the case of the fourth. We do not need to prove this list here and now. We only need to specify that this is the view of Aristotle. Aristotle's *Ethics* contains a larger list, including such things as liberality, easy friendliness, and magnanimity – a list of eleven moral virtues and three intellectual virtues. He entertains some things and sets them aside. For example, he says that shame, a sense of shame, is not truly a virtue because the gentleman would not do something of which to be ashamed. We might, however, say that it is a hemi-semi-demi-virtue, because if someone does something shameful we would rather that he be ashamed than that he be shameless. There is a difference between the ancient view of the virtues and the modern view. Mouthing an old saying, we say that "virtue is its own reward," but we do not mean it. What we mean, for example, is that moderation is good because gluttony makes you lose health, strength, and beauty. To say that, however, is to say that moderation is not good in itself; it is only instrumentally good. As Immanuel Kant (Germany, 1724–1804) explained in his *Foundations of the Metaphysics of*

Morals, the saying that "honesty is the best policy" is not at all to speak of honesty. If a storekeeper calls back a customer to give him his change, it may be for the purpose of improving business. That is not the same thing as honesty, as justice, as wanting another human being to have what is rightly his. The old saying, that "virtue is its own reward," meant that one developed and practiced the virtues not to get something for them, either here or hereafter, but to have them. One is moderate not to stay slim and beautiful, but to be moderate. Since Machiavelli early in the sixteenth century we have understood ethics and politics as two different and separable things. This is not so with Aristotle. They are, as it were, chapters of the same book. One simply cannot discuss morality in the absence of a discussion of politics, for the *polis* is the essential condition of the development of the good life, the life lived in the practice of the virtues. Likewise, one cannot discuss politics in the absence of a discussion of morality. Hard-boiled political realism is, to repeat a figure of speech, *Hamlet* without Hamlet. Likewise, a post-Kantian airy ethics, detached from human ends, is Hamlet without *Hamlet.* Thus, Kant got it half right.

We shall return to Aristotle's *Politics* in due course. For the moment, it is enough to finish our incomplete enumeration of the aspects of the *polis.* The *polis* is natural (although not accidental nor inevitable), it aims at the good or noble life, it is complete in itself, it acknowledges and builds upon the natural inequalities of man, and it must be of the right size – not too small and not too large.

One problem cannot be left behind as we move to the next chapter. In the opening eight lines of *Politics,* Aristotle says that the *polis* is the community that aims at the highest good.

We need to repeat here and to emphasize a problem we just canvassed. Does Aristotle mean the highest good, simply, even as to the good of the gods, or does he mean the highest human good? We have already dismissed the first and the second possibilities. If he means the second of these two, then there would be nothing beyond the *polis* in the light of which to judge between the good *polis* and the bad *polis,* and we would have the spectacle of a philosopher who sees politics as superior to philosophy. The philosopher knows the innate superiority of philosophy. It is the highest life for man. He also knows that the good life, not to speak of the noble life, and surely not to speak of the philosophic life (the life of pursuit of the truth wherein, as Plato shows in *Phaedrus,* the philosopher glimpses the ultimate truths quite as the gods do), is a life utterly dependent on the *polis* and, in fact, on the good *polis.* Philosophers are therefore not intoxicated with such a sense of superiority that they are destructive of the *polis.* They may look down on politics in a way, but they are not sneeringly contemptuous of it or of their *polis.* They need their *polis,* so they are patriots of a sort, although perhaps from self-interest, or with a view to the interest of their interest group, the philosophers. Touching close to this point, Leo Strauss has offered this explanation:

> [From one point of view] "political philosophy" means primarily not the philosophic treatment of politics, but the political, or popular, treatment of philosophy, or the political introduction to philosophy – the attempt to lead the qualified citizens, or rather their qualified sons, from the political life to the philosophic life.[12]

That point of view opens up to us a new insight into Aristotle's *Politics*, and even into Plato's *Republic*. Both may be seen as opening the door to philosophy, although the *Republic* opens it wider than does the *Politics*. The arguments Socrates makes to Glaucon and Adeimantus in the *Republic* may be seen as enticements to them to rise from their place as mere gentlemen into the more exalted place of philosophy, if indeed they are capable of such an ascent, but Book Ten offers them – and us – an out if the ascent is too steep. The *Politics* seems even more modest in its goals. It may be that it aims first of all to develop in the gentlemen a cheerful tolerance of philosophy, leaving it to those among the gentlemen for whom "the shoe fits" to nominate themselves for the higher calling.

Machiavelli and many others since have spoken of both Plato and Aristotle as though they were, on the one hand, irrelevant idealists and, on the other, absolutists who are intolerant of any *polis* but the ones they have dreamed up. These are great mistakes. Properly read, even the *Republic*, and surely the *Politics*, offers counsels of political moderation. Properly read, they also make clear that no one who has ever studied politics is more generous or more open-minded than are Plato and Aristotle.

Politics, then, as we see from our glancing touch of Book One of Aristotle's *Politics*, means of or pertaining to the *polis*, the things of the *polis*. Each *polis* has its own, unique *politeia*, or constitution, or regime, but a useful scientific or philosophic inquiry requires sorting the several *politeias* into the smallest possible classification. As Book Three of the *Politics* shows, this proves to be a list of six classes of *politeia*, three good ones and three bad ones. The *politikos*, the politician or statesman, is simply the one who does politics. He does the things of the *polis*. Once again, for Aristotle, it is the second-highest calling.

---

[12] Leo Strauss, *What Is Political Philosophy?* Glencoe, IL, 1959, Free Press, pp. 93–94.

4

The Origin of Political Philosophy

Marcus Tullius Cicero (106–43 B.C.), a lawyer, orator, statesman, and philosopher, was likely the greatest intellect of the ancient Roman republic. He is usually called a "Stoic," after the group of postclassical philosophers who carried on their disputations while taking their ease under the *stoa*, or porticos, of Athens. Cicero calls himself such, but questions have been raised as to whether he fit in with the other Stoics or departed from them by way of a return to stricter adherence to the philosophic principles of the classical thinkers Socrates, Plato, and Aristotle. These three are, of course, the three great figures of political philosophy at its beginnings. Aristotle (384–322 B.C.), the last of the three, wrote treatises. A treatise is a work that endeavors to offer demonstrative proofs regarding the matters treated. He seems to have meant this method as an improvement on the work of his teacher, Plato (427–347 B.C.). All of Plato's writings that have come down to us (other than a few letters) are called "dialogues." The dialogues look a bit like plays and they have something of the poetic quality of plays. Plato was the first political philosopher to leave behind a body of writings. He was the most prominent follower of Socrates (469–399 B.C.), who left no writings. The oldest academic joke explains that Socrates "didn't get tenure" because he didn't publish anything.[1] Cicero was the first to say that Socrates founded political philosophy. He wrote:

[F]rom the ancient days down to the time of Socrates, . . . philosophy dealt with numbers and movements, with the problem whence all things came, or whither they returned, and zealously inquired into the size of the stars, the spaces that divided them, their courses and all celestial phenomena; Socrates on the other hand was the first to call philosophy down from the heavens and set her into the cities of men

---

[1] This is a variation on the complaint of professors hoping for tenure in their teaching positions. The usual phrasing is "Publish or Perish." Catholic priests following academic careers ring the changes on this by describing their lives as "Publish or Parish."

and bring her also into their homes and compel her to ask questions about life and morality and things good and evil.[2]

What we know of Socrates we learn from the writings of his contemporaries – his close associate, Xenophon, and the comic poet, Aristophanes, as well as his greatest adherent, Plato, and, once removed, Plato's pupil, Aristotle. We can begin to see the origin of political philosophy by reading the Aristophanes comedy the *Clouds*; the Platonic dialogue that preserves for us the defense speech of Socrates at the trial that ended in his being given the death penalty, Plato's *Apology of Socrates*; and the Platonic dialogues *Crito* and *Phaedo*, which give accounts of the life of Socrates between his trial and execution.

Comedies are comedies. They are funny. We cannot help but laugh at the ridiculous figure cut by Socrates as Aristophanes portrays him in the *Clouds*, but we need the sobriety wrought by the cold shower of acknowledging that that play contributed to the guilty verdict and death penalty meted out at the trial of Socrates and by reminding ourselves of that other verdict rendered at the moment of his death by the friends of Socrates that he was, of all the men of his time, "the best and wisest and most just."[3] Even the prison guard who brought the lethal drug to Socrates said, "I have found you . . . the noblest and gentlest and best man" who has ever come to the prison, and then the guard turned away and burst into tears.[4]

The dramatis personae of the *Clouds* add up to more than a dozen characters (two of whom are the personifications of the Better Speech and the Worse Speech), but the three of greatest interest to our account here are Strepsiades, his son Pheidippides, and Socrates. Pheidippides is a carefree youth who wastes the family wealth on the horses. Strepsiades is naturally worried about his son's conduct. He reasons that if he studies at a place called the Thinkery for a while to learn the Better Speech and the Worse Speech he might wriggle out of his equine-engendered debts by twisting the law. He enrolls at the Thinkery, but he is soon expelled because he is too old and too rustic to learn, so he sends his son there in his place to study under Socrates. Socrates undertakes his researches and teaches his pupils from a gondola suspended from the sky by a hook. In addition to examining the things of the earth below, Socrates, from his conveniently elevated vantage, examines also the things of the heavens above. Obviously, the chief things of the heavens above are the gods. What is more, Socrates teaches what some law professors today teach, namely how to win law cases by fair means or foul, that is, how to speak persuasively to make the Worse Speech appear

---

[2] Cicero, *Tusculan Disputations*, V. iv. 10. The translation is by J. E. King, Loeb Classical Library, Cambridge, MA, 1945 (original publication 1927), Harvard University Press, p. 435.

[3] Plato, *Phaedo*, 118a.

[4] Ibid., 116c, the Harold North Fowler translation, Loeb Classical Library, Cambridge, MA, 1966 (original publication 1914), Harvard University Press, p. 397.

the Better. Thus, Socrates is represented in the play as being both a physiologist and a rhetorician, a researcher of natural philosophy and a teacher of speech. As was just intimated, to pursue natural philosophy – to enquire into the things below and the heavens above – is to be, among other things, a theologian. Thus Socrates, on high, looks down on the gods.

Pheidippides goes home one day from his studies at the Thinkery of Socrates and beats his father. Now this is one of the two most grievously unjust and shockingly impious acts imaginable. One's parents are, after all, gods, or will be so hereafter.[5] Having done this terrible thing somehow as a consequence of his schooling at the hands of Socrates, Pheidippides, having learned also the two speeches, then makes a persuasive speech to his father that it was, in fact, quite just for him to have beaten him. Given the "progress" of education since the *Émile* of Jean-Jacques Rousseau (1712–78), it cannot confidently be said that what Pheidippides learned from Socrates takes the cake for bad schooling, but surely the upshot of the burlesque by Aristophanes is to make Socrates out to be not so much laughable as he is the most corrupting force in all of Athens.[6]

Whether Aristophanes wrote his play in good fun and it just "got away from him," or he meant deliberately to libel Socrates, at least it is clear that the play acknowledges that Socrates is a most sought-after teacher and that his teaching has consequences for both private and public life. In his defense speech before the court that tried him, Socrates links his indictment to the earlier attacks on him by many slanderers. On reflection we see that his *Apology* is not only a defense of himself, it is a defense of philosophy itself. As we read that defense, we catch a glimpse of the necessity of the coming into being of political philosophy, Socrates elsewhere explains the reason for that movement from philosophy of nature to political philosophy, which Cicero had cited in the passage quoted earlier. The explanation by Socrates helps us to see more keenly the antipathy between philosophy and the polis.

Beginning with Thrasyllus (d. A.D. 36), the works of Plato were sorted into tetralogies.[7] The first of these tetralogies places the *Euthyphro*, the *Apology*, the *Crito*, and the *Phaedo* together. The *Euthyphro* is a short dialogue that

---

5 The other of the two most unjust and most impious acts imaginable is unfit even to be mentioned in decent company. Fortunately, although a tragedy has been written about it, nobody has yet had the bad taste to make a comedy of it. The nearest thing so far is a glancing reference to it in the Mel Brooks motion picture *History of the World, Part I*. In keeping with the comic genius of Brooks, that movie achieves, designedly, the summit of bad taste.

6 The word "Thinkery" in this paragraph is the translator's choice in the Thomas G. West and Grace Starry West translation of the *Clouds* in their *Four Texts on Socrates*, Ithaca, NY, 1984, Cornell University Press. Some others have translated the word used by Aristophanes for the place where Socrates holds forth as "think tank." West's "Thinkery" is much closer to being a literal translation from the Greek.

7 See Book III, "Plato," in Diogenes Laertius, *Lives and Opinions of the Eminent Philosophers*, tr. R. D. Hicks, Loeb Classical Library, Cambridge, MA, 1925, Harvard University Press, vol. 1.

portrays Socrates at the office of the King Archon answering the indictment laid against him. This attendance is on the order of what today would be called an "arraignment." He meets Euthyphro there. Socrates is responding to the charges made against him, but Euthyphro is *making* charges, charges against his father for impiety. This accusation by Euthyphro is, in present-day usage, what we would call "ironic," for, other than the beating of Strepsiades by Pheidippides, few things could be as impious as taking legal action against one's father. This leads to a conversation in which Socrates tries to understand the nature of piety or holiness. This conversation is a matter of utmost importance to Socrates – a matter of life or death, as it turns out – because the indictment that brings him to trial has as a principal element the charge of impiety. Although Euthyphro is quite emphatic in his action against his father, which he attributes to his piety, he is quite befuddled in his understanding of the nature of piety. Not surprisingly, the *Euthyphro* culminates not in an answer to but only in a degree of clarification of the question as to that nature.

"Apology" is another word that confounds the modern reader. We have been reared to mean by the word a speech or writing that says one regrets some action. That is not its original meaning. The Greek word ἀπολογία (*apologia*) of which the English word "apology" is a straightforward transliteration, means defense speech, an oration not asking forgiveness for but in defense of one's actions, a speech that maintains that one has not broken the law as charged. When an Athenian was charged with a crime, a court was convened by drawing from among the citizens a large number of men by lot. There was no judge as distinct from this number. All were both judges and jurors – or it would be better to say that their duties did not distinguish between these functions as does the English system of law courts, and, following it, the American. In the case of Socrates, the court that was convened consisted of 501 men. Although one might in Athenian jurisprudence engage the services of a rhetor, that is, an orator (or of a rhetor's teacher, a rhetorician), to write a persuasive defense speech, one could not hire a speaker (a lawyer or a barrister in modern English-speaking usage) to be his advocate or counsel at the trial. Socrates therefore had to argue his case himself, and he chose not even to employ someone else to write a speech for him, perhaps regarding it as more honest to speak plainly and extemporaneously – or perhaps simply more prudent.

John Burnet edited a critical edition of the Greek texts of the *Euthyphro*, the *Apology*, and the *Crito*, first published in 1924.[8] Socrates, in his defense, denies any knowledge of the proper legal forms, but Burnet shows that the *Apology* in fact follows such forms. He divided the speech of Socrates into some nine parts. Following Burnet, we shall look at the text one part at a time.

---

[8] Consulted here is a recent reprint of the 1924 book, Oxford, 1979, Oxford University Press.

Part I, The Proemium (17a1–18a6)[9]

In the Proemium (or Preface) Socrates describes the argument made to the court by his accusers. That argument, he says, is a deliberate attempt to mislead the court. We do not have their arguments, but we know that the charges were brought by Anytus, Meletus, and, to a lesser extent, Lycon.[10] Socrates says that among the many lies[11] they told was the one that warned the court to beware because Socrates was a persuasive speaker. He was not any such thing, he said. We are inclined, however, to accept as true the characterization of Socrates by his disciples that he knew just about everything of use that anyone knew, and so surely knew forensic rhetoric. Furthermore, Plato's dialogues *Phaedrus* and *Gorgias* represent Socrates as being thoroughly versed in both private and public rhetoric – that is, in both erotic speech and in deliberative and forensic speech. Socrates, however, had to deny rhetorical skill, because to let his accusers' statements stand would be to admit the very charge laid against him that he was one of those Sophists who used rhetorical skill to undermine public order. Of course, if speaking plainly is speaking cleverly, then the shoe fits, for speaking plainly is what he intends to do, but such speaking would not (or at least ought not) to have been unlawful, unless the substance of the speech were forbidden. He asks his judges not to judge the manner of his speech, but simply to consider whether what he says is just or not. If the court accepted his defense it would acquit him, or perhaps, in modern legal language, dismiss the case against him for want of a cause of action.

Part II, The Prothesis (18a7–19a7)

The modern, American equivalent of the ancient Greek "prothesis" is defense counsel's opening argument to the jury. There being no defense counsel, Socrates of course makes this argument for himself. The prothesis is appropriately short, about one page in the Stephanus edition and also about one page in English translation. Socrates calls attention to the fact that there are two sets of accusers – the first accusers and the later accusers, and he states that he will counter those accusations in turn. There had been accusations made against him to the Athenians for many years, and he says that he fears them (i.e., fears the effect of those early accusations on the minds of the jurors) even more than he fears the accusations by Anytus and those in concert with him who had made the accusations that brought

---

9 The page and line numbers of the Stephanus edition of the works of Plato are explained in Note 1 to the Prologue herein.

10 Brief articles can be found on Anytus and Meletus, but none on Lycon, in *The Oxford Classical Dictionary*, Oxford, 1949, Oxford University Press.

11 See the *Apology*, 17a6. Socrates does not mince words.

about the trial. The jurors had not come to the trial with open minds. Those earlier accusers had gotten hold of the Athenians from childhood and persuaded them "that there is a certain Socrates, a wise man, a thinker on the things aloft, who has investigated all things under the earth, and who makes the weaker speech the stronger."[12] Thus, the jurors had already a mind-set to find him guilty of being an investigator of "things aloft" and a teacher of how to make the worse appear the better cause. Because the gods *are*, and because they are aloft, and because the polis has authoritatively identified and defined them, to "investigate" them means to question their being or at least their authoritative identification and definition. This is blasphemy, and it is sedition. It undermines the most precious parts of the law and turns one's pupils into seditious citizens, the sort likely to bring about by force or fraud the destruction of the whole political order and all the laws. In addition, the charge of being a corrupt teacher of rhetoric further accuses him of being what we would call a "smart aleck" who sneers at and causes his pupils to sneer at the law and the legal process. Thus, in both substance and form, he threatens the city, threatens to tear it down completely, and he does so knowingly and willfully. He is public enemy number one.

What we have tried to clarify in Chapter One, namely, the distinction between genuine philosophy and merely so-called philosophy, is not what is at stake here. The many do not make such fine distinctions. In one neat package, the charges against Socrates point to the fact of a mortal and unresolvable conflict between philosophy itself and politics. The fact of the conflict is indisputable. The question that might conceivably remain open is whether that conflict is mortal and unresolvable. Since the philosophic movement begun in the seventeenth century that is called "the Enlightenment," we been lulled into believing that the problem has gone away. It has not. Philosophy, like Socrates, is on trial for its life. At most times in history, philosophy has had to "go underground" to avoid burning at the stake or, at best, banishment. At all times since Socrates, philosophy has had to confront the problem of accommodation to politics. If it succeeds too well, it does so simply by telling ignorant public opinion what it wants to hear. That is not accommodation; that is surrender. In contrast, if philosophy simply flouts the law, simply acts in contempt of the polis, it is everything that the earlier and the later accusers of Socrates maintain. Philosophy deserves to perish. One route to a proper understanding of philosophy is to look at the various attempts philosophy has made over the centuries to accommodate itself to politics, to reach a lasting cease-fire.

Socrates acknowledges the nearly insurmountable difficulty confronting him. He does not have any illusions about his fate, but he cannot simply throw up his hands in despair. To do so would be at once to abandon

---

[12] The *Apology*, 18b7–10. The quoted passage is from the West translation, *op. cit.*, p. 80 n. 6 in this chapter.

philosophy and to prove his accusers right that he thinks the polis, the law, and the multitude are beneath his answering the charges. He closes the prothesis by saying, "Let this proceed in whatever way is dear to the god, but the law must be obeyed and a defense speech must be made."[13] If one were to judge him according to this speech, it would appear that he does believe in gods, perhaps even in the gods Athens believes in, and he is law-abiding. Still, he would face the accusation that he does not believe in the gods as the poets present them.

All present-day students who take their studies seriously, who love life, and who wish truly to be just, owe it to themselves and to the good to weigh all of their teachers in this balance. Are they as Socrates claims to be, or are they as the accusers of Socrates say he is? Are they law-abiding, or are they charlatans, smart alecks, wise guys? Common sense suggests that some will pass the test and others will not. Be warned. These will not be easy tests. Even coming to the conclusion that a given teacher fails the test cannot be done without proper respect and consideration of the claims of the teacher to be a sort of moral and political savior. In contrast, claiming to be a "philosopher," as we suggested earlier when defining philosophy, does not make one such. Nor are appeals to the natural altruism of young people in the name of "getting involved," "making a difference," or "bringing about change" to be taken at face value. One should "get involved" only after proper study of the problems and their alternative answers. One should attempt to "make a difference" only after reflecting on the existing state of affairs to judge whether it is truly defective. This involves, for example, genuine study of the array of alternative states of affairs – possible political regimes – and the cost and difficulty of their correction. One should never bring about change just for the sake of change. Change should only be change for the better, and even in such a case the probable human cost of the change may counsel leaving things alone. Not everyone who feels strongly is a paragon of wisdom and moral virtue. Not everyone who has preceded us – not our parents, not the founders of our country, not all the philosophers of old – are to be held as complete fools nor are they all to be judged as venal self-seekers. In the light of these remarks, it ought to go without saying (but in fact it must be said) that this book means to teach. Did the teacher who wrote it do so for the sake of money? Did he do so to stroke his vainglory? Did he do so simply because pedantry is what professors do? All these things must be judged, but it is in the best interests of the student to judge them fairly and cautiously. If it is proper, in one's own best interest, to judge these matters in the case of teachers in the present day, so also must the defense of Socrates, the greatest figure in the history of philosophy, and the founder of political philosophy, be judged. Confronting these questions is hard work.

---

[13] The *Apology*, 19a7, from the West translation.

Part III, The Defense of Socrates

A. The Defense against the Old Accusers (19a8–24b2)

Socrates proposes to "take up from the beginning" the old accusations that brought into being the slander[14] that ensured that his jurors would prejudge him. The source of that slander or prejudice must be seen as an accusation just as though it had been in the form of a sworn statement (19b2–4). Socrates takes those old accusations and for the benefit of his jurors puts them in the form of a legal, sworn statement, a statement that would be akin to the basis of a present-day grand jury indictment: "Socrates does injustice [i.e., violates the laws] and is meddlesome, by investigating the things under the earth and the heavenly things, and by making the weaker speech the stronger, and by teaching others these same things." Socrates had spoken of "many" old accusers. It seems that neither Socrates in his defense nor any historian or commentator since provides us with their names or even a guess as to their numbers. Apparently, however, the slander had been so widespread that a whole generation of Athenians had been imbued with it and took it as simple truth. This would not be hard to imagine. Just as in the present day when accusations and insinuations in the press and on television can move a large part of the population to try and then to condemn in public opinion some prominent figure, so it was possible in ancient Athens for a wide portion of the public to hold in suspicion someone of the stature of Socrates. At his trial, Socrates names Aristophanes as a principal accuser. Aristophanes' comedy, the *Clouds*, had been written about twenty-four years before the trial. It may be presumed that many of the judges/jurors in this trial had seen the play performed. To understand Socrates and his circumstance, one may for the moment forget about the many slanderers. One need only reflect on the power of poetry as evidenced by the motion picture industry. It can, for good or for ill, "educate" the public. It can exonerate or condemn without the inconveniences of due process of law and, along the way, hide behind a screen of poetic license. Because his jurors already knew his guilt, the defense of Socrates was well-nigh hopeless, yet he had to go on. He had to exonerate something higher and better than himself.

Socrates denies any expert knowledge of the things below and above, and he likewise denies that he teaches for money, although it would be, he says,

---

[14] "Slander" is West's translation of the Greek word διαβολή (*diabolé*) that appears in the *Apology* at 19a (the last line). Fowler, whose translation of the *Phaedo* is cited at p. 79 n. 4, translates *diabolé* here at 19a in the *Apology* as "prejudice." It is unfortunate that there is not an English word that encompasses both slander and prejudice. The West or Fowler translation is the best choice, because, if, instead of translating, either had simply transliterated *diabolé* into the English word "diabolic," the end result would have been misleading.

a fine or noble[15] thing to be able to teach human beings, and he names three prominent Sophists – Gorgias, Prodicus, and Hippias – as those who do so.[16] Even this praise of the Sophists named seems as much to be a praise of their ability to earn money as of their ability to teach (19e5–20a2). That is, there is something tongue-in-cheek about the praise. His tongue seems to remain in his cheek, for he then says that he had once asked Callias, the son of Hipponicus, and one who had spent more money on Sophists than all the others, who it is that he would hire to teach his two sons to be good men, what is the teacher's city, and how much does he charge. Callias had answered, "Evenus from Paros, Socrates, five minae." The taciturnity, not to say gracelessness, of that answer suggests that perhaps Callias is a rustic, and not much of a judge of better and worse Sophists.

Socrates then supposes that his jurors might ask him, in effect, "What is it about you, Socrates?" He says that he is not joking and that perhaps he does have a kind of wisdom, and he asks them not to make a disturbance while he explains. Chaerephon, the comrade of Socrates from their youth and also the comrade of the democrats, those who now rule and whose court Socrates faces, had gone once to Delphi and had asked the god there through his priestess whether anyone was wiser than Socrates. We clever, secular moderns regard asking a pagan god in this way as the equivalent of asking the Magic Eight Ball, or a Ouija board, but Socrates, whatever he may think, presents his argument as though he takes altogether seriously the accepted gods (in this case, Apollo) and their oracles. The priestess, speaking in the name of the god, answered Chaerephon that no one was wiser than Socrates. Socrates tells the jurors that when he heard this from Chaerephon he wondered at it because he knew that he lacked wisdom, but because it was not possible that the god might lie, he wondered what he could have meant, for the gods do speak in riddles. He then began a search that he explains to the court.

In his search he first questioned statesmen, then poets, and then artisans as to what wisdom they had, and he discovered that none of them had wisdom but none of them knew that he had no wisdom, whereas he, Socrates, was, in a way, wiser than they because, although he had no wisdom, he had at least the wisdom to know that he had no wisdom. Socratic wisdom is knowledge of ignorance, an apprehension of the greatest questions and of the elusiveness of their answers. He realized that he had become hateful to those he questioned (21d2, e2). Certainly he had. He had, we see, shown

---

[15] The Greek word καλός (*kalos*) can be translated as "fine," "fair," "beautiful," or "noble." The opposites are obviously "coarse," "foul," "ugly," or "base." In other words, a *kalos* thing is deserving of praise, and its opposite, *aischron*, is blameworthy.

[16] Plato's dialogue *Gorgias* shows Socrates questioning Gorgias, who, although he lacks the understanding of Socrates, seems to be fundamentally a decent man. His two pupils, Polus and Callicles, however, show themselves to be such good pupils of Gorgias that they seem to have lost any decency they may have had.

them up, shown what vain fools they were. One does not forgive this without becoming a convert who turns to serious inquiry. Such an outcome is, to say the least, rare. It takes a degree of open-mindedness and self-awareness to say, "By Zeus, Socrates is right."

The politicians, the poets, and the artisans disclosed subtle differences one from the others according to the account given by Socrates of his conversations with them. The politicians seemed simply not to know what they were doing. The poets could not explain what they had done. The artisans seemed to know their several crafts, but they made the mistake of thinking that they were therefore wise in other things – rather like a motion picture actor in our day publicly offering advice on how foreign affairs should be conducted. In particular, we are concerned here with the ignorance of the politicians because questions about that are especially the concern of political philosophy.

Part III, The Defense of Socrates

B. *The Defense of Socrates against Meletus (24b3–28a1)*
Socrates now turns to the present accusers. He takes up the sworn statement of Meletus, which is to the effect that he, Socrates, does injustice by corrupting the young and by not believing in the gods in whom the polis believes but believing instead in new *daimons*.[17] It is, Socrates says, Meletus who is the wrongdoer for he brings lawsuits against others lightly, pretending to care about things for which he had never cared. This is to make frivolous charges – to make what today would be punished as a malicious misuse of the instruments of justice, something that is, in itself, a crime.

Part III, The Defense of Socrates

C. *The Interrogatory of Meletus (24c10–28a1)*
Socrates calls Meletus forward and asks him if he believes that it is important that the youth be the best possible and Meletus answers that he does. Then Socrates asks, because Meletus had charged that he, Socrates, made them worse, who makes them better. Meletus hesitates, and Socrates calls attention

---

[17] There were three ranks of gods in the understanding of the Greeks: gods, heroes, and demons. The proper definition of a hero is a being one of whose parents was a god, the other a human. He is thus a demigod. In Christian usage, "demon" always denotes something evil, a thing to be exorcised. In the pagan usage, the word was neutral. One could have a good *daimon* or a bad *daimon* (to "have" one is to be invested with it). The English word "enthusiasm" comes from the Greek *entheous*, to have a god within, to be possessed. Socrates had said that he had a *daimonion*, a demonic thing that prompted him. It was as an inner voice that never prompted him to do anything but always warned him against injustice. This voice was the new *daimon* that Meletus charged him with adding to the accepted ones.

to his silence and then asks again, and Meletus answers, "The laws." Socrates insists that he is asking not what they are but who they are who make the youth better, and Meletus answers that it is "these men," namely, the judges/jurors, the members of this very court trying Socrates. Socrates then leads Meletus through a series of questions asking whether all the 501 judges and even all the spectators and even the members of the Council and even the whole Assembly[18] teach the young to be good. Meletus agrees, and when Socrates says that then all the Athenians except himself make the youth gentlemen,[19] Meletus agrees "vehemently."

In all, Socrates asks Meletus questions or responds to his answers nearly twenty times, and what is most remarkable about this forensic exchange is that it mirrors perfectly the habitual, dialectical method of Socrates as that method is portrayed in the dialogues of Plato. Meletus is led to contradict himself over and over again. That Socrates helps Meletus make a fool of himself in front of the other jurors – or perhaps it would be more precise to say in front of us who now read his defense – in no way redounds to his exoneration, however. If anything, the tide turns against Socrates precisely because he shows the emptiness of the charges by Meletus, for to do so shows the emptiness of the prejudice of his jurors, and no one likes to be made a fool of in public, especially not the public itself. Herein, and perhaps especially herein, lies the unresolvable opposition of philosophy and politics. Also herein is shown the power of politics over philosophy for, although both philosophy and politics understand the tension between them, only philosophy understands the need each has for the other. The polis, the multitude – and, in a way, they are the same – would be glad enough to be rid of philosophy. It is an annoyance. Philosophy reminds politics of its shortcomings. Thus, Socrates cannot simply turn his back on Meletus and the court. Full well

---

[18] West's footnote points out that the Assembly of Athens consisted of whatever "adult male citizens" happened to attend an Assembly meeting. (Of course, all citizens were adult males, but not all adult males were citizens. Not everyone *in* the city was *of* it. Citizenship depended upon qualification. Still, among the citizens, some ranked higher and some lower. Aristophanes, in his play, the *Ecclesiazusae [The Assembly of Women]* pointed to the fact that Assembly meetings were attended principally by rather lesser folk who lined up to serve merely to get the two obols pay. In the play, several women borrow their husbands' cloaks and slippers and attach false beards to their faces to disguise themselves as men, and they get to the Assembly early to be sure of places in it for the day's doings. During the session, the leader of the women, Praxagora, proposes that "we men" have ruled poorly and ought to turn the government over to the women. The women and enough of the ne'er-do-well men make up a majority and pass Praxagora's motion. ·

[19] The Greek words *kalos kai agathos* are normally translated into English as "noble and good," but the Greek contraction of those words into *kaloskagathos* is the nearest equivalent of the term "gentleman" which, in predemocratic Europe, signified a member of the better class of people. Because gentlemen were, among other things, relatively well off, they had horses, and because the Spanish word for horse is *caballo*, the word for gentleman is *caballero*. Likewise, the words in French are *cheval* and *chevalier*, respectively; the latter is often translated into English as "knight." The English word "chivalry" has its roots there. The nearest Greek word for gentleman, cavalier, or caballero is *kaloskagathos*.

knowing the ineducability of the polis and the multitude, he is nonetheless compelled to teach, and, as well, the defense speech must be made because the law demands it. If we are thoughtful, we see through the interrogation of Meletus by Socrates that whether the laws make men better depends on the goodness of the laws and so on the goodness of those who make the laws. Even if the laws are defective (and one must suspect that nearly always they will be defective), laws – almost any laws – are in some degree salutary. The likelihood that laws will be defective is the consequence of the fact that the multitude that makes the laws is educated at best by the poets and, more likely, by those who pass for poets – in the present day, the authors of bumper stickers. Curious as it may seem, neither Socrates nor philosophy is contemptuous of the law, not even of defective law, although the "job description" of the philosopher calls for searching examination of the laws.

Socrates had in the course of his interrogation brought Meletus to admit that he, Socrates, believed in demonic things, and he closes that interrogation with the following speech:

Therefore if I do believe in *daimons*, as you say, and if, on the one hand, *daimons* are gods of some sort, then this would be what I say you are riddling and jesting about, when you say that I do not believe in gods, and again that I believe in gods, since in fact I do believe in *daimons*.

On the other hand, if *daimons* are certain bastard children of gods, whether from nymphs or from certain others of whom it is also said they are born, then what human being would say that there are children of gods, but not gods? It would be as strange if someone believed in children of horses or asses – mules – but did not believe that there are horses and asses. But, Meletus, there is no way that you did not bring this indictment either to test us in these things, or else because you were at a loss about what true injustice you might charge me with. There is no device by which you could persuade any human being who is even slightly intelligent, that it is . . . the part of the same man to believe in both *daimonia* and divine things, and further that this same man believes in neither demons nor gods nor heroes (27d2–28a1).[20]

Part IV, The Divine Mission of Socrates (28a2–34b5)

John Burnet, in the line-by-line, word-by-word editorial comments in his edition of the Greek text of the *Apology*, remarks at this point thus: "Having disposed of Meletus, Socrates makes his serious defence. In form, it is a digression; in fact, it is the most important part of his speech."[21]

Socrates opens this part of his defense by stating simply that he has not done injustice according to the indictment by Meletus but says that he has

---

[20] This is West's translation except for the last sentence, which I modified by deleting the word "not" (where the ellipsis now is) because it seemed to me that leaving that word in turns the sentence into a self-cancelling self-contradiction.

[21] *Plato's Euthyphro, Apology of Socrates*, and *Crito*, Oxford, 1979 (originally 1924), Oxford University Press, p. 197.

incurred much hatred, and it is this hatred rather than the charges in the indictment that will convict him. Then he poses a question that someone might put to him asking if he is not ashamed of having done what he did thereby risking the death penalty. Except for the indictment itself, he is the first to mention the death penalty. One would have thought that the more prudent course would have been to speak only of the risk of conviction and not to prejudge the likely punishment. Both the system of criminal procedure and, it seems, something in the mind of Socrates lead him to go directly to the most extreme imaginable conclusion of the process. In following this course, he is led to make a statement that is bound to anger the jurors even more, for it shows even more his sense of superiority to the ordinary Athenian. He says that what would be truly shameful would be to abandon one's station out of cowardice:

> For thus it is, men of Athens, in truth; wherever a man stations himself, thinking it is best to be there, or is stationed by his commander, there he must, as it seems to me, remain and run his risks, considering neither death nor any other thing more than disgrace.

> So I should have done a terrible thing, if, when the commanders whom you chose to command me stationed me, both at Potideia and at Amphipolis and at Delium, I remained where they stationed me, like anybody else, and ran the risk of death, but when the god gave me a station, as I believed and understood, with orders to spend my life in philosophy and in examining myself and others, then I were to desert my post through fear of death or anything else whatsoever.[22]

Socrates goes on to say that if he were told that he would be let go on condition that he cease to philosophize, he could not cease. He would continue, although it meant death. To say the very least, this is bold talk. It is defiant. Moreover, the claim that he acted as he did as the consequence of the god's having stationed him and ordered him to philosophize is the claim of a divinely wrought superiority. It is calculated to appear to the jurors as a kind of swagger.

Socrates could not help doing what he did, but he asked no quarter. Just as a couple of instances in his life – for example, his refusal when performing certain civic duties to allow (contrary to law) the trial together rather than separately of several generals – so the whole life of Socrates may be described as a continuing self-examination. (This is not to be confused with the almost universal self-absorption that obtains in the wake of Sigmund Freud.)[23] He

---

[22] The *Apology*, 28d12–29a2, in the Fowler translation.

[23] A notion of self-examination developed within Freudian psychology in the twentieth century that is the polar opposite of the Socratic advice to "know thyself." It might be proper to draw the contrast by saying that the Socratic guidance calls on one to study human nature by introspection and so to know one's possibilities, one's limits, and one's duties as well as to know one's fellows – to know the nature of man – whereas what developed in the twentieth century is what Allan Bloom called the descent into the "sub-basement" of the mind, a descent that paralyzes action and shifts responsibility for one's failings to others.

knew what he had to do and what he must not do because the god at Delphi told him to philosophize, and his demonic thing, his inner voice, kept him from injustice. Following that voice never led him to make a plea for a free pass, however. He had to do the right thing, come what may. This firm stand was one more straw on the camel's back. It further angered the jurors. Who did he think he was, saying that the god spoke to him, and that whatever the court might say, he would not cease to do as the god had ordered?

Rubbing salt in the wound, Socrates says that he supposes that "until now no greater good has arisen for you in the city than my service to the god." What was that service? He had spent his life whipping the souls of his fellow citizens and now he tells them he deserves thanks. It bears an eerie resemblance to Pheidippides in the play of Aristophanes, having learned from Socrates to beat his father and, then, having learned from Socrates how to do so, making a persuasive speech to him holding that it was just for him to have beaten him. We are all calmly certain that the conviction and sentence of Socrates were unjust acts and we preen ourselves on the assured belief that we would never condemn anyone to death out of sheer envy and hatred. We are morally superior and we know it, but suddenly a shudder of doubt afflicts us, and, if we truly wish to emulate Socrates, must we not question our smug certainty? Does not the very defense speech of Socrates, the whole of it, show at least that human weakness, envy, and shallowness have a toehold that enables the jury to race precipitously to the verdict that in fact they shortly reached? Our love of Socrates prevents us from resting on moral equivalency – Socrates did what he had to do, and the jury did what it had to do. On one hand, what they did was wrong. On the other hand, clearly, Socrates goaded them into their wrong judgments. Why did he do so? Was this also something he had to do?

This part of the *Apology* concludes with the statement by Socrates that if he was, indeed, corrupting, and had, indeed, corrupted any of the young, they ought to have been brought forward as witnesses against him or, if they had all been fully corrupted and so were unable to testify against him, then at least the relatives of those corrupted should have been brought in to testify. There is, however, no one with firsthand knowledge to testify, because he had not ever corrupted anyone. If Meletus had forgotten to bring in such witnesses, Socrates offers to yield the floor and let such witnesses be brought in now. None is introduced.

Part V, Epilogos (34b6–35d8)

Socrates says that he will not attempt to appeal to the sympathies of the jury by mentioning his family, even though others in like circumstances might do so. If he did so he would be asking them to rule contrary to their judgment after they had sworn an oath. To do this would be to demonstrate that his beliefs were the opposite of everything he had said in his defense, for it would be to show that he did not believe in gods and that he attempted to teach the jurors not to believe in gods. These things would show that his whole life had been a falsehood. He would not stoop to begging. He would not break the trust with his companions who believed and should believe that his whole life, including this immediate part of it, was just as he said it was.

Part VI, The Antitimesis (35e1–38b9)

The "antitimesis" is a counterproposal. The thing that it counters is not presented by Plato. The work is known as *The Apology of Socrates* and that is all it is, and, for the most part, the context of that apology has to be understood or figured out. Plato does not put, in square brackets, as it were, that the jury had found Socrates guilty and that Meletus had proposed the death penalty, but that is what had happened. By Athenian law the one convicted had a right to make a counterproposal, and then the jury would choose between the two proposals. Socrates says that for him to propose a penalty of any kind would be to admit his guilt and this he could not do, so in the place of a counterproposal he offers a further slap in the face to the jurors: Because he had actually benefited the city, he suggests that the jury award him free meals in the Prytaneum.[24] He says that he has no money for a fine – perhaps only one *mina* – and then, at the urging of those of his friends and followers who are present and who offer to pay for him, he suggests a fine of thirty *minae*. It is difficult to estimate the equivalent in British pounds or U.S. dollars, but, considering the seriousness of the charges, the sum proposed would have to be regarded as relatively small. This was another affront to the jury. The next thing is easily guessed. The jury awarded the death penalty.

Part VII, After the Sentence (38c1–42a5)

Socrates tells the court and the accusers that what they have done is wrong and that they will come to rue their actions. He then asks those present who had voted for his acquittal to stay a bit for a conversation with him. He tells them that he knows that he did the right thing, because when he left the house that morning, the sign of the god did not oppose him, and even throughout his defense speech the sign did not warn him against anything he was about to say.

---

[24] The place where the chief magistrates met daily to consult and to take their meals. The suggestion by Socrates is the equivalent of someone today who, having been convicted of a crime against the United States, suggests during the sentencing phase that the sentence awarded be that he or she be given meals every day at public expense in the Executive Dining Room in the White House.

Socrates comforts his friends. Death is not a bad thing. Either it is a great and perpetual nothingness, the greatest imaginable peace, or it is a migration of the soul from one place to another. If it is the latter, would it not be wonderful to be together with all the notable human beings of the past and to converse with them? Reading this, we might be led to ask, will Socrates then, in the House of Hades, question everyone reputed to be wise and will he discover that some of them are not so? Could the gods make mistakes in the meting out of rewards and punishments? Is Socrates wiser than the gods themselves? Twenty-four years earlier, Strepsiades, in Aristophanes' *Clouds*, had implied that that is how Socrates saw himself.

A curious omission in Socrates' list of those he would enjoy in engaging in conversation in the afterworld speaks volumes. The dead whom he names include judges, poets, those who lost their lives because of unjust judgments, and some notable figures from the Trojan War, but he does not mention a single dead philosopher. Are they all beneath consideration as fit partners in conversation, like the present poets, politicians, and craftsmen? Is this a final insult hurled by Socrates, or do those described as those who lost their lives because of unjust judgments mean philosophers?

The grouping together of the Platonic dialogues *Euthyphro*, the *Apology*, *Crito*, and *Phaedo* as a tetralogy in the manner of their presentation by Diogenes Laertius is eminently sensible. They present both a historical sequence and an intelligible argument in precise order. The *Euthyphro* had shown Socrates in the pretrial process. The *Apology* presents his defense speech at the trial. The *Crito* relates a conversation between Socrates and Crito in the prison, and the *Phaedo* presents a conversation between Phaedo and Echecrates in which Phaedo recounts the conversation between Socrates and several of his followers in the prison on the last day, the day he takes the lethal drug and dies.

Plato's *Apology of Socrates* is presented in the manner of a transcript of the defense speech of Socrates. It is, in literary terms, presented in the first person. We learn the content of the charges against Socrates by his repeating them in the course of his defense. The charges that brought on the trial were to the effect that he did not believe in the gods that Athens believed in but brought in new gods and that he had corrupted the youth of Athens. Socrates complicated matters by calling to mind the "old accusers," and those accusers, the slanderers, had charged that he meddled with things above and below. In his defense, Socrates denied that he was an atheist, but that only strengthened the charge against him for the charge against him had only accused him of not believing in the correct gods. Perhaps his changing the terms of the argument was a sort of lawyer's trick that enabled him to make his case better. We think not. The other matter of which we need to remind ourselves is that it was he, not the later accusers, who brought in to consideration the old accusers, those who had accused him of being a physiologist or physicist. In his defense speech he said that he never knew anything about that sort of thing. It turns out, however, that the flat denial is misleading. In the *Phaedo*, Phaedo recounts to Echecrates that, in the conversation with his followers on his last day in the prison, Socrates had said to Cebes that when he was younger he was eager to pursue questions of natural philosophy (96a6ff.). Then he recalled that at one point he encountered someone reading from a book by Anaxagoras,[25] and the reader said that Anaxagoras held that it was intelligence that was the cause of all things. Socrates was pleased with this and began to read Anaxagoras eagerly. However:

> My glorious hope, my friend, was quickly snatched away from me. As I went on with my reading I saw that the man made no use of intelligence, and did not assign any real causes for the ordering of things, but mentioned as causes air and ether and water and many other absurdities. (Fowler translation, 98b8–c3)

So great was his disappointment with the physiologists that he turned away from such studies and began his "second voyage" (99d1), studying speeches. Thus began what Cicero called the turning of philosophic attention to the human things, the beginning, that is, of political philosophy.[26] Perhaps it is not possible, however, to turn one's soul altogether away from philosophy proper. Perhaps the intellect persists in beckoning one to questions of number and calculation, and the heavens above, and the earth below.

John Burnet raises a question that had exercised the minds of commentators for a long time: What is the relation between the Socrates presented

---

[25] Anaxagoras was born about 500 B.C., so he was about thirty when Socrates was born. He died about 428 B.C., or when Socrates was about forty.

[26] A comment on the literary aspect of the text is appropriate here. Leo Strauss often remarked to his students that he had noticed in his studies, perhaps because it has so been taken for granted, something on which no one had in commentaries remarked. It was that, whereas we moderns tend to "put first things first," ancient authors tended to put central things in the center. Thus, in careful reading, noticing what an ancient author put in the center of a writing often – but by no means always – signaled an intention to emphasize what had been so placed. What holds true for a whole writing is also true when enumerations of things occur – say, the third of a set of five speeches. *Phaedo* appears chiefly as a conversation between Phaedo and Echecrates, but a substantial portion of it consists of quoted conversations between Socrates and Simmias and Cebes. Such is the case for a good portion of the first half of the dialogue. Then there is an interlude of conversation between Phaedo and Echecrates (88c7–89a10) followed by Phaedo's report of the continuation of the conversation between Socrates and others, this time, at first between Socrates and Phaedo, and this blends back into conversation between Socrates and Simmias and Cebes. Then there is another interlude consisting of a resumption of conversation in the "present" between Phaedo and Echecrates. This latter interlude lasts from 102a4 to 102a11. In between the two interludes, pretty near to the center of the book, lies the reminiscence by Socrates of his move from natural philosophy to moral and political philosophy – from the attempt to pin down physical causes to the examination of speeches. In other words, some of the most substantial parts of the conversation are sandwiched in between outer layers of conversation. Sometimes in reading seriously a serious work, one must peel away more than one layer to get at the heart of things.

to us by Plato's dialogues and Socrates himself? Burnet acknowledges that the representation of Socrates in the dialogues may have been, in general, an attempt to present him as nearly as possible as he was and to put into his mouth speeches such as he might have made in the circumstances portrayed, but in the single case of Plato's *Apology of Socrates*, the representation is, as nearly as may be, a verbatim transcript of the actual defense speech of Socrates.[27] Plato was at the trial, as Socrates himself calls to our attention in his apologia. Following Burnet, we here treat Plato as a straightforward journalist capable of taking accurate and complete notes and doing so in the case of the *Apology*. Such a transcript, without any editorial asides on such matters as the purported lifelong absence of interest in the things below and the things aloft, leaves it to us readers to uncover and ponder the problems raised by the defense speech.

As it happens, Plato was not the only one to report to us the defense speech of Socrates. Plato's report of the speech is presented, as we observed earlier in this chapter, in the first person. Xenophon also gave us a report, and it differs in form from Plato's. It is written in the third person. Xenophon says out of his own mouth – although what he says he had heard mostly from Hermogenes – that Socrates did such and such and that Socrates said so and so. This allows for some useful commentary on the speech, commentary that characterizes and questions what was said.

This is as good a time as any to call attention once more to the enormous problem of translation. If a scholar is a nice, English or North American gentleman, suffused with decency and with a kind of pious regard for the old books, it may be that Socrates is seen as some sort of saint, and the presentation of him in translations may reveal him to us as such. This is not to say that the translator must be accused of deliberate fraud. He just gives us what he sees as he sees it. Still, some lesser blame may attach. On the first page of Xenophon's *Apology of Socrates*, Xenophon uses the word "*megalegoria*" three times. The Loeb Classical Library translation by O. J. Todd of the University of British Columbia renders that word first as "the loftiness of his words," then as "his lofty utterance," and then as "the sublimity of his speech." To render it such is not so much to translate as it is to render, that is, to suppose that one has come to a perfect understanding of the overall intention of the original author that allows the translator to present what the author "must have meant." Here, at least, the effort is misleading. A straightforward, literal translation would help the reader of English to make up his own mind as to the author's intention. The Greek word *megalegoria* means, very simply, big talk. To read it that way enables us to see clearly that Socrates seems deliberately to have provoked the jurors. In his defense speech he "struts." Xenophon, by speaking of the "big talk"

---

[27] See Plato, *Euthyphro, Apology of Socrates, Crito*, edited with notes by John Burnet (originally published 1924), Oxford, 1979, Oxford University Press, pp. 143–48, especially 143–44.

of Socrates, indicates a sort of "in-your-face" boasting by Socrates of his superiority to ordinary men, such as the men who were his judges. The bowdlerizing translation by Todd does not make it impossible, but it does make it difficult, to understand Xenophon. Xenophon raises for us the possibility that Socrates wanted to be convicted and wanted to be given the death sentence. Xenophon offers some reasons why this might have been the desire of Socrates, better reasons, that is, than that he just wanted to be what we would call a "show-off."

If we did not see it in our first reading of Plato's *Apology of Socrates*, reading Xenophon's version helps in our second reading of Plato's version to see that Socrates did, in fact, talk big to the jury. Reading, and rereading, the old books in a nitpicking way, with a dose of respectful skepticism, helps us to reach the great problems of politics and to see them and the alternative answers in a less smug, self-assured, less partisan way. What more, other than divine intervention, could we ask?

We get a glimpse in the *Apology* of the nature of political philosophy. At the beginning of Book Four of his *Politics*, Aristotle gives us a sound statement of the necessary parts of a complete syllabus of political science. In due course we shall examine that syllabus. Let us here extrapolate from what we see in the *Apology* and note that the tension we see there between philosophy and politics ought not to be lightly dismissed on the grounds of the churlish stupidity of the Athenians. Driven by a wholesome prejudice, by love of country, and by an imperfect view of justice as unquestioning obedience to the laws, and by a simple piety taught by the poets, they perceive philosophy as, to borrow a term from modern psychology, "threatening." The philosopher asks the nature of the gods, and the political philosopher thus suggests that their nature is not such as the polis has decreed. The pursuit of a true answer to the question of justice is clearly an indictment of the city's answer, the laws. Because the laws are made by the rulers, to look for better laws is to ask "Who should rule?" That question is simply a variation on the question "What is the best regime, the best political order, the best *politeia* of the polis?" Turning these questions this way and that, we see that a summary statement of these questions might be, "What is right? What, in the nature of things, is right? What is right simply? What is natural right?" Be careful. The modern doctrine of "natural rights" is only a version of the ancient quest. It is not the equivalent of it. In fact, it is nearly 180 degrees from the original statement of the problem. A first step in understanding is that one should not skip lightly over the difference between "right" and "rights." The modern doctrine is, it must be said, selfish. It turns the question of the public good into a mere mathematical calculus of private, that is, privately perceived, goods.

Political philosophy, then, is the free and radical pursuit by unassisted human reason of the good regime. It is the attempt to find truly what is by nature right, to identify those truly fit to rule. It began with Socrates. As things recede further into the past, we tend to compress them in our minds so that something said by Socrates in 399 B.C. appears to us a straightforward answer to a question raised twenty-four years earlier. If we look beneath the surface of what Socrates said at his trial, however, we see that, despite his denial, he had indeed pursued questions about "the things aloft and the things below," much as the comic caricature by Aristophanes portrays him, but then he came to see the futility in such an endeavor. He turned his attention, as Cicero said, away from the things that philosophers had pursued and to the things they had disdained to study, the human things, the things of the household, the market, and the city. This startling innovation by Socrates was the epochal moment in philosophy. In the next chapter we shall look at the first great writing that confronts these questions and therefore at the first proffered clarification of a sound accommodation of the tension between philosophy and politics.

Before we turn to that next chapter, however, we cannot restrain ourselves from a modicum of speculation. We began the present chapter with reference to Cicero's attributing to Socrates the beginning of political philosophy. Cicero does not in that place offer an explanation as to why Socrates brought about that innovation. Our problem is even more difficult than that faced by Cicero. We are twenty centuries further away from Socrates than Cicero was. The whole sense and temper of classical times are lost or forgotten or, worse, hackneyed by supposed familiarity, for us. As we did earlier, we can here take a small step back historically to try to appreciate, by analogy, a factor we are likely to overlook. A small step takes us to the American Founding, a mere two centuries or so ago. Accepting that "or so" as sufficiently precise, we often commit the grievous error of treating the Constitution itself and what we call the "Bill of Rights" – that is, the first eight, or perhaps the first ten, amendments – as "contemporaneous," but they were not. One need only reflect on the past couple of years of political history to appreciate that two years constitute an eternity of sorts. It is absolutely futile to try to understand the "bill of rights" without understanding that they are amendments, and it is impossible to understand amendments without a clear understanding of the unamended thing the amendments amend. Generally, that is not at all what we do in history or Constitutional law classes. Now think again about Socrates as the founder of political philosophy. Think about the twenty-four years between the lampooning of him by Aristophanes in the *Clouds* and the confession by Socrates to his friends on the day he took the poison, as that is reported to us in the *Phaedo*, that indeed he had once been interested in the things above and below but that he had changed. If his denial in his *Apology* now seems less than straightforward, might it not also be the case that his explanation to his friends as to why he changed direction is less than complete? Think about the troubles of Socrates, year in and year out for twenty or more years, confronting the hatred and suspicion of the Athenians because of his infernal questioning and, yes, his open swagger. Examine in your imagination the gradual change in direction of his inquiries. At what point and why is that change complete? Following the suggestion of Strauss that political philosophy is just as much a political defense of philosophy as it is a philosophic examination of politics, might it not be that the philosopher is compelled, in the interest of philosophy, to turn his attention to politics, and that that defense of philosophy is the primary definition of political philosophy? In fact, might we not speculate that the disappearance into the mists of the pre-Socratics rests on the fact that philosophy is not complete until Socrates completes it in the turn from the things above and below to the things of the polis? Maybe the pre-Socratics are the prephilosophers and Socrates is the founder of more than political philosophy. Maybe he is the true founder of philosophy.

Then again, maybe not. Let us exercise a certain modest restraint. Let us now turn to Plato.

PART TWO

THE PROBLEM OF POLITICAL PHILOSOPHY

Introduction to Part II

In Plato's *Laws*, in the course of developing an imaginary city, a detailed description is given of the various officials to be established, and laws are proposed covering every aspect of human concern: marriage, procreation, the nurturing and education of children, and so on. At one point the Athenian Stranger explains to Clinias of Crete and Megillus of Sparta that babies, while awake or sleeping, should be kept constantly in motion and their ears constantly filled with soothing sounds. These things are necessary to counteract the internal motions of fear and frenzy (790c–791b). What, then, may be the underlying causes of that fear and frenzy that the argument of the dialogue presupposes are, by nature, found in all babies? Why, throughout all of history, have there been lullabies? Why do young children race about such as to exhaust a watching adult? Why do they chatter, and why do they endlessly recite sing-song ditties? Are these things a shield? To the extent that they are beset by fears, and particularly the fear of death, human societies (whether political or merely tribal) have fashioned a thousand remedies from incantations to stave off the inevitable to poetic traditions that promise rewards in the hereafter for good conduct here

In Book Ten of the *Republic*, Plato makes Socrates persuade Glaucon and Adeimantus that there is life after death. He then relates a story of someone who, it was said, died and was then allowed to return to life to report to the living that those who had comported themselves well in life travel hereafter to an upper realm in the House of Hades that is blissful and that those who had comported themselves ill here travel downward there to a realm that is most unhappy. After a thousand years, most from both realms in the House of Hades return to life by way of metempsychosis. That is, they are embodied again, some in human form, some in another animal form. What is especially interesting in the story is that even those who had been for a thousand years in the bliss of the upper realm approach their return to life with eager anticipation. Why? Perhaps life itself, even a rather unhappy life, is sweet. Perhaps the pleasures of the flesh, even such gentle pleasures as the inner sense of well-being while walking in a beautiful garden on a warm spring day, are more to be desired than the millennium-long unrelieved bliss of the upper realm of the House of Hades. Perhaps what is missing there is striving, pursuit – in a word, *eros*.

It may be that there is some seemingly unfathomable connection between death and *eros*. In the *Phaedrus*, Plato presents for us the spectacle of Socrates and Phaedrus conversing in an idyllic place on the bank of the Ilissus River, just outside one of the city gates of Athens. Phaedrus had just come upon a courtship speech written by Lysias, and he was much taken with it. It seemed to him the very model of erotic rhetoric wherein the lover persuades the beloved to yield. Socrates, however, is critical of the speech. Although it appears to casual view that *eros* is the desire of a body for a body, it is in fact a much loftier thing. *Eros* in the most profound sense is the desire of a soul for a soul. In fact, the soul of the lover yearns for something higher than both itself and the soul of the beloved. It yearns for something "up there" in the heavens that is reached through reflection, or perhaps through refraction, by way of the soul of the beloved. It is, let us call it, beauty, or perhaps we should say "the beauties." They sound rather like what in the *Republic* Socrates calls the "ideas." These are beings, intangible beings. They are what constitutes reality. The tangible, the visible, things only seem to be real. The soul yearns, it aches, to see the true beings. It wants to be with them. All human beings have within them the seed of philosophic *eros*, the desire to know, truly to know, but souls are embodied. The body weighs the soul down, preventing it from getting up there to see what it most wants to see. For most human beings, the weight is so great that they are distracted into thinking that the inner urge they sense is merely the desire of body for body. Perhaps it would be better to say that most people reach this opinion without thinking at all. Perhaps this is how most people reach most of their opinions. Perhaps appreciating this leads us toward an understanding of that saying of Socrates that "the unexamined life is not worth living." Perhaps the real beginning of philosophizing is asking oneself, "What do I desire?"

Only a few succeed in stretching their necks and getting fleeting glimpses of the beauties, the ideas. In fact, as Socrates puts it in the *Phaedrus*, what makes the gods gods is simply that they are constantly in the company of the things most desirable to contemplate. They get to apprehend them as much as they like, whereas human beings must struggle against the weight of the body to catch momentary glimpses of the beauties, the true things, the beings, the ideas. One does not seek them for the sake of something else. They are not instruments used for the reaching of good ends. They are good in themselves. They are hidden by clouds. It is a great struggle that few are equipped and even fewer both equipped and inclined to make to part those clouds and gaze even for a moment on those beauties. When one confronts the truly beautiful, the lesser things fade from view.

There is in the Museum of History and Art in Anchorage a painting of a small body of water surrounded by forested Alaskan mountains. The painting is called *The Silent Pool*. It was painted by Sydney Lawrence in about 1930. It is a painting of surpassingly beautiful natural scenery imitated to perfection by the painter. Many people who encounter the painting are both calmed and transfixed by it. They cannot turn away. They do not ask what it is "good for." It seems to them simply good.

This is, in a manner of speaking, an inkling of the definition of philosophy. Philosophy simply, unequivocally, unrelentingly wants to know. It loves the truth, not the humdrum, ordinary phantasms of truth that the many mistake for the truth. Here is another place where our present habits of speech blind us. We say, "I have an idea." Nobody ever has an idea. The ideas are. They are beings that subsist independently of us. They are "up there." The eye of the body, when it sees a tree, does not have the tree within itself. Having a glimpse of the tree, it has an impression. The mind has a perception of the tree. In like fashion, when the eye of the soul apprehends an idea, the soul does not swallow up the idea, it merely has a conception of it. The conception of beauty, like the perception of the tree, must be refreshed over, and over, and over again. Similarly, it is not sufficient to have seen *The Silent Pool*. One must see it.

The philosopher understands this. Philosophers do not store up truths in their souls. They have to work hard for their pleasures. The problem is the body. The demands of the body constantly drag the soul down, keeping it from its beloved. That is why in the *Phaedo*, Phaedo, recounting to Echecrates his recollection of Socrates on his last day in the prison, tells of Socrates saying to Simmias and Cebes, "Other people are likely not to be aware that those who pursue philosophy aright study nothing but dying and being dead" (Fowler translation, 64a).

Two threads of our inquiry intertwine at this point. First of all, we can now appreciate that the "big talk" of Socrates at his trial was only a confirmation of the near truth at the base of the antipathy of Athenians toward him. His whole life is a double reproach to the city and to its citizens. To insist that the truth is the one truly worthy thing is to say that the city and all its citizens are in pursuit of what is unworthy. This is a great reproach. Second, to define truth as the exact opposite of everyone's notion of the truth, and to define it in such a way as to be unintelligible to all but the initiated, that is, to those he has "corrupted," seems madness. Furthermore, impliedly to excuse the city's faults on the grounds that, after all, he, Socrates is someone special, someone with a god-given grasp of things, and therefore such that ordinary people cannot be expected to follow, is to add insult to injury. Socrates is the most intolerably boastful, self-loving man in the city. There is no place in the city for someone who is not of it. Socrates, although an Athenian by birth, is by his nature an unwelcome foreigner. There was in the ancient polis a practice called "banishment." Tyrannies and democracies especially, but finally all cities, found a human being of supreme excellence a threat and so sent the threat away. If Socrates had followed the suggestion of his friends, he would have allowed them to bribe his prison guard and then he would have run away. That is, he would have banished himself. To understand this problem, it is necessary to read in the *Crito* (50a–54e) the dialogue Socrates imagines having with the laws as to whether he should run away. Some have wondered if the character called the "Athenian Stranger" in the *Laws* is Plato's way of showing us how Socrates would have appeared had he run away to Crete rather than taken the lethal drug in the prison.

We raised previously the problem as to why scholars are prone to lump all the philosophers prior to Socrates together under the name "pre-Socratics." Not all do this, of course, but with regard to those who do, we need to seek the reason. All of the pre-Socratics had been held in suspicion by the city. We need to remind ourselves that the caricature of Socrates put forth in the *Clouds* by Aristophanes had shown him as impious and a corrupting influence – that is, a threat to the civil order. We need also to remind ourselves that that caricature was drawn twenty-four years before Socrates was put on trial and that Socrates admitted to his friends while in prison that he had, indeed, been interested in those things attributed to him in the *Clouds*. To stretch the meaning of words a bit, perhaps we could say that the younger Socrates had been just one more pre-Socratic. It would then be sensible to say that philosophy has not yet matured until it examines itself and confronts its place in the city and the tension between itself and the city. Thus, the beginning of political philosophy by Socrates is the true completion of the beginning of philosophy. Political philosophy is the bar mitzvah of philosophy.

The merit of such a conclusion just suggested is that it explains political philosophy as well as anything we might formulate. It may seem odd to have prefaced this by speaking of "the problem of political philosophy" rather than speaking of "the problems of political philosophy." This choice seems to make sense, however, because, after all, the place of philosophy in relation to politics is, in fact, simply *the problem*, the problem that philosophy confronts that is solved by the origin of political philosophy. All the other definitions of the problems of political philosophy amount to ringing the changes on this formulation. Because philosophy is the highest pursuit of man, to ask the question "What is the best regime?" is simply to ask, "In what political order is the highest human pursuit free to carry on its search for truth?" To ask, "What is justice?" is to ask how lives should be arranged so that human beings, and especially philosophers, get to do what is proper to them. As we shall see in the next chapter, that is the subject matter of the *Republic*. To ask, "What is by nature right?" is not to ask what is the right order of nature. Nature is what it is, and no amount of study, no great feat of engineering, will change it. To ask what is by nature right is to ask what that arrangement of lives is that is truly in keeping with the nature of man and with the natures of humans. To ask, "Who should rule?" is, again, simply to ask what is that political order most in concord with and most supportive of the highest human activity, most congenial to philosophy, the highest pursuit of man. Granting the premise that philosophy is, indeed, the highest human pursuit and therefore the end that is served by such means as statesmanship and generalship, every attempt to reformulate the problem of political philosophy ends as simply a rephrasing. Political life is the necessary condition of philosophy, but the polis is lost in a sea of anger and appetite unless it is oriented to what is higher than itself. It is precisely this relation between the political and that which stands above and in judgment of it that Machiavelli jettisons at the beginning of the sixteenth century. The true helmsman is the philosopher. The ultimate truth about *eros* is not that body hungers for body but that soul hungers for truth. The problem of political philosophy is the problem of the reconciliation of politics and philosophy. The first great offer of an answer to that problem is made in Plato's *Republic*, to which we now turn.

5

The Best City

The *Republic* is the true *Apology* of Socrates, for only in the *Republic* does he give an adequate treatment of the theme which was forced on him by Athens' accusation against him. That theme is the relationship of the philosopher to the political community.

Allan Bloom[1]

Since the death of Socrates a little more than 2,400 years ago, there have been many thousands of books written about politics. Many scholars would argue that the best is Aristotle's *Politics*, but others believe that the best is the book that we know as Plato's *Republic*. I agree with the latter group. The "Republic" is the most penetrating, the most thorough, and the most beautiful book ever written on the subject of politics, on the nature of philosophy, on the tension between the two, and on the resolution of that tension. It ought to be read over and over again. It is a book of such transcendent excellence that each new reading opens the problems of politics to clearer and better understanding and appreciation.

Some time after Plato's death, scholars attached the subtitle *On Justice* to it. To accept uncritically both the title "Republic" and the subtitle "On Justice" is to burden oneself with some hindrances to proper understanding of the book. These things and the numerous misdirections that various translators impose must be peeled away. It is my earnest desire that the following sketch does not also introduce such hindrances.

Let us spend a moment on each of the three things just mentioned. First, the title. Cicero, the Roman statesman and philosopher, wrote a dialogue fashioned after Plato's book but adapted to Roman politics and understanding. He gave to that adaptation the Latin title *De Re Publica*. A literal translation of that title into English would be something like "of the public thing," that is, of the nature of the political order and of better and worse

---

[1] "Interpretive Essay," in *The Republic of Plato*, 2nd ed., Basic Books, 1991, p. 307.

sorts of it. With the spread of the Roman Empire, which facilitated the spread of Christianity, Europe came to be the core of Christendom. Latin was the language of the Church and of the law, so it became the common literary and scholarly language of educated Europeans. So thoroughgoing and so deeply imbedded became this usage of Latin that even on into the present one can find an ancient Greek text printed in a critical edition of the *Oxford Classical Texts* with the body of the work in the original Greek and the editor's introduction not in English (the language of the editor and the publisher), but in Latin. It is no wonder, then, that Plato's Greek book comes down to us, whether in Greek or in translation into French, German, or English, with Cicero's Latin title, *De Re Publica*. We then, in English, settle for an English word which is even at that only an approximation of the Latin, namely, *the Republic*. Nobody quite knows what "republic" means, except that it means not a monarchy. What then are we to make of the annoying fact that, in the "Republic," the city Plato causes Socrates to make in speeches as an illustration of the best city ends up looking very like a monarchy?

We are constrained to use the English translation of Cicero's Latin because, as the long quotation from Harry Jaffa in Chapter Three shows, we just do not have convenient English equivalents for all of the Greek words that explain politics. Plato gave to his book the title ἡ πολιτεία, that is, *The Politeia*, the structure, form, or constitution of a *polis*. Now, obviously, that he titled his book *The Politeia* clearly implies that the subject matter of the book is the correct *politeia*, the truly good *politeia*, the best regime. This is the one and only right political order. Every other makeup of a *polis* is a deviation from the true and the good one. All such deviations will be sources of evil and sorrow.

It would be presumptuous to fancy ourselves the ones to correct a couple of thousand years of usage by insisting on calling the book *The Regime*. Let us continue to call it "The Republic," but let us remind ourselves that in doing so we have taken one step off to the side. When we write it here, instead of putting the title in italics as in the case of a proper title, let us leave it in Roman script and encase it in quotation marks. Such will be our continuing reminder.

Second, the subtitle, "On Justice," is, although not simply wrong, an imperfect guide to the contents. Common sense suggests that what the book is on is amply indicated by the title, *The Regime*, although such a common-sense suggestion may in some cases turn out to be misleading. Political or other circumstances often compel a serious author to hide things behind a misleading title. In this case, however, either casual or penetrating reading of the "Republic" shows that it is, as the title suggests, really on the best political order. This is not surprising inasmuch as the first formulation of the nature of political philosophy is the search for the best political order. Political philosophy *is* the search for the best regime. As we closed the previous chapter, we suggested that the very definition of political philosophy is political argument or action in defense of philosophy. Perhaps these two different definitions are not really altogether different.

The book is evidently on the subject of justice in that justice would surely be a necessary attribute of the best regime, but let us check ourselves! It is so easy to say that word, "justice"! Everybody is cocksure he knows what justice is. Every hallway of every building on every campus is festooned with posters urging everyone to work for justice. There is no need to study what it is. We just know! Ask any lawyer, preacher, politician, or college student you encounter, and that person will assure you that he or she already knows. How comes it, then, that the first of the ten books of the "Republic" is an exchange of several opinions as to what it is? None of those opinions is quite right, yet none of them is simply wrong. Perhaps what makes us so sure of ourselves in the present day is that if one is asked what he thinks about something he is quite likely to answer that he feels that justice is equality, and so saying is meant to close the subject. Since Rousseau in the eighteenth century, it has become common to regard feeling as the equivalent of or as somehow superior to thinking. It is not. Aristotle had said that man was a political animal because he is endowed by his nature with *logos*. Rousseau, in contrast, treats sentiment as the defining feature of human nature. Sentiment and reasoning are not one and the same. The sentiment that leads us to feel that to mean well is to be right is a misleading sentiment. Here is another place where a little sober reflection has at least some chance of improving our political understanding.

The first great codification of laws in the West was that compiled on the demand of the Roman Emperor Justinian and completed in about A.D. 533. It is known as "Justinian's Code." One of the three great parts of the Code is titled "The Institutes," and it begins with a proposition that no one would deny: "Justice is the constant and abiding will to give to everyone what is his." This, as a matter of fact, is the ages-old definition of justice in civilized places, but to pronounce this pious generality raises more questions than it gives answers. What Plato's "Republic" does is peel away the layers that encrust justice, so as to give us a greater appreciation of the difficulty of the question, "What is justice?"

At the very surface of things, I take Justinian's formulation means that whatever it is to which one has proper title will, if taken from him, be restored to him. My pencil, my automobile, my real estate, or my bank account is mine. No one should take it. If someone does take it, the rest of us should earnestly desire that, and the law should assure that, it is returned. Was it just in the first place, however, that title to the pencil, the auto, or the house came to be mine? That is only the next layer down. Those "on the right" warmly subscribe to the first proposition and its corollary that the laws, and particularly the laws regarding property rights, be strictly enforced. Those "on the left" subscribe warmly to the implications of the second proposition, namely that if the world were a just place, there would be a wholesale redistribution of wealth. As the "Republic" shows, there is even a third, a deeper, level to the question of justice. It is easy to say that flautists should have their flutes returned and farmers their plows. It is even pretty easy to follow the second proposition that flutes ought to go to flautists and plows to farmers. The putative solution to the deeper question, however, is that those who ought to play the flute ought to become flautists and those who ought to farm ought to become farmers. Just think: Implementing this would involve not just a redistribution of material wealth, but a redistribution of everything – a redistribution of lives. The first thing would be a complete destruction of the family. If we subscribe to the proposition that might does not make right, then we would want the redistribution of lives to be truly right. Oops! We are back to the original question: What is justice? Think for a moment what scientific skill and what scientific certitude we would need to move a child from one family to another more suited to the child's nature. Would we not need some sort of litmus test? Would we not have to be able to dip children of, say, six months of age, into just the right solution, and if they turn blue send them to a family of farmers; if they turn orange send them to a family where they will be educated to become scholars of eighteenth-century British poetry; and if they turn green, soldiers; and so on. Anyone so foolish as to think he or she has answers to these and all the attendant questions should be forbidden to speak in any public forum. In contrast, anyone who admits that he lacks answers to these questions had best "lighten up" a bit in his ardor regarding the first and second levels of the search for justice. Both Plato and Aristotle have sensible, limited expectations of politics. Neither expects to see justice, in the full sense of that word, to be found in any of the *politeias* likely to be encountered in actuality. Reading Aristotle's description of that *politeia* which he calls, simply, *Politeia*, that which Polybius later characterizes as the "mixed *politeia*," and the one Aristotle regards as only the third-best regime, behind kingship and aristocracy, but the best regime most places can hope for most of the time, we would not be amiss to attribute to Aristotle the view that not justice, but merely moderation, a moderation of countervailing injustices, is the true virtue of politics. The strange thing is that the idealists, the utopians, who are so willing to control the lives of other people on the basis of what they feel is right seem to forget that the human beings so controlled themselves have feelings and that sound political action is compelled to take into consideration those feelings. A mother loves her son in a way that no one else can be schooled or paid to love him. We should only wish to take that son away to some place better for him in the most extreme circumstances, but we would then turn from one question to another: What is better and what worse? What is better and what worse in each of a multitude of instances? From caring and being well-meaning we turn ourselves into bureaucratized busybodies.

The desire of well-meaning people to straighten out all political problems and to put everyone in his proper place makes two serious mistakes. First of all, it overlooks or perhaps hopes to overcome, the element of chance in human affairs. A college student probably had a choice to make from among two or more colleges that accepted him. No matter how satisfied he is with the fact that he is enrolled in College A, he cannot help but wonder what it would have been like to be at College B. He may not realize it, but his choice to be a political science major here at College A might rather have been a choice to major in chemistry had he gone to College B. The reason for this is clear. The attractiveness of some professors in one place as distinct from that of others in another is influential. Also, the differential attractiveness, quite by chance, of certain fellow students in one place or another influences such choices. Ask any fifty-year-old about his life and, as he reflects, a hundred accidents – the advice of relatives and teachers, the motion pictures that caught his fancy, the chance encounters that make up a large part of anyone's life – come to mind. Trying to figure all that out is about as easy as tracing why it is that a particular molecule of water in this river ended up in the sea rather than in somebody's garden hose. Some students seem to know from infancy that they want to be a doctor, a lawyer, or a soldier, but for a great many, the freshman and sophomore years are moments of discovery that pull this way or that, allowing the intellect and the inclination to taste many possibilities. Everywhere one goes offers a different smorgasbord of options and problems. Another thing the would-be managers do not see is that it does not really matter whether one ends up being an optician or a traveling salesman, as long as there is some reasonable freedom to choose and as long as some choices offer themselves. Of course the big differences in the course of one's life do matter. Reading the "Republic," we need to translate in our minds the small-scale differences used by Plato to illustrate the division of labor among individuals into the large-scale differences that characterize the division among classes that is the result of the argument of the book. These differences are important, but the notion put forth in the dialogue that this sorting can be achieved rationally has to be seen for what it is, exaggeration.

The search for justice that is conducted by the characters in the "Republic" is carried on at progressively deeper levels of analysis. To help in the appreciation and grasp of those different levels, a good companion reading would be the account Xenophon gives of the young Cyrus of Persia, visiting along with his mother, Mandane, his grandfather, Astyages, the king of the Medes. After a time, Mandane tells Cyrus that they must leave so that the boy can resume his education. He likes his grandfather and the horses he gets to ride, and he wants to stay, but Mandane says that, because he will one day be king, he must learn about justice. "Oh," Cyrus responds, "I already know about that." The ensuing conversation between Mandane and her twelve-year-old son is a beautiful illustration of the different depths to which the search for justice takes us.[2] The "Republic" prods the enquiring mind and compels it to go down, down, down, to ever deeper levels of the search for justice. We begin cocksure and we are gradually widened into an appreciation of the complexities.

The third of the three problems we raised is that concerning translation. An excellent, and perhaps the best, translation of Plato's "Republic" is that by Allan Bloom. Bloom endeavors to provide a literal translation and, in his preface, he shows decisively why such a translation is the right one. There is room here for only one illustrative warning regarding the problem of translation. In Book One of the "Republic," an old man named Cephalus mentions justice, and it turns out that the meaning of that is not easy to establish. In fact, in seeking the answer to this question, it is necessary for Socrates and his interlocutors to make up a city, to talk a city up, to make a city in talkings, a city in speech – a *polis* in *logoi*. That's all it is, a talked-of city, a city in speech, the best city, the best city one can speak of. At no time, never, not even once, does the Greek text call it "an ideal city," much less "an ideal state." The word "ideal" means, by definition, of or pertaining to an idea. Now examination of the beings called "ideas" or "forms" makes up a large part of the text of the "Republic" and is in fact the very core of the search for truth. At no time, not once, not ever, do Socrates or the others speak of "the idea of the city." Socrates speaks of the "idea of the man" and of its reflection in the city, but not of the idea of the city. It appears there is no such thing. Beginning in the nineteenth century, nice, English gentlemen started to translate the expression *polis in logoi* into the English expression "ideal state." What an "ideal" is in customary English usage is a thing to which one aspires. Although one may not be able quite to reach it, one ought to strive mightily to achieve as near an approximation to it as one can. No doubt there are circumstances in which reaching for the ideal is praiseworthy, even noble, but think of something where that is not the case. Suppose one comes to a chasm a hundred feet wide at the bottom of which, a thousand feet down, there are jagged rocks. Should that person jump as much of the chasm as is possible, or would seeking an alternative be advisable? Would it not be wise to accommodate oneself to the necessity of remaining on this side of the chasm?

If you start by accepting the translation "ideal state," your whole reading of the "Republic" leads you up the garden path. You are confident that Plato means his book as a how-to-do-it handbook. You take him to mean that you should endeavor to bring about in deed what can perhaps only be talked up. That makes you an idealist – that is, a murderous, damned fool. Being an idealist makes one feel self satisfied, but pressing on with such schemes can subject thousands, even millions, to misery and then to a

---

[2] Xenophon, *Cyropaedia*, I, iii, 13–18.

miserable death. I know that this is harsh talk. It is not a nice thing to throw ice water on that wonderful throbbing sensation in the breast when one thinks of doing brave deeds and of undoing all the harm done in this world by the selfishness and ignorance of his parents and his parents' generation. Sooner or later, however, it is necessary to confront the fact that there is no Santa Claus, no Easter Bunny, no Tooth Fairy, no Superman, and no Batman and that the dream of becoming a really clever lawyer who goes abroad to talk to the lawyer for the terrorists and brings about in one great "deal" the coming into being of perfect, permanent, just peace is just that, a dream. Some time in the 1940s there was a nice cartoon in *New Yorker* magazine showing a six-year-old boy, dressed up in his cowboy suit and brandishing his popgun, imagining himself arresting Adolf Hitler. Somehow maturity has to be understood as a middle ground between the folly of thinking all the world's problems can be solved if we "just talked" and indifference to those problems. Maturity involves relentless labor informed by study and fortified by virtue combined with the expectation of limited success. If Western civilization manages to hold its own, you will have earned the gratitude of your grandchildren. This, of course, is not to promise that your grandchildren will show any gratitude. If you do not, why should they?

You would certainly not be the first reader to ask, "Well, if Plato didn't really mean it, why did he write it?" The short answer to this question is, "Ah, yes. Well, let us see!" The longer answer takes patience and strenuous effort. Our first task is to try to understand the text. Let us make a beginning. A good prelude to the "Republic" is the rollicking comedy by Aristophanes titled *The Ecclesiazusae*. This title is usually translated into English as "The Assembly of Women" or sometimes as "The Congresswomen." In the play the women of Athens, by a stratagem, take over the rule of Athens and they fix everything. There is perfect equality of the sexes (well, not perfect, because the women run everything), and there is perfect communism, which includes free love. Well, not perfect, and not free. In traditional circumstances, the young, the strong, and the beautiful are dominant. In the wonderful communism established by the revolution there is a kind of affirmative action that gives the dominance to the old, the weak, and the ugly. There is a touching scene in which a cool young stud and an achingly beautiful young girl are holding sweaty hands looking for a convenient private place, but there is no privacy in the wonderful, new, communist scheme of things. In addition, a series of ugly, wrinkled, old women – each uglier, older, and more wrinkled than the one before – claim priority in the enjoyment of the handsome young man. Plato's "Republic" is, in a way, an answer to the wonderfully funny but not promising play of Aristophanes.

All of Plato's dialogues are just that, *dialogues*. A dialogue is a talking-through of a problem, but if one is not talking to himself there must be two or more talkers. The merit of such a talking-through is that we all have opinions about myriad things. As was suggested earlier, everyone knows what justice is.

If there are two people, however, likely enough there are two opinions. The talking-through therefore appears as a talking-against. The Latin word for that is *contradictio*, which means against-speech, contradiction. One opinion contradicts or counterspeaks another. The contradiction leads toward some resolution or other, some provisional agreement, and therefore a third and perhaps a better opinion, an opinion better than that with which either of the talkers began. If, as appears here to be the case, opinions fall short of the truth but are generally not altogether false, and if we add a third and a fourth speaker, we may get a pretty good range of possible half-truths. The dialectical process would then likely lead to a quite improved approximation to the truth, and those engaged in the dialogue – but nobody else – might gain improved appreciation of the partiality, the mere partisanship, of their original opinions. At the very least, it might make political argument more tolerant. It might achieve that political moderation that Aristotle praised. Because this benefit accrues only to the talkers, the wonderful benefit of the Platonic dialogue is that it enables the reader to step into the pages and take part in the argument. If we do not do that, if we treat the dialogue as though it were no different from a textbook, we end up regarding Plato as just one more "dead white male" who, although entitled to his opinion, has nothing to say to us, who, having come along much later are, obviously, a lot smarter than he. After all, we have databases. We have, therefore, comfortably achieved a closed mind. Why, then, do we fritter away our time and our parents' retirement fund by going to college? Why do we not do what is naturally pleasant – drink whiskey, chase sexual partners, and get the perfect tan?

The Platonic dialogues are of two sorts. Some are "performed" thus:

Socrates: "What is justice?"
Jones: "Getting the better of the other fellow in a contract."
Socrates: "How about things that don't involve contracts?"
Smith: "Well, who cares? What is just in one place is unjust in another."

The performed dialogues look rather like a play, except that there are no stage directions. The other sort of dialogue is "narrated." Thus, the narration of the "Republic" begins with Socrates saying, "I went down to the Piraeus yesterday with Glaucon, the son of Ariston, to pray to the goddess," and it goes on for hundreds of pages with Socrates being the only speaker whom we hear, so that the speeches of all the others come to us, as it were, in quotation marks. There are certain benefits to this, one being that Socrates can report to us nonverbal attributes of the other speakers. There is a certain added burden for the reader, however. At the most advanced level of reading, we might wonder whether Socrates accurately relates to us what it was that Glaucon, Adeimantus, or Thrasymachus said in a given instance, and we would have to ask the really gritty question, "What's in it for Socrates?" Hans Morgenthau (1904–80) relates in his *Politics Among*

Nations the story that, at the Congress of Vienna (the meeting in 1814–15 that settled a degree of peace in Europe for the next hundred years), news was brought to Prince Metternich, the Austrian representative, that the Russian representative had dropped dead of a heart attack in his lodging. Metternich is said to have stroked his chin and mused aloud, "I wonder what could have been his motive." This sort of digging to the very bottom of things is a most advanced level of analysis of a dialogue. We mention it here only to suggest the depth, the layers, of understanding that one finds in the "Republic." We said earlier that it is the best book ever written on politics. We stand by that evaluation.

Every writing worth reading has certain attributes of style attending it. In the case of the "Republic," we need to take especial note of three such elements of style. These are analogy, abstraction, and exaggeration. Abstraction may well be an attribute of all scientific inquiry. The problem with abstraction is that it rips the studied thing out of its context to focus on and magnify it. Such is the case in looking at a tissue sample under a microscope. That focus and that magnification falsifies the object of study. To understand the studied thing properly, one has to make the mental exertion of putting it back in its proper place and in its true size. We shall need to keep each of these three literary methods in mind in our sketch of the argument of the "Republic," and we need to put things back into their normal place and shape in our minds to come to a practical conclusion about the book. This takes patience, sweat, and reflection. No computer, no matter how invested it is with artificial intelligence, can do this for us.

According to the narration of Socrates, he had gone down "yesterday" to the Piraeus with Glaucon to see the festival of the goddess and to pray to her. If the English translation could capture the word order that is dictated by the Greek syntax, the first sentence in the English would begin with the word "down-I-went." The Piraeus is the port of Athens. Other than the obvious fact that sea level is "down" from any place in the land, or, as appearance suggests, from the "high seas," what is "down" about the port town? It is, in fact, the place where some people who seem essential to the city but who are not welcome in the city are allowed to live. These include foreigners, merchants, and sailors. They are relegated to this place because they would corrupt the city if they were allowed to tarry in it. Their corruption lies in the fact that they do not do "as we do." Why then do Socrates and Glaucon go down there? Are they "slumming"? Is it necessary to dig down beneath the city to understand it? The goddess whose festival is being held is, obviously, a foreign goddess. Are not foreign goddesses the wrong goddesses? Are not our goddesses the right ones? One might say in defense of Socrates, that, although he prayed to her, he really was not worshipping that foreign goddess; was just curious. Would not that in turn mean that he viewed the gods not with piety, but as objects of cold, scientific inquiry? Would that not mean that he was, let us call it, a student of comparative religions? Is that not the very opposite of piety? Is it not the sort of study that would be undertaken by someone who simply does not believe in the gods, or even in gods? When later (i.e., later in his life than the moment portrayed in the "Republic") Socrates asserts at his trial that he was not interested in "the things above," was he perhaps swearing to something that was not the whole truth? Why would he say one thing in one place and another in another? This is a good question and one that must be asked, because the Socrates portrayed by Plato in the dialogues does just that repeatedly.

Just as Socrates and Glaucon are about to leave the Piraeus and walk back up to Athens proper, they are overtaken by Polemarchus and some others who first invite and then, playfully, compel the two to abandon their walk home and to accompany Polemarchus to the home of his father, Cephalus, so that they can have some good talk. After all, Socrates is the most engaging talker in the whole city. The bait is cast that, in addition to talking, they will have dinner and then come back out afterward to see the torch race. It is noteworthy that the remainder of the "Republic" is a kind of transcript of the talking, and it does not take a mathematician to notice that it goes on for several hundred pages and would certainly engage those conversing at least until dawn of the next day. They never see the torch race. They never eat or drink anything. This is a narrated dialogue, so we learn from the mouth of Socrates some things about how the interlocutors sit, when they move, and things of that sort, but at no time does Socrates report one of the interlocutors saying, "Wait a minute. Don't anybody say anything interesting. I have to excuse myself for a few minutes." The whole of the dialogue is a radical abstraction from the needs of the body. An actual conversation of that length would take place in a context that accommodates the needs of the body. To take seriously, therefore, the conclusions to which the conversation comes, the reader would have to add back in the body and its needs that the conversation, as reported, neglects. However much Plato may "mean it," he cannot mean simply what is on the surface of the conversation. What this means we can see by an analogy. If you call your bank to find out something about your account, a robot answers. Recorded questions are asked, and you have to give answers from a list of preapproved ones. You never find out what you want to know unless you insistently "press zero" until a live, human being comes on the line. The characters in the Platonic dialogue are splendid characterizations of real types of people, but they are, after all, somewhat like mannequins, or like the robots at the bank "who" answer your call. To get the full meaning of the dialogue, we have to infuse it with those human attributes that it, for good reasons, leaves out.

The "Republic" is composed of three conversations. The first is between Socrates and Cephalus and then his son, Polemarchus; the second is between Socrates and Thrasymachus; and the third is between Socrates on the one hand and the brothers Glaucon and Adeimantus on the other.

Having just above used an analogy, we are obligated here to show the use of analogy in the "Republic." We cannot get to the analogy, however, without following the same route to it that is followed in the dialogue. When Socrates and the several others get to Polemarchus's house, Socrates pays his respects to the old man, Cephalus, by asking him what old age is like. The reason he gives for his question is that Cephalus is at "what the poets call, 'the threshold of old age.'" By this he does not mean that Cephalus has reached a point just short of old age. Cephalus is already old. He means rather that Cephalus has reached that threshold constituted by old age, namely, the threshold of death.[3] It is as though Cephalus, being far advanced in age, can perhaps better "see" to the "other side." The dialogue begins exactly where it will eventually end, with a discussion of the point where life and death meet. Cephalus, who is a rather decent old fellow, says that it is not so bad to be old if one has good character, that is, if one possesses piety and justice. Socrates maneuvers Cephalus into admitting that he has substantial wealth, but Cephalus sensibly says that wealth is the necessary but not the sufficient condition of good character. Socrates then asks what part wealth does play in this and what justice is. Cephalus answers that it frees one from having to cheat, having to lie, and having to fail to pay a debt to a human being or a sacrifice to a god. One might notice two things here: first, that the old man defines justice in altogether negative terms; and second, that his definition makes piety or holiness a mere subcategory of justice. The politeness of Socrates gives way to his philosophic curiosity. He takes the old man's answer apart, and this leads to Cephalus admitting that there might be some circumstances in which not repaying a debt to a man is the just thing. We might ask whether that would also apply to sacrifices owed to a god. That question, however, does not arise precisely because Cephalus leaves the conversation to go into the courtyard to continue prayers and sacrifices. What happens instead is that the son, Polemarchus, leaps to uphold the original definition given by the father. Justice is, indeed, returning things. Among other things, this development shows us that in any conversation things may turn this way or that. There are always choices, and choosing one thing means ignoring others, and it also means that a whole train of argument follows that is different from the train that would have followed if another choice had been made. Polemarchus, quoting the poet Simonides, insists on the customary view that justice is returning things. He is led to say that this means giving benefits to friends and harms to enemies, but Socrates talks him into agreeing that the just man will never harm anyone. Justice is, in its nature, beneficent. The dialogue does not, at least for the time being,

---

[3] We see here that when Socrates wanted to raise with Cephalus the prospect of his death, he quoted a poetic indirection as a kind of gentle courtesy. The discourteous alternative would have been to say bluntly, "Hey, old fellow, you've got one foot in the grave, haven't you?" It is certainly not always the case that courtesy is foremost in his mind.

pursue the question whether severe punishment might, in some cases, benefit someone. In the case of someone whose soul is drenched in evil, would
the death penalty perhaps be a benefit? The conversation does not turn
to this question. The response Polemarchus makes to the suggestion by
Socrates that the just man will never harm anyone is a great joke. Using
a specifically military term, Polemarchus says that he will "join up" with
Socrates to beat anyone who does not agree with them that Simonides must
not have meant that justice includes harming enemies. Polemarchus here
proposes a double injustice. Not only would it involve harming someone, it
would harm one who might be innocent and therefore a friend, because we
had by no means shown conclusively that what Simonides meant was what
Socrates and Polemarchus agree he should have meant. Again, however, a
fork in the road of argument is reached. Thrasymachus, a rhetorician, is so
enraged by what a simpleton Polemarchus is for having capitulated so easily
to Socrates that he enters the argument in a burst of anger.

The turn taken in the argument is that Thrasymachus insists that justice
is the interest of the stronger, that is, getting the better of the weaker, and
the one who does this best is not the small criminal, but the great criminal,
the tyrant, who gets the better (actually, the Greek word means to get the
more) of a whole city. Socrates never quite persuades Thrasymachus to the
contrary, but he trips him up so often that he shames him into admitting
that exactly as the art of medicine is for the benefit of the patient, not for
the benefit of the physician, so, by analogy, the art of ruling, so far as we are
talking about ruling itself, is always for the benefit of the ruled and never
for the benefit of the ruler.

So ends Book One. The remaining nine books consist almost entirely of
the third conversation, that which Socrates has with Glaucon and Adeimantus. These two, brothers of Plato, are both more sophisticated than is Polemarchus and more gentlemanly than is Thrasymachus, and they are also
brighter than either. They press Socrates as the others had not. They ask
him if he really wants to persuade them that justice is simply preferable to
injustice, and Socrates insists that he does, indeed, want to persuade them of
this. They press harder. Does he mean that the just man, who is mistakenly
thought to be unjust and so is cruelly punished, is better off than the unjust
man who gets away with it and is praised and honored? Adeimantus adds
something: Do not give us any of that pie-in-the-sky nonsense about rewards
for the just and punishments for the unjust in the hereafter, because, clearly,
the injustice of the unjust man brings him wealth, and he can buy off the
gods with ample sacrifices. The gods can be bribed. Show us, the brothers
demand, that the just man is better off than the unjust, both here and hereafter, even after their characters are stripped of the appearances that hide
what they truly are. This, too, is a radical abstraction. They ask Socrates to
abstract from justice and injustice the rewards and punishments normally
attendant upon them. Leave that stuff out! If we think about it, this is a

question impossible to answer. The whole of the remainder of the dialogue, the bulk of the dialogue, consists of Socrates' answer to this impossible, this unanswerable – and, one might say, this unjust – question. It is unjust because, although it appears to treat the just and the unjust man equally – to give them a "level playing field" as one would now say – in fact it treats them radically unequally, because the just man wants to appear as he is, whereas the unjust man wants to appear the opposite of what he is. Taking the appearances away from both gives an unfair advantage to the unjust man, just as such an unjust man would desire. It is every vile criminal's dream come true. To get at reality itself, the dialogue scrapes away appearances. This scraping away is the first necessity if one is to understand the discussion of the ideas that runs from the latter part of Book Five to the beginning of Book Seven. All well and good, but if we do not remain aware of this abstraction, the dialogue misleads us, because the fact is that appearances are also important, perhaps as important as actualities.

With characteristic irony, Socrates claims to be incapable of meeting the demands of Glaucon and Adeimantus, and then promptly proceeds to meet them. Here he employs the analogy that becomes the master analogy of the entire dialogue, the analogy that pervades and dominates the argument. Socrates points out that a man and a city are alike and, because the city is larger than the man, it will be easier to see justice there in the larger than it would be to see it in the smaller. What makes a city and man alike is that the soul of each is composed of three parts, three like parts, and so, having found justice in the larger, it would be much easier to discern it in the smaller. Socrates proposes that they make a city in speech, that they talk up a city, and when they find justice in it they will then be able to look back at the man and find justice there.

Be forewarned! As you continue on with study of the dialogue, take with great seriousness the tripartite division of the man and of the city. The soul of the man consists of a reasoning part; an irascible, or spirited, part; and an appetitive part. So also the city.

The first "draft" of their city provides for a division of labor, just as we asserted earlier in trying to grasp the nature of the *polis*, but it barely provides for the necessities of life. It is minimal. It is most unlikely that any but the simplest soul would settle for such a city. Glaucon is anything but simple. He is a cultivated gentleman. He is also very spirited, very manly. He is *andreiotatos*, ever so manly, manliest, most courageous. He dismisses what Socrates has so far wrought. It is, he says, a "city of pigs," and he demands improvements. Socrates yields and adds comforts, sauces, and spices. The result of this is that the simple city is replaced by a second city, a luxurious city, a bloated city – so bloated, in fact, that a whole army has to be added to protect it from the envy of other cities and to take from those other cities whatever appetite demands. This bloated, luxurious city is unsatisfactory in the other extreme, so what we might call a "third draft" produces a purged city, a city purged of its excesses. The word "Spartan" comes to mind. Despite the purging, however, the army stays, and, like any army, it bears watching. With great effort, a fourth-stage city is developed. This is the best city. It may be said to be a city of beauty, a city so perfect in its composition that, although the text does not say it in so many words, we are inclined to call it the beautiful city, beautifully complete, beautifully proportioned, beautifully just.

Socrates had said that a city would be talked up so that justice could be found in it and then one could discern justice in the individual, but, turning the analogy inside out, Socrates and the others actually find the three parts of the soul in the individual first, and in each part its own virtue is found. The reasoning part possesses wisdom, the spirited part courage, and the appetitive part moderation. These are three of the cardinal virtues. Where is to be found the fourth, justice? It turns out that justice is found in the proper relation among the three virtues found. As the argument develops, we see that justice in the individual consists in the absolute rule of reason over appetite with that rule supported wholeheartedly by spiritedness. This conclusion is not easy to resist. How, then, will the just city, the best city, the perfected city in speech, look?

Not only does it take four drafts to get to the best city, the full development of that best city takes a great deal of argument. In all, it requires Books Two, Three, and Four to work through the development. At the very beginning, the city of utmost necessity – the one Glaucon called a "city of pigs" – had manifested a division of labor. The character of that division had required a strict rule of "one man, one art," on the grounds that it would be better if one man grew foodstuffs and another built houses, and another made shoes, and so forth. This strict rule ensured good food, good houses, and good shoes, but it also necessitated some means of exchange, or barter, or trade. The fully developed city continues this strict principle, except that it is not one man, one art, but one class (or group or classification) that relates to one art, job, or calling. Just as there had been found three parts of the soul of the individual, it turns out that there are three distinguishable classes in the city as a whole. By the master analogy of city and man, there are found in the city a reasoning class, a spirited class, and an appetitive class. Because there is no such thing as a disembodied reason walking around, this requires a bit of reformulation. The upper, much the smallest, class has, of course, spiritedness and appetite as well, but its chief mark is its possession of reason. The second group, a sizeable minority, although it does not possess reason of the sort possessed by the uppermost class, it certainly has appetite, but what stands out about it is its spiritedness. The largest group, the remainder of the population, lacks both reason and spiritedness. It is marked by appetite alone.

Where is justice in the city? Sure! Right there before our eyes. It is in the harmony of the three classes. The reasoning class (which is very small, consisting of a very few individuals, or perhaps even of only one individual) is invested with absolute, unquestioned rule of the city, and that rule exists without any restraint of law. It is unrestrained because wisdom itself needs no external restraints. Its rule will be what is good for the whole city. The second class, the spirited class, the sizeable minority, has a sufficient understanding (or at least ingrained training) that it accepts and supports the rule of the wise. The support is essential, because the second class constitutes the armed force of the city and, as it develops, that force turns both inward and outward. That is, not only does it protect the city from outside threats; it also protects the regime, that is, the system of rule of the wise, from any disorderly threats that would otherwise develop in the third class. Apparently, all weapons in the best city are in the hands of the spirited, the courageous class. Nobody in the third class appears to take any part in defense. The weapons that those of the second class have are essentially all that they have, however. The soldiers have no private property at all. To understand this last point we have to delve just a little deeper below the surface of the argument.

The problem with the analogy is in the tendency to take it literally, to take it seriously, to exaggerate it, to treat the man and the city not as somewhat like each other but as identical to each other. Is there to be found anywhere, however, a purely appetitive class? Has anyone ever even seen a single human being who is so simply defined by his appetite that it can be said that he or she is altogether wanting in the qualities of reason and spiritedness? It is one thing to say that the healthy human being is one whose appetite is controlled by his reason but to say, by analogy, that there is a reasoning class that should rule without question over an appetitive class is to lay out a scheme for politics that the thoughtful reader should confront with caution. Perhaps this is a place where we should recognize the literary device of exaggeration. Perhaps we should take this conclusion with a grain of salt.

The whole course of the city's development now proceeds by way of what Socrates calls "three waves of argument." They are waves because as the arguments progress they wash over and engulf the participants with stunning revolutionary propositions. The first wave is that there will be complete equality of the sexes. Except for the poetic imagining of a nation of Amazons, nobody had ever broached the suggestion that women might do such an unwomanly thing as bear arms and fight, much less the obviously crazy suggestion that they might think and rule. The equality does indeed reach to equality in the upper two classes, but it does not apply to the appetitive class. The interlocutors of Socrates press him for details as to how this would all work, and this leads to the second wave, which is that there will be complete communism. It will be complete in that it will be not just a communism of material goods, but a communism of sexual partners and parentage. This sounds pretty attractive to the young men who make up the group (remember that old man Cephalus has left the conversation to attend to the pieties), and they press Socrates for more and more details. They are in for some disappointment, because it turns out that it will not be open season on the women for the men. The need to maintain and improve the stock of thinkers and soldiers necessitates a strictly enforced system of positive eugenics, so that who breeds with whom will be dictated according to the wisdom of the wise. This is one place where one might expect *eros* to rebel against its chains, so it is decided that the breeders – the best with the best most and the least with the least least – will be told a little white lie, namely, that it was the gods who chose the couplers, their choices by the rulers being divined by the drawing of lots. To explain this by talking in present-day military terms, we must imagine the troops out on the drill field at oh-six-hundred hours for quarters for muster and the sergeant major coming out, calling them to attention and ordering in his sergeantly voice, "All right, male number 164 and female number 19: into the pen to perform your civic duty . . . March!" We are asked by the dialogue to believe that the fact that the troops, males and females mixed, would perform their calisthenics naked in close-order drill every day will not in the slightest involve their being troubled by private inclinations. The ground for swallowing this tall tale hook, line, and sinker is that this is just one more instance of the radical abstraction of the whole argument from the natural needs of the body, and one more instance of extreme exaggeration of the human possibilities. The only love our troops are allowed is love of country.

Commentators are sometimes equivocal about the equality and the communism, but it is quite clear from the text of the "Republic" that these principles apply only to the two upper classes. There is no equality of the sexes or communism for the third class, the appetitive class. The members of this class, the great majority of the population, will have their own houses, their own husbands or wives, their own children, and their own money and other properties. They will give annual allotments of food and clothing, and these sparingly, and just about nothing else to the two upper classes. You might wonder, along with Adeimantus, how Socrates can give complete control of the city to these two upper classes and yet expect them to get nothing for themselves out of it and be perfectly satisfied with their lot. It turns out that it will be necessary to tell them a couple of whopping lies. These two lies are known to scholars as "the myth of autochthony" and "the myth of the metals." According to the autochthony myth, they are to be made to believe that what they thought was their education and training were really only parts of a dream, that in fact they were sprung full-grown, fully trained, and fully armed from the very soil of their motherland. Thus, their love of the motherland is indistinguishable from love of mother. Their patriotism is more than natural. It is the gift of the gods. They will never be subject to a divisive or seditious thought. Since everyone in the city is born "of it," all are brothers. Thus, the care for the safety and well-being of the productive class comes naturally to the auxiliaries, the soldierly class. The other part of the lie, the myth of the metals, is that all of them have metals in their souls by their natures. The wise class has gold in its souls, the courageous class has silver, and the others have bronze and iron. The upper classes will be incorruptible. They will believe that material gold or silver would weaken the gold or silver in their souls and so they will never covet the material goods held by the bronze and iron class. There will be no class envy.

The interlocutors challenge Socrates, but he shifts the burden. He asks Glaucon if he can somehow find a way to bamboozle everyone at the founding of the city to believe these wild lies. Glaucon's answer is that maybe those at the beginning can not be brought to believe them, but their grandchildren can be so persuaded. Indeed, this is the way of such stories (414b–15d).

Stop! The greatest difficulty in reading an ancient book is not that it is ancient. It is that we carelessly read it with modern eyes. Despite the fact that the "Republic" makes it eminently clear that the two upper classes in the city in speech have no property whatsoever and that the lower class has all of the wealth in the city, more than half the students in a present-day class seem bound and determined to see this through a certain astigmatism. They look right at the words in the text and, as though they were drugged, or perhaps busy exchanging text messages, they see this in terms bequeathed to us by Karl Marx, the terms of the "class struggle" of the downtrodden, poor proletariat and the oppressive, rich bourgeoisie. Grade inflation will boost the self-esteem of such students, but nothing, it seems, will educate them. A sensibly selfish student will strain every muscle to break free from that mental astigmatism.

These two stories, the two salutary or noble lies and the two principles – equality and communism – that are shored up by the lies are not nearly as shocking as the third wave. Socrates suggests that, when he pronounces it, everyone will laugh at him. If you think of these suggestions being made not to these intelligent gentlemen but to the citizens of Athens at large, the third wave would not elicit laughter but a lynch mob. The third wave is that the wise in whose hands the rule is put are none other than philosophers. The entire salvation of the city rests on the rule of philosophers. "What?" rejoins Adeimantus. "Is it not the case that all philosophers are either weird, or vicious, or, at best, utterly useless?" Socrates agrees. Indeed they are – now – but in the good city that they establish, the city in speech, philosophers, that is, true philosophers, not those who now pass themselves off as such, would be willing to rule, would be accepted as rulers, and would be the very salvation of the city and all its people. This leads to the necessity of explaining who are the true philosophers and what will be their education.

Ideas

Throughout Books Two, Three, and Four, an education for the gold and silver classes combined had been laid out. It consisted of music (i.e., the things wrought by the Muses) "for the soul" and gymnastic "for the body." As it develops, both music and gymnastic are for the proper development of the soul, for the development, that is, of moderation and courage. Now, however, it is necessary to separate in our discussion the gold class from the silver class and describe the education proper for the gold, the true education of the philosophers. The whole bunch had been called the "guardians," but we come to see that the silver class deserves only to be regarded as "auxiliaries." The only ones who deserve to be called guardians are the gold class. They are the true guardians, the perfect guardians. They are the saviors of the city. They must be educated so that their souls are fixed on the highest things, the ideas, the beauties. This is what real philosophy is made of. This examination of the education of the reasoning class occupies Books Five, Six, and Seven, and the heart of the matter is the adequate explanation of the "ideas," or "forms." This is difficult for Socrates to explain to the others, so the second most important analogy of the "Republic" is employed. The "Idea of the Good" is likened to the Sun. Every activity of the intellect is explained by analogy to the activities of the physical senses. This is more easily understood if we think about what we do every day in conversation. Repeatedly, we turn to one another after stating or arguing something and ask, "Do you see what I mean?" Of course we do not. Nobody has ever "seen" what somebody else meant. We cannot, however, understand the things of the soul without talking off to one side about the things of the body, in this case, talking about the eyes to refer obliquely to the intellect. It may be that nothing ever written in the whole history of the human race comes close to explaining this as well as the "Republic" does. This explanation takes place from the end of Book Five to the beginning of Book Seven and includes the figure of the divided line and what traditionally has been called the "allegory of the cave." To follow it, one needs to reread this section even oftener than the required often rereading of the "Republic" as a whole. The rewards are correspondingly great.

To sum this up, the best city is the city wherein philosophers, the gold-souled ones, rule absolutely and without restraint, and the rule is enforced by the armed ones, the silver-souled ones. Justice is defined as everyone minding his or her own business. One class, one task. Those whose souls are infused with bronze and iron do not meddle in making war or in ruling, and the silver-souled ones do not meddle in ruling.

A series of troublesome surprises follows all this. The interlocutors have repeatedly badgered Socrates for assurance that the city in speech might be brought into being in deed. By the end of Book Seven he can no longer put them off. This is no problem, for the answer is simple. To make a new city, we cannot start with empty hands. We shall need some Greeks. Unfortunately, all existing Greeks are miseducated. They are corrupt. It is too late for them. No decent city could be made with them as citizens. Don't worry. Be happy. All we need to do is banish everyone older than ten years of age. They must be persuaded to pack up and leave the city, and to leave those ten or younger, their children, behind. Sure! No problem! They will all say, "Oh. Okay." They will leave their children and their property behind. They will voluntarily accept banishment because we ask them nicely to do so. If you believe this, we need to talk about a bridge over the East River that I own and will shortly put up for sale at a rock-bottom, closeout price. The fact is that this answer by Socrates is irrefutable proof that Socrates and Plato both know that the bringing into being in deed of the best city, the city in speech, cannot ever come to pass, or, if it is ever to come to pass, it must be the consequence of some remarkable accident. It cannot, by skill and effort, be brought to pass.

More, Books Eight and Nine show that if the city in speech did actually come into being, it would, in due course, inevitably disintegrate. It is bound to be degraded. The city in speech, if it were ruled by one philosopher, would be called a "kingship." If it were ruled by a few philosophers, it would be called an "aristocracy." Either way, it is the rule of wisdom. The rule into which the city in speech deteriorates has to have a name made up for it by Socrates because rules of this second kind, such as those in Sparta and Crete, are falsely called aristocracies. They are not truly rule "by the best," which is the exact meaning of "aristocracy." Socrates has to invent a name for this second-best city. Because it is rule by the silver class, he dubs this second rule "timocracy," or the rule of honor, because it is rule by the class that is motivated not by the search for truth but by the love of honor. The silver class usurps rulership from the gold class because it has, over time, drifted away from its subordination to wisdom. Carried away by its love of combat ribbons, chevrons, gold bars, and silver eagles, and intoxicated by the honors bestowed on it, it gets the strange idea that it is fit to rule. This rule, in its turn, soon deteriorates into rule by the moneyed class, which shows itself as the first rulership with a dispossessed class, the poor. This rule of the moneyed class is called "oligarchy," or "Plutocracy." It in turn deteriorates into democracy, and democracy soon gives way to tyranny.

Three observations need to be made here. First of all, it is a mistake to accept this as a prediction of a fixed sequence or to read into the text some notion of historical process, or historical necessity, or historical determinism. It ought perhaps to be understood simply as a scheme that allows a description of and contrast among the several major classifications of *politeias*. Once again, our astigmatism hinders us. Again attributable to Karl Marx is the notion that revolution is a straight-line process. It goes in one direction. It goes ineluctably to a predetermined end. It goes always from "right" to "left." When it gets there, revolution ends. All one has to do, however, is think of the tachometer on a dashboard. It measures revolutions per minute, revolutions by the thousands per minute. The fact is that revolutions revolve. The several points in a revolution are visited over and over again. I think that all that is meant by the description in Book Eight of the deterioration of the city in speech, the best city, into the several varieties of defective city is that one sort of city can change into another sort because of inherent defects in each variety and that transformation can be from any sort to any sort. This does not deny that the explanation of the down spiral from the best to the worst has an immediate, understandable, common sense to it. But, lo! Does it not also mean that our city, the best city, has some fault in it? The route to understanding this is to take the peculiar "number" that is described at 546b to 547a near the beginning of Book Eight and reflect on it in the light of the abstractions that help to form the whole argument. Correcting that fault shines a completely new light on the whole argument of the "Republic."

Second, although it is shown that kingship or aristocracy is surely the best *politeia* and tyranny is surely the worst, the line between the two is pencil thin. Moving from the worst regime to the best would be far easier than moving from Timocracy, oligarchy, or democracy to the best regime. The reason for this is that the Just King and the Tyrant share one vital characteristic: Each of them is driven by *eros*. Their lives are driven by intense desire. The reason Plato makes Socrates argue that the route from tyranny to kingship is the shortest is twofold. On the one hand, the Tyrant already has that complete control of the city that is essential to the Just King. On the other hand, although it is true that he is like the Just King in that he is driven by insatiable desire, he does not know what it is that he wants. He does not know what the truly desirable is. The Tyrant is like you and me when we keep going back to the refrigerator and rummaging about in it. We know *that* we want, but we do not know *what* we want. The life of the philosopher is a life of professed ignorance, but it is a life aware of its ignorance. That is, it is wiser than all the other lives because they are lives of ignorance multiplied by ignorance of their ignorance. The philosopher is the one human being who truly knows what is truly worth knowing. If we could only turn the appetite of the Tyrant, if we could educate him, if we could show him what it is that he hankers, for, if we could subject him to what might be called a "conversion of the soul," we would move instantly to the best *politeia*, the absolute rule of the wise. Sure! Maybe if we got hold of the dozens of tyrants who now abuse their peoples and sent them to the American College of Tyrannical Reformation, the whole bunch of them would break their bad habits. I can see it now, the logo of ACTR: a weeping tyrant laying aside his beheading axe and his bloody sword, and beneath it the slogan, "You Know You Really Want To." Maybe we could make a lot of money selling a medical patch that, like a quit-smoking patch, when stuck on the tyrant's arm, would weaken his desire to butcher babies and nursing mothers. Then again, maybe not. With repeated apologies for deflating the invigorating idealism of youth, perhaps we should regard this as another instance of exaggeration by Plato's Socrates. Here is another place where reading some Xenophon is a good accompaniment to reading Plato. His dialogue, *Hiero*, shows the poet Simonides at the court of the tyrant Hiero. Whereas the "Republic" begins with Socrates asking Cephalus, "Say, Cephalus, what's it like to be old?" *Hiero* begins with Simonides asking Hiero, "Say, Hiero, what's it like to be a tyrant?"[4] Simonides goes on to show Hiero that if he truly knew what he wanted he would be transformed into a just king.

The third observation is that, in describing the four deviant regimes, Socrates excoriates democracy severely. Many modern commentators have, rather self-righteously, said of this that Plato disapproved of democracy and that his scheme merely spouts a call for the establishment of a regime patterned after that of Sparta. This is a mistake for several reasons. The first reason is that Plato does not advocate anything. We cannot guess from reading a dialogue, in which all speeches are made by identifiable speakers, what it is that Plato is for or against. Another reason this view is mistaken is that, as we suggested earlier, the dialogue, no matter to whom you credit the things said, does not advocate any political action whatever. A third reason is that this accusation against Plato and Socrates presupposes that all decent people will agree that democracy is good. The fact is that until very recent times no sensible observer spoke well of democracy. Democracy is bad rule. Whereas oligarchy is bad because the few oppress the many, democracy is bad because the many oppress the few. It is only marginally less bad than oligarchy because fewer people are oppressed. To explain why we so facilely praise democracy in the present is again to confront our mental astigmatism. To understand this, we would have to say something that is now quite unfashionable in academic circles, namely that democracy simply looks good to our skewed vision because the United States created the very first self-moderating democracy in the whole of history. To understand this, one needs to read and reflect on the discussion of "faction" in *Federalist* No. 10. In principle, "democracy" means exactly what its name says: rule by the *demos*, the great multitude of uneducated and unrestrained people who are defined by their appetites and who are lawless. No one could call that good rule.

Is the disapproval of democracy by Socrates all there is to it, however? Those who call Plato antidemocratic make a parallel error in speaking of Aristotle as though, contrary to Plato, he were a nice, cuddly democrat. Both of these views misread their subjects. Aristotle is certainly not an unequivocal

4 This can be found in the Loeb Classical Library volume of Xenophon titled *Scripta Minora*. The companion to the Xenophon dialogue is a commentary by Leo Strauss titled "On Tyranny," the revised and enlarged edition of which was published by The Free Press, 1963, Glencoe, IL, and includes a translation of the work by Xenophon.

fan of democracy, and Plato is not (nor is Socrates) simply an opponent of democracy. Plato's "Republic" and Aristotle's *Politics* are remarkably alike in their practical conclusions. In both cases, if one reads the text with reasonable care, it appears that the authors give similar, and carefully measured, half approval of democracy. If we read the harsh description of democracy in the "Republic," we see that salted away in it is an acknowledgment that some measure of justice abides there. What is justice? The "Republic" offers the definition (toward the end of Book Four) that justice is everyone minding his own business. On the principle of one class, one job, the job of the philosophers is, unfortunately, to rule. This is unfortunate because the true job of the philosophers is, essentially, to philosophize, to pursue the truths, to seek to glimpse the beauties, to apprehend the ideas. They get to do "their thing" in the best city (but only after retirement from the rigors of ruling), because wisdom itself rules that city. The city in speech is the only safe haven for philosophy. That city in speech is not likely to be seen by any of us in deed, however. It is curious that the only other city in which philosophers get to philosophize at all is the democratic city, because there everybody gets to do "his thing." The curious lawlessness of democracy allows philosophy a measure of leeway. Only a measure! This is, however, at least better than oligarchy, timocracy, or tyranny. In each of those regimes the antipathy of the rulers to philosophy is thoroughgoing. In a way, the text allows a grudging acknowledgment that although true kingship or true aristocracy is the best regime, perhaps democracy is the second best. Plato puts something in his text that is akin to a playful treasure map. He could have had Socrates rank the deviant regimes any way he liked, but he lets Glaucon rank them thus: (1) kingship (or aristocracy); (2) timocracy; (3) oligarchy; (4) democracy; and (5) tyranny. Accompanying this ranking, Socrates makes an offhand reference to Hesiod's "races" (546e).[5] Hesiod had identified historical epochs by the races of men that ruled in them. The first was the golden race (like the philosophers in the city in speech); the second was the silver race (like the auxiliaries); the third was bronze (corresponding to half of the description of the multitude in the city in speech); and the fifth was the iron (corresponding to the other, the harsher, half of the description of the multitude in the city in speech); but the fourth race in Hesiod's account is the "Race of Heroes," a hero being the offspring of one god and one human, that is, a demigod. What is more, Plato shows us in a parallel part of the argument that Glaucon is a defective ranker of things. Perhaps his ranking of the cities is flawed.

Perhaps this ranking by Glaucon, held alongside the ranking by Hesiod, is meant to suggest that, all things considered, democracy is the second best rule. Certainly it and the city in speech, are the only two regimes in which philosophy can be found. In the city in speech, philosophy is a certainty. In

[5] Hesiod, *Works and Days*, from about line 130 to about line 204.

democracy it at least might have a chance. We are not permitted to forget, however, the cold historical fact that it was the democratic Athens that meted out the death penalty to Socrates precisely because he philosophized. We must not, however, forget that Socrates "got away with" philosophizing until he was seventy. The harsh characterization of democracy by the Socrates portrayed in the "Republic" conceals a muted, half approval of democracy. Here again, one may ask, "If that's what Socrates thought, why doesn't he just say so?" That is a good question, but not an unanswerable one. One or more possible answers will occur to the thoughtful reader, the reader who puts himself into the middle of the speakers in the dialogue. Such a reader will not let Socrates "put one over on him" as Socrates repeatedly "puts one over on" Glaucon and Adeimantus. Just when Socrates fools his interlocutors, the careful reader will stop him in his tracks and demand that he answer. The reader who does this may suddenly feel a strange sense of euphoria, thinking that he hears Socrates talking to him, saying more than can be found on the printed page of the "Republic." The first words out of the mouth of Socrates might likely be, "In the name of Zeus, man, have you forgotten who condemned me to death? Come talk to me in my office, later."

If the condemnation of Socrates that we see in Plato's *Apology of Socrates*, which adds up to the trial of Socrates in the court of public opinion, is the very definition of the problem of philosophy, then the apology of philosophy, the defense of it in a private conversation with intelligent gentlemen, most of whom show a measure of cultivation and good character, is the equivalent of the search for the best regime, the regime, the city, where philosophy is safe. Justice is everyone minding his own business. The business of philosophy is free and radical pursuit of the truth. The business of political philosophy is the search for a secure place for that pursuit.

The *Apology of Socrates* shows the problem. Plato's "Republic" is the first answer: Philosophers must be kings. The crux of the answer is that the two higher classes, the gold and the silver classes – let us rename them here, the philosophers and the gentlemen – must work together to establish and maintain rule over themselves and all the others. Two practical observations are necessary: Make no mistake, it must be the philosophers who rule, and there must never be opened a fissure between the philosophers and the gentlemen, for, if there is, the multitude will rush into the breach and start meddling in rulership, which is not its business.

We began with a kind of easygoing open-mindedness. We wanted to know what political philosophy is. Somehow or other we have stumbled onto the proposition that political philosophy is the search for justice, the search for what is right by nature. It turns out that the question, "What is justice?" is identical to the question, "What is the best regime?" This is the same as asking, "Who should rule?" The first answer that we come across is the strange and shocking propositions that philosophers themselves should rule (even though their proper calling is philosophizing); that their rule should be without any restraint other than their own judgment; and that they should be supported unquestioningly by the gentlemen, who are the only others capable of reasonable acceptance of the rule of philosophy. It follows that it is necessary to track this alliance between the gold and silver classes over the centuries.

6

Moderation

The city in speech that Plato has Socrates build in the "Republic" is the best city imaginable. The road to it is paved with the abstractions and analogies we discussed in the preceding chapter and with the exaggeration of those abstractions and analogies. It lays up or discovers, however, a pattern in the heavens. Although the pattern is not in the form of an "ideal" for which we are bidden to strive, it does suggest to us that if we rectify the chief analogy so that we see it as an analogy and not as a perfect likeness, if we rectify the chief abstraction by bringing back into the equation the needs of the body, if we reduce to reasonable levels the exaggeration of both of these literary devices, and, finally, if we take into account the force of *eros* and the force of *thumos*, or spiritedness, and a host of lesser matters, we have something of a practicable pattern. It is still only a pattern, however, and the task of statesmanship, the chief element of which is prudence, or practical judgment, is to find the best dilution of the already rectified pattern that will make the best of the raw material – the human beings – at hand, so that some sort of decent city that is law-abiding and stable might come about and bring a degree of justice to all. The first thing to forget is the widespread, present-day notion that "justice" and "equality" are interchangeable terms.

We can only rectify the chief abstraction if we first understand it. As we argued in the preceding chapter, every abstraction falsifies that which is its focus, but the focus here is itself the abstraction. To understand this abstraction, we have to appreciate that the "needs of the body" add up to what we call "economics," or household management. Now anyone who thinks that politics and economics can be set altogether apart from each other is mistaken. We need to abstract from economics, however, if we are to get a clear understanding of politics itself. If we do not rejoin them in the practice of politics, however, unhappy results will be incurred. The man who properly turns our attention to the practicable is Aristotle. He sees that trying to make a city where reason rules simply and absolutely is a fool's errand, but he also sees that the only truly good city will be one where good judgment holds the highest place in the political order. The communism of the "Republic" is an absurdity. Adeimantus asked how Socrates expected the gold and silver classes to have the city entirely in their grasp and yet be willing to take no material benefit from that fact – to live in monastic poverty. The answer Socrates gives seems to "put one over" on Adeimantus, but we need not be taken in by the answer. Here, very pointedly, we see that we need to take part in the dialogue to profit from it. Aristotle sees that it is still the case that, although property is in its nature private, its employment ought to be for the public good. A watered-down diminution of the wealth of the wealthy is a practicable, achievable goal, but we have to support our understanding of both Plato and Aristotle with the reminder that any such diminution is critically dependent on there being actual rule by the wisest members of the community, and to be well-intended and ardent or to be equipped with a doctrine, a prepackaged "ism," is not the same thing as to be wise. Platonic communism among human beings – marriage, procreation, and the like – is altogether destructive. The family is always potentially divisive of the city, but it is also essential to the city because the affection of kinfolk is the only thing that can give assurance of the well-being of people. To speak in modern terms, "day care" just "doesn't cut it." Somehow the family's divisiveness and its contribution must be balanced, and this balance is always a difficult task for statesmanship. Shakespeare's *Romeo and Juliet* shows how difficult it can be. Finally, although it is not the case that there are three neatly demarcated classes – the rational, the spirited, and the appetitive – it is the case that there are three broadly distinguishable elements in the city, and the good city is one in which they are in a proper state of balance. That balance too will be a challenge, but the first necessity in approaching the problem is to remind ourselves of the need to rectify the chief abstraction of the "Republic." The notion prevalent since the nineteenth century that the classes are simply sorted out as the "rich" and the "poor" is an error. It is an error that turns the relation between politics and economics upside down. If we follow Karl Marx on this matter, or even such a "soft" heir of Marx as Charles A. Beard, our chance of reconciling the naturally antagonistic classes is made much more difficult. The perpetual juggling of these problems is a task of statesmanship, insofar as it turns its attention inward. We do not mean to deny that there are poor people and rich people in any city. Nor do we overlook the fact that, until recently, in every country the poor were far more numerous than the rich.[1] We mean only to state emphatically that politics cannot be reduced to economics. Here, as in many other things, Aristotle is a clearheaded guide.

---

[1] To understand why this is now less true in some countries, it is useful to read Chapter 5, "On Property," in the second of John Locke's *Two Treatises of Government.*

In Chapter Three we were guided by the teaching of Aristotle in Book One of the *Politics*. Here we must follow a sentence or two of Book Two and some portions of Books Three and Four. Ernest Barker (England, 1874–1960) wrote a translation of Aristotle's *Politics* published by Oxford University Press in 1946. His translation gives to Book Two the title "Ideal States in Theory." This is wrong for two reasons. The second of the two reasons is that, as we explained earlier, the words "ideal" and "state" are not to be found in Plato or in Aristotle. The first reason is easier to state. The "Books" of Aristotle's *Politics* have no titles at all. Indeed, the fact that the work is divided into books is simply dictated by how many words can be written on one roll of paper, that being a "book" in the ancient sense. If not Aristotle himself, then some early scholar "numbered" the "books." The Greeks "numbered" their books with letters of the alphabet. The second book is Book β, that is, beta. Even though Ernest Barker was both a fine gentleman and an excellent scholar, whose translation of the *Politics* is both good and useful, readers of this book can quite rightly see these problems and name them as errors. H. Rackham,[2] of Christ's College in Cambridge University, made a translation of Aristotle's *Politics* published by the Loeb Classical Library in 1932. Rackham does not give names to the books, but he does on the first page of Book Two use the word "ideal" in the same incorrect way as Barker. Despite this, his translation is useful also.

Aristotle's criticism of Plato's "Republic" runs from 1260b27 to 1264b25 (or, following traditional usages, the first five "chapters" of Book Two) of the *Politics*. Aristotle treats the communism in the "Republic" both as though it had been meant to be followed in actual practice and as though it applied to all parts of the city in speech, not just to the gold and silver classes. When I first read the Barker (and then the Rackham) translation of the *Politics* in 1955 I was dumbfounded by this. Because I thought the opposite to be true, I could not see how Aristotle could think such things. I reasoned that I must be mistaken, the translations were radically defective, or perhaps Aristotle had some salutary purpose behind what he was doing. Early in my teaching career, a senior colleague in a different academic department came to me and asked me to read the manuscript of a book he had written and to comment on it. I was embarrassed by the request, he being my professional senior. There was, however, no way out of the problem. I did read the manuscript. To my amazement, my colleague asserted therein that Aristotle did not understand Plato, whereas he, my colleague, did. How could my colleague (a true, old-school gentleman and a sound and congenial colleague), a mere liberal arts professor, make such a bold claim?

---

[2] "H. Rackham" of Cambridge University is not to be confused with "Horace Rackham" (1858–1933) a lawyer and a generous benefactor of the University of Michigan, and especially of its classics programs.

Aristotle had, after all, been a pupil of Plato for twenty years until Plato's death. What is more, he was one of the half dozen greatest minds in all of history. It would take someone nearly on his own level – an al-Farabi, Niccolò Machiavelli, Thomas Hobbes, Friedrich Nietzsche – to dare to say that he understood Plato better than Aristotle did and be taken seriously. A mere, nice, college professor saying this could not be taken seriously. I had by then already become aware that St. Thomas Aquinas had figured the problem out in the thirteenth century, but it would have added to the discomfort of the situation for me to have pointed this out to my colleague. A little polite, incoherent stammering was the only way out. I took it.

What explains Aristotle's seeming error? The answer is straightforward. Aristotle treats Plato in this way to show how disastrous it would be if one were to follow Plato as though he did in fact mean us to bring into being in deed the city in speech. Also, Aristotle well knew that many young people (some of them Plato's former students) might be intoxicated by the Platonic dialectic. Aristotle knew that it is easy for us "intellectuals" to sneer at the "losers" in Plato's dialogues and to continue by sneering at all of our fellow citizens and believing that, if only *we* managed things, we could straighten out the whole political order. Aristotle's poker-faced critique of Plato has the effect of sobering Plato's pupils, his own pupils, and his readers. Perhaps he actually sobered his own pupils also by counsel that is nowhere published, but the *Politics*, being published, is addressed to an audience much wider than Aristotle's immediate circle of pupils and, indeed, might fall into the hands of an even larger group, and he had to deal with them in a politically responsible way. Even if, as some say, the *Politics* is not a book by Aristotle but a transcription of his lectures by his students, he certainly must have known that what he said would reach farther than the schoolroom door. He had to act responsibly because Aristotle, like Plato, understood that although political people often regarded philosophers as the city's enemies, philosophers knew that the city was not simply their enemy, because the city is the precondition of philosophy. To say this is no more than to state the obvious: Smart people are likely to understand things better than ordinary people.

Aristotle's sobriety in recognizing the seductive power of a mind as over-powering as Plato's is a good reminder. We shall say here more than once that Plato is the great creative genius of classical antiquity. Machiavelli, whom we shall shortly consider, was the great creative genius of modern political philosophy. Friedrich Nietzsche may be regarded as the great creative genius of what has come to be called postmodernism. We shall in due course consider him. Now it happens that Plato was the most distinguished follower of Socrates, and these three geniuses – Socrates, Machiavelli, and Nietzsche – were, each of them, founders of what we might call "youth movements." Socrates, himself, in his *Apology*, acknowledged that some of his followers might lack prudence and turn into smart alecks and trouble makers. Again, Aristotle was right to caution his pupils – and us – about Plato's book.

Book Three of the *Politics* is divided between a treatment of citizenship and a treatment of the several imaginable regimes. Let us skim quickly over the first of these matters and then concentrate on the latter.

In 1865, after the American Civil War, an attempt by Congress to write a civil rights act encountered the problem that many doubted that Congress had Constitutional authority to pass such an act, and so the Fourteenth Amendment was fashioned. In the early stages of its development in Congress, the language of the amendment began with an empowerment of Congress to secure to all citizens due process, equal protection, privileges, and immunities. It struck someone that such an empowerment of Congress would not secure any rights to the blacks newly freed from slavery by the Thirteenth Amendment because of the ruling in the Dred Scott case in 1857 that no negro, whether free or slave, could be a citizen in the sense in which that word is used in the Constitution. Therefore, the empowerment-of-Congress language was dropped into a new Section 5 of the amendment, Section 1 was completely rewritten, and there was prefixed to the whole the following: "All persons born or naturalized in the United States and subject to the jurisdiction thereof are citizens of the United States and of the State wherein they reside."[3] We have difficulty understanding Aristotle; for kindred reasons he would have difficulty understanding us. He would have quite a bit of difficulty understanding our Fourteenth Amendment, and if we are to understand his treatment of citizenship, we will have to see why our scheme would not make sense to him. Once again, we have to put on our historian's mental eyeglasses to correct our mental astigmatism.

The human beings who made up the ancient city were free people and slaves, men and women, adults and children. In no city were all those born there or admitted to residence regarded as citizens. In none of them were children or slaves citizens, and, if there were cities where free women, or some of them, were citizens, it would take some devoted scholarship to figure out what that meant. As far as free men were concerned, the portion of them that ranked as citizens varied from city to city. Only in the most democratic of cities were all the free men citizens. Aristotle notes that the several definitions of "citizen" in the several cities do not offer a clear statement that explains what citizenship is. In one city, for example, the definition of citizen was the "son of a citizen father," but Aristotle asks, what about the citizenship of the father, or of the father's father? We cannot tell how a city really defines citizenship without knowing why the first citizens were citizens. One can approach this by analogy. If we go to an art gallery

---

[3] *Dred Scott v. Sandford,* 19 How. (60 U.S.) 393 at 403, 406, 418, 421, 425–27 (1857), and see Francis Canavan, "A New Fourteenth Amendment," *Human Life Review,* vol. 12, no. 1 (Winter 1986), pp. 30–48.

and see a painting of Adam, we notice with surprise that he has a navel.[4] Why? He did not need one. He was not born of woman. God fashioned him from dust (*Gen.* 2:7). The only explanation of Adam's belly button that I have read that is plausible runs like this: God knows everything, that which is yet to be as well as that which is. He knows that a snake will beguile Eve and that Eve will entice Adam to eat of the fruit of the tree of the knowledge of good and evil that is in the middle of the Garden in violation of His explicit commandment. He knows that He will banish them from the Garden, and one thing will lead to another, generation after generation will be born,[5] and all of them will have navels, so God in His grace, gave a navel to Adam. I hope that we shall not be thought irreligious if we smile at this strained effort to explain away what is perhaps only an oversight of some painters by our saying, "Oh, so God wanted Adam to be one of the guys!" Aristotle has something in mind that is not unlike this Adam's navel problem when he says that none of the definitions of citizenship one hears makes any sense at all. The true definition of a citizen, and one that fits any city whatsoever, is, Aristotle says, "sharing in decision and office" (1275a23). Thus, one who may vote, is judge, or may sit in the assembly, or is eligible to hold any office whatever, is a citizen. The others, even if native born, are not. The first thing we need to grasp, therefore, if we are to have any understanding of the ancient city and of the several regimes Aristotle discusses, is that not everyone *in* the city was *of* it. Just as Aristotle's definition fully and adequately explains citizenship, that definition is the ground of the definitions of the several regimes. There is more to Aristotle's discussion of citizenship, such as what its virtues are, but it is better if we turn now to the latter part of Book Three to look at the several regimes.

Aristotle's classification of regimes is exhaustive and irrefutable. It is also almost too neat to be satisfying. He tells us that rule is either by one, by a few, or by the many. So far, that makes three rulerships or regimes, or *politeias*, but he soon doubles that number by noting that rule is either good or bad. It is good rule if it is rule by the rulers for the benefit of the whole city. It is deviant rule if it is rule by the rulers for their own benefit. That is quite straightforward, and no one could argue with it. It is, among its other virtues, exhaustive. Surely there are subcategories, but

---

[4] In *The Book of Art*, 10 vols., New York, 1965, Grolier, at p. 118 of vol. 4, *German and Spanish Art*, there is a reproduction of an engraving by Albrecht Dürer (1471–1528) titled *Adam and Eve* (1504). The engraving can be found in the British Museum in London. In it, Adam unquestionably is shown with a navel. This should be compared with a small painting done by Dürer in 1502 of a hare. It is painted with exact fidelity to its subject. With scrupulous care, every single hair on the animal is painted, hair by hair. Even if one considered no other aspect of the painting, this alone would merit a description of it as a work of great beauty. Although Eve was fashioned from one of Adam's ribs, I have not encountered any explanation for her navel in art.

[5] More! God Himself commanded Adam and Eve to "be fruitful and multiply." *Gen.* 1:28.

it is impossible to imagine a seventh major category, a type of rule that falls outside of Aristotle's list. A few amplifications suggest themselves to us immediately, however. We realize that to speak of "a" few is to imply that there are two or more "fews," distinguished from each other by some substantive characteristic – for example, there are the few who are wise and virtuous and there are the few who are merely well-to-do. In contrast, there is only one "many." Two or more "manys" would add up to more than 100 percent. But, if there is only one "many," we seem to be back down to five *politeias*, as Plato had had Socrates list them, not six as Aristotle lists them!

Aristotle's categorization lends itself to being set out in a matrix, and, if we follow that possibility and give to each of the six the name that Aristotle offers, even more things come to light. Aristotle not only lists the six *politeias*, he names them and ranks them. In his own name and with his own pen, he ranks them. It will be remembered that the ranking of the five regimes in Plato's "Republic" was not by Plato, nor even by Plato's Socrates, but by Plato's Glaucon. We can not know from the text where Plato stands. We cannot even know where Socrates stands. Glaucon's ranking was, it will be remembered, kingship/aristocracy, timocracy,[6] oligarchy, democracy, and tyranny – or at least it was apparently so, and a couple of hints force us to think the matter through for ourselves and perhaps to change the ranking. In the *Politics*, on the contrary, you know what the several regimes are and you know how Aristotle ranks them. Let us draw up for ourselves, then, the suggested matrix, numbering the several regimes according to Aristotle's ranking, and let us think the whole scheme through (Table 6.1).

Table 6.1. *Politeias*

Number	Good	Bad
One	(1) Kingship	(6) Tyranny
Few	(2) Aristocracy	(5) Oligarchy
Many	(3) Politeia	(4) Democracy

Several things come to mind. First of all, it appears that Aristotle cannot think of a commonly used name for a good rule by the many. There is a good reason for this. No thoughtful person ever called rule of the many "good." Therefore, just as Socrates had to invent the name "Timocracy," Aristotle has to make up a name for rule of the many that is good rule. He gives to this rulership the generic name for all rulerships. This has led some commentators to suggest that this shows that Aristotle regards a certain kind

---

[6] The proposition that kingship and aristocracy are the same except for a slight quantitative difference and the giving of the name "Timocracy" to the rule of the spirited class were the doing of Socrates, but the ranking of the five *politeias* was by Glaucon.

of rule of the many as so good a *politeia* that it deserves the name *politeia* itself, as though it is the one, the true *politeia*, the best regime. Thus, the many, if they are good, make for a good rule, and the many, if they are bad, make for a bad rule. If, however, there is only one "many," *the* many, this answer fails.[7] Besides, Aristotle plainly states that kingship is the best rule.

The latter half of Book Three and all of Book Four are devoted to the characteristics of the several regimes, including various subspecies of each of them, and to their establishment and their preservation. We need to take special note here of the first few pages of Book Four to understand Aristotle's ranking and to see its relation to the three major subdivisions of a population.

Book Four begins with a description of the capabilities of a gymnastic trainer and, by analogy, shows what would be the complete syllabus of instruction that would characterize an adequate political science study of regimes. A rather long quotation from Aristotle's text is called for at this point:

So it is clear that, with regard to the regime, it belongs to the same science to study what the best regime is, and what quality it should have to be what one would pray for above all, with external things providing no impediment; which regime is fitting for which [cities] – for it is perhaps impossible for many to obtain the best, so neither the one that is superior simply nor the one that is the best that circumstances allow should be overlooked by the good legislator and the political [ruler] in the true sense; further, thirdly, the regime based on a presupposition – for any given regime should be studied [with a view to determining] both how it might arise initially and in what manner it might be preserved for the longest time once in existence (I am speaking of the case where a city happens neither to be governed by the best regime – and is not equipped even with the things necessary for it – nor to be governed by the regime that is [the best] possible among existing ones, but one that is poorer; and besides all these things, the regime that is most fitting for all cities should be recognized . . . one should study not only the best regime but also the regime that is [the best] possible, and similarly also the regime that is easier and more attainable for all.[8]

We shall continue to quote from Aristotle in a moment, but it is first necessary to make a few observations on the excerpt just presented. First, notice the fidelity in the description of political science to the analogy with gymnastic training and the fact that such fidelity could be maintained in a description of medicine, shipbuilding, or any other art. Second, notice that Aristotle counsels a study of the best regime. That means that a good political scientist ought to make a serious study of such things as the city in

---

[7] None of this is to deny that the many in one city may be more law-abiding and decent than the many in another city, but this question is not at the center of Aristotle's thoughts at this point.

[8] These two paragraphs are from the Carnes Lord translation, 1288b10–39. The phrases in square brackets are interpolations by Lord.

speech built by Socrates in Plato's "Republic." Furthermore, notice that the political scientist ought to study even a poorer regime and how not only to establish one but also how to preserve it. Does this not mean that the political scientist needs to be able to give advice even to a tyrant on how to preserve his tyranny? Of course it does, but does it mean that the good political scientist will, in fact, give such advice to a tyrant? Well, perhaps it does, but the precise nature of the advice that enables a tyrant to maintain his rule is perhaps advice that makes his rule less tyrannical, for tyrannical rule is inherently self-destructive. We are reminded of the advice Xenophon's Simonides gives to Hiero. What is more, a little reflection reminds us that to know how to preserve a tyranny is also to know how to destroy it. Caution! We must not read backward into the past a notion that prevails in the present. Nothing whatsoever in Plato or Aristotle calls people to the barricades. Not until the American and French revolutions at the close of the eighteenth century was there ever an overthrow of an existing regime based on a philosophical doctrine. One cannot even imagine an angry crowd in ancient times ranging through the streets of Athens with placards that read "Onward to the City in Speech!" or one that read "Burn, Tyrant, Burn." There is more than one reason for the absence of philosophic revolutions in the past, but the one that needs to be noted here is the great difference between the ancient understanding of the relation between theory and practice and the modern understanding of the relation between theory and application. The ancients understood that theory is higher and better than practice. The fact that one cannot bring into being in deed the city in speech does not mean that one need not contemplate the city in speech. The modern notion that theories are to be applied means that if the city in speech cannot be brought into being in deed it should be driven from our thoughts, and we should, in characteristic modern parlance, "go back to the drawing board." We need to remind ourselves that the ancients knew, given the understanding that speech is better than deed, that any political practice would necessarily be a dilution of what is possible in speech, but knowing what is possible only in speech is also knowing which way is up. (This observation does not contradict what was said previously regarding patterns. As we said, statesmanship consists in the prudent dilution of a pattern. Furthermore, the dilution will not simply be quantitative in character; it will be qualitative.)

Another observation is useful here. Several commentators in the past century or two have dismissed Aristotle (as well as Plato) as an "absolutist." This is a handy epithet to brandish at someone you do not want to bother to understand. The folly of this dismissal can be seen by simply reading what Aristotle says. He is the most open-minded student of politics one can find. For example, as we just read, he shows that anyone who would try to bring into existence a regime that is better than the one suited to the raw material – the human beings – is foolish. Therefore, a regime that is by Aristotle regarded as quite defective may still be one that he would recommend in a given instance. This is not an abandonment of principle – only an idealist could foolishly call it that – it is rather common sense. Here is a good place to reflect on the analogy between political science and gymnastic science. If an elderly college professor who has led a sedentary life, is a little overweight, and suffers from some respiratory problems should go to a gymnasium and tell the gymnastic trainer that he would like to "get in shape," and the trainer accepts him as a pupil and then has him join a group of sturdy young men training for the Olympics, it would quite simply kill the old man. The gymnastic trainer would be guilty of negligent homicide.

Each of the elements of political science recommended by Aristotle in Book Four fits and explains one of the several imaginable regimes named in Book Three and explains its rank order. This can be understood by following Aristotle's detailed descriptions and evaluations of the regimes that are to be found in Books Three and Four and in portions of the remaining books of the *Politics*. Aristotle explains that kingship is the best regime, simply, but he shows that it is only called for if there were one man who is so superior in wisdom and the other virtues to all the other human beings in the city combined that he is "like a god among men." The only sensible thing to do with him would be to give him absolute rule because any diminution of his rule by the opinions of those inferior to him would worsen the city. Certainly, he, being superior, ought not to be ruled by a law made with concessions to the inferior ones. Indeed, even the rule of law in the best sense might be problematic because full practical wisdom requires for its effectiveness a latitude of discretion that law's uniformity and catholicity impede. If we acknowledge, however, that no rule – not even the best rule – is good rule if it is forced, the other requirement for rule of the one best man is the presence of a multitude capable of accepting such rule and, by definition, that means a multitude that is not really a multitude, for there is perhaps no multitude anywhere on earth possessed of such understanding and moderation. Here is a place where we need to "do the math." How likely is it that the first condition might be met, that there is to be found in the city one man who is "like a god among men?" Let us reach up and pull a figure right out of the ether. Let us say that the chance of finding such a man is "one in a million." Now ask how likely it is to find such a general population that would meekly say, "Oh, all right, let's let him rule absolutely." Again, maybe there is one chance in a million. In other words, given our suppositions, the arithmetic result is that the chance of such a rule is one in a million million[9] cities. We would have to count in quite a few extraterrestrials to find the best city. How likely is the coming into being in deed of Aristotle's very best rule? It is a bit more likely than the coming

---

9 British and American terminology differ here. What Americans call a "billion," the English call a "thousand million." What Americans call a "trillion" the English call a "million million." To avoid misunderstanding, I have in the text written "million million."

into being in deed of the city in speech talked up by Socrates in Plato's "Republic," but not much more.

"Democracy" means rule of the *demos*, the great multitude, the many. Reflection reminds us that they are poorer when it comes to material goods, and examination indicates that they are also poorer when it comes to human excellences. Perhaps there is even a link between "virtue" and "equipment." Perhaps, as Aristotle says, virtue "requires" equipment, but the link is not a sure thing. It would be sensible to acknowledge that equipment is the necessary but not yet the sufficient condition of virtue. "Oligarchy" means – the very word means – "rule of the few." The word in its origins is morally neutral, but it came to be that everyone understood that when we say "the few" without qualification, the qualification tacitly understood is "the few who are merely rich." The few who are good are called just that, "the few good." "Aristocracy" is the name of rule of the few good. This is not a mere judgment open to dispute by those with a different point of view. This is a flat statement of fact. That is what the word itself means. The Greek word for "the best" is οἱ ἄριστοι (*hoi aristoi*). If we add the suffix "cracy," which is a Greek form that means rule, the result is "aristocracy," or rule of the best. It is understood that this does not mean "the best gymnast"; it means "best with a view to ruling," namely possessing more than others the virtues necessary for ruling well. These are, of course, probity, courage, and prudence or practical wisdom. Now the regime that Aristotle labels *politeia* is the one he ranks as the least good of the three good regimes. The one called "democracy" he ranks as the least bad of the three bad regimes. There is no room to quibble here. Oligarchy and democracy, not to mention tyranny, are bad regimes. They are such because those are the names of regimes wherein the rulers rule for their own benefit, not for the benefit of the whole city. Most of the Greek cities in antiquity were either oligarchies or democracies. Some, and Athens was one, alternated between oligarchy and democracy, the rule of one of them giving a measure of respite from the rule of the other. Democracy is less bad than oligarchy for the simple reason that there are more democrats than oligarchs; therefore, the number who suffer from partisan injustice in a democracy is fewer than the number who suffer in an oligarchy. That is certainly praise of democracy, but it is rather faint praise. Democracy is still bad rule. When the oligarchs are in power, they trample the democrats. To use an old British expression, the oligarchs "lord it over" the many. When the democrats are in power, they dispossess the oligarchs, and, worse, they banish them, and they even banish the few who are truly good, the "aristocrats" in the strict and correct meaning of the word. The operative sentiments of the oligarchs are contempt and distrust of the many; the operative sentiments of the many are envy and hatred of the few – even of the few good. These explanations of oligarchy and democracy are explanations of the political faults of partisanship. It is a mistake to view Aristotle as simply an advocate of democracy. The most one can say is that democracy is less bad than oligarchy because its (admittedly defective) criterion of citizenship, namely freedom, is somehow more political (in Aristotle's sense of that term) than is oligarchy's criterion of wealth.

Politeia, the least good of the good regimes is, in Aristotle's ranking, the third of the six. In Aristotle's syllabus for the study of political science, the *politeia* that he names *politeia* fits what he describes as the best rule one can hope for for most cities most of the time. It is a great mistake, however, to jump from that and say that "democracy" is Aristotle's "ideal" or "best" regime.

If "politics is the art of the possible," then in rather poor circumstances even oligarchy, a quite poor regime, may be the best one can hope for, and, in somewhat better circumstances, one can hope for something better than either oligarchy or democracy, and that *politeia* is *politeia*. Aristotle goes on to say that in somewhat more fortunate cities, a somewhat more aristocratic regime is that for which one might hope, but what in the world *is politeia*? Also, what does "aristocracy" add that improves on *politeia*?

Much ink has been spent analyzing the differences between Plato and Aristotle. Surely they differ in some matters that belong to what is called "metaphysics." When it comes to politics, however, it may be that the differences are more apparent than they are actual or consequential. One thing that has to be considered is the sobriety, the pervasive sobriety, of Aristotle. Reading Plato is pleasant. It is not uncommon for students to sit around together in the dorm to read the "Republic" aloud, even sometimes taking parts, as though they were rehearsing a play. I do not believe that I have ever encountered anyone who lit up a cigar and poured himself a brandy before sitting down to savor an Aristotelian text. Reading the "Republic" alone at night can dispel drowsiness and can lead the reader to flights of fancy, stopping at this or that point in the text to daydream a bit, just as though he were joining one of the cast of characters to dispute another. That daydreaming can be productive, but it can also lead to manic excesses. Having read the "Republic," we need the antidote, Aristotle's *Politics*. If we take into account the sobriety of Aristotle, it appears that he does not altogether disagree with Plato. He largely agrees with his description of the parts of the city, but he turns our attention away from the best, and altogether fanciful, city and draws our thoughts to the second best city. It is a city still not easily achieved, but is one that can hold the attention of the more sober students. This can be appreciated by reading a passage of the *Politics* that comes a couple of pages after the two paragraphs excerpted earlier in this chapter. In the later passage he repeats his syllabus for a complete political science but, in the course of the sequel, leaves something out that was essential to the syllabus as first related:

[W]e must distinguish, first, the number of varieties of regimes, if indeed there are several kinds both of democracy and of oligarchy; next, which is most attainable and which the most choiceworthy *after the best regime*, and if there is some other that is aristocratic and finely constituted but fitting for most cities, which it is; next, which of the others is choiceworthy for which [cities] – for perhaps democracy is more necessary for some than oligarchy, and for others the latter more than the former; after these things, in what manner the one wishing to do so should establish these regimes – I mean democracy in each of its kinds and likewise oligarchy. [1289b12– 22, Lord translation. Italics added by present author.]

We have italicized four words in the passage quoted to emphasize that Aristotle, while recognizing in the first accounting of the syllabus the necessity of studying the best regime, pointedly omits that part in his second statement of it. Why? The short answer to our question is "sobriety." The slightly longer answer involves our recognizing the particular audience to whom Aristotle addresses the teaching in the *Politics*.

The clue to understanding *politeia* is the catalog of the several kinds of democracies and the several kinds of oligarchies that Aristotle gives. He offers that catalog not once but twice. He does so from one point of view the first time and from another the second time, and in the process something slips through the cracks. In the first cataloging Aristotle lists five sorts of democracy (1291b29–92a4) and arrays them for us in such a way that we see that they range from the most radically democratic regime (where all citizens are part of the ruling element but they rule without any restraint of law, and, being led by "popular leaders," i.e., demagogues, who rule almost as would a tyrant) to a democracy at the other extreme that is noticeably restrained by law and leans in the direction of oligarchy. Thus the former of these rules, the most extreme democracy, hardly deserves to be called a "regime," just as tyranny is not so much a regime as it is rule by the immediate and immoderate appetites of the tyrant. (In a regime, one can count on certain things from one day to the next. This is what leads us to say that, even in a rather poor regime, any law, even a partisan law that is unjust in many respects, provides some sort and some degree of justice. Under a tyranny or under a radical democracy one cannot guess what the tyrant's whim will be from one minute to the next.) Thus, there is something inherently tyrannical in democracy. The list of five democracies may be laid out by us in such a way as to display that range along a line, from the most moderate to the most extreme. Then Aristotle sets out an array of oligarchies. There are four of them, also ranging from the most moderate to the most radical. These four may be added to the line of democracies. If you put the most radical of the four oligarchies at one end and the most radical of the five democracies at the other, and you show the moderation of the democracies and the moderation of the oligarchies progressing toward the center of the line, you get a sense of relief as though you had found the gentlest and most decent regime. Suddenly, however, you are struck by the asymmetry of the array. Why are there five democracies and only four oligarchies? There might be a simple, sensible answer to this question without immersing ourselves in numerology. Still, it does not hurt to muse a bit.

The first thing you notice is that the most moderate democracy barely qualifies as a democracy. It hardly fits the description of rule by the sheer force of the multitude employed for its own and not the public's good. The second thing you notice is that when Aristotle repeats the array of several kinds of democracies and several kinds of oligarchies, there are only four of each. (See the two listings at 1292b24–93a10 and 1293a13–34, respectively.) It occurs to you that perhaps the least democratic of the five democracies first listed is simply not quite a democracy.

Because five of Aristotle's six regimes have intelligible names and can be explained by statements of qualities and characteristics, whereas *politeia* seems not to have any qualities or characteristics distinct from those of the other five, and because Aristotle cannot even give it a name other than the generic name for all the regimes, namely "regime," "constitution," or *politeia* itself, perhaps there is no such thing, or at least no such distinct thing as *politeia*.

The remainder of Book Four gives a detailed statement of the parts of oligarchies and democracies and of the ways in which their characteristics and presences make up the several subclassifications of these two major sorts. Also included is a discussion of *politeia*, which revolves entirely around a mixing of the attributes of democracy and oligarchy. Aristotle may be described as the discoverer, the inventor, or at least the first chronicler of a regime that one can add to the list of the other five.

The best regime that one can hope for in most cities is the mixture of the two commonplace bad regimes, democracy and oligarchy. It has no characteristics peculiar to itself other than that it is built on a mixture of the characteristics of two others, more or less as the color green is understood to be simply a prismatic blending of two of the three primary colors, namely yellow and blue. We may add here mention of one of the literary characteristics of Plato's "Republic" that we left unmentioned in the previous chapter. The conversation in Books Two through Ten of the "Republic" takes place between Socrates on the one hand and the two brothers, Glaucon and Adeimantus, on the other. If one follows the course of that conversation, noticing both what is said and what is shown, it is clear that the brothers differ from each other in some respects. Glaucon is described as being preeminently endowed with the virtue of courage, and Adeimantus is shown as being most moderate. The text of the "Republic" declares the need in the city in speech for an education that will develop in the auxiliary class, that is, the silver class, the proper balance between those two virtues. As the conversation flows along, one also notices that Socrates deliberately develops moderation in Glaucon and deliberately teases Adeimantus into becoming somewhat more daring. In other words, he draws the two somewhat disparate brothers closer together. We come away with the sobering thought that perhaps the best practical definition of justice is reconciliation, reconciliation of and balance between two necessary but contrary human elements.

Just as in the "Republic," the reconciliation of the contrasting character-istics of Glaucon and Adeimantus had silently proposed to us a limited but practical expectation for a sort of justice, it appears that the union of democracy and oligarchy in Aristotle's *Politics* offers the appealing and also practical prospect of *politeia* displaying a realistic kind of justice. Beneficial consequences appear likely. Moderate property ownership among the many lessens the prospect of class conflict and therewith gives the voice of virtue at least a chance of being heard. In the realm of the practicable politics of the here and the now, reconciliation itself appears as a species of justice. Here, as elsewhere, one may say to the idealist who thinks he knows what true justice is and who wants it right this minute, "You came to the wrong planet." The name Aristotle gave to this political mixture was *politeia*, but this ought to be a clue that it is not, in itself, a distinctive other regime. There are only five distinct types of regime. The two most common are oligarchy and democracy. Both of these are defective regimes, regimes wherein the rulers rule selfishly. The merit in mixing them is that the vices of each tend to offset the vices of the other. It is not so much a good regime as a standoff between two opposing injustices. On the whole, that is not too bad. It was Polybius, a historian who was born about 120 years after Aristotle died, who gave it the name "mixed regime" or "mixed constitution." The mixed regime was the standard adhered to by political philosophers for at least 1,800 years, up to and even including Machiavelli. It persisted even longer in the case of actual regimes. Montesquieu claimed to have discovered the "separation of powers" in his examination of the British constitution in 1740. I think he may have been mistaken. It may be that what he saw in Britain was a decay-ing mixed regime, a regime the mixed character of which has continued to fade even up to the twenty-first century. In contrast, some political scientists and historians have described the work of the American founders as hav-ing established a mixed regime. I believe that this is incorrect. There was nothing to mix at the time of the American Founding. During the colonial period there had been a steady democratization of conditions based on a pervasive and increasing spirit of equality. I think that the true answer is that the "separation of powers" Montesquieu had thought he discerned in British constitutional monarchy is actually what in America largely filled the place of the mixed regime as a means of moderating rulership. So much for Aristotle's *politeia*. What, then, may be said of a somewhat more aristocratic regime?

It would be pleasant, I suppose, if a philosopher never had to talk to anyone but other philosophers. Unfortunately, the number of philosophers is small. Also, there is no secret handshake whereby two philosophers know each other as members of a fellowship. There is also a greater reason why this isolation is undesirable, however. Philosophers could not live in a place where there were no nonphilosophers. Philosophers need, and philosophy itself needs, other sorts of people. Therefore, the better among the other sorts need to be courted and persuaded to be friends and supporters of philosophy.

In the "Republic," Plato had identified three classes of people: one the embodiment of wisdom; the second the embodiment of courage, spiritedness, and honor; and the third everyone else. These were characterized as the gold, the silver, and the bronze and iron classes. There are no such embodiments anywhere, however. In any actual city, the good of the city depends on a realistic appraisal of the human beings. The actual classes are not philosophers, soldiers, and everyone else. The actual classes are the truly thoughtful (in which are included the few who are indeed philosophers), a larger minority who may be designated "the gentlemen," and, third, everyone else.

Those in the "everyone else" class sow and reap the grain; construct, maintain, and repair houses and machines; and do all the other things necessary to the material condition of the city. They are the source of all the material necessities and comforts of the city. Those in the "thoughtful" class perhaps need no explanation. The city would die if the public administration were without some element of prudence. The intermediate class, the "gentlemen" class, does need some description. The possession of moderate wealth certainly is a factor. Such wealth enables the class to avoid exhausting labor and thereby enables it, first of all, to learn good manners. This learning occurs in the household and depends on the young learning from the elders, who teach by example and pronouncements. This general introduction to sound character is the groundwork for later, more formal teaching in ethics, politics, and the liberal arts. Those in this class most fit to do so transcend the class of mere gentlemen and are found to be the more thoughtful ones, including the few philosophers. The remainder learn the necessities of political management and also learn to appreciate and respect their intellectual betters. They may think that the philosophers are a bit odd, but they glimpse their goodness, support them, and are sufficiently successful pupils of them to appreciate the character and necessity of philosophy. By analogy, they study just so much of the flute and the lyre to appreciate them and understand their music without becoming skilled players of the flute or the lyre. The same is true of their appreciation of sculpture and painting; they recognize beauty when they see it.

The studies just mentioned may compendiously be described as "music," that is, the things wrought by the Muses – history, poetry, and the like. The gentlemen cannot replicate Homer, but they can read him, remember him, and live a life fashioned by the moral principles imparted by his teaching. Along with the music, they learn gymnastic. That is, their bodies come to be erect, strong, and more beautiful, and they become agile and able to endure discomfort. The combination of music and gymnastic and its consequences for the souls and bodies of the gentlemen is what is properly called "cultivation" or "culture." The corruption of the word "culture" so that it just means "surroundings," whereby we are able to talk of the culture of youngsters in street gangs or to speak of popular culture, whereby "music critics" appraise cacophony, misleads us. Culture is what the cultivated have, and only a minority can have it. Natural capacities and material conditions are vital underpinnings of it. An important ingredient is long habit and tradition. The habits and opinions of the gentlemen are old habits and opinions. Likewise, their wealth is old wealth, unlike the hurriedly and hungrily amassed wealth of merely industrious and commercial people. The gentlemen are distinguished from the merely well-off. Now is a good time to remind ourselves that when Aristotle spoke in Book One of the several parts of economics, that is, household management, he raised the question of whether the getting of wealth was part of household management, merely ancillary to it, or perhaps altogether separate from it. He concluded that there were in fact two sorts of wealth getting. One sort was indeed part of household management, was natural, and was limited. As we said earlier, no householder in his right mind would feverishly set himself to acquire as many plows as he could lay hands on. The other kind of wealth getting is not part of household management, is not natural, and is not limited. Aristotle says, however, that gentlemen do not discuss such things. Indeed, there was not much in the way of discussion of that kind of economics until John Locke inched into it in 1690. After the cat was out of the bag, Adam Smith came along in 1776, and modern economics arrived, putting its dear mother, household management, away in a nursing home. Oh, well, we have to live our lives, don't we? After all, isn't life about getting things?

The gentlemen are not, as are those of the silver class in the "Republic," just soldiers, tough as nails and contemptuous of injury and death. They do not believe the "myth of autochthony" promulgated in the city in speech, that they had sprung from the very soil of their country making that country virtually their mother, but they are in excellent physical condition; they have learned and taken to themselves the moral and intellectual virtues; they know that their habits and traditions are good; and, loving their country, in a way as much as they love their mothers, they are willing to fight and die for her. Having wealth, they have equipment for heavy infantry and horses for cavalry, and having patriotism and good character, they gladly contribute their wealth to and stand ready to form a part of the armed force of the city when such a force must be called into being. Their gymnastic exercises, their games, and their hunting keep their military excellences ready for the call to action. It is not by accident that the word for "gentleman" in Spanish is *caballero*, that is, "horseman." One French word that is the equivalent of the English word "gentleman" is the straightforward cognate *gentilhomme*. That is translated as meaning gentleman or nobleman, but then the equation of those two is, in a decaying way, the same in English. It must not be overlooked that the French word *chevalier* translates as "knight," which means, of course, a noble rank, or the rank of gentleman, and, translating literally, the word *chevalier* means "horseman." In Italian, the word *cavallo* means "horse," and, drawing from that, *cavalière* means "cavalryman" or "knight" (i.e., someone who can answer the call equipped with a horse), and *cavalièria* means "chivalry" (i.e., conduct becoming a gentleman). Thus, historically, the political rank of gentleman or nobleman fit someone who did, indeed, have a degree of wealth, but the mere economic fact of wealth was not the sufficient condition of that rank. It is the political fact that defines aristocracy, not the economic accompaniment.

It should not surprise us if we noticed that just as there are some true aristocracies and also many political systems that take that name but are not in fact aristocracies, not in fact ruled by the few who are truly good and wise, there are also various sorts of regime called "kingship" that do not live up to the strict definition Aristotle gives. In the latter part of Book Three, Aristotle describes five varieties of kingship, but only the last in his list may truly be called by that name. The whole discourse runs from 1284b35 to 1288a32. The description of the true kingship runs from 1287b36 to 1288a32. Aristotle treats this sort of kingship as, although unlikely, capable of being brought into being in deed. Readers of different and better capacities may surely differ from me, but as I read the description I conclude that although Aristotle's account cannot be refuted, the coming into being in deed of that which he describes as complete and true kingship is little more likely than the coming into being in deed of the city in speech built by Socrates in Plato's "Republic." Still, even the city in speech is presented by Socrates as one that could, in fact, come into being in deed, but its actualization cannot be effected deliberately. It could happen only by chance, sheer chance. It could only come into being if by chance a king, let us say a king with tyrannical powers, or perhaps more likely the son of such a king, took to philosophy. Maybe some time somewhere a philosopher might accidentally become king. It would have to be accidental, because what it takes to seize kingly power, including an occasional murder (which, as Lady Macbeth learned, leaves an indelible spot) cancels out what it takes to be a philosopher. This is harder for us moderns to grasp because modern science, including modern social science, has fairly well convinced us that chance can be mastered. We just need to keep going "back to the drawing board." The progenitor, the founding father, of modern political science was Machiavelli (1469–1527). Long before Doris Day sang "Que será, será," "what will be will be," Machiavelli dismissed as nonsense the notion that our affairs are governed by God and by Fortune. *Fortuna*, he argued, is, after all, a woman, and a strong man knows how to bend her to his will. Even Machiavelli, however, does not go so far as those of us since Francis Bacon (1561–1626) have gone. Machiavelli admits, perhaps grudgingly, that half of our affairs are, indeed, governed by chance. Only a criminally foolish politician is oblivious to the consequences of chance.

In summary, for Aristotle as for Plato, the best city is not at all likely. The second-best city, Aristotle's aristocracy, is more likely – or perhaps one should say, less unlikely. The best one can hope for in most cities is the third-best city, *politeia*, the *politeia* that mixes oligarchy and democracy and pits the vices of one against the vices of the other. That sets the bar rather low. What can make *politeia* more decent and more just is infusing it with a measure of aristocracy.

Aristotle left Athens shortly after the death of Plato, perhaps in part because of some political troubles brewing there. He stayed away for about ten years, from 345 to 335, and then returned to Athens, where he rented lodgings on the outskirts of the city and opened his school, the Lyceum. It throws some light on what we said earlier respecting citizenship to note here that he, being a resident alien, was not allowed to own real property. He understood his circumstances as a tolerated alien, and he was, moreover, always keenly aware of the tenuous position of philosophy in the face of politics. He left Athens a second time shortly after the death of Alexander in 323, it is said, "to keep Athens from sinning against philosophy a second time." This awareness is a clue to reading the *Politics*. It is subphilosophic in character. It is, some say, a collection of the transcripts of lecture notes taken by several of his pupils. It is what it is because it was addressed to his pupils. A few became distinguished in one way or another, but many were mere gentlemen, and Aristotle saw them as such and spoke to them in such a way as to contribute to their education in the liberal arts and to their favorable disposition toward philosophy. The word "philosophy" occurs only three or four times in the *Politics*. All this suggests that we are justified in trying cautiously to read between the lines a bit.[10]

In Plato's *Apology of Socrates* we encountered the problem of philosophy, the enmity that in part defines the relation between philosophy and politics, between the philosopher and the city. The resolution of that enmity is found by Plato's "Republic" to consist in the absolute rule of the philosophers. The vehicle for the solution in the "Republic" was the alliance between philosophers and a second group, the spirited class, the class that we later learn from Aristotle to call "the gentlemen." Make no mistake here. The alliance in the "Republic" is not on equal terms. Philosophy rules absolutely. It never consults the spirited class on what is to be done. The spirited class accepts without question the unrestrained rule of philosophy and, in its military capacity, it not only defends the city from other cities, but also it defends the philosophers from the internal threats that might come from

---

[10] See *Politics* at 1279b, where he mentions "philosophy" once and 1282b where he does so twice. As far as I can tell, these are the only three instances. If there is a fourth instance, I cannot find it. The biographical data in this paragraph are drawn from Martha C. Nussbaum's article, "Aristotle," in Simon Hornblower and Antony Spawforth, eds., *The Oxford Classical Dictionary*, 3rd ed., Oxford, 1996, Oxford University Press.

the third class, the bronze and iron class. The silver class is composed of such strong and fit men and women, and they are so well trained in the arts of war – and they are the only ones in the city who are armed – that it would never cross the mind of someone in the third class to babble some such nonsense as "one man, one vote." The city in speech in the "Republic" is a pipe dream, however.

We are all now liberal democrats. At first glance we do not even like the solution in the "Republic." Sobered by reflection and study, we see the need for such a solution. The sober Aristotle is our second teacher. In a watered-down way, as necessity dictates, the solution in the "Republic" is preserved in the second-best city, Aristotle's aristocracy, and even in measure in his third-best city, *politeia*. If you want more than that, clutch the "Republic" to your breast and catch the next UFO to another planet. Do not misunderstand me. I do not mean in the slightest to speak ill of the "Republic." It is, as we said at the beginning of the last chapter, the greatest book on politics ever written. In fact, the extraterrestrial driving your UFO could not break free from the grip of gravity were it not for the "Republic."

PART III

THE PERMUTATIONS OF POLITICAL PHILOSOPHY

7

Ancient and Medieval Political Philosophy

Again we must pick a word apart. The word "history" is nothing more than the English descendant of the Latin *historia* which, in turn, is the cognate of the Greek word ἱστορία, that is, *historia*. Its meaning in both Greek and Latin is a narrative of "the things." Things happen. The historian takes note of their happening. History is not the things themselves, nor, with one possible exception, did anyone in the West prior to the eighteenth century see any rational system to the sequence of those things. This or that written or reported history has some meaning, and surely one historical event alters the landscape such that prudent men can make reasonable estimates of other events which might follow, but, absent reference to divine providence, the overall sequence of things was not thought to be discernible. Things happen. That is all. History is the inquiry into or the narrative about things that have happened. At some point in time the word "history" came to be used to delineate the sequence. History became reified. It became itself a thing. Of all the strange things imaginable, it came to pass that, as in the title of a book by Hegel (1770–1831), we find someone speaking of the *Philosophy of History*. If, as we said, philosophy is the pursuit of the truth about things, then the "philosophy of history" would mean the discovery of the truth about that sequence. Hegel states it straightforwardly this way: "the history of the world, therefore, presents us with a rational process."[1] To say when this notion of history as a thing itself, as a process, rather than as an inquiry into or narrative of things, came into being is itself a historical question. It will be most convenient to defer that question for yet two more chapters.

Speaking of the "history of philosophy" and so, of the history of political philosophy, is, of course, different from speaking of the philosophy of history. Whereas one may doubt that history has "meaning," there is no doubt

---

[1] G. W. F. Hegel, *The Philosophy of History*, J. Sibree, tr., New York, 1956, Dover Publications, p. 9.

at all that there can and must be some inquiry into and narrative of the several political philosophers. The problem is that the notion that there is a "historical process," when applied to the things of philosophy, may lead us astray. The problem of the philosophy of history thereby intertwines with the problem of the history of philosophy.

History and philosophy as activities of the mind are complementary. Philosophy deals with general propositions. It pursues universal truths. It is in principle altogether uninterested in particulars. It mentions particulars only as examples. One can say, for example, that energy is translated from one form to another without ever paying the slightest heed to how my house is lighted, or one can say that "democracy is a deviant form of *politeia*" without ever mentioning Athens or any other particular *polis* by name. History as a narrative of or inquiry into the things, on the contrary, is entirely composed of proper names, dates, and incidents – that is, of particulars. There are no universals in it. It is one thing to counsel, as General George S. Patton (1885–1945) did, that military officers should read a lot of history. There are indeed lessons to be learned from the experiences of our predecessors. The reason for this is that historical incidents are particulars and reflecting on them may shed light on universals, say, successful cavalry tactics. Rather, it is not the incidents that shed light; it is the thoughtful student's reflection on the universals illustrated by the incidents. It is another thing altogether to believe that history is "going some place" and that its route and destination can be figured out. Certainly it is true that one can discern clusters of events and trends that enable prudent statesmen to anticipate events yet to occur, but one does that only to step in and influence those events. Why else study them? To imagine a historical process that has about it an inevitability is to align oneself with a kind of fatalism. Along with a number of other nonsciences that arose in the twentieth century, there began to be departments of "futurology" in some American universities, as though one could study the history of that which had not yet occurred.

The doctrine of historical inevitability leads to a strange bundle of illusions. If we discover the "process" of history, we can study not only the past, but the future. We can examine something that has not yet come to be. Our modeling in science or social science leads us to a conclusion. That conclusion is some sort of possibility – but then, almost anything is possible. For some unfathomable reason we call our conclusions the "truth." Without having yet seen the future, we "know" it. We are like gods! We are omniscient. Yet we are not omnipotent. So far from being omnipotent, we are unable to influence the future. We are mere spectators. We can watch the historical process unfold and predict the future, but the future we predict is inevitable. *Que será será.* What will be will be. Like children rather than like gods, all we can do is giggle nervously. Recognizing our impotence, our inability to have any effect on the outcome of the historical process, because of the ultimate inevitability of things, it occurs to us that there is no need to bother about laws, restraints, or obligations. "The world is," as Macbeth said, on hearing of the death of Lady Macbeth, "a tale told by an idiot, full of sound and fury, signifying nothing." Paradoxically, finding the meaning of history is finding the meaninglessness of history. We cannot help but see, then, that Socrates was a fool to insist on obeying the law. Our soundest counsel is to do, in language coined in the past century, "whatever turns you on." The whole of one's life becomes a tiresome sequence of frivolities. The unspoken assumption that underlay the invention within popular usage in the 1960s of the neologism "lifestyle" is that the question as to how people should live is a matter of mere fashion, that life itself is a tiresome sequence of trivialities, and so to do something "positively outrageous" is to do something interesting and so, if only evanescently, praiseworthy.

It is possible to become a watered-down Hegelian, a watered-down Marxian, or a watered-down Freudian without ever having read a page of Hegel, Marx, or Freud. It is possible to be affected by an intellectual tendency that pervades the atmosphere without going instantly to the extremes just suggested. That does not mean that we are safe from all the bad effects of those tendencies. To say that there is a history of political philosophy might mean only that political philosophy was pursued by philosophers, and philosopher are human beings, and so they were born and then died, and some lived and died after others. One might as well consider them in the order in which they lived – although we should not preclude doing so in some other order. As far as historical order is concerned, it makes perfect sense to suppose that a philosopher in the tenth century A.D. might have been aware of and understood something a philosopher fourteen centuries earlier had written. It is convenient, but not necessary, to consider them in that order. The chief benefit is that doing so enables us to understand the allusions that one philosopher makes to a philosopher who has gone before. This is true of writers of all kinds. For example, it does not take a learned person to guess that a book by Robert Kagan titled *The Return of History and the End of Dreams*, published in 2008, is some sort of answer to a book by Francis Fukuyama titled *The End of History and the Last Man*, published in 1993. Like Adam, who perhaps had no navel, or like the first citizens of a city to whom Aristotle refers us, there were philosophers who had nothing to go on. They had to break the ground in the first instance. So surfeited are we with history and with the historical process that we think of Plato as "a Greek." This obscures from us the fact that Plato, and Socrates before him, rose altogether above Greekness. To believe otherwise is to see them as products of their culture, which means that they were no better than you and I are. Are we not products of our culture? Are not all cultures equal? Just as modern Americanness thinks through me, so ancient Greekness thought through Plato. We do not need to take Plato seriously. All we need to do is to browse Greekness. Actually, nobody ever thinks. There are thoughts but no thinkers. It is "the times" that exude thoughts.

It was not Plato but Greekness that did the thinking, and Plato was merely its instrument, its puppet. Thinking, in fact, is not possible. Although this notion incubated over time, it was in the middle of the nineteenth century that Marx and his collaborator Engels asserted that philosophy itself was not truly possible, that what we had called philosophy was nothing more than a "superstructure" put forth by the particular underlying material structures of "the times."

All this is comforting. Even though I have never thought through the nature of opinion, or anything else for that matter, I am just as much entitled to my opinion as Aristotle is. Aristotle "felt" one thing. I "feel" another. Why should I care what he thought or felt – or what you feel or think? Each of us is entitled to our own opinion, but none of us needs pay the slightest attention to anyone else. What is more, there can be no such thing as philosophy. There can be, at best, only a wan, historical cultural anthropology, but because every second in the passing of time has its own zeitgeist, its own "spirit of the time," its own thinkerless thoughts, we have to impose arbitrary boundaries for the eras or ages to which we arbitrarily ascribe some defined spirit or culture. We must never admit the arbitrariness of our studies, for then we would be out of our academic, political, or journalistic job. There is no tenure for those not on the "cutting edge" of fashionable thought, but perhaps there is a starting point for a road back from this intellectual dead end. We are, after all, compelled to admit that there are a few timeless things like eating and being praised. All of us must eat and most of us are glad of praise. These two things do not say much about human nature, but they at least affirm that there is a human nature, a nature which cannot be defined by the times.

What if Plato actually thought?

Our salvation begins with acknowledgment that Plato's "Republic" is a lot more interesting than a Greyhound bus schedule. Building on this introspective insight, perhaps we can for ourselves resurrect philosophy. Our first step is to gird ourselves with a healthy skepticism about the history of political philosophy. We have to take a given philosopher seriously. We have to suppose that he was serious himself, that he meant something by what he wrote, and that it was he, striving to rise above his culture, rather than the culture, who did the thinking. The truly interesting thing about his culture is that that is what he had to confront while trying to get to the bottom of things. No doubt we too must try to understand the culture in which he strove – no easy task, by the way – not, however, to dismiss his thought as attributable to that culture (not, i.e., as we learned – also in the 1960s – to speak to and so to dismiss each other by saying "I see where you're coming from"), but the better to approach an understanding of his thought. The contrary view, the view that cultures are ventriloquists and that those once called philosophers were really nothing but puppets cannot, after reflection, be held. It cannot be held because it is self-canceling. If they could not think, then we cannot think. If we cannot think, then it must be because our culture is the ventriloquist and we are the puppets. To think that there were thoughts but no thinkers is not to think that there were thoughts but no thinkers, for to think that is to think that one cannot think. Perhaps the sensible thing is to eat, drink, and make merry.

In the middle of the twentieth century, it was commonplace for college political science departments to require all of their majors to take a two-semester sequence in the history of political theory. Textbooks about the history of political theory were written to supply those courses. One that was in wide use was George H. Sabine's *A History of Political Theory* (New York, 1937, Holt). The first paragraph of the Preface illustrates this acceptance of the notion that not thinkers but "the times" produce thoughts. In consulting those textbooks, you need to confront each one with the question whether it treats the philosophers examined as philosophers or as culture-puppets. Perhaps it will appear that the authors of such books are the only true puppets.

One text must be mentioned because of its steadfast avoidance of that self-cancellation. In 1963 Leo Strauss and Joseph Cropsey edited a volume called *History of Political Philosophy*, which we have already mentioned. Among the several merits of the book is the fact that each philosopher is examined by an author who, with the requisite language skills in Latin, Greek, German, French, Hebrew, Arabic, or Italian, as the case may be, had spent a long period of study and had devoted especial effort to understanding the particular philosopher about whom he wrote. Another is the fact that all the contributors are agreed that the philosophers need to be taken seriously and not dismissed as products of their times. The self-contradiction in the view that all thought is a product of its times is the unexamined notion that we, now, even though products of our time, can understand the several times that purportedly spoke through those products. The several contributors to the Strauss-Cropsey *History* are also agreed in that they do not presuppose that modern political philosophy is the inevitable evolution of an incremental stream of the history of political philosophy. Thus they see that the same words do not necessarily say the same things in the works of two or more philosophers, because different philosophers, actually thinking, are "up to" different things. This is the same as to say that philosophers, rather than being products of their times, are critics of those times.

Two examples of failure to try to understand philosophers as they understood themselves are worth noting here, both having to do with Thomas Hobbes (1588–1679). Because Hobbes speaks a good deal about natural rights and frequently about the laws of nature it is sometimes said that he is simply a continuation of the natural law tradition. These commentators do not notice that there is a difference between the phrase "natural right" and the phrase "natural law," and there is a stark difference between the phrase "natural rights" and either of the former. The correction of this error is easily begun by crediting Hobbes with seriousness when he asserts that, in a condition of mere nature, nothing is just or unjust – that is, there is no natural justice.[2] Hobbes is apparently the originator of the modern notion of natural rights. His view is in stark contrast with the ancient natural right view and of its largely Christian offshoot, the notion of "natural law." For a dozen reasons this is often overlooked. A second assertion fraught with problems is that which holds Hobbes to be a devout Christian because he quotes the Bible a lot. The reader needs to read slowly and carefully and note the context of those quotations and the use to which they are put and also to notice other passages which easily might lead us to characterize Hobbes as an atheist. Without meaning to charge Hobbes with the worst crimes, we need only remind ourselves that the Devil himself "can cite scripture."[3]

If all of this sounds drearily like a sermon, summarize it as follows: Do not think you are so wise; do not suppose that you are wiser than those whose works you read because you came later in the stream of history. Think it possible that there is a good reason Plato's writings are still in print, and read him and the others with an open mind. That sounds easy, but it is not.

If philosophers write in response to or at least in awareness of the times, different times will elicit different responses. Indeed, even the same philosopher may say different things to different readers. This is not so difficult to fathom as it appears. If your adolescent son stays out late one evening, you will speak to him about the dangers of bad habits, and you will speak in a certain way. If a fellow levels a pistol at you and demands your money, you are not likely to speak to him at all of bad habits, and, if you venture to do so, you will surely not replicate the diction or the tone of your admonition to your son.

Traditionally, there have been three eras or ages of political philosophy that the writers discuss: ancient, medieval, and modern. Now there has come to be a fourth one, called "postmodern." We can satisfy the needs addressed by this and the next two chapters by briefly characterizing each of these so as to assist in the entry into the study of the philosophers identified with those eras. Hold on! Let us be clear. This is not because we have forgotten what was just said and are prisoners of the notion that the so-called thinkers were merely mouthpieces for those times. Quite the contrary. It is because the truly serious thinker bucks the times and we cannot enter into his thinking unless we come to grips with the established opinions of an historical period so that we can see how the serious thinker goes about bucking his particular times. We need to see "what he is up to."

Ancient Political Philosophy

The origin of political philosophy is in the person of Socrates. He appears to have been a philosopher before he became a political philosopher. That can

---

[2] Hobbes, *Leviathan* (1651), the 13th paragraph of chapter 13.
[3] Shakespeare, *The Merchant of Venice*, I, iii, 99.

mean only one thing: He was at first a natural philosopher, a physiologist. It seems that he was driven to turn his attention to political things because of the threat posed by political life to philosophy. Political philosophy then is in one respect philosophy in the act of self-defense. The remarkable things about the earliest philosophers are their intrepidity and their originality. It may be that the only way really to understand philosophy is to encounter the first practitioners before philosophy becomes encrusted with a thousand names, a hundred thousand books, and half a million academics, many of whom bring to mind those lawyers who commit barratry or champerty and those who are "ambulance chasers." The philosophers who are akin to our mention of such lawyers were described by the Platonic Socrates in the course of the defense of his assertion in the "Republic" that genuine philosophers should be kings. He describes the impostors thus:

Do you suppose . . . that they are any different to see than a little, bald-headed worker in bronze who has gotten some silver, and, newly released from bonds, just washed in a bathhouse, wearing a new-made cloak and got up like a bridegroom, is about to marry his master's daughter. ("Republic," 495e, Bloom translation)

Just as there were those of the silver class, who, caught up in their attachment to honor, usurped the place of the gold class in Book Eight of the "Republic," so there are in every age and in every calling those who yearn for the appearances without due concern for the substance, and so there are those who pursue philosophy for the sake of the honor attached to it and who, like that "little, bald-headed worker in bronze," cling to the appearances. It is for this reason, above all others, that the works known as "the classics" – those now fashionably dismissed as merely the works of "dead, white males" – are the works one most needs to read, and it is because they are so fresh in their breaking of new ground that it is almost, but not quite, fair to speak of all later works as mere footnotes to the originals.

Because brief commentaries on Aristotle's *Politics* and Plato's "Republic" were offered in Chapters Three, Five, and Six, a brief bibliography will serve here as a general tally of classical political philosophy. The thirty-four Platonic dialogues together constitute a comprehensive canvass of the whole of philosophy and a far-reaching critique of philosophers. Among these are the *Meno*, which raises the question whether virtue can be taught, and the *Timaeus* and the *Critias* on physics. The dialogues of most immediate interest to the student of political philosophy are three, even the titles of which identify them as such, the "Republic," the *Laws*, and the *Statesman*, as well as the tetralogy covering the trial and death of Socrates, the *Euthyphro*, the *Apology*, the *Crito*, and the *Phaedo*. Next would come the *Gorgias*, which examines public (i.e., deliberative and forensic) rhetoric; the *Phaedrus*, which examines private (i.e., erotic) rhetoric; and the *Symposium*, covering *eros* itself. Because Plato makes Socrates speak in the "Republic" of the "old quarrel between philosophy and poetry" (607b–08b), one should read the short dialogue *Ion*, wherein Socrates converses with a rhapsode regarding poetic inspiration. Finally, because war is an inevitable part of political life, one might read the *Laches*, a conversation with some generals on generalship.[4]

Indispensable are the two great historians, Herodotus on the Persian Wars and Thucydides on the Peloponnesian War.

Of the works by Xenophon, those most necessary as adjuncts to Plato are the *Cyropaedia* (i.e., the *Education of Cyrus*), the *Memorabilia*, the *Apology*, the *Symposium*, and the *Hiero*.

In his comprehensive reach and his encyclopedic detail, Aristotle rivals Plato. He wrote works on metaphysics, physics, the elements of philosophic inquiry, poetry, rhetoric, ethics, and politics. Those most necessary to the student confronting political philosophy are the *Rhetoric*, the *Nicomachean Ethics*, and the *Politics*.

Reading modern, English literature is barren if one cannot follow the allusions to the Bible and to Shakespeare, to mention only the two sources on which greatest reliance is placed. In the same way, it is difficult to read the classical political philosophers without some familiarity with the poetic sources to which they allude. Aesop's *Fables*, some of which have been traced to sources older than Aesop, are helpful. Next come Homer's *Iliad* and *Odyssey* and Hesiod's *Theogony* and *Works and Days*. No doubt it would help to know all the tragedies and all the lyric poets, but we especially mention two comedies by Aristophanes here because of the immediate connection one of them has with Socrates, and both of which serve as foils for Plato. These are, as befits comedy, coarse and racy. Bowdlerized translations should be avoided. They take all the fun and half the meaning out of the plays. The *Clouds* should be read as a preface to Plato's *Apology of Socrates* and the *Ecclesiazusae*, that is, *The Assembly of Women*, as a preface to the "Republic."

Of the Latin authors, the one most necessary is Cicero (106–43 B.C.). Cicero was a philosopher, a statesman, and an orator. To appreciate his range, a mere quantitative comparison is helpful. The works of Plato take up twelve volumes in the Loeb Classical Library series. The works of Aristotle take up twenty-two volumes in that series. The works of Cicero take up twenty-nine volumes. When we consider that, with the possible exception of one volume, none of the Cicero volumes can be considered as falling within

---

[4] It is worthwhile to mention here that the English word "strategy" is a form of the Greek word *strategos*, which is translated into English as "general." This explains why it grates on some ears to hear someone speak glibly of "marketing strategy." People selling breakfast cereals may lie, but so far there is no record of any of them killing a competitor. The "business" of generals is to lead soldiers to kill other soldiers. Strategy is the thoughtful pursuit of that end through the conceiving of comprehensive battlefield, territorial, and circumstantial aims.

natural philosophy, one might say that there is more than twice as much of Cicero than of Aristotle and a lot more than twice as much than of Plato that may be said to touch on or relate to political philosophy. Perhaps one who aspires to be a classicist should read all his works. The most that we are competent to recommend are *De Re Publica* and *De Legibus* (both of which come down to us incomplete). It would also be good to read *De Officiis* (i.e., *Of Duties*) and at least to browse the *Tusculan Disputations*.

I know of almost no one who has grasped and maintained a thorough understanding of all the above-mentioned works, so we all need to rely on reference works. Two that should be at the top of a student's list are the *Oxford Classical Dictionary* and *Everyman's Classical Atlas*.

Medieval Political Philosophy

What about the Stoics? No doubt some will criticize this book for mentioning only Plato, Aristotle, Xenophon, Herodotus, Thucydides, Cicero, and a few poets in the foregoing section on ancient political philosophy. We must at least deflect that criticism here. But for one thing, it might be possible to leave out of account not only those who followed for a few hundred years in the train of Plato and Aristotle but also the whole range of medieval thought, thereby reducing our classification simply to "Ancients" and "Moderns." Thus, disregarding not only the Stoics and all the others in the three hundred years after Aristotle, it would almost be possible to speak of classical political philosophy as remaining intact for nearly two thousand years, from the midpoint in the life of Socrates until the midpoint in the life of Machiavelli. It would be possible to speak of Plato and Aristotle as the whole ground of political philosophy for that two-thousand-year period and so to brush aside all the academics, commentators, embellishers, and deviators as of less than secondary importance. But for that one thing it could readily be argued that medieval philosophy does not stray from the Platonic-Aristotelian pattern. That one thing, however, is divine revelation and the religions established in its light. That is a large "but."

Even accounting for revealed religion, the changes to philosophy seem on the surface to be few: The measured acceptance of the pagan classics joined to an attempt at accommodation of them to the demands of revealed religion and a change of focus from the *polis* as the irreducible object of political study to the nation and the empire. It will come as no surprise, however, that others considering the same facts weigh them differently from the way we weigh them here. Harry Austryn Wolfson (1887–1974), for example, says this:

Taken altogether [the] principles of medieval philosophy constitute a radical departure from ancient pagan Greek philosophy – they radically change its theory of knowledge, by introducing into it a new source of knowledge; they radically change its metaphysics, by introducing a new conception into the nature and causality of God, who is the main subject of metaphysics; they radically change its physics, by introducing a new conception into the working of its laws; they radically change its ethics by introducing a new source of morality.[5]

Still, whatever the difference in weight attributed, there is agreement between what Wolfson says here and what we just said, namely, that the source of the principal difference is revelation. This leaves the main problem as one of the contrast between unassisted human reason and the interposition of the revealed word of God.

If revealed religion had not appeared and spread, the dissemination of philosophy to distant places would perhaps have occurred at a slower pace. More importantly, philosophy itself would have needed to confront only one of the two changes that we notice in medieval philosophy. Even that one, namely the application of the word "political" to whole nations and to empires, might not have been necessary in the absence of revealed religion. Philosophy concerns itself with universals. It may have, as in our view, originated in Greece, but it is not just for Greeks nor is it just about Greek things. In the absence of revealed religion, its spread is hindered only by the varying antipathies to it that might be found in different polities and their different views of things (especially, no doubt, their views of the gods) and by the absence of any imperialistic or proselytizing tendencies in philosophy itself. Because philosophy is addressed to a small minority and religion addresses all souls, it is not likely that philosophy would spread far and wide and rapidly without the motive force of its confrontation with revealed religion. We can here offer only the summarization that, prior to the radical break wrought by Machiavelli, the only determining factor in the historical modification of philosophy was the need to accommodate it to the new religion.

At this point, a compendious paragraph or two of sheer narrative history will be useful.

In 500 B.C., the Persian Empire under Darius the Great (Darius I, 558–486 B.C.; king, 521–486 B.C.) extended from northern Libya and Egypt and from the eastern reaches of Greece through Anatolia and Mesopotamia to the western third of present-day India and from the Black Sea on the north to the Indian Ocean on the South. In 499 B.C., Hellenic cities along the western coast of Anatolia and the islands along that coast rebelled against the Persian rule, and an alliance of cities on the Greek mainland gave their support to those rebellious cities, so the Persian Wars began. The wars continued for twenty years, and by 479 B.C. the Persians, who had reached to the heart of Greece, were pushed back by the alliance of Greek cities. A

---

[5] Harry Austryn Wolfson, *From Philo to Spinoza: Two Studies in Religious Philosophy*, New York, 1977, Behrman House, p. 34. I am indebted to Rabbi Tovah Stevens for directing my attention to Wolfson.

new international balance then persisted for more than a hundred years. Alexander III of Macedon (356–323 B.C.) succeeded his father, Philip II, as king in 336 B.C., and in the thirteen years between his ascension and his death he conquered nearly the whole of the Persian Empire. Because of the intellectual achievements of the Athenians as well as of the Ionian Greeks and those in southern Italy, there had developed beginning in the fifth, if not already in the sixth, century B.C. a growing hegemony of Greek learning and language over southeastern Europe and the western parts of Anatolia. The establishment of Alexander's empire, which reached Egypt and conquered in 331 B.C. a town he renamed Alexandria, strengthened and extended that Hellenization. On the death of Alexander in 323 B.C., his empire was divided among his three chief generals. Seleucus took the rule from Syria to Persia. Antigonus assumed the rule of Macedonia, Greece proper, and parts of Anatolia. Ptolemy assumed rule over Egypt and Libya and established the Ptolemaic dynasty. What historians are wont to call the "Hellenistic Period" of history is marked as beginning with the death of Alexander in 323 B.C. and ending with the death of Cleopatra, the last Ptolemy monarch, the last Pharaoh, in 30 B.C.

Aristotle died in 322 B.C. Some sixteen years later, in 306 B.C., Ptolemy began construction of a library at Alexandria which was then stocked with books from everywhere, many from Greece and from those places where Greek was the dominant intellectual language. It became the greatest library in the whole world, headed by chief librarians who were themselves noted scholars, and it became the haven of scholars from all over. The library building was destroyed in A.D. 642 by Muslim Arabs in their march across the north of Africa. Different accounts can be found of what may have happened to the million or so books (i.e., scrolls) in the library. One suggestion is that perhaps the books were shipped off to libraries in Baghdad, Aleppo, and Damascus. Surely much of classical learning was preserved by Muslim civilization over the centuries, and it has been suggested that the encounter with that great learning by Europeans was a collateral effect of the Crusades and, furthermore, that the rediscovery led to the Renaissance of classical learning in Christian Europe.[6] At the beginning of the present millennium, the library at Alexandria was rebuilt; behind the rebuilding was the expressed intention of making it once again the greatest library in the world. In becoming so it will compete in consequence with the British Library and the Library of Congress of the United States.

At the beginning of 2007 the population of the world was estimated to be about 6.6 billion. A rough calculation suggests that 4.6 billion were, at least nominally, Jews, Christians, or Muslims. These 4.6 billion people have as

---

[6] See the magazine *Archaeology Odyssey*, vol. 6, no. 4, July/August 2003, p. 24 at p. 29. (In 2006, *Archaeology Odyssey* was merged for economic reasons with its sister magazine, *Biblical Archaeology Odyssey*.)

their religious source the *Torah*, the *Torah* and the *Gospels*, or the *Torah*, the *Gospels*, and the *Qu'ran*. Perhaps. 1.2 billion more are Hindus and Buddhists. The 4.6 billion souls found in the following of the patriarch Abraham constituted therefore about seven-tenths of the human population, and the proportion continues with the growth of the world's population. Within the remaining two billion there may be some whose religions pose the same problems of accommodation for philosophy that are posed by Judaism, Christianity, and Islam. The author's acquaintance with the tenets of the 1.2 billion adherents of Hinduism and Buddhism is so minimal that it does not permit him to entertain the question whether such a problem troubles them. Simply calculated, if we think only of Jews, Christians, and Muslims, about two-thirds of present humanity then are those whose religions pose significant problems for classical political philosophy.

Risking a charge of presumptuousness, we are compelled here to offer the sketchiest account of those three religions. If we attempt to follow the doctrine of traditional adherents of those religions, we may be guilty of ignorance but we shall be acquitted of any charge of impiety because we are merely trying to give our account with a sort of reportorial simplicity that is not opinionated and that lacks all embellishment. Histories have beginnings, and beginnings have dates attached to them. Modern physical science estimates the age of the earth to be about 4.5 billions of years, and the presence of humans on earth in what, in Darwin's scheme of things, is regarded as his present state of development, to have run a bit more than three million years. Biblical accounts mark the earth as much younger and offer a precise date for its origin and for the appearance of man. According to calculations stemming from the *Torah*, God created the heavens, the earth, and all the creatures on it 5,760 years before what in common usage is now called the year 2000.[7] Accepting the account of time by physical scientists or that by Biblical scholars involves in either case an act of faith. Accepting the Biblical account *arguendo* as a means of beginning this part of our study, we are still left with the need for scholarship to assign particular years for the life of Abraham. The *Torah* states that God formed Adam out of dust (*Gen.* 2:7) and gives accounts of the generations leading up to Noah who, having been forewarned by God, built an ark and, with his sons Ham, Shem, and Japheth, and the wives of these four, along with pairs of all the animals, embarked in it to ride out the forty days and forty nights of rain that flooded the earth and killed all those not in the ark (except, of course, we suppose, for the creatures whose home is in the seas) as a punishment for all the wrongdoings of man. Thus the whole present population of the earth is understood to be constituted of descendants

---

[7] Before the arrival of intercultural sensitivity this year would have been called, by Christians and by many others in predominantly Christian countries, "A.D. 2000," that is, the "2000th Year of Our Lord."

of those three couples who sailed in the ark with Noah and survived the flood.

The genealogies presented in the *Torah* at first report a life span of some 900 years (*Gen.* ch. 9), for later generations 400 years, and then 200 years (*Gen.* ch. 11). We are told that Terah begat Abram (*Gen.* 11:26) and that Abram took Sarai to wife (*Gen.* 11:29). In due course God tells Abram that thenceforth he will be called Abraham (*Gen.* 17:5) and Sarai will be called Sarah (*Gen.* 17:15). Sarah had been barren, but, even though she and Abraham were both advanced in age (Abraham was 99 and Sarah 90 [*Gen.* 17:17; this would have been about 1810 B.C.]), God promises that she will have the child much desired by the two. Upon hearing this from God, Abraham laughs and silently doubts God, but he is not punished for his doubt or for his levity. Sarah does conceive and bears a son, Isaac. When Isaac had grown to be a young boy, God tests Abraham by ordering him to sacrifice Isaac, his only son. Abraham dutifully prepares to do so. At the last moment, God stays Abraham's hand and tells him not to sacrifice Isaac (*Gen.* 22:12). Although the accepted founding of the Jews as a nation is the leading of them out of captivity by the Prophet Moses and then the Covenant God makes with them through Moses at Sinai five hundred years after Abraham, it is at the moment of Abraham's unquestioning obedience to the word of God that the ground of Judaism is laid. Whatever may be tallied up as the six, eight, or thirteen fundamental principles of Judaism, this one thing, absolute obedience on the part of Abraham to the revealed word of the one God, is the signal identifying mark of the religions that begin with Abraham, that is, of Judaism, and ultimately of Christianity, and then of Islam. This event occurs at that point where the great difficulty of pinpointing the dates of the early genealogies in the *Torah* ends and there begins a time which can be subjected to historical research, which research, even without divine guidance, can give a good approximation of the date of a Biblical event. The moment when these three great religions have their origin is, then, a moment that is historically intelligible. God had indeed spoken even to the first humans, Adam and Eve, and had punished them both (along with the serpent that had beguiled Eve) for violating his express commandment, and there had been a covenant of God with Noah (*Gen.* 6:18), but it is the covenant with Abraham that introduces an established and cumulative body of revealed truths and divine law, and therefore a religion that adheres to that truth and that law and a liturgy for the worship of their Author.

The revealed word of God authoritatively records beginnings, explains beings, defines truth, and orders our lives. It would seem that the "theory of knowledge," the "metaphysics," the "physics," and the "ethics" mentioned by Wolfson do not merely reorient philosophy as Wolfson tells us. What had been the search for truth is reduced to a deductive process from truths that are freely given by God's grace. Philosophy, it would seem, is out of a job.

The Hebrew language, like any other, is subject to having the meaning of its words confused over time. Such is the case with the word *goy* (plural: *goyim*), which is the equivalent of the Latin *gens* and the Greek *ethnos*.[8] This equivalency can be traced by the translations from the Hebrew Old Testament, the Greek New Testament (and the Greek translation of the Old Testament, the *Septuagint*), and the Latin translation of both the Old and New Testaments (*the Vulgate*) into the English word "nation" (or "people"). To begin with, the word *goy* is used in the Old Testament to refer to any people, including "this" people, the Jews. By the second book of the *Torah*, *Exodus*, this people calls itself by its proper name, "Israel" or "the Jews." Over time, common usage tends to forget the core meaning of the common noun *goy*, and the word tends to be confined to usage as a reference to *other goyim*. Hence it is that American Jews now characteristically use the word *goyim* (or, from the Latin, "gentiles") as though its meaning were simply "the others," those peoples other than the Jews.

Watching with care this language usage, we can make sense of the observation that at first the covenant that God makes with Abraham and "his seed" is naturally understood to be a covenant made with that people, the chosen people. A profound alteration occurs in that re-formation of Judaism wrought by Jesus. Although his followers are, in due course, properly so called, Jesus himself is not a Christian. He tells his listeners in the Sermon on the Mount, "Think not that I am come to destroy the law, or the prophets; I am not come to destroy but to fulfill"(*Matt.* 5:17). He sees himself, it seems, not as a founder of a new religion but as one who corrects what are then explained as errors that the priests have committed in their stewardship of the existing religion – in their stewardship of the law. It appears as a consequence of that re-formation that the followers of Jesus are able to understand their religion as one that can be spread to other nations, other peoples, other *goyim* or gentiles. Hence it is that St. Paul comes to be known as "the Apostle to the Gentiles." I do not know to what extent Jews had hitherto proselytized, but with Christianity there comes into being a positive duty to do so. It is the commission, the mission, of Christians to spread "the Word." If it were not for that spreading in modified form the religion of Abraham to the corners of the earth, first by Christianity and then differently by Islam, the tension between religion and philosophy might have been confined to a few people in a small space, and that tension might still, even today, escape widespread notice.

Abram's wife Sarai had a maidservant named Hagar. About fourteen years before God by His grace enabled the ninety-year-old Sarah to conceive, she, about at the age of seventy-six (then being called Sarai), had given Hagar

---

[8] There is a Latin cognate of the Greek *ethnos*, but in the sense in which the English adjective "ethnic" descends from the Greek noun *ethnos*, so to the same effect does the English adjective "gentile" descend from the Latin *gens*.

to Abram as a surrogate mother so that his seed might continue.⁹ Hagar did conceive, and when she knew that she had done so, "her mistress was lowered in her esteem." Sarai was therefore angry with Hagar, so Abram told Sarai to do as she pleased with her. She treated her harshly, and Hagar ran away. An angel of the Lord intercepted her and instructed her to return to Sarai and submit to her. Then he told her that she would bear a son and he instructed her thus:

You shall call him Ishmael, for the Lord has paid heed to your suffering. He shall be a wild ass of a man; his hand against everyone, and everyone's hand against him.¹⁰

Thus, Ishmael, the son of Abram and Hagar, was about fourteen when Isaac, the son of Abraham and Sarah, was born, but the primacy of Isaac over the older Ishmael was demanded by Sarah and granted by Abraham.

In A.D. 570, in Mecca in the Arabian peninsula, Mohammed was born a member of the Koreish tribe, which traced its lineage to Ishmael. At about the age of forty Mohammed proclaimed himself a prophet and founded a new religion, which he named Islam, which is Arabic for "submission to God." This, too, presents itself as a continuation and correction of what had gone before. At first the religion was propagated by persuasion, and it soon had followers across the Red Sea in Ethiopia. The early years saw Islam pitted against heavy odds and strong resistance from the several traditional religions of Arabia, and especially from Mohammed's kindred in the Koreish tribe in Mecca, and about the time he was fifty-two, he and some adherents had to flee Mecca. He and a faithful companion, Abu Bekr, in fact fled by night and traveled secretly to Medina. That flight is known as the Hejira, and the year of the Hejira – A.D. 622 by the Christian calendar – is acknowledged by Muslims as the first year by their reckoning. The Muslim calendar begins with that moment, so that the year calculated as A.D. 2000 by Christians is approximately the year 1421 in the Muslim calendar. (That this "doesn't add up" results from the fact that the Muslim calendar measures lunar years as contrasted with the solar years of the Julian and then the Gregorian calendars.) Although it began with persuasion, the eventual spread of Islam across the globe was more the result not of persuasion but of the sword. Its spread in its first century was breathtaking. Before the end of that first century, it had enveloped Africa north of the Sahara and much of Spain. By the thirteenth century, although having lost some ground in Spain, it

---

⁹ This is a matter of the deepest concern. Many things in modern life lead us to suppress consideration of what may be the deepest desire, the desire – nay, the aching need – of a man to leave something of himself in his wake. Reading of Sarai's awareness of and deference to this need in Abram, and reading of a similar reflection on the part of Lot's daughters (see *Gen.* 19:30–36) opens the mind to this need, a need which has now become almost improper to mention in polite company. I am indebted to Rabbi Tovah Stevens for getting the terminology right.

¹⁰ *Gen.* 16:11–12. Jewish Publication Society translation of the *Torah*.

spread in southern France and had moved northward through the Levant to Syria, Mesopotamia, and Armenia, and thence eastward, enveloping Persia, Afghanistan, the north of India, and a portion of central Asia, as well as northwestward through Anatolia (present-day Turkey) and into the Balkans. By the sixteenth century, Indonesia and the southern part of the Philippines had been taken. By the latter part of the seventeenth century, the push through the Balkans took Islam to the outskirts of Vienna. The relative scarcity of Muslims in present-day Spain is readily explained. In the latter part of the fifteenth century, Isabella of Castile and her husband, Ferdinand of Aragon, were joint sovereigns of both of those realms. Before Isabella funded the famous voyage of Columbus in 1492, Ferdinand had established the Inquisition, and he had driven both the Muslims and the Jews out of Spain. Now, in the twenty-first century, Indonesia, with a population of more than two hundred million, is the largest Muslim country, and there is now a renewed Muslim occupation of France and a new occupation of Germany, one Muslim at a time. There are now about 1.25 billion Muslims in the world.

As with Judaism and Christianity, so also with Islam, for those who have faith, the revealed word of God is simply the truth and is simply the law. For the nearly two thousand years since the spread of Christianity, Jews and Christians – and, since Mohammed, Muslims – have had to confront the question of whether philosophizing is at all permitted by the law and, if so, within what limits.

As was noted earlier, what is called the "Hellenistic" period runs from 323 B.C. until 30 B.C. Although Republican Rome had an expansionist thrust, the Roman Empire is understood to have begun at the time of the assassination of Julius Caesar in 27 B.C. and the ascension of Caesar Augustus. Because educated Romans had been Hellenized, the cultural empire of Greece continued for some time after the military, legal, and political empire of Rome had begun. The Empire split into two parts in the fourth century and began to disintegrate in the fifth century.

As the Roman Empire came into being, some writings by Jews were in Aramaic (the language spoken by Jesus), but much was in Greek, usually in that form of it known as Koine Greek, the language of the New Testament. Philo Judaeus of Alexandria, that is, Philo the Jew, lived from about 20 B.C. until about A.D. 50. He was a philosopher in the tradition of classical antiquity and seems to have been the first to reflect on the confrontation of philosophy and the religion of Abraham. He wrote in Greek. Philo's near-contemporary, Josephus of Jerusalem (A.D. 37–100), who took to himself the Roman praenomen Flavius, was a historian who was to the Jews what Titus Livius ("Livy") was to the Romans. Josephus wrote in Greek. The high point in philosophical endeavors by a Jew is found in Moses Maimonides (1135–1204). Maimonides wrote some of his works in Hebrew, some in Arabic, and some in a form of Arabic that used Hebrew script. Joseph Albo

(1380–1444), a Jew in Spain, wrote about law, but did so not simply as a jurist but philosophically. He wrote in Hebrew. We shall have to slight Albo, but we will return to Maimonides. Let us start with Philo the Jew and Augustine the Christian. Then we shall concentrate on philosophers within Islam.

The Jews were a distinct people. Some time after Moses led them out of Egypt they settled in a territory on the eastern shore of the Mediterranean Sea. Under Saul, then under David and Solomon, their country covered somewhat more territory than the present state of Israel. The general area encompassing present-day Israel and parts of present-day Jordan, present-day Lebanon, and present-day Syria, subsequently subjected to the suzerainty of the Roman Empire, was called by the Romans "Palestine," after Philistia, a country approximately coterminous with present-day Gaza. The people of Philistia, the Philistines, according to some accounts, were an Aegean people who arrived in what became the country of Philistia by way of Crete. Thus the Jews, whose country enveloped the greater part of the area that was loosely called "Palestine" were "Palestinians." Because of refusal to submit to elements of Roman rule that ran counter to their law they were driven out of their country, Palestine, by the Romans and were dispersed. The element of Jewish history that is of the greatest consequence is that dispersion, or Diaspora. What is remarkable to one who looks at that history from the outside is that the Jews, as perhaps no other people in history, survived as a people for two thousand years without a homeland. They were dispersed first of all by the force of Roman arms. Those Jews who, in due course, came to be known as Christians, being at first individual Jews rather than whole communities, suffered not so much dispersal as persecution by the Romans. The persecution began under Nero, emperor from 54 to 68, and continued for 250 years. Armenia was a province at the eastern reach of the Roman Empire. Tiridates III was restored to the throne of Armenia under Roman protection in 298, and in about 301 Tiridates was converted by Gregory – later St. Gregory – to Christianity. His country followed in his train. Armenia thus became the first Christian country. Then in 311 Roman persecution of Christians ended with the deathbed proclamation of the Emperor Galerius who had himself been a vigorous persecutor. Constantine, who had succeeded in 306 as Emperor of the eastern portion with its capital in Byzantium, was the successor to Galerius in 311 and was therefore Emperor of the whole of the Roman Empire from that point until his death in 337. In 312, the year after the proclamation of Galerius, Constantine was converted to Christianity. There then began the extension of Christianity throughout the Empire and beyond. In due course the whole of Europe stood as the heart of Christendom.

We have already spoken of Philo Judaeus. The most prominent of the early Christians to undertake philosophic endeavors was St. Augustine of Hippo (354–430). His greatest work is *The City of God*. Many Christians regard it as a work in the Platonic tradition, modified, of course, by Christian principles.

The Goths were originally a Scandinavian people along the southern shore of the Baltic Sea. They moved southward and eastward across Europe. The Huns were a people of Mongolian origin who moved westward and southward through Asia and into Europe. These two peoples, each in its way, confronted the boundaries of the Roman Empire, and they also confronted each other. In time, the eastern Goths (the Ostrogoths) yielded to the suzerainty of the Huns, and the western Goths (the Visigoths) confronted the western part of the Roman Empire on its northern edges. The Romans and the Visigoths were, variously throughout the third and the fourth centuries, at war and at peace. The Emperor Theodosius who reigned from 379 to 395, by his straightforward dealings, developed a stable and reasonably pacific relation with the Visigoths, but after his death and the consequent division of the Empire between Eastern and Western rulers, the relation between the western Empire and the Visigoths worsened, and in 411 the Visigoths inflicted military defeats on the Romans, culminating in the sack of Rome itself. Some Romans blamed the vulnerability of the Empire on its turn to Christianity, a "soft" religion. The view that a manlier Rome, strengthened by its traditional gods, was superior to Christianity, was resuscitated and broadened eleven hundred years later by Machiavelli. Despite the conversion of Tiridates in Armenia and then Constantine in Rome in the second decade of the fourth century, and the effect of these conversions on the religion of the Armenians and the subjects of the rest of the Roman Empire, and despite the tribulations in the fifteenth century of the Spanish Inquisition, Christianity is fundamentally a religion that addresses itself not to peoples but to persons, one soul, one conversion, at a time. St. Augustine, who denied that Rome's fall was the consequence of Christianity, resolved the question of the community of Christians that follows from the existing political order by conceiving in the *City of God* of a worldwide community of Christians that does not replace or replicate the political communities but which altogether transcends them. It would be, one may say, a community of the spirit, not a community of the flesh.

The stretch of time that historians call the "Middle Ages" runs from Augustine late in the fourth century until the fourteenth and fifteenth centuries, the latter of which is the period of that revival of classical learning that we call the Renaissance. The roster of medieval Christians notable in philosophy includes Dante (1265–1321) and Marsilius of Padua (1275–1342). The high point of philosophy among medieval Christians is St. Thomas Aquinas (1225–74).

As we saw, the foundation of Islam began with Mohammed's Hejira from Mecca in 622. Principal figures confronting the intersection of Islam and classical philosophy included al-Farabi (870–950) from Transoxania (or Transoxiana), now Uzbekistan; Avicenna (980–1037) from Bukhara, in

Transoxania; Avempace from Saragossa in Spain (late eleventh century to 1138); and Averroës (1126–98) from Córdoba in Spain.

Let us scratch the surfaces of these three confrontations between philosophy and religion (Judaism, Christianity, and Islam), taking in the order of their appearance, al-Farabi, then Averroës, then Maimonides, and then Aquinas, first noting the observation by Ernest Fortin (1923–2002) that the greater reliance on Aristotle's *Politics* by Christian authors and on Plato's "Republic" and *Laws* by Muslim and Jewish authors rests on the need of Muslim and Jewish authors, as distinct from Christians, to make a positive defense of philosophy. He explains this by saying:

The most distinctive feature of Islam and Judaism is that they both present themselves first and foremost as divinely revealed Laws or as all-inclusive social orders.... Christianity on the other hand first comes to sight as a faith or as sacred doctrine, demanding adherence to a set of fundamental beliefs but otherwise leaving its followers at liberty to organize their social and political lives in accordance with norms that are not specifically religious.[11]

The defense of philosophy prior to its confrontation with Judaism, Christianity, and Islam is in its classical origins a confrontation with politics, with the *polis*, although it is clear that the tension between Socrates and Athens is understood also as the tension between Socrates and the gods of Athens. Prior to the moment when philosophy encountered the God of Abraham, its encounter with the pagan gods was mediated by the *polis*. Revelation introduced a transformation, the coming into being of a new complexity. For reasons that are themselves complex, it is easier to recognize this in the case of Christianity. Jesus himself draws for us a distinction between the "things that are Caesar's" and the "things that are God's."[12]

Political Philosophy and Islam

In 1996, Samuel P. Huntington of Harvard published *The Clash of Civilizations and the Remaking of World Order*. The book discusses the state of international affairs resulting from the apparent end of the Cold War that was coincident with the dissolution of the Soviet Union in 1991. As the title of Huntington's book indicates, it is not likely that another "world war" of states against states will occur. What is likely is the violent confrontation of one entire way of life with another. In this respect the clash would be reminiscent of that between Christendom and Islam that brought about the Crusades from the eleventh to the fourteenth century and the expulsion of Muslims from Spain late in the fifteenth century. The later development of

---

[11] Ernest L. Fortin, "St. Thomas Aquinas," in Leo Strauss and Joseph Cropsey, eds., *History of Political Philosophy*, 3rd ed., Chicago, 1987, University of Chicago Press, especially pp. 249–51.

[12] *Matt.* 22:21.

Islam comes with the inception and growth of the Ottoman Turkish Empire. It was the Turks who besieged Vienna in 1683. That Ottoman Turk Empire collapsed at the end of World War I. It was as a consequence of that collapse that the modern state of Turkey came into being. Since 1923 Turkey has striven to become and remain a secular state, even though its population is overwhelmingly Muslim. This striving is an exception to the Muslim rule, and the results are still fragile. It would not be far from the truth to suggest that the very notion of the nation-state, a notion that perhaps had an implicit beginning in the sixteenth century and developed in Europe as a consequence of the French Revolution, is antithetical to Islam. The clash of civilizations of which Huntington spoke seems indeed much like what we now observe early in the twenty-first century, although President George W. Bush and many other well-meaning Americans and Britons made and continue to make an effort to draw a distinction between militant "Islamists" or "Islamofascists" from the main body of Islam and so to claim that the ongoing clash is between Western civilization (or maybe between civilization as such) and the Islamists and not with Islam itself.

Bernard Lewis, born in 1916, professor emeritus of Near Eastern studies at Princeton, is widely and properly regarded as the single greatest scholar in the Western world in the fields of Near Eastern, Arabic, and Islamic studies. In a brief work of his, *What Went Wrong?*, published in 2002, he argues that the present confrontation between the West and Islam, or a significant part of Islam, may be the consequence of the realization that Islamic civilization, which once was the highest civilization, is now in the posture of a poor relation of the West. The envy and resentment fostered by this reversal of fortune is difficult for us to grasp. First, we wonder why Islamic countries, are not very (some of them not at all) tolerant of Jewish and Christian minorities. Isn't tolerance good? Isn't "diversity" good? Don't they know that? We have to understand that in Islamic countries, religion is not a choice. In fact, Islam is not a religion in the Western sense. It is a life. It is the law, the law is given by God himself, and God does not offer options. Insofar as Islam is a religion, there is one true religion and it is Islam. Plain and simple, all other religions are false. Not to be a Muslim is, perforce, something to be corrected.

Our second difficulty is that, apart from a few scholars, we find the suggestion that Islamic civilization was great at a time when Christendom was peopled by superstitious illiterates and book-burning priests is not just a problematic suggestion; it seems downright foolish, and undeserving of a second thought. Our ignorance in this regard is illustrated in a matter close to our immediate concerns here. We mentioned earlier the textbook assigned most widely in the middle of the twentieth century in that widely required college course, the course in the history of political theory, namely George H. Sabine's *A History of Political Theory*. My copy of that book, the book assigned to me in graduate school in the 1950s (but not, of course, by Leo Strauss), was the 1950 edition. That book is 932 pages long. The index takes up the last 20 of those 932 pages. The names al-Farabi, Averroës, Avicenna, and Avempace do not appear in that index. Neither do the words "Islam" or "Arab" or any form of either of them appear. The nearest thing is the entry "Averroism" that simply reads "see Latin Averroism." How one can know what "Latin Averroism" is without knowing what "Averroism" is or without having any idea who Averroës was rises almost to the rank of a mystery, if not to the more exalted rank of comedy. Turning to the entry "Latin Averroism," we find that it points to five places in the text. Going to those five places one finds only that some "Latin" writers (i.e., Christians who, being cultivated Europeans, wrote their books in Latin) were in some respects rather like Averroës, but there is not a syllable to suggest who Averroës was, what he wrote, what he argued, or what it would be to be "like" him.

Ralph Lerner and Muhsin Mahdi published, in 1963, a collection of illustrative examples titled *Medieval Political Philosophy*. The works of al-Farabi that are presented in that book are *The Enumeration of the Sciences*, *The Political Regime*, *The Attainment of Happiness*, and *Plato's Laws*. These four works present themselves as a natural sequence of subjects. Stop to think! Within Islam, that entity concerned with human affairs, insofar as it is not the whole of mankind, is not, as it was for the ancient pagans, the *polis*, that is, the "city." The nearest equivalent of the *polis* in Muslim thought is the nation or that complex of nations, the empire. Political science, or the science of the *polis*, that preoccupation of the political philosopher, could not possibly be of human concern. What matters is the application of the Law, the Law of God himself, to nations and empires. Furthermore, science itself, as the search for truth, would seem to be superfluous. We know the truth. Science is still respected, but its nature has changed. Likewise, it is not profitable to read what Plato may have said about laws. There is only one Law. It is the Law given by God out of the mouth of his Prophet, and there is need for only one primary book on Law, the *Qur'an*. We state these things in the most radical way to discover the intellectual context in which al-Farabi was compelled to work in turning to these old books of the pagans, now rendered obsolete by the new dispensation revealed by God himself through Mohammed.

al-Farabi

Very nearly in defiance of Islam, al-Farabi follows Aristotle in turning his attention to the city. As does Aristotle, he sees the end, the aim, of the city to be human happiness, although he is compelled to acknowledge the happiness understood by Islam, which of course consists in submission to

God followed by the enjoyments that are his gifts in the hereafter as a reward for that submission. To get to the *polis*, al-Farabi must navigate something a thousand times more complicated and more delicate than the operating system of a personal computer. He has to enumerate the sciences in order to include and justify political science, and only then may he speak of the political regime and, much as Aristotle had done, classify the sorts of political regimes, and then he is able to speak of the attainment of happiness, at least temporal human happiness, as some consequence of sound politics. Finally, because sound laws are the basis of that happiness, it becomes permissible to see what Plato had taught about such things. Why? What can those laws possibly have to do with *the* Law? Here we have again the spectacle of a man, perhaps an unbeliever, who seems to flout the Law and corrupt his pupils. It is not possible to encounter the story of this man's life and work without seeing the ghost of Socrates. Al-Farabi's business is a delicate business that requires a kind of rhetorical choreography.

Al-Farabi turns the reader's attention to the "political regime" in the following way:

Man belongs to the species that cannot accomplish their necessary affairs or achieve their best state, except through the association of many groups of them in a single dwelling-place. Some human societies are large, others are of medium size, still others are small. The large societies consist of many nations that associate and cooperate with one another; the medium ones consist of a nation; the small are the ones embraced by the city.[13]

He goes on to speak of the three faculties of the soul – the rational, the imaginative, and the appetitive – which perforce makes us think of that tripartite division of the soul offered by Plato's Socrates in the "Republic." A few pages later he relates these faculties to their presence in different men. Thus:

[W]hat is intended by man's existence is that he attain happiness, which is the ultimate perfection that remains to be given to the possible beings capable of receiving it. . . . Man can reach happiness only when the Active Intellect first gives the first intelligibles. . . . However, not every man is equipped by natural disposition to receive the first intelligibles.[14]

Happiness appears to be the intellection of the beings – in other words, philosophy – and this is the preserve of the few, for most men are unable to "cognize" those things. For them there must be imitations, imaginations, or similitudes of the beings. We cannot help again thinking here of the tripartite division of the gold-souled, silver-souled, and bronze- and iron-souled portions of the population in the city in speech in the "Republic."

---

[13] Al-Farabi, "The Political Regime," Fauzzi M. Najjar, tr., in Lerner and Mahdi, eds., *Medieval Political Philosophy*, Ithaca, NY, 1963, Cornell University Press, p. 32.

[14] Ibid., pp. 33 and 35.

Al-Farabi continues with what can hardly be thought anything other than apostasy:

Consequently, there may be a number of virtuous nations and virtuous cities whose religions are different, even though they all pursue the very same kind of happiness. For religion is but the impressions of these things or the impressions of their images, imprinted in the soul.[15]

Muhsin Mahdi summarizes this as what Averroës later explicitly calls the "three kinds of brains," first, the wise, the philosophers, who know the natures of beings and give demonstrative proofs; second, those capable of following those demonstrative proofs; and third, everyone else.[16] Further study of al-Farabi would necessarily explore the question whether (and if so, how) he preserves the classical conclusion that the solution of the political problem lies in the alliance between the two upper classes – those who can make demonstrable proofs of the highest truths and those who, although they cannot make such proofs, can follow them – in ruling over the others, those others who, in the complete sense of the saying, cannot "listen to reason."

Putting two and two together, one might conclude that, by allowing for different religions, al-Farabi implicitly denies that Islam is the one, the true, religion, but Muhsin Mahdi draws a different conclusion. What is clear is that fundamental aspects of Plato's and Aristotle's views remain intact in al-Farabi despite, or perhaps even in rhetorically cautious denial of, the religious and political understanding that philosophy is at best unnecessary and at worst the high-water mark of apostasy.

Averroës

The twelfth and thirteenth centuries constituted a pinnacle in the medieval efforts to come to grips with the problem of the confrontation between religion and philosophy. Averroës (1126–98) was born in Córdoba. He spent his life in the study of law and philosophy and in judicial posts in Spain and Morocco which, from about 1145, when Averroës was 19, until 1269 were under the rule of the Almohads, a dynasty inclined toward reform of Islam. Some politico-religious considerations, however, led the rulers, who were normally sympathetic to philosophy, to censure Averroës and exile him from Córdoba and confine him to a small town nearby. The article on Averroës in the eleventh edition of *The Encyclopædia Britannica* puts the matter this way:

But science and free thought, then as now, in Islam depended almost solely on the tastes of the wealthy and the favour of the monarch. The ignorant fanaticism of

[15] Ibid., p. 41.
[16] Muhsin Mahdi, "Alfarabi," in Strauss and Cropsey, *History of Political Philosophy*, at p. 210.

the multitude viewed speculative studies with deep dislike and distrust, and deemed any one a Zendik (infidel) who did not rest content with the natural science of the Koran. These smouldering hatreds burst into open flame about the year 1195. Averroës was accused of heretical opinions and pursuits, stripped of his honours, and banished to a place near Cordova, where his actions were closely watched. At the same time efforts were made to stamp out all liberal culture in Andalusia.[17]

Among his works that ranged from jurisprudence to grammar and philosophy, the work by Averroës clearly addressing the matter under consideration here is that titled *The Decisive Treatise, Determining what the Connection is Between Religion and Philosophy*. He begins that work thus:

The purpose of this treatise is to examine, from the standpoint of the study of the Law, whether the study of philosophy and logic is allowed by the Law, or prohibited, or commanded – either by way of recommendation or as obligatory.[18]

"The Law," of course, is the Law of God pronounced by the Prophet and explained by his followers. Averroës promptly answers the question he has posed. Citing Sura 59:2 of the *Qur'an*, he says the fact that "the Law summons to reflection on the beings, and the pursuit of knowledge about them, by the intellect is clear from several verses of the Book of God."

Even for outsiders such as we are, our reading of English translations of Sections 1 through 4 of Sura 59 is bound to make us wonder if Averroës has not explained 59:2 as he would like it rather than as it is. He hangs his argument that the Law summons to reflection on the last sentence of 59:2, "Reflect, you have vision." This is Hourani's translation. We do not presume to question it, but we point to a different translation, that in the Oxford World's Classics translation of the *Qur'an* by M. A. S. Abdel Haleem that we might flesh out the context. This first part of Sura 59 speaks of "those of the People of the Book who broke faith." They, as it turns out, were those who breached their agreement with God, and the Sura goes on to state that God, obviously through his prophet, Mohammed, punished them severely and will do so more severely in the hereafter, namely with "the torment of the Fire." The Sura refers to those who had broken faith and were punished as mistakenly believing that their "fortifications" could resist God, again, obviously meaning resist his agent, the Prophet. Unless the Sura uses the word "fortifications" figuratively, the whole passage refers to an instance where Mohammed had defeated an opposing force militarily. The crucial sentence, in Haleem's translation is, "Learn from this, all of you who have insight." Accepting "reflect" and "learn from this" as equally

[17] *Encyclopædia Britannica*, New York, 1910, Encyclopædia Britannica Co., vol. 3, p. 58. Andalusia is the southernmost part of Spain. It was the Muslim-Arabic or Moorish portion of Spain from early in the eighth century until 1492.
[18] Averroës, "The Decisive Treatise, Determining what the Connection is Between Religion and Philosophy," George F. Hourani, tr., in Lerner and Mahdi, *Medieval Political Philosophy, op. cit.*, p. 165.

correct translations of the Arabic, and accepting "you have vision" and "all of you who have insight" also as equally correct, still, the admonition of the sentence, read in context, rather than "summoning to reflection on the beings" (i.e., philosophizing), offers a veiled threat to those who dare to oppose God, that is, God who speaks through Mohammed, and who acts through the armed force of Mohammed. If one does not like to represent a holy book in such harsh terms, one might still construe the first four verses of Sura 59 as offering prudent counsel to those who acknowledge the omnipotence of God. Either way, it does not look like a call to speculative study except insofar as, in Haleem's translation, it speaks of "you who have insight," that is, those whom Averroës describes as being capable of "demonstrative proofs" or at least capable of understanding such. It does look rather like turning from the word of God and philosophizing in the way we defined philosophizing in Chapter One.

We shall have to leave it unresolved as to whether Averroës stretches the *Qur'an* to his purposes, but how he does whatever he does reminds one of the Hebrew word *pilpul*, which is used to describe commentary on *Talmud* that tortures a whole page of meaning out of a syllable of text.

Averroës continues his argument by saying that the law renders study of the beings by the intellect obligatory. That is, if you can philosophize, God orders you to do so (shades of Socrates and the Oracle of Apollo!), but he says that only those who have both the intellectual capacity and the proper moral character should do so, and he adds to this ten pages later with an argument that reminds one of the Roman Catholic provision for an "Index," which is a listing of books that might invite those who lack the rigorous intellectual training of the priesthood to lose their faith. Such books must be kept from the laity. The Catholic understanding implicit in the Index appears to be that such books should be kept rather than burned because they might be safe to read for those with the intellect and the religious strength. Those, the priests, may need to read them in fact to arm themselves against various errors and heresies. Those books should be locked up, however, to keep the weaker souls from exposure to them.

Democratized as we are, we Americans do not much like the idea of some sort of elite group telling us what we may and may not read. At the drop of a hat, an American who has never even been in the same room with a copy of the U.S. Constitution will indignantly cite the First Amendment and, following the most extreme interpretations of that amendment, assure anyone who listens that it forbids both the United States, and the states, as well as all of the subdivisions thereof to engage in any form of censorship. A little common sense, however, opens our thoughts to the wisdom that lies at the core of the Index and at the core of the argument of Averroës. People have diseases. Doctors study diseases to treat them. Many doctors specialize in the treatment of particular classes of disease. Women constitute a group with a particular class of diseases. The doctors who specialize in those diseases are called "gynecologists." Gynecologists need to study and to keep studying every imaginable gynecological problem. There are books devoted to such things. Those books are filled with discussions and pictures. Some of those pictures are disturbing, even disgusting, to look at. Still, gynecologists need to look at them. It would be wrong and crazy to forbid such books, but would it not be at least as crazy to have paperback editions of them on sale on a rack in the Greyhound bus depot?

We shall venture one bit of analysis here that may or may not be persuasive. To get some sense of Muslim law it might be best to work by analogy with the more familiar Anglo-American law. What is called the English common law is an accretion of decisions of the common courts of England beginning some time in the century following the Norman conquest in 1066. At times there have been sharp contests between the courts and the Crown, and then between the courts and Parliament, over who it is that rightly pronounces the law. We say "pronounces" because the courts surely did not claim to "make" law. They "found" it. Therefore, the contests involved indignant denial by the courts that Crown or Parliament could compete with the judges in finding it. One of the most interesting moments in this contest appears in the strong critique in the seventeenth century by Thomas Hobbes of the opposition to the authority of the Crown by Sir Edward Coke, the most celebrated judge in all of English history.[19] This contest has flared again and again over time. Its heir and counterpart is the somewhat muted contest between the American continuance of the Common Law on the one hand and the statutes and then the codification of statutes by the state legislatures on the other hand. The law is certainly a "mysterious science." To get a genuine feel for it would take, I should think, much more than three years of study at a law school. It would be the work of a lifetime.

Muslim law is the *Shari'a*. Within Islam, the law at first came from God through his prophet Mohammed, who not only pronounced the law in the decision of cases; he legislated. Within Muslim law, there has been no legislation since the Prophet. (Some Muslim countries now have only *Shari'a* for law; others have made municipal law by legislation, without, of course, challenging the law of *Shari'a*.) There have been numerous scholars of the law, jurists, within Islam. Idris al-Shafi'i (767–820) was a notable jurist, just as was Averroës some four hundred years later. Early in the ninth century al-Shafi'i formulated what are called the *usul al-fiqh*, the four "roots of the law." These are the Qur'an; the tradition of the Prophet; the consensus of the community in the past; and finally, analogical reasoning from these three.[20]

---

[19] See Thomas Hobbes, *A Dialogue between a Philosopher and a Student of the Common Laws of England*, Joseph Cropsey, ed., Chicago, 1971, University of Chicago Press.

[20] This summary is drawn from the section on law in the article "Islam" by Charles J. Adams of McGill University in Montreal, in *Encyclopedia Americana*, Danbury, CT, 1985, Grolier, vol. 15, pp. 499–500.

Being twenty-first century Americans, when we see the word "law," we at most think of the Constitution, the statute law, and court decisions. "Politics," "religion," and the "sense of the community" are thought not to be encompassed by the expression "the law." It is only with difficulty that we make ourselves think of law as being understood elsewhere quite differently. For Muslims, however, the law is the law of God and as near as one can come to understanding "politics" in the context of Islam is to think of "the law." To a Muslim, the thought of a legislature or a court "making" law is an aberration. When Averroës speaks of "the Law," he does not mean what we would mean if we spoke of the law. He means *Shari'a*, and that means the whole way of life of Muslims – their prayers, their conduct, and their judgment of the good and the bad and the just and the unjust. The content of *Shari'a* is, as we have reported, the *Qur'an*, the tradition of the Prophet, the sense of the community in the past, and the analogies drawn by rational inference (by the jurists, of course) from the other three elements.

To finish our speculation here, we quote at some length from the *Decisive Treatise* of Averroës:

We say: the purpose of the Law is to teach true science and right practice; and teaching is of two classes, [of] concepts and [of] judgments, as the logicians have shown. Now the methods available to men of [arriving at] judgments are three: demonstrative, dialectical, and rhetorical; and the methods of forming concepts are two: either [conceiving] the object itself or [conceiving] a similitude of it. But not everyone has the natural ability to take in demonstrations, or [even] dialectical arguments, let alone demonstrative arguments, which are so hard to learn and need so much time [even] for those who are qualified to learn them. Therefore, since it is the purpose of the Law simply to teach everyone, the Law has to contain every method of [bringing about] judgments of assent and every method of forming concepts.

Now some of the methods of assent comprehend the majority of people, that is, the occurrence of assent as a result of them [is comprehensive]: these are the rhetorical and dialectical [methods] – and the rhetorical is more comprehensive than the dialectical. Another method is peculiar to a smaller number of people: this is the demonstrative. Therefore, since the primary purpose of the Law is to take care of the majority (without neglecting to arouse the elect), the prevailing methods of exposition in the Law are the common methods by which the majority comes to form concepts and judgments.[21]

Recall now the "three kinds of brains," understood in similar ways by al-Farabi and Averroës. Remember that the demonstrative brain is the superior one. Remember, as al-Shafi'i had taught, that the roots of the law include the "sense of the community," the community clearly including a majority who can at best follow "similitudes." Does Averroës here implicitly teach that philosophy is superior to the Law? Can one take the next step and wonder

---

[21] Averroës, "The Decisive Treatise," in Lerner and Mahdi, *op. cit.*, pp. 179–80.

if he does not teach that philosophy is superior to all the law, to all its roots, to the Prophet, to the *Qur'an*, to Islam itself?

Reading through the "Decisive Treatise," it is possible to conclude (as indeed some commentators have concluded) that he solves the problem of the tension between philosophy and Islam – that is, between reason and revelation – by coming down squarely on the side of reason. Serious study of Averroës would culminate in at least a tentative agreement or disagreement with that view. Making progress toward that end would help the student, because there are always pieties. Every college and university, both of the past and of the present, is a great nest of pieties. A present-day college student easily ridicules the pieties of his parents and grandparents while at the same time mouthing the present pieties – that equality of rights is the only true first principle of political life, that diversity and affirmative action are salutary, that the earth is warming and is doing so because of human actions, that cigarette smoking is the crime of the century – in hushed and reverent tones. Questioning the pieties is a daring enterprise. Averroës shows that he is daring, perhaps as daring as Socrates.

We mentioned earlier the blind alley down which the Sabine *History of Political Theory* led us with its index entry on Averroism that directed us to "Latin Averroism." Perhaps Averroism is an appeal to philosophy at the expense of faith. Perhaps Latin Averroists are Christians who follow Averroës in answering that appeal. Perhaps Sabine was too polite or too prudent to say so.

There is always need for questioners. We can offer only one reassurance to those who would question: You may not be graduated; you may not be widely liked; you may not get a job; if you get a job, you may not keep it; if you aspire to academic life, you may not get in; if you get in, you may not get tenure. But be of good cheer: At least in some places you will not get the hemlock and you will not be burned at the stake or beheaded. Things really have gotten better in some respects within Western civilization. Remember, however, that questioning the pieties does not require discourtesy or intolerance. It is possible that you are just as mistaken as the pieties you question. The invitation to philosophy is not an invitation to be a smart aleck, a trouble maker, a law breaker, or one who holds all priests, all politicians, or all ancestors in contempt. It is an invitation to think, to be open-minded. It may be that at the heart of some pieties there really is truth, and it surely may be that this is what Averroës teaches. "Reflect, you who have insight."

Political Philosophy and Judaism

Inasmuch as the medieval period is generally defined by historians as the range between the fourth and the fourteenth centuries, and inasmuch as Joseph Albo (1380–1444) and Isaac Abravanel (1437–1508) stretch those bounds and, more to our purpose, present us with much less in the way of systematic treatment of the tension between reason and revelation that so marks the medieval period, our treatment of medieval political philosophy and its relation to Judaism will rest on brief remarks on Moses Maimonides.

Moses Maimonides

Moses ben Maimon (c.1135–1204) was born in Córdoba in the Muslim part of Spain. The language there was Arabic. Maimonides and his family were compelled to emigrate in 1148, when he was thirteen. Eventually they settled in Cairo. In some places at least, Jews were safer under Muslim than under Christian rule, and there was no third choice. Friedländer explains the flight from Córdoba this way:

> So much is certain [about the early life of Maimonides], that his youth was beset with trouble and anxiety; the peaceful development of science and philosophy was disturbed by wars raging between Mohammedans and Christians, and also between several Mohammedan sects. The Moravides, who had succeeded the Omeyades, were opposed to liberality and toleration; but they were surpassed in cruelty and fanaticism by their successors.[22]

"Their successors" were the Almohades. Cairo was a refuge for Maimonides and for his scholarship. The mature Maimonides was a philosopher and he was a rabbi of wide repute, being an unrivaled scholar of *Torah* and *Talmud*. Like Aristotle, he was also a physician,[23] and in Cairo he came to be appointed physician to Saladin (1138–93), a great military leader of Kurdish lineage who became the sultan of Egypt and Syria. The brother of Maimonides died when a ship in which he was traveling sank, so, in addition to being rabbi, philosopher, and physician, Maimonides perforce became manager of the family's finances and affairs. Despite the mundane burdens he shouldered, he was a supremely accomplished philosopher and rabbinical scholar. Among his works in the latter field are the *Mishneh Torah*

---

[22] Michael Friedländer, in his introduction to his 1904 translation of Moses Maimonides, *Guide for the Perplexed*, New York, 1956, Dover Books, p. xvii. The dates of the birth and death of Maimonides are perhaps imperfectly fixed by the tradition. See the first several pages of Chapter 1, "Maimonides' Life," in Herbert A. Davidson, *Moses Maimonides*, New York, 2005, Oxford University Press.

[23] Back when ethnic jokes were not the crime of the sensitive century, Jewish stand-up comics developed a multitude of jokes revolving around Jews. Jewish mothers are famous for doting on their children, and they often make chicken soup as a cure-all for minor illnesses. After penicillin was developed in the 1940s, some Jewish stand-up comic thought of calling chicken soup "Jewish penicillin." Now it happens that a group of pious Jewish physicians in New York had begun the work of translating and publishing all of the medical works of Moses Maimonides, and about twenty years ago Rabbi Tovah Stevens, knowing my fondness for ethnic jokes and discovering one of these works to be a marvelous precursor of the Jewish Penicillin joke, procured for me a copy of Maimonides's *Treatise on Hemorrhoids*. Guess what Dr. Maimonides prescribed in the twelfth century as a cure. You're right: chicken soup.

(a compendious commentary on *Torah*) and the *Commentary on the Mishnah* (the *Mishnah* being a part of the *Talmud*). His greatest work, however, was a book in the form of an exceptionally long letter in answer to an inquiry by a young man perplexed by the tension between philosophy and the law. The pupil had asked whether it was permissible to study the books of the pagan philosophers. Maimonides's book was written in Arabic. Its title in that language is *Dalālat al-hā'irīn*. The English translation of the title is *Guide of the Perplexed*. Maimonides warns readers that the *Guide* is not addressed to ordinary people, that the language in it has been chosen "with great exactness and exceeding precision."[24] Taking Maimonides at his word, I shall play it safe and largely confine myself here to relaying the gist of Ralph Lerner's chapter on Moses Maimonides in the Strauss and Cropsey *History of Political Philosophy* and to the chapter on Maimonides in the Ralph Lerner (1925–) and Muhsin Mahdi (1926–2007) *Medieval Political Philosophy*.

In his chapter on Maimonides in the Strauss and Cropsey *History*, Lerner notes the neglect of the study of medieval Jewish political philosophy and suggests that the reason for this neglect might be that "a people that for more than a millennium was unable to lead an autonomous political life and that for the most part was excluded from governance and administration is not a likely source of independent political reflection." Such speculation, however, "has never been a preserve open only to statesmen and full citizens." The concern for political things is in part explained by the fact that the Jews regarded the diaspora as an abnormality. Their repentance for the sins that had brought on that dispersion would lead to the restoration of the Jewish commonwealth (p. 228). The simple, observable fact, however, is that one is hard pressed to speak of Jews and political philosophy in the same breath for the "more than a millennium" of which Lerner speaks, that is, from Philo Judaeus in the first century up until Maimonides in the twelfth, that being the span to which Lerner perhaps refers.

As is true later in the case of Islam, Judaism is understood as adherence to the divinely ordained law of *Torah* that, as Lerner puts it, "aims at prescribing and regulating, down to the smallest detail, the conduct and beliefs of an entire community."[25] "Community," of course, means not this or that town or local community, but the community of the whole Jewish people. This community, which during the commonwealth went beyond all localities, even during the Diaspora, and passed all boundaries and all political entities. We add that this community seems akin to that which St. Augustine describes in his *City of God* as a community of all Christians that subsists despite the numerous base cities of man, except that the transcendent community

---

[24] Ralph Lerner and Muhsin Mahdi, introduction to their translation of excerpts from the *Guide of the Perplexed*, in their text, *Medieval Political Philosophy, op. cit.*, p. 191.

[25] Lerner, "Moses Maimonides," in Strauss and Cropsey, *History of Political Philosophy*, 3rd ed., p. 229.

Augustine sees he sees as one that will last through all eternity, whereas what the Jews see during the diaspora is a community that once had and will have again its own distinct commonwealth.

Two of the works just mentioned, the *Mishneh Torah* and the *Commentary on the Mishnah*, are described by Muhsin Mahdi as a "comprehensive attempt to represent the immense complexities of talmudic legislation in a clear and systematic fashion." Mahdi continues, saying, "In the *Guide of the Perplexed* Maimonides addressed himself to the challenge posed by Greek philosophy to the believer in a divinely-revealed law."[26]

There is another work attributed to Maimonides that, if truly his, helps to describe the breadth of his learning. In response to an inquiry from a "man who is described as an authority on the sciences based on the law [i.e., the law of Islam] and an authority on Arabic eloquence," Maimonides, according to a widely accepted opinion, had written, at the age of sixteen a *Treatise on the Art of Logic*. Chapter 14 of that *Treatise* is devoted to political science.[27] Thus it would appear that a natural sequence of subject matter implicit in the fact of this inclusion in the work of Maimonides would be similar to that in the sequential character of the works of al-Farabi listed earlier, the *Enumeration of the Sciences* and the *Political Regime*. The chapter on political science accepts as a given the expansion of the focus of political science from that of the ancient political philosophers, namely the *polis*, to a focus that includes the "nation" and even "the nations."[28]

Herbert A. Davidson published recently a comprehensive study, *Moses Maimonides: The Man and His Works*. After a thorough treatment of the life of Maimonides, he provides an analysis of his rabbinic works. He then deals with the philosophic works. He begins the first of the chapters on that topic with a proper disposal of the silly uses of the word "philosophy," a disposal that is similar in spirit to the treatment we offered in Chapter One of this work. He then points out that Maimonides clearly has a more precise understanding of what philosophy is. Davidson argues, however, that there are philosophic threads even in certain of the rabbinic works, the *Commentary on the Mishnah* and the *Mishneh Torah*. One work that is clearly philosophic and that is, as just noted, widely accepted as the work of Maimonides, the *Treatise on Logic*, is not, Davidson persuasively argues, in fact by Maimonides. He then devotes more than one hundred pages to an analysis of the most comprehensive philosophic work by Maimonides, the *Guide of the Perplexed*. He takes, essentially at face value, the argument of Maimonides in that text and, in so doing, he confronts the more esoteric reading given it by Leo Strauss. He treats, altogether dismissively, that approach from esotericism.

---

[26] Lerner and Mahdi, *Medieval Political Philosophy, op. cit.*, p. 188.
[27] Ibid., pp. 188–89.
[28] Ibid., p.189.

The student who wishes to weigh this dismissal responsibly should include in his studies an examination of *Persecution and the Art of Writing* by Strauss.[29]

In 1963, an English translation by Shlomo Pines of the *Guide of the Perplexed* was published by the University of Chicago Press. Leo Strauss wrote an introductory essay to that new translation, titled "How to Begin to Study the Guide of the Perplexed." Because we have mentioned Davidson's dismissal of Strauss's method, a few words from the introduction to the *Guide* will be proper here. After itemizing the parts of the *Guide*, Strauss begins his essay by quoting Maimonides's own introduction as saying that the work "is a key permitting one to enter places the gates to which were locked." Then, however, Strauss goes on to say that the work as a whole "is not merely a key to a forest but is itself a forest, an enchanted forest." The first premise of the book, Strauss says, is "the old Jewish premise that being a Jew and being a philosopher are incompatible things." Maimonides starts his inquiry from the vantage point of acceptance of *Torah*. His book, then, is chiefly "biblical exegesis." Because "many biblical terms and all biblical similes have an apparent or outer and a hidden or inner meaning . . . the Guide is then devoted to . . . the secrets of the Law." The most important of these secrets are "the Account of the Beginning . . . and the Account of the Chariot."

As is made plain by the pupil's question that elicited the *Guide*, the *Guide* is a confrontation of the tension between revelation and reason. Strauss shows the approach of Maimonides to that tension by the fact that, although "the Law forbids one to seek for the reasons of the commandments, yet Maimonides devotes almost twenty-six chapters of the Guide to such seeking." Maimonides "transgresses the Law . . . in order to uphold or to fulfill the Law." One cannot help but recall here the distinction that Averroës had made between philosophy's address to those only with understanding and the Law's address to all. Maimonides's transgression of the Law must be kept secret, but how can that be achieved in as much as the *Guide*, although addressed to a particular pupil, is open to all? It must be at once open and not open. One means of its being so is that Maimonides, as he had warned at the outset, chose every word "with exceeding care" and few men "read with exceeding care."

It would be a vain exercise for the present author to pretend a workable understanding of Maimonides or to attempt a coherent teaching of him. It is enough to take note that, as Strauss points out, Maimonides calls attention to the fact that there is in his day an obstacle that the ancient philosopher did not encounter, namely the habit of relying on revered "texts." This shows us that Maimonides consciously confronted the tension between revelation and reason, and, although this much does not put us in possession of the

[29] Herbert A. Davidson, *Moses Maimonides: The Man and His Works*, New York, 2005, Oxford University Press, pp. 305–22. The analysis of the *Guide of the Perplexed* will be found in pages 322–428. For his dismissal of the reading by Strauss, see pp. 393–402.

key to this difficult study of the most difficult questions, it at least leads us to the gate, and one clue is offered as to the place where the key may be found. Strauss says that "Maimonides introduces Reason in the guise of Authority."[30]

Political Philosophy and Christianity

It may be that St. Augustine and St. Thomas Aquinas are the two most celebrated figures within Christianity to enquire into its relation to philosophy – that is, pagan philosophy – which we know as "ancient" or "classical" philosophy. We considered St. Augustine briefly earlier, but it will be proper to add a few words here. From the chapter by Father Ernest Fortin (1923–2002) on Augustine in the Strauss and Cropsey *History of Political Philosophy* a few passages must be cited. Father Fortin says that Augustine's works "may be said to constitute at once a philosophic defense of the faith, whose reasonableness they emphasize, and a theological defense of philosophy." "His chief objection to the pagan philosophers," Fortin says, "concerns not so much their doctrine of the naturalness of civil society and the need for justice within it as their inability to bring about a just society." Fortin then goes on to say that the pagans knew perfectly well that the just cities they could erect in speech they could not bring into being in deed. Only a most concentrated study of Augustine would confront and answer the question of whether this does not mean that his understanding of the pagans was incomplete. In any case, we might add here that the failure so far of any political community – pagan, Christian, or any other – to achieve simple justice suggests a superior understanding by the pagans of the political problem. The answer to this difficulty may lie hidden somewhere behind the fact that, according to Christianity, human beings are radically equal in the sight of God whereas political prudence shows that men are radically unequal in the politically crucial respects. It makes sense to suggest the wisdom of Augustine in setting his City of God against the many cities of man, because perhaps from a Christian standpoint therein lies the only hope for justice. As Fortin puts it, "The City of God is none other than the community of the followers of Christ and the worshipers of the true God. It is made up entirely of godly men and its whole life may be described as one of pious acquiescence in the word of God. In it and in it alone is true justice to be found." The hopeful words of Augustine are indeed a counsel of perfection. Are we not "all miserable sinners," however? Perhaps this explains why Jesus reminded his disciples that "the spirit indeed is willing but the flesh is weak."[31]

---

[30] Leo Strauss, "How to Begin to Study the Guide of the Perplexed," in Moses Maimonides, *The Guide of the Perplexed*, Shlomo Pines, ed., Chicago, 1963, University of Chicago Press, vol. 1, pp. xiii–xvi, xx, xxiii.

[31] Strauss and Cropsey, *op. cit.*, pp. 179, 181, 195, and see *Matt.* 26:41 and *Mark* 14:38.

St. Thomas Aquinas

Thomas (1225–74) was born in Roccasecca and first studied at Monte Cassino. These towns are very close to Aquino, whence comes the name by which we know him. All three towns are dots on the map about midway between Rome and Naples along the inland road that is traced by the route of the present Autostrada A2. After Monte Cassino, he went to the University of Naples, where he encountered members of the order that had been founded by Dominic in 1215. From that encounter he became a member of the Dominican Order, the order of Friar Preachers. He studied then with Albertus Magnus, first at Paris and then at Cologne. He was canonized by Pope John XXII in 1323, less than fifty years after his death. He is known as "Doctor of the Church" and as "the Angelic Doctor." Likely he is the most famous of all those called "Scholastics," a label attached to certain thinkers since the time of Charlemagne (742–814). The most famous of the works by Thomas is the *Summa Theologica*, an encyclopedic study of Christian doctrines of theology. Thomas is said to have solved the riddle of reason and faith, producing a synthesis of the two.

   Thomas never learned Greek. Fortunately, he began his studies just at that time when the whole corpus of Aristotle's works in Greek, having come back into the reach of the West, began to be translated into Latin by William of Moerbeke with whom Aquinas established a collaboration. The result is best characterized by Allan Bloom who, in the Preface to his translation of Plato's "Republic," wrote the following:

> My goal – unattained – was the accuracy of William of Moerbeke's Latin translations of Aristotle. These versions are so faithful to Aristotle's text that they are authorities for the correction of the Greek manuscripts, and they enabled Thomas Aquinas to become a supreme interpreter of Aristotle without knowing Greek.[32]

   The interpretations of Aristotle that Bloom had in mind were Thomas's *Commentary on the Ethics* and *Commentary on the Politics*. A matter of style comes to mind. There are occasional light, even comic, moments in Plato's dialogues. We mentioned earlier the incident in Book One of the "Republic" where Polemarchus, having been persuaded by Socrates that the just man will never harm anyone, promises to join up with him militarily to punish those who do not agree with them about the meaning of a saying of the poet Simonides. The effect of this is to force us to wonder whether the thing to which Socrates had made Polemarchus agree is the whole, the simple, truth.

   In contrast, if Aristotle has a sense of comedy at all we would be hard put to find evidences of it in the *Ethics* or the *Politics*, not to speak of his

---

[32] Plato, *Republic*, Bloom, tr., 2nd ed., Basic Books, 1968, 1991, Preface, p. xi.

writings on natural philosophy. The sobriety of St. Thomas, however, makes Aristotle look like Mel Brooks by comparison.

We had intimated earlier that the centuries-old scholarly view that St. Augustine was an adequate expositor of Plato is at least subject to reservation. A similar question may be framed regarding Aquinas. Father Fortin, in his chapter on Aquinas in the Strauss and Cropsey *History of Political Philosophy*, explains him in relation to Aristotle in the following way:

Although Aquinas looked upon Aristotelian philosophy as the most perfect expression of natural truth and as the philosophy which was most congruent with the truth of Christianity, he was fully able to coordinate that philosophy with the Christian Faith only by transforming it both in content and in spirit. For present purposes the precise nature of that transformation is perhaps best illustrated by the fact that, whereas Aristotle never speaks of natural law but only of natural right, Aquinas has generally come to be regarded as the classic exponent of natural law theory in the Western world.[33]

Another significant departure to which Fortin calls our attention is the fact that whereas for Aristotle ethics, politics, and economics are aspects of the same science, Aquinas makes them separate sciences. We might add that Machiavelli, at the beginning of the sixteenth century, separates ethics and politics so that we moderns are able to imagine an ethics liberated from every concrete political fact and a politics, especially in application to international relations, that is wholly free of ethical considerations.[34]

Thus, although as recently as September 12, 2006, Pope Benedict XVI, in his speech at the University of Regensburg, affirmed the harmony of Christian faith and reason, there may be, from the standpoint of philosophy, as such, some doubt regarding the synthesis attributed to Aquinas, some doubt, that is, whether philosophy and faith – reason and revelation – are capable of a perfect accommodation.

Marsilius of Padua

Although the 1950 edition of Sabine's *A History of Political Theory* fails, as we noted earlier, to give an account of al-Farabi, Averroës, Avicenna, or any other philosopher within Islam, it does speak of "Latin Averroists." Chapter 15, "Marsilius of Padua and William of Occam," devotes a full

[33] Strauss and Cropsey, *op. cit.*, p. 253, and see pp. 257–58. Perhaps the difference between classic natural right and what came to be called natural law may be brought to mind by the fact that, although Aristotle devotes the whole of Book V of the *Nicomachean Ethics* to justice, barely half a page deals with natural justice. (See pp. 1134b18–1135a5.)

[34] Fortin, at p. 258. Cf. Kant, *Foundations of the Metaphysics of Morals*, the twentieth century "realists" in international relations, American "civil rights activists" who claim that legislation motivated by moral opinion derived from religious faith is "unconstitutional," and Adam Smith's foundation in *The Wealth of Nations* on the modern science of economics.

fifteen pages to Marsilius. Marsilius was born about 1275 (biographical dictionaries differ on the year of his birth) and died in 1342. I settle for 1275 as the correct year of his birth for no better reason than that there is a kind of poetic orderliness to his being born the year following the death of Aquinas inasmuch as his philosophic views are a kind of sequel to those of Aquinas. His chief work is the *Defensor Pacis* (1324). Dante (1265–1321), whom literate Westerners know from his *Comedy*, had written only one straightforward work in political philosophy, the *De Monarchia* (often translated as *Of World Government*). In that work he accepts the Medieval extension of the "political" beyond the confines of the *polis* so as to include the nation and in fact the world. He accepts the view that there ought to be one government of the whole world (although perhaps he means only the "world" encompassed by the ancient bounds of the Roman Empire), and he argues for the necessity of monarchical rule of that world. He may be described as an "imperialist," not in the sense of the present usage by students of international relations, but simply in the sense that he contends the world should be ruled by the emperor, the *Imperator*, and not by the pope. It must be remembered that for a long stretch of time there was a three-way political struggle, between emperor and pope, between emperor and kings, and between kings and pope. Marsilius takes a view similar to that of Dante.

The *Catholic Encyclopedia* begins its article on Marsilius by identifying him as "Physician and theologian," both of which characterizations are correct, but to call him a "theologian" is not to mention the fact that his theological arguments are subordinated in the *Defensor Pacis* to an overarching political philosophy. The position taken by Marsilius – that the pope does not have plenitude of power, that the clergy has no control over worldly affairs, that all priests (including the pope) are equal, that no one can authoritatively declare orthodoxy or brand heresy, and that the pretensions of the pope to rule the Church are effected in derogation of the true power of the General Council of the Church (the "Church" being, of course, not the establishment or the hierarchy but the whole body of the faithful) – naturally was opposed by the pope. The article in the *Catholic Encyclopedia* states plainly that the "pope was stirred by these heretical doctrines." He excommunicated Marsilius and some four associates, including Louis of Bavaria (who was both the king of Germany and the Holy Roman Emperor), who had opposed himself to the political claims of the pope.[35] What distinguishes Marsilius from Aquinas is chiefly that Marsilius's response to the tension between reason and revelation is, instead of a doctrine of fusion, a clear recourse to Aristotle. It is this that merits the appellation "Latin

[35] *Catholic Encyclopedia*, vol. IX, New York, 1910, Robert Appleton Co., Nihil Obstat, October 1, 1910, Remy Lafort, Censor, Imprimatur. +John M. Farley, Archbishop of New York. The Marsilius article can be found at http://www.newadvent.org/cathen/09719c.htm.

Averroist," that is, a Christian follower of Averroës – Averroës not without reason having been branded a heretic within Islam because of his following of Aristotle's doctrine despite any conflict between it and Islam. Marsilius's fidelity to Aristotle includes his denial of the doctrine of "natural law" that is forwarded by Aquinas. Leo Strauss argues that Marsilius departs from Aristotle in that he makes Aristotle appear to be more democratic than he is and he distinguishes between the "sovereign people" and the government, whereas Aristotle had held that the government *is* the sovereign, but then he shows that Marsilius, having used his populist argument in the service of his anticlericalism, gradually returns to a stricter adherence to Aristotle as his argument progresses into what is more plainly political philosophy.[36]

As brief and thin as are these sketches of the medieval political philosophers, we must turn now to the modern era.

---

[36] See Leo Strauss, "Marsilius of Padua," Strauss and Cropsey, *op. cit.*, especially pp. 277–78, 280–81, 283, 291–92, and the sources in Marsilius's *Defensor Pacis* cited in support of Strauss's interpretations. The distinction between the people as legislator and the government as subordinate to it is foreign to Aristotle's view. It is more consistent with the modern view that distinguishes between "state" and "society." Marsilius provisionally adopts the distinction for the purpose of subordinating the clergy, including the pope, to the whole body of the Christian faithful. In doing so he anticipates not only the modern notion of the "state," but also the modern notion of subordination of the ecclesiastical power to the civil power. For Aristotle there is no such thing as "the state." The *polis* is composed of form and substance. The substance is the *polis* as a whole. The form identifies that part of the city that is sovereign, the governing part.

8

A Kind of Betrayal

"Betrayal" is a strong word. No doubt someone seeing the title of this chapter might charge it with being combative and judgmental. We are obliged to explain its usage. Beginning in the nineteenth century and solidifying in the twentieth, there came into being the view that the sum and substance of political theory was the "history of political theory." The thrust of this view was that "theory evolved." From this point of view it would not be possible for one theory to be a betrayal of another. Change of any sort was progress, and in everything progress was inevitable. A certain "process" determined things: a "historical process." Like all accepted views, however, this view deserves to be questioned. We need to consider the possibilities that (1) somewhere along the line there was a conscious and deliberate reversal, and (2) the possibility that a given new view is in fact a betrayal or at least a reversal, a deliberate reversal of an old one. We need to be open to the possibility that thought does not think itself and does not simply happen as part of the historical process of thought. Maybe sometimes somebody actually thinks, and thinks purposefully. This is not to deny that some thought is careless.

For nearly two thousand years, from Socrates up to and including Machiavelli, philosophers adhered to the Platonic and Aristotelian notion of an alliance between the thoughtful and the powerful as the best political order. The Platonic core of that alliance was the iron-clad insistence on the absolute supremacy of the thoughtful over their allies, the powerful. For those two thousand years, every philosopher who gave attention to politics adhered to that Platonic core. This adherence persisted despite the fact that throughout the Middle Ages – roughly from the fourth to the fourteenth century – philosophy stood not only in a state of tension with politics but also in a state of tension with revealed religion.[1]

---

[1] If one follows the Old Testament acceptingly, the origin of the world occurred about 3,760 years before Jesus, but the confrontation of revealed religion and philosophy seems only to have occurred after Jesus. I do not know that Plato or Aristotle, for example, had ever heard

Moses Maimonides (c. 1135–1204), the greatest of the Jewish philosophers, referred to al-Farabi (870–950), surely one of the greatest philosophers within Islam, as the "Second Master," that is, the teacher second only to Aristotle in his endowment of surpassing excellence. In continuing the tradition since antiquity of regarding the alliance between the thoughtful and the powerful, al-Farabi, in a way reminiscent of Plato in the "Republic," classified the three sorts of people according to their "three kinds of brains." Aristotle's method of argument is called "demonstration." He seemed to regard that philosophical method as a surer means of proof than Plato's dialectical or dialogical arguments. Al-Farabi accepts Aristotelian demonstration as the correct means of philosophical proof. In distinguishing the three kinds of brains he describes the first kind as being capable of demonstrative reasoning. The second kind is not able to undertake demonstrative proofs, but can understand and accept the demonstrations offered by the first kind of brain. They can, that is to say, function successfully as the pupils of the demonstrative class. They are capable of undergoing liberal education. They are the "gentlemen." The remainder of a population can neither make nor follow demonstration and so must be taught by "similitudes." That means that by agreement between the two higher classes of brains, the others, the many, must be brought to willing obedience to the laws by stories, wholesome stories, that invest that unthoughtful majority with wholesome prejudices. This reflects the very basis of the argument Socrates had made in Book Two of the "Republic" when he calls attention to the necessity that the poets must be censored in the city in speech. They need to be censored not because they tell lies. Of course they do. That is the very meaning of the word "poetry." Poets "make things up." Their fault, Socrates argues, is that they do not tell salutary lies, that is, wholesome similitudes. According to al-Farabi, prophets or philosophers create those similitudes. This, by the way, implicitly likens prophets to poets. The gentlemen read those stories and willingly promulgate them to the many.

This is an appropriate time to glance again at Plato. You will recall that in the "Republic" Plato makes Socrates, in the course of perfecting the city in speech, assert that the founders of that city must tell an enormous lie to the people of that city. The lie was twofold. First there was the myth of autochthony and next was the myth of the metals. Not only was it acknowledged that this would be a lie; it would be a big lie. It was also said that it would be a noble lie, a fine lie, a beautiful lie, a salutary lie of which we can therefore approve. You will also remember that the third stage or phase of the development of the city was the purging of the excesses that characterized the second-stage city, the luxurious city. A crucial element of

of the Jews. We must not overlook the fact that the encounter resulted from Hellenization – the intellectual hegemony of the Greeks – and then as an accompaniment of the spread of the Roman Empire.

that purgation was the sanitizing of the works of the great poets (Homer, Hesiod, Pindar), the tragedians, and all the rest. In educating those who at that point were still called the "guardians" (i.e., all of the two upper classes), the lies the poets told would have to be cleansed of things that formed the souls of those in the two upper classes badly.

Poets claim to be inspired by muses. They claim that the muses speak through the poet's mouth or, later, write through the poet's hand. Of course, the work of the poet is to tell retail lies that insinuate a wholesale truth. In fact, what we call "taste" is the ability to distinguish between good poetic works – those that plant a wholesale truth – and poor ones – those that plant a false, ugly, unwholesome, wholesale lie. Poetry, of course, in its primary sense means all of what we today call creative writing, epic stories, lyric poems, odes, tragedies, and comedies.

The conclusion reached by the first phase of the supervision of the poets in the city in speech is a threefold theological doctrine that is pronounced, namely that the stories told by the poets must never present the gods as the creators of both the good and the evil but only of the good, and they must never portray them as liars, nor may they be portrayed as wizards who change themselves into clouds, beasts, or what you will. This doctrine is laid down shortly after the "correction" of the poets that begins in Book Two of the "Republic" at 377b. We must have poets, but only poets who tell wholesome lies. It is in that context that the big lie that Socrates says must be told to the guardians is described as a "noble" lie, and it appears to be this sort of thing that al-Farabi has in mind when he speaks of similitudes as the guide for those with third-class brains.

Now it is necessary to confront another probable objection. "Oh," it will be said, "talk like that is elitist." All brains are equal. All humans are equally rational. All understand the most complex matters "if they are just told the truth." All must be cleansed of prejudice. You have to think a bit, however. Look in the mirror and remind yourself of the statement of Socrates that "the unexamined life is not worth living." Look around you at your fellows in the classroom and weigh them and what they say. Walk into a neighborhood bar and look at a bunch of regular fellows and listen to them talk about sports, politics, women, or automobiles. Do their understandings rest on demonstrative proofs? We note also that demonstrative proofs cannot be learned casually nor can they be learned by everybody. Therefore, the aim must not be the utopian one of a population without prejudice. It would seem that Plato and al-Farabi, among many other thoughtful people, believe in the inevitability of prejudice and so the necessity of wholesome prejudice, salutary prejudice.

At the beginning of the sixteenth century, a new way of thought appears. The place of sober practicality that Aristotle filled is usurped by a philosopher more practical than anyone before or since. Niccolò Machiavelli (1469–1527) dismisses the likes of Plato and Aristotle as mere dreamers.

Those dreamers are seen to be of no use to citizens or statesmen. Machiavelli offers an altogether practical alternative to those dreamers, and although he adheres to the traditional philosophic insistence on the alliance between the thoughtful and the powerful, he inverts it. The statesman or politician takes the leading place. This statesman is not the "Gold" one described by Plato's Socrates. He is not the philosophic one. He is the powerful one, the one ruling. The one with true wisdom, or even the one with a noticeable degree of practical wisdom, finds his place as the servant of the powerful one. The prince is what he is because he can be. The official "intellectual" tells the prince how to get what he wants, not what should be wanted. The seventeenth-century offspring of this inversion by Machiavelli is Francis Bacon's assertion that "knowledge is power." That means that knowledge is not the judge of power; it is the servant of power. It enables power. I have seen a prominent banner over the office of the Mathematics Department in a very-well-thought-of college that reads "MATH IS POWER." One learns not to know but to get the better of others. If one learns math, one gets the better of everyone. Is this education or is it pandering to appetite?

Machiavelli was himself a statesman for a time, serving in the chancellery of Florence. His intellect was remarkable. In addition, he was more clever perhaps than anyone since Plato. He combines some of the talents of an Aristophanes with some of the talents of a Plato, as well as some of the talents of a Winston Churchill. He wrote both plays and treatises – treatises in philosophy, and history, and on the art of war as well as plays that on their face appear to be comedies of manners but which in fact are part, along with the treatises, of his overall philosophic project. If Plato may be regarded as the great creative genius of antiquity, Machiavelli may perhaps be regarded as the great creative genius of modernity, but to regard him so does not suggest that he is the moral or intellectual equivalent of Plato. Machiavelli's two most famous political treatises are the books we know as *The Prince* and the *Discourses*. The full title of the latter is *Discorsi sopra la prima deca di Tito Livio*, or *Discourses on the First Ten [Books] of Titus Livius*, or *Discourses on Livy*. It would be profitable to devote a whole semester – perhaps several semesters – to the study of these two books. Because of the density and the subtlety of them, we can at best make our point here regarding the tension between politics and philosophy by a partial examination of *The Prince* in the hope that this glimpse will draw some students into serious study of it and of the *Discourses*.

First, a word about the title. It has become so commonplace to accept the title *The Prince* that even Italian editions now publish the book under the title *Il Principe*. Machiavelli's book, however, the body of which was in Italian, had its title and its chapter titles in Latin. The title of the book was *De Principatibus*. As Leo Paul de Alvarez explains that Latin title in the introduction to his translation, it more properly might be translated into English as *Of Principate*, although de Alvarez, too, bowing to the dictates of tradition, settles for the title *The Prince*. If in our mind we see the translation of the Latin title as "Of Principate" or "Of Princedom," or, spelling it out, "Of How One Acquires State and Keeps It," it becomes a bit easier to follow Machiavelli's argument. The title directs our attention not so much to the person of the prince as to his doings. In the case of *The Prince*, as in the case of the "Republic," we shall put the title in Roman script, enclosed in quotation marks, as a constant reminder that it is off to one side of Machiavelli's intention. We also remind ourselves here that literal translation of the text leads us less astray than does "rendering the Italian into English." I believe that the translation by de Alvarez of the University of Dallas, now published by Waveland Press, and the translation by Harvey C. Mansfield, Jr., of Harvard University, published by the University of Chicago Press, are clearly the best. No doubt there are some other acceptable ones, but I have seen a few, including one by a translator with a decidedly Italian surname, that are defective.

Because we do not pretend here to offer an exegesis of the "Prince," but mean only to make one point related to the three kinds of brains and the traditional doctrine of alliance between the two superior ones, we can be reasonably brief. We shall emphasize a handful of passages.

The Epistle Dedicatory to Machiavelli's 1513 *De Principatibus* is addressed to the "Magnificent Lorenzo Medici." This is a bit of tongue-in-cheek flattery inasmuch as it was the addressee's grandfather (1449–92) who was known as "Lorenzo the Magnificent." The grandson (1492–1519) to whom Machiavelli dedicates his book had yet to make a name in public affairs. [In fact, the name he "made" was rather made possible for him by his uncle, Pope Leo X; Giovanni di Lorenzo de Medici, 1475–1521; (Pope Leo X, 1513–1521) who created him Duke of Urbino in 1517. The young Lorenzo was wounded in 1516 defending the seized Urbino from an attempt by the ousted duke to recover it. He died of his wounds in 1519 after prolonged suffering.]

In the latter part of the second paragraph of the Epistle to Lorenzo, Machiavelli says that he does not

> wish it to be thought presumptuous if a man of low and mean state dares to discuss and to regulate the government of princes; for just as those who sketch the country-side place themselves below in the plain to consider the nature of mountains and high places, and in order to consider the low places put themselves high on the mountains, similarly to come to know well the nature of the people one needs to be a prince and to know well that of princes one needs to be of the people.[2]

There is some legerdemain here. If it were not for the fact that Lorenzo might be too flattered or too dumb to catch it, he might be insulted. As it is,

[2] The passage quoted here is from the translation by Leo Paul S. de Alvarez, Prospect Heights, IL, 1989, Waveland Press, p. 2. Reprinted by permission of Waveland Press, Inc., from Niccolo Machiavelli, *The Prince* (Long Grove, IL; Waveland Press, Inc., 1980 [reissued 1989]). All rights reserved.

it is a nice little joke shared by the author with us, his readers. It would be one thing to "sketch" a prince, but Machiavelli admits he means to "regulate the government" of the prince, that is, to tell Lorenzo how to conduct his affairs, how to acquire state, and how to maintain it. To do this, he needs to know not only the prince, as the people can know him; he needs also to know what princes know, namely peoples. He needs to know both what the people know of the prince and what the prince knows of the people. He needs to know the art of rule. Thus, princes and peoples have partial knowledge. Machiavelli knows both sides of the equation. Notice that this presupposes in somewhat different form the three sorts of people one finds in Plato's and al-Farabi's formulations. Machiavelli is more a prince than any prince. Despite the fact that he has not acquired state, in a manner of speaking, he has. He, the party of the third part, is superior to both the prince and the people. If there are three kinds of brains, his is surely the highest of the three.

I have spoken earlier of bad translation. I apologize if I seem to be carrying on at length, but so that we might appreciate Machiavelli's argument in the "Prince," we need to see persuasively the impossibility of doing so if we are subjected to careless translation of it. Because all the major European languages – English, French, German, Italian, and Spanish – share a great deal of their roots in Latin and Greek, the speaker of any one of them can go a long way in protecting himself from bad translations if he has barely a smattering of knowledge of the language translated and has a dictionary. Let us see this by looking at a bare six words in the Italian original of the "Prince," and then let us look at several misleading translations of those six words, two of the six that are nouns having straightforward cognates in all the European languages. Let us then reflect on the opposition of those two nouns in Machiavelli's syntax, and then on the repeated playing on that opposition throughout the book. The various mistranslations lead us down various garden paths. The correct translation leads us along a straight line, a bright red line, from the beginning to an intelligible end.

Chapter One consists of 117 words. That is, it is just less than fifteen times as long as the title of the chapter. The title, in Latin, consists of eight words. For both de Alvarez and Mansfield it takes fourteen words to give a fair translation into English. (Prepositions such as "by" and "of," which are necessary in the English, for example, are simply folded into the forms of the Latin nouns or verbs.) The translation of the title by de Alvarez is this: "How Many Kinds of Principates There Are and by What Modes They Are Acquired." The chapter itself is, for the most part, unexciting, rather as what one would expect in a schoolbook. Reminiscent of Aristotle's classification of the six regimes, Machiavelli ticks off republics and principates and the different sorts of principate. As to the acquisition of principate, he says . . . Wait a minute! *Acquisition*? Yes, acquisition! Machiavelli is talking to Lorenzo, a would-be prince, and the theme of his book *seems* to be how one acquires princedom, a principate, or a principality. That is, how he gets "state" or status as a prince. One cannot help imagining Lorenzo going to the Amazon.com Web site, finding a book titled *Usurpation for Dummies*, and saying, "Ah, just the ticket!"

Machiavelli ends the first chapter saying, "Dominions [that are] acquired are either habituated to living under a prince or are used to being free; and they are acquired either with the arms of others or with one's own, either by fortune or by virtue." The last six words here are a translation of the six words in the Italian original, "*o per fortuna o per virtù.*" It requires almost willfulness to get this wrong. These two phrases, separated by a comma, are alternate ways of stating the same thing. The two phrases are what in grammatical or syntactical analysis are called a "parallelism," which is rather like a proportion or an equation. If A and B are the two substantive things in the phrase before the comma, and C and D are the two substantive things in the phrase after the comma, it is clear that C is the equivalent of A and D is the equivalent of B. That is, C *is* A; D *is* B. Acquisition by the use of others' arms is acquisition by fortune; acquisition by the use of one's own arms is acquisition by virtue. The definition of the terms amounts to this: What is in one's own control is virtue; what depends on someone else's control is fortune. If it is yours, you are in control of it. If it is someone else's, it is subject to being taken from you at a moment's notice. If you want to take something, make sure that you have what it takes to take it. Note well: The whole of the argument of the "Prince" is a continuation and perfection of what is implicit in this parallelism.

Translators who are nice chaps who smoke pipes, sit at desks, get tenure, and chat with other nice chaps either do not believe a reader can understand this or do not believe that Machiavelli could mean this. Why not? If a reader of Italian can read this, why can't a reader of English read it in English? Also, Machiavelli must mean it. He said it. If, as is a reasonable possibility, he says what he does not mean, we are obliged to explain why he does that. What is he up to? If he means what he says, we are obliged to think through the consequences of that meaning. We need to examine the possibility that Machiavelli is deliberately teaching us a new meaning of the word "fortune," a new meaning of the word "virtue," a new meaning of both, or a new meaning of the relation between the two. Maybe we have all become soft. Maybe the usual meaning of "virtue" is for sissies. Maybe our salvation lies in getting tough. Maybe we need to root out the cause of our softness. Maybe politics requires that we throw off debilitating traditions. Taking Machiavelli seriously opens the door for us to see both his supreme excellence, his virtue, and his frighteningly dark side, his vice. Only thereby can we both learn from him and yet maintain our decency. If we do not take our study seriously we will fall into one of two sorts. One sort turns away in shock from Machiavelli's indecencies. The other winks at them. Neither learns.

Machiavelli uses the word *virtù* over and over again in the "Prince," and he seems to mean something different with each usage, but there is a common thread which must be seen if we are to understand the whole cloth of his argument. Virtue is what is yours; fortune is what is another's. The man of virtue is not the man possessed of all those Sunday school niceties. The man of virtue is the man who has what it takes. Translators seem to have devised a thousand ways to keep from confronting the two sides of Machiavelli. A sampling of mistranslations of these two words will illustrate the problem. Edward Dacres translated the words this way: "either by fortune, or by valor" (1640; republished in 1905 by David Nutt, London); Henry Morley this way: "by his good fortune or conduct" (London, 1889, George Routledge and Sons); N. H. Thompson this way: "either by good fortune or by merit" (The Harvard Classics, vol. 36, New York, 1910, P. F. Collier and Sons); Luigi Ricci this way: "by good fortune or special ability" (New York, 1950, Modern Library [Random House]); and Peter Bondanella and Mark Musa this way: "either through Fortune or through cleverness" (New York, 1979, Viking Press and Penguin Books. This instance is of special interest because Bondanella and Musa capitalize "Fortune" whereas Machiavelli's Italian consistently uses the lowercase *f* in *fortuna*). In Chapter Twenty-Five, the next-to-last chapter, Machiavelli even puts the word *fortuna* in the Latin chapter title and then uses it again seven times in the Italian text of the chapter. Now it happens that the Italian word *virtù* is a lineal descendant of the Latin word *virtus*, and the root of that word is *vir*, which is the Latin word for man – not mankind, but man, the male of the species. *Virtus* means both virtue in the generic sense and manly virtue, manliness, virility. Thus, to have virtue is to have virility, to be manly. There is in Latin a different word altogether for what in English is "mankind," namely *homo*. The same is true in Greek. There is a word for mankind, *anthropos*, and a separate word for man, the male of the species, *aner*. An orthographic change takes place in order that a variation of this latter word be pronounceable, so the word for courage is *andreia*, that is, manliness.

In the seventh and last usage of *fortuna* in Chapter Twenty-Five, namely in the last paragraph thereof, and after numerous repetitions of the word throughout the book, and just after speaking of the necessity of impetuosity in acquiring state, Machiavelli reminds us that *fortuna* is a woman. He still does not capitalize the word, but this clearly is an allusion to the personified fortune, the goddess Fortuna. He says, "I am very much of this judgment: that it is better to be impetuous, for fortune is a woman, and if one wishes to keep her down, it is necessary to beat her and knock her down."

With apologies for the offense to our "feminine side," we cannot bowdlerize Machiavelli if we are to understand him. The acquisition of principate may conceivably be achieved by way of fortune or by way of virtue. The one who wishes to seize principate would be a fool to trust to fortune, and he would likewise be a fool to send his lawyer over to see if something might be worked out. To seize it he must seize it, and to do that requires that he be impetuous. Impetuosity is an attribute of virtue, and virtue is another name for manliness. Fortune is a woman, and, like all women, she rather likes to be slapped around a bit. When she wants a man she wants a man. If you bring flowers and ask her nicely, she will grow coy and find a thousand ways to put you off. Conquest of the political kind, as that of the other kind, is not for softies. "What will be will be" is nonsense! Machiavelli's advice for aspiring princes seems to be that one should either settle for his present lot or be a man!

Lest these illustrations heighten our enthusiasm for finding fault with our own country and with English speakers in general, it is comforting to note the foibles of translations into other European languages. Let us look at one example. In honor of the quincentenary of Machiavelli in 1969, a Spanish translation of *The Prince* was published in Mexico, along with a tribute to Machiavelli by Antonio Gómez Robledo of the Colegio Nacional. The first part of the sentence in question is translated into Spanish literally. The latter part of the sentence is translated thus: *"y se adquieren por las armas propias o por las ajena, por la suerte or por la virtud."* In English, this comes to: "and are acquired by one's own arms or by [those of] others, by chance or by virtue." Reading Machiavelli in this translation is a hopeless task. First of all, notice that the parallelism is scrambled. Instead of A:B = C:D we get B:A = C:D. "One's own arms" becomes the counterpart of "chance" and "the arms of others" becomes the counterpart of "virtue." To this difficulty is added the fact that although the translator properly translates the Italian *virtù* into its perfect Spanish cognate, *virtud*, for some reason known only to his Muse he translates the Italian *fortuna* into the Spanish *suerte*. *Suerte* means in English "chance," and that is a good enough substitute for "fortune," but why he so translates is a mystery, given the fact that there is a perfectly fine cognate for the Italian *fortuna*, namely the Spanish *fortuna*. The translator's desire to be more "interesting" and so to shop around for words deprives the reader of the possibility of appreciating the rhythm and the drumbeat of Machiavelli's argument and of appreciating the long-delayed punch line about virtue or manliness knocking around the willingly submissive woman, *fortuna*.[3]

This is stunning. By that, I mean it shuts down your brain. Once in the 1970s I was in Montreal. I went into a drugstore to get some aspirin. There was a customer at the pharmacy who spoke only Spanish who was getting medication for her child who was evidently ill. The pharmacist spoke only French. He appealed to me in French to tell the woman in Spanish what dosage was prescribed for her child. Not being good at either French or

---

3 *El Príncipe*, Mexico City, 1985, Editorial Porrúa. It appears that Professor Gómez Robledo's introduction was written in Rome in 1969, the 500th anniversary of Machiavelli's birth. I cannot tell who wrote the translation.

Spanish, I froze in my tracks. (Earlier that day in a café I had ordered in French a ham sandwich and a beer and was served a croissant and a hot chocolate.) I did my best to accommodate the pharmacist. Listening to him with a half-French ear, I translated into English and thence into my half-Spanish, and in my best Spanglish advised the mother as to the prescribed dosage. To this day, I have often wakened in the night trembling, wondering if I got that right. The same dire consequences may be feared reading this Spanish translation of Machiavelli's Italian. Studying philosophy is a little like walking down a bad street in a tough neighborhood on a dark night. It is fraught with the danger of being mugged. As difficult as in its nature philosophy is, translators should not add to the student's burdens.

A last illustration is worthwhile. The student should beware the pitfalls of "Notes" sold in bookstores that have the effect of confounding and corrupting them. Glancing at the *Monarch Notes* on *The Prince* and *The Discourses*, I perceive that commentary on both Chapters One and Two of the "Prince" is combined in one paragraph. Not a single word in that paragraph mentions "fortune," "virtue," or the contrast between them. Perhaps there is some use to be gotten out of the pamphlet, but this grievous oversight conjures up the possibility of "Notes" on Shakespeare's *Hamlet* that describe the clothing of Rosencrantz and Guildenstern, the pedantry of Polonius, and the good looks of Ophelia but never once mentions Hamlet.[4]

Discussion of fortune and virtue is only one, but it is one vital, aspect of considering the "Prince." Before turning to another aspect, we will touch on Chapter Fifteen.

Chapter Fifteen is critical for seeing what Machiavelli is "up to" in teaching us a new meaning of the word "virtue." The Latin title of the chapter is *De his rebus quibus homines et praesertim principes laudantur aut vituperantur.* Of all the things that come to mind in explaining that title, the first and most obvious is that, in going around Robin Hood's barn, it takes Machiavelli eleven words to say what, but for one thing, could be said in four. That "one thing," however, is Machiavelli's purpose, so simply to raise the question is to intimate the answer. Professor Mansfield perfectly translates Machiavelli's Latin into English thus: "Of Those Things for Which Men and Especially Princes Are Praised or Blamed." If it were not for the fact that it takes two English words – "for which" – to translate the one Latin word *quibus*, Mansfield would even have been able to use the same number of words as Machiavelli. Also, except for the fact that Mansfield could perhaps have strained a bit and used the rather cumbersome "lauded" and "vituperated" for the Latin *laudantur* and *vituperantur*, every other English word of his is the inescapable English translation of Machiavelli's Latin.

---

4 Robert Sobel, *Niccolo Machiavelli's* The Prince *and* The Discourses, Monarch Notes, New York, 1965, Simon and Schuster, pp. 11–12.

In thinking this through, we ask ourselves, What are those things for which men, and especially princes, are praised or blamed? Students may fall into a trap here if asked for what things men are praised. They might answer, "being handsome," or "singing well," and understanding Machiavelli then becomes a futile guessing game. If we start not with praise, however, but with blame, the solution comes easily. Why are men blamed? Does anyone ever blame a man for being ugly or for singing poorly? Certainly not. The one thing for which men are blamed is being bad, for being vicious, that is, for having vices. When we see this, it is clear that the things for which men are praised are virtues. Now the why or wherefore of Machiavelli's circumlocution becomes evident. He wants the reader to see that all that old-fashioned talk of virtues and vices is off the mark. We need to come to grips with a new, more practical, understanding of the virtues and the vices. For the thoughtful man, they are not the things that Grandma called virtues and vices. By way of analogy, Machiavelli teaches politics by saying that a strong man will knock a woman around because that is the only way to bring her around to his point of view. The political analog of that is that the would-be prince must knock a few heads around and murder an occasional baby. If he does this well, he succeeds. (Wait a minute! Is it possible to murder a baby well?) In addition, the one thing that is sure to garner praise is success. Men are praised for success. The road to success is being practical, being a realist. As Josef Stalin said, "You cannot make a revolution with silk gloves."

I do not suppose that Machiavelli himself deserves all the praise (or blame) for it, but the fact is that five centuries of his influence have made us hesitant to speak at all of virtues. The word sounds preachy, sissified, or, worse yet, religious. As recently as five or six decades ago, a graduate of an ordinary, public, secondary school in America, when asked to name the cardinal virtues, could properly answer, "Prudence, Courage, Moderation, and Justice." That is no longer true. As the late Allan Bloom remarked, the only virtues now even mentioned are the softer ones, the feminine ones – things like chastity, caring, and sensitivity.

This aversion to plain talk yields a self-inflicted ignorance. Let us remind ourselves of a matter treated earlier. One can begin recovery from that ignorance by resurrecting the word "virtue." We can do this by using the analogy of an inanimate object, a knife. What one desires in a knife can be expressed either by speaking of its use or by speaking of its essential quality. The use of a knife is to cut, but it cannot be used effectively unless it is sharp. The essential quality of a knife is sharpness. The virtue of a knife is sharpness. If a knife becomes so dull that it cannot even be sharpened, it cannot cut. It is no longer really a knife. It only looks like a knife. It reminds one of a knife, but it is not a knife. A knife cuts.

A human being is a thousand times more complicated than a knife. The first thing is that a human being has both body and soul. I do not know whether one can speak properly of the virtues and vices of the body, because it may be that the good or bad condition of the body, within certain limits, is the consequence of the virtues and vices of the soul (and it does not seem fair either to praise or blame those conditions of the body that are outside those limits; for example, one would not in decency call someone a bad person because he or she was born with one short leg). If we cannot speak of the vices of the body, we can speak figuratively at least of the good conditions of the body as "virtues." They are, quite simply, strength, health, and beauty. They are the qualities wanted in a body. Nobody wants to be weak, ill, or ugly. The virtues are what one wants. To want vices is to want what is not good for oneself. One need not be embarrassed to speak of the virtues. The virtues are by nature simply the wanted things.

As for the virtues of the soul, they had been considered in prephilosophic discussions from time immemorial, but a searching examination of the cardinal virtues came in Plato's "Republic." It is, however, left to Aristotle to make a demonstrative and exhaustive study of all of the virtues of the soul. He does that in the *Ethics*. There seems to be implicit in Plato's treatment a distinction between moral virtues and intellectual virtues. Whether what seems to be implicit in Plato is truly there, it is certainly the case that Aristotle makes the distinction between moral virtues and intellectual virtues explicitly. He defines moral virtue as a "mean" between two vices, one an excess and one a defect. This definition is more plainly seen in the case of those virtues, such as liberality, that have a measurable, quantitative aspect to them, but Aristotle offers the mean as a measure of them all. Aristotle lists eleven moral virtues: courage, moderation, liberality, magnificence, greatness of soul, proper ambition, gentleness, truthfulness, wittiness, friendliness, and (separated out for more extensive treatment) justice. It is necessary to repeat here, in speaking of Machiavelli's "restatement" of Aristotle, that what might appear to be a twelfth, namely shame, Aristotle will not call a virtue, because the complete gentleman will not do anything of which to be ashamed. It is rather an emotion somewhat like a virtue because, if the gentleman does do something shameful, it is better that he then be ashamed than that he do a shameful thing shamelessly. Machiavelli, in recommending a whole catechism of shameful deeds, never mentions the word "shame."

The intellectual virtues come to three: prudence, science, and wisdom. It would require some work to examine these, but because it is not to our purpose to do so here, let us ignore them except to put "prudence" aside to be brought back into the discussion to see how Machiavelli deals with it.

Machiavelli's treatment of the things for which men and especially princes are praised or blamed is a deliberate burlesque of Aristotle's *Ethics*. The evident purpose of that treatment is to have his readers dismiss the traditional views of virtue and vice with contempt. Accepting Machiavelli's revision, Aristotle comes off as laughable. He is simply an old fogey. In language invented in the twentieth century, he is just one more of those execrable "dead, white males." Machiavelli, without ever mentioning Aristotle, employs as a literary device an arithmetic measure contrasting his and Aristotle's catalogs of virtues that can be seen by the reader who is careful. By an "arithmetic measure," I mean that to understand what Machiavelli is doing we have to count. Because Chapter Fifteen is only three paragraphs long, let us pace our way through all of it. The first paragraph begins thus:

It remains now to see what the modes and government of a prince ought to be with respect to his subjects and his friends. And because I know that many have written on this, I fear that I shall be taken to be presumptuous in writing about this again, especially in my departing from the orders of others in the disputation of this matter. But since it is my intention to write a useful thing for him who understands, it seemed to me to be more profitable to go behind to the effectual truth of the thing than to the imagination thereof.

After a polite, apologetic bow to those "many" who "have written on this," without wasting more time, Machiavelli points out that what they all wrote was mere exhalation from their imaginations. He will write the truth, if not for the first time, at least effectually. He spells out their imaginings like this:

And many have imagined republics and principates that have never been seen or known to be in truth; because there is such a distance between how one lives and how one should live that he who lets go that which is done for that which ought to be done learns his ruin rather than his preservation – for a man who wishes to profess the good in everything needs must fall among so many who are not good. Hence it is necessary for a prince, if he wishes to maintain himself, to learn to be able to be not good, and to use it and not use it according to the necessity.

It appears that virtue, properly understood, is doing the things for which men and especially princes are praised sometimes, and at other times doing those things for which they are blamed. There must then be something or other that enables a prince to know which is which. Clearly the one thing that will not tell him this is the *Boy Scout Handbook*. The second paragraph spells out the things that elicit praise or blame. Where Aristotle had set out three things in each case, a virtue and the two vices on either side of it, the virtue being a mean between the vices, Machiavelli sets out pairs of things. How is it then that he, somewhat like Aristotle, treats virtue as a mean of some sort? In arithmetic terms, we must say that it "doesn't add up." The second paragraph begins thus:

Omitting, then, the things about an imagined prince and discussing those which are true, I say that all men, whenever one speaks of them, and most especially princes, since they are placed so high, are noted for some of those qualities which bring them either praise or blame.[5]

---

[5] Reprinted by permission of Waveland Press, Inc., from Niccolo Machiavelli, *The Prince* (Long Grove, IL; Waveland Press, Inc., 1980 [reissued 1989]). All rights reserved.

For the sake of simplicity and clarity, instead of finishing this paragraph by a direct quotation of the balance of it, let us set out those qualities in a table. The qualities, in pairs, are:

> Liberality or *Misero* (i.e., meanness or miserliness)
> Givers or Rapacious
> Cruel or Full of Pity
> Faithless or Faithful
> Effeminate and Pusillanimous or Fierce and Spirited
> Human or Proud
> Lascivious or Chaste
> Open or Cunning
> Hard or Easy
> Grave or Light
> Religious or Skeptical

Note some things about this list. First, notice that the customarily praised thing is sometimes listed first and sometimes it is the customarily blamed thing that comes first. Second, there are eleven pairs. Perhaps if we combined some things in the list there would be fewer pairs, maybe only ten. In contrast, one of the pairs is a pair of pairs. Wouldn't it fit the whole list better if the pair of pairs "Effeminate and Pusillanimous or Fierce and Spirited" were split into two pairs, thus: "Effeminate or Fierce" and "Pusillanimous or Spirited"?

If we did so split that pair of pairs, however, would that not give us twelve pairs instead of eleven? If we were one of those translators who likes to "fix" Machiavelli's "errors," could we not edit this whole list and make it neater, with nine, ten, twelve, or maybe thirteen pairs? It almost seems as though Machiavelli wants us to count. Let us count, then, but take into account some aspects of Aristotle's list, so that we can contrast the two lists.

There are ten triads in Aristotle's list in Book Two of the *Ethics*, but if we note that a whole book, Book Five, is devoted to another virtue, and accepting Aristotle's distinction between moral and intellectual virtues, it is clearly included in the moral category. That virtue is Justice. Also, if a prince followed Machiavelli's advice he would often do things for which an ordinary person would be ashamed. Aristotle discusses Shame but does not include it among the virtues. We sensibly add Justice to the ten moral virtues in Book Two, making Aristotle's list add up to eleven. Shame is a knottier problem. Aristotle does not think it proper to call it a true virtue, but then again he treats it as a kind-of-sort-of virtue. Surely if we bent Aristotle's list to accommodate the shameful acts that Machiavelli positively recommends, we might be wise to promote Shame to the rank of an actual virtue. That would make Aristotle's list swell to twelve triads.

Oh, well, let us admit that we cannot do these things. Aristotle's list is Aristotle's and Machiavelli's is Machiavelli's. Machiavelli, however, seems to taunt us into comparing the two lists. If we were to consider Machiavelli's remark in the first paragraph that his "intention is to write a useful thing for him who understands," let us aspire to be among those who understand and put what he has written to use. Compelled as we are to count things, let us note that the two lists are numerically matched, eleven for Aristotle and eleven for Machiavelli. There are two things strikingly absent from Machiavelli's list, namely Justice and Shame. Machiavelli's list cannot include justice or shame. Justice, at least in the ordinary sense, seems not at all to be a great concern of Machiavelli, although saying that opens a difficult line of inquiry, well beyond the reach of this introduction. Maybe Machiavelli is concerned about Justice but, to see how, we would have to wrack our brains in examining the whole of his writings. Then again, maybe he really does not care about this. Also, is it not clear that Shame can have no place in Machiavelli's list? By forcing us to think of Aristotle's *Ethics* does he not want us to see the irrelevance of Shame in politics rightly understood? After all, in acquiring state, what is so shameful, for example, about murdering an occasional baby if that is what it takes? That is surely a thing for which men are blamed, but, although it cannot be called a virtue, it must not be called a vice. On reflection, if we accept the acquisition of principate as a given, being able to do what must be done to so acquire must, in some higher Machiavellian sense, be understood silently – perhaps winkingly – as virtue.

Machiavelli's burlesque of Aristotle's *Ethics* is part and parcel of his reformation of those moral understandings that are inseparable from the traditions both of classical political philosophy and of Christianity – that is, of those traditions from which Western civilization itself is inseparable. For Machiavelli, virtue is what works. To translate *virtù* a dozen different ways is to hide his argument from us. The endeavor of Mansfield and of de Alvarez to present to us in English exactly what Machiavelli gave us in Italian is the indispensable means by which we who cannot read Italian have the slightest chance of an entrance into the thought and significance of Machiavelli. What is the possible consequence of a successful entrance? Will it not be either a conscious and knowing acceptance or rejection of his teaching? Will it not enable us to profit from his wisdom while escaping his corruption, if indeed that is what he proffers? We can only nibble here at the edges of this last-named consequence.

Some time after nuclear weapons came into being at the end of World War II, some hardheaded commentators began to use the expression "thinking the unthinkable." Perhaps we should not close our eyes to the possibility of coming under nuclear attack. Perhaps we should not be so squeamish about considering the use of such weapons ourselves. The moment we do think these unthinkable things we are ashamed. How could we even entertain such thoughts? Perhaps there is no alternative. What Machiavelli has done so far in the "Prince" is make us think things we wish we had not thought. Perhaps he has begun to corrupt us. Maybe in the final analysis, that is his purpose. Maybe he wants his more thoughtful readers to shake off all those sissified moralisms that have come down to us from the past, a past filled with the imaginings of dreamers. Machiavelli wants those of his readers "who understand" to embrace the "effectual truth." He wants us to become what have come to be called "realists." If we take ourselves and the lives of our children and grandchildren seriously, we are almost inclined at this point in our study of Machiavelli to say, "Let us pray."

We can forego quoting the remainder of Chapter Fifteen. Let us simply think for a moment about the intellectual virtues that Aristotle discusses. We recall that there were three: prudence, science, and wisdom. If we had to reason it out we would see that prudence, or practical wisdom, is the one that most fits Machiavelli's pursuit of political practicality. We need not guess about this because, at the end of Chapter Fifteen, he says that it will be necessary for the prince "to be so prudent that he will know how to avoid the infamy of those vices that would lose him his state" but that "he should not concern himself about incurring the infamy of those vices without which it would be difficult to save the state." Notice that for the first time in this chapter he uses the word "vice," he uses it twice, and he uses it as ordinary people use that word. Then, for the first and only time in the chapter, he uses the word "virtue," and he uses it as ordinary people do. He does so only to say that there are times when it is necessary to avoid virtue.

For Machiavelli, true virtue is the prudent choice between virtue and vice. For Aristotle, virtue was a mean between two vices, two extremes in each of the triads he treated. For Machiavelli, virtue is also a sort of mean, but it is rather a perverse sort. Because there are only two terms in each of his listed contrasts, there is no middle term. Virtue then is a mean only in the sense that it is knowing when to act according to the customarily praised thing and when to act according to the other, the blamed thing. Prudence, instead of being that intellectual capacity that was understood as enabling one to find the good in human affairs becomes that capacity that enables one to figure out when to be good and when to be bad. It becomes reducible to calculation, to low cunning. The safe, comfortable, and in fact the chief route to teaching that is, for Machiavelli, through circumlocution and euphemism. We probably could not bring ourselves to learn these lessons by straightforward means. If Machiavelli tried to teach us in a straightforward way, we would turn away in shock and in shame. Even Machiavelli's chosen way is shocking enough. He has to seduce us. He wants us to learn that the annoying nuisance that religion, and particularly the Christian religion, has inflicted on us is that it has made us too weak to do what needs to be done. Others who do not suffer from that crippling inability will be our masters. Therefore, we must not say "virtue" or "vice." We must say "those things for which men and especially princes [used to be] praised or blamed." Those who are put off by the shocking surface of his teaching will turn away and rebuke him. Those who can see through to the "effectual truth" and "understand" will perhaps nod ever so wisely and join him. Given the acknowledged brilliance of Machiavelli, we are almost embarrassed to ask ourselves if it is possible that he cannot envisage a third sort of reader, one who understands but does not join. Is it now clear that in reading Machiavelli we must not read what we want to find in the text but what is in it. When he writes "virtue" we must read "virtue," and we must confront the inconvenience that we have to work hard to figure this all out.

We need now to turn to Chapters Nine and Twenty-Two after some introductory observations.

Following Chapter One, which set out the contrast between fortune and virtue, several chapters follow the taxonomy offered in that first chapter in detailing the acquisition of state in each of its different kinds. Chapters Four and Five have titles that are long circumlocutions (like the title of Chapter Fifteen) that immediately alert the reader to the need for extra caution in interpretation. Chapter Six is titled "Of New Principates Which by One's Own Arms and Virtue Are Acquired." The chapter is of middling length as far as the "Prince" goes. It is one and one-half pages long in one edition of the complete works in Italian. The Italian text is divided into five paragraphs as is Mansfield's English. The English of de Alvarez is divided into eight paragraphs. In the Italian, the word *virtù* or a form of it occurs thirteen times. *Fortuna* occurs four times. Three of those mentions of *fortuna* involve direct contrast with *virtù*. *Prudènte* occurs twice. Machiavelli speaks of four "princes" who have come to their state by virtue rather than by fortune. The four he lists are Moses, Cyrus, Romulus, and Theseus. This may be the first instance in the history of Western literature where an author has treated Moses as just one more "prince." He mentions, but dismissively, that Moses had been the executor of "things that were ordained by God," but goes right on treating him as a prince who, like the others, had acquired state by virtue (virtue, that is, in Machiavelli's new sense of the word). Thus, he treats the Grace of God as a species of mere chance, and by slighting it he effectively denies that Moses was a prophet. To top it off, he diminishes the stature of Moses, along with that of Cyrus, Romulus, and Theseus, by tossing in Girolamo Savonarola (1452–98), a Dominican priest who had been tortured, hanged, and burned for sedition and heresy, as one who, had he been armed, would have succeeded and so would deserve to be likened to these four who acquired state by their own virtue. Worse, he lists Hiero, the Tyrant of Syracuse, as of the same ilk as these four. He even hints that Moses was not really a Jew, an argument the completion of which waited on the psychological doctrines of Sigmund Freud (1856–1939) and maybe even on the cinema of Walt Disney's heirs.[6] Oh! We must not overlook the fact that Romulus and Theseus have not been proved to

---

[6] See Niccolò Machiavelli, *Tutte le Opere*, Florence, 1971, Sansoni, pp. 264–65. The genealogy of Moses that Machiavelli seems to ignore is reported at *Exodus* 2:1–10. I take a chance in mentioning Disney. It is hearsay to me. I welcome editorial correction from a reader.

be actual historical figures. Perhaps they are only legendary accumulations each of the characteristics or attributes of several persons (not to mention the unlikelihood that Theseus made war against the Amazon women, a rather doubtful race). Does Machiavelli want us to wonder whether Moses really existed? Maybe he is just a figment of Scriptural imagination.

Chapter Seven, continuing in the same theme, is "Of New Principates Which by the Arms of Others and Fortune Are Acquired." It is here that, in the course of a backhanded encomium to Cesare Borgia, he tells us that it was not Cesare, but his father, Rodrigo Borgia (i.e., Pope Alexander VI, 1431–1503; pope 1492–1503) whose power made possible the acquisition of the Romagna. Cesare did, indeed, have sufficient virtue that he might have been able to hold on to the acquisition, had it not been for an excessive malignity of fortune (namely that his father died at an inconvenient moment). *Fortuna* appears in the chapter nine times in addition to being in the chapter title. *Virtù* appears seven times. The two are placed in direct contrast four times. In speaking of his virtue, Machiavelli says "there was in the Duke such ferocity and such virtue" that "had he been healthy" he "would have stood up to every difficulty." Proof of his virtue is put forth in the following account:

And because this part is worthy of notice and of imitation by others, I do not want to omit it. The Duke, having taken the Romagna, found it commanded by impotent lords who had been quicker to despoil their subjects rather than correct them, and who gave them matter for disunion, not for union. As the province was full of robberies, of factional quarrels, and of every other reason for arrogance; he judged it necessary, wishing to reduce [that province] to peace and obedience under the princely arm, to give them good government. So that he placed there Messer Remirro de Orco, a cruel and expeditious man, to whom he gave the fullest power. That man, in a little time, and with very great reputation, reduced it to peace and unity. The Duke then judged that such excessive authority was not necessary, because he did not doubt that it would arouse hatred; and he set up a civil judiciary, in which every city had its own advocate, in the midst of that province, with a most excellent president. And because he knew that the past severities had generated some hatred, in order to purge the minds of that people and to gain them all to himself, he wished to show that if any cruelty had been done, it had not come from him, but from the harsh nature of his minister. And he found an occasion: he had him placed one morning in the piazza in Cesena in two pieces, with a piece of wood and a bloody knife alongside. The ferocity of that spectacle left the people at the same time satisfied and stupefied. (de Alvarez translation, pp. 44–45)[7]

Three paragraphs later, Machiavelli says, "Summing up all the actions of the Duke, I would not know how to find fault with him." Now this is said not without qualification, but the first reading – and the lasting impression – is that sending someone in to do your "dirty work" for you, then ostentatiously

[7] Reprinted by permission of Waveland Press, Inc., from Niccolo Machiavelli, *The Prince* (Long Grove, IL; Waveland Press, Inc., 1980 [reissued 1989]). All rights reserved.

contracting a "hit" on him and leaving him, cut in two, in the piazza so as to "satisfy" and "stupefy" the people is the "way to go."

Chapter Nine shares with Chapter Eleven the distinction of having the shortest title: three words. The title of Chapter Nine is *De principatu civili*, "Of the Civil Principate." It begins:

> But coming to the other part, when a private citizen neither by wickedness nor other intolerable violence, but with the favor of his fellow citizens, becomes prince of his fatherland (which one can call a civil principate; nor is it necessary to attain it either wholly through virtue or wholly through fortune, but more nearly [through] a fortunate astuteness), I say that one ascends to this principate either with the favor of the people or with that of the great. For in every city these two different humors are to be found: and it comes of this that the people desire not to be commanded or oppressed by the great, and the great desire to command and to oppress the people; and of these two different appetites one of three effects issues in the cities – either a principate, liberty, or license.[8]

Aha! The people are wrongheaded because not only do they not want to be oppressed, which shows their good side, but they also want not even to be commanded, which shows their bad side. Also, not only do the great want to command, which is proper, they want to oppress, which is not. It seems that each of the two "humors," factions, or parties is half right. Here, the good result – virtue – is not the result of choosing between that which garners praise and that which garners blame, but some third thing. If the people had their way, the result would be license – the very lawlessness that Cesare Borgia found upon his arrival in the Romagna – and if the great had their way, the result would be principate. Is principate the opposite of license? Is "liberty" the good thing, the mean? Is it, rather than being like Machiavelli's prudent choice between a pair of alternatives, truly like Aristotle's "mean" between two vices? Does Machiavelli show here, and fling it right in the face of Lorenzo, that principate is a blameworthy regime? Harking back to Aristotle's six choices, does Machiavelli mean us to understand that there is no such thing as good rule by one? Is the solution – given the existence everywhere of these two "humors" – something reminiscent of Aristotle's *politeia*? Is it a mean between two vices? Is it a standoff between two truly blameworthy alternatives? Is it what Polybius named the "mixed regime?" Is this, however, settling for Aristotle's third best regime? Are we, in consummate Machiavellian practicality, simply forgetting the two better regimes about which those old fuddy-duddies of antiquity insisted on dreaming? In short, because Machiavelli's two humors include a "great" that is nowhere described as being "aristocratic," that is, of being "gentlemen," do the two parties come down to the few and the many, and are both parties corrupt? The political opinions of both parties are simply representations of their

[8] Reprinted by permission of Waveland Press, Inc., from Niccolo Machiavelli, *The Prince* (Long Grove, IL; Waveland Press, Inc., 1980 [reissued 1989]). All rights reserved.

"appetites." If we think of the three classes in the city in speech in Plato's "Republic," where is the wise class; where is the spirited class? There is a painting (a print of which my wife forbids me to hang in the house lest visiting grandchildren be terrified) called *Portrait of a Venetian Gentleman.* The original hangs in the National Gallery of Art in Washington. Looking at it you see not a gentleman but a man wholly given to avarice. The artist(s) made a magnificent, although covert, statement by titling the painting as the subject would have it but showing the subject as he is.[9] Venice was noted as most emphatically a commercial city, but not only was the sixteenth century in the midst of the "High Renaissance" in all of Italy, it was also the period during which that new class, dubbed in the eighteenth century by Rousseau the "bourgeoisie," blossomed. Could it be that Machiavelli recognized the absence of a class of gentlemen and the presence in its place of a moneyed class "passing" as an aristocracy? In Machiavelli's view, is there no "silver class"? Is spiritedness reducible to the desire of the man on horseback to acquire state? Is wisdom replaced by Machiavellian prudence, a kind of low cunning? Our examination so far does not answer these questions, but it does sharpen them. Chapter Nineteen is, without contest, the longest chapter of the "Prince." Its subject matter is conspiracies against princes. The chapter title refers to this subject matter indirectly: "Of Avoiding Contempt and Hatred." It should be read in conjunction with the longest chapter of the *Discourses*, Chapter Six of Book Three, which is titled "Of Conspiracies." This chapter in the "Prince," Chapter Nineteen, blandly encourages Lorenzo to think that the odds are on the side of the prince and against the conspirators, but the evidence he gives shows the contrary. This literary device occurs often in Machiavelli and puts us on the alert to work at figuring out his real argument. The title of Chapter Twenty-One, "What a Prince Should Do That He May Be Esteemed," promises a subject matter the counterpart of the subject matter promised by Chapter Nineteen. He begins the chapter with ironic praise of Ferdinand, the Spanish king known as "Ferdinand the Catholic." In the middle of that mock praise he speaks of Ferdinand's "pious cruelty" in "driving out of his kingdom and despoiling the Marranos." The Marranos were Jews who had overtly converted to Christianity to avoid persecution, but who covertly continued as Jews. Machiavelli does not hesitate to pronounce judgment. He calls the action of Ferdinand one than which "there cannot be a more miserable and rare example." The last paragraph of Chapter Twenty-One is difficult

---

[9] The painting is attributed to Giorgione (1478–1511) and Titian (1477–1576). Perhaps one began it and the other finished it. We note that Titian lived to be almost one hundred. Giorgione only lived to be thirty-three. Experts date the painting as being done in 1510, a year before Giorgione's death. I have not found a picture of it in the two histories of art ready to hand, but it can be found at "Olga's Studio," online at http://www.abcgallery. com/G/giorgione/giorgione20.html.

not to take at face value. It is reminiscent of the advice the poet Simonides gives to the tyrant Hiero in Xenophon's *Hiero,* namely that the only way the tyrant can achieve what he really desires is to cease being a tyrant and to be instead a just king. It is said that the name "Old Nick" for the devil comes from Machiavelli's first name, Niccolò. This last paragraph of Chapter Twenty-One compels us to consider the possibility that, although he surely is no angel, he may deserve a reputation better than that of the devil himself.

Chapter Twenty-Two is not the shortest chapter in the book – Chapters One and Two deserve first and second honors in that regard – but it is surely short, just more than half a page in the Italian text. The chapter title is "Of Those Whom Princes Have as Secretaries." (It is clear that "secretary" means what we would call "first minister.") Some commentators assert that the chapter proves that Machiavelli's whole purpose in the "Prince" was to curry favor with and solicit appointment by Lorenzo. We are inclined to think otherwise. The chapter turns our attention back to the Epistle Dedicatory, in which Machiavelli spoke of the prince and the people and so compelled us to think of a third party (Machiavelli himself), and to Chapter Nine, in which Machiavelli spoke of the "two humors" in each city and so made us think of a third party (namely the party capable of appraising those two humors). Here in Chapter Twenty-Two, without mentioning either Plato or al-Farabi, Machiavelli says this:

And because there are three kinds of brains: one understands on its own, the other discerns that which others understand, the third neither understands on its own nor through others; the first is most excellent, the second excellent, and the third useless.[10]

Machiavelli argues that a prince will be esteemed prudent if he has the sense to appoint as secretary someone of the first rank (the prince evidently being only of the second rank himself). The chapter as a whole is in a backhanded way complimentary to Lorenzo, but holding it at arm's length to read, it is clear that Machiavelli is, seemingly with the blandest of expressions on his face, insulting Lorenzo. It is by its show of contempt for Lorenzo and, by extension, for all ambitious politicians, a recruiting speech to Machiavelli's potential disciples – and in the past half millennium he has had thousands of those, they being the sort of followers that Aristotle tried to guard against in the case of Plato. What the chapter adds up to is this: Look, Lorenzo, I know that you hunger for state. You have no idea why you want it, you just want it. However, you do not have any idea how to get it, and if you did stumble into it you would not know how to keep it. Hire me, listen to me, and you will succeed.

---

[10] Reprinted by permission of Waveland Press, Inc., from Niccolo Machiavelli, *The Prince* (Long Grove, IL; Waveland Press, Inc., 1980 [reissued 1989]). All rights reserved.

Chapter Twenty-Three is titled "In What Mode Flatterers Are to Be Avoided." With the same bland expression on his face as in the preceding chapter, Machiavelli then proceeds to shower Lorenzo with honeyed flattery. This chapter, also, and perhaps the whole of the "Prince," although overtly addressed to Lorenzo, is truly addressed to intelligent readers who might be enlisted in pursuit of the greatest acquisition in the history of humans, the conversion of the human race to a wholly new moral and political understanding. In this, Machiavelli exhibits a high self-regard unmatched in history. In Chapter Six, when speaking about the four "princes," he had said that no "unarmed prophet" had ever succeeded. This compels us to remember Jesus. Remembering him now, we are led to suspect that Machiavelli wants to rate himself at least potentially a bit above Jesus. Machiavelli is the most practical philosopher ever to have written. Those dreamers of antiquity imagined cities that could never be brought into being in deed. By lowering the standard, Machiavelli presents a scheme that, once adopted, cannot fail to succeed. In great measure his scheme did succeed, but, as Plato needed a follower like Aristotle, so Machiavelli needs a follower who can reduce his teaching to textbook method and textbook proportions. In due course there was such a follower.

As Leo Strauss has definitively shown, Machiavelli is not just after a job with Lorenzo. His purpose is far grander. He seeks to open altogether new vistas in political philosophy. He conceives of himself rather as the Christopher Columbus of the mind. He leads the second of three great youth movements, Socrates having led the first and Nietzsche leading the third. Machiavelli makes it clear that he does not expect to succeed in bringing about his new modes and orders during his lifetime, but he believes that he might be able to "carry it far enough so that a short road will remain for another to bring it to the destined place."[11] One needs to remember Machiavelli's listing of Moses as a new prince. We do not denigrate Moses because he did not make it all the way to the promised land. Speaking of Moses, one odd thing comes to mind. Machiavelli tells us that there is a change of religion two or three times in every five or six thousand years.[12] Let us "do the math." The possible stretches of time suggested would be (1) three times in 5,000 years, or 1,666 years; (2) three times in 6,000 years, or 2,000 years; (3) twice in 5,000 years, or 2,500 years; and finally (4) twice in 6,000 years, or 3,000 years. If we leave completely out of consideration Islam, which Machiavelli does not mention here, the midpoint would be somewhere in the neighborhood of 2,200 to 2,300 years. If we calculate a midpoint between a dozen years before the death of Socrates (that would be 411 B.C.) and the publication of the *Discourses* in about 1520, the span

[11] *Discourses on Livy*, Harvey C. Mansfield and Nathan Tarcov, tr., Chicago, 1996, University of Chicago Press, Preface, at the end.
[12] Ibid., Book II, ch. 5, para. 1.

between the origin of political philosophy and the Discourses would be 1,931 years. Maybe he wants us to think not so much of a new religion as of the success of a new philosophy – his philosophy – with a reasonable expectation that such success might take another three or four hundred years. If we think again of the suggestion mentioned earlier that just as Plato's political dialogues needed to be followed by the more textbook-like works of Aristotle, so also Machiavelli needed a successor, and if we further see that successor as Thomas Hobbes, whom we shall discuss in Chapter Nine, next, then Machiavelli here speaks cautiously, for Hobbes's *Leviathan* follows the *Discourses* by only 130 years.

Machiavelli is, it seems, the first philosopher to betray philosophy. He keeps the notion of an alliance between the thoughtful and the powerful, but many things are broken in his version. He sees himself as the first genuine political philosopher, although he leaves it to a seventeenth-century successor to make that claim openly. Philosophy, made more practical, has dropped altogether any concern for the things "up there," the really good city, the city of transcendent beauty and justice. More, rather than continuing the alliance of the thoughtful and the powerful as a defense of the thoughtful (for the good of all, by the way), the alliance is conceived as a means of assuring the goals of the powerful. Whereas in the ancient scheme, wisdom ruled because wisdom and rule coincided, being held in the same hands, Machiavelli seems to think that there can be a convenient division of labor and if the wise flatter and cajole the powerful they can be the "power behind the throne."

Many have hoped to be the power behind the throne. It is a job without tenure and often without a "safety net." Henry Tudor (1491–1547), that is, Henry VIII, king of England from 1509 to 1547, surely had what Machiavelli calls "state," but he was troubled also by that other appetite of his. Cardinal Thomas Wolsey (c. 1475–1530), who was Lord Chancellor to Henry (1515–29), tried to "manage" Henry and at the same time manage England's foreign policy. He came to an unhappy end. In his play *Henry VIII*, Shakespeare puts a pitiable speech in the mouth of Wolsey when he is driven from office. It is worth reading that speech in the present context (see at III, ii:350 *et seq.*). Sir Thomas More was appointed in Wolsey's place. He fared worse than Wolsey. Henry, having married Catherine of Aragon (1485–1536), the daughter of Ferdinand the Catholic in 1509 by way of a dispensation of Pope Julius II (1443–1513; pope, 1503–13), cast her out in 1531, and she lived out the rest of her life in religious devotion and in fear of poisoning. Henry failed to enlist More in his campaign to get a new dispensation, this time from Pope Clement VII (1478–1534; pope, 1523–34), to divorce Catherine so that he could, with the blessing of the Church, bring Anne Boleyn (1507–36) to bed. Finally, More was dismissed because he would not swear an oath to an act which proclaimed Henry head of the Church in England, an act that dismissed the pope as head of the Church there. More was beheaded. In due course Henry and Anne were married, but then, Henry tiring of her, Anne was beheaded. The unhappy ends to the lives of Catherine and Anne are mentioned here merely as an aside. Our real purpose is to illustrate the difficulty of "secretaries to princes" in keeping their princes on the straight and narrow.

We are reminded by a saying of Sir Francis Bacon (1561–1626), "Knowledge is power," of the hope of Machiavelli that philosophers might maneuver princes. I have heard that saying quoted favorably a thousand times by people with business, law, or political science degrees. Some who have lived by that slogan have lived to regret it. Worse, this proposition, which is the legacy of Machiavelli to his intellectual heirs, is a reversal of the ancient view, the view that the function of knowledge is to sit in judgment of power, not to join it or to yield to it.

Philosophers who hope to be the power behind the throne inevitably find out that the seat of power is the throne, not the study. Rulers listen for a while, but then they rule. For reversing the relation between wisdom and power, Machiavelli deserves to be remembered as the first philosopher to betray philosophy. There have been others since. The word "since" reminds us of time and so of history. We must consider that subject in the next chapter.

9

Modern Political Philosophy and Postmodern Thought

Modern Political Philosophy

If philosophy did, indeed, originate with the Greeks and if Thales, who lived from about 636 to about 546 B.C., was the first of those to whom the appellation "philosopher" applies, then that origin appears at some point in his lifetime, some moment late in the seventh or early in the sixth century. In the Ionian cities and the other cities of southeastern Europe and western Asia Minor where it began, philosophy appeared as a discordant element. As Plato makes Socrates show us in the allegory of the cave in Book Seven of the "Republic," all cities are necessarily such that their denizens are immersed in darkness and are therefore suffused with prejudices, believing that the shadows they see are the truth itself. As for the denizens of those cities we call "Greek," their understandings of the good and the bad, the just and the unjust, and the noble and the base were fashioned for them by the poets, the great creative geniuses, beginning with Homer who lived perhaps in the ninth century B.C. or, if the historian Herodotus is right, perhaps as early as the twelfth century B.C. Philosophy appeared as discord because it countered the settled opinions, the prejudices, the shadows within any and all of the cities, that is, the opinions promulgated by the poets. With the advent of philosophy there came to be a natural suspicion of it in the minds of the cities and their peoples. The philosophers appeared as impious and disturbing. The suspicion of philosophers pervaded all the cities. As was said earlier in this volume, Anaxagoras (c.500–c.428 B.C.) was the first to be prosecuted at Athens for philosophizing. The next and the more celebrated case of the tension between philosophy and the city was Socrates. As we showed, Socrates was portrayed by the poet Aristophanes in the *Clouds* as being an unsavory character who looked down on the gods and who corrupted the youth by teaching them to do the same. The culmination of that comedy is that Socrates' pupil, Pheidippides, along with his father,

Strepsiades, accompanied by the god Hermes, the *very* god Hermes, himself, burn down the thinkery where Socrates holds school and drive Socrates and his pupils away. At his trial, about twenty-three years later, in which he was charged with not believing in the gods believed in by Athens, believing in other divinities, and corrupting the youth, Socrates blamed long-standing envy of and slander against him for the fact that he had been put on trial. The ground of that envy and slander lay, he said, in "a certain comic poet." He formulates the slander as a resuscitation of the old accusations against philosophers, namely that he looked into the things aloft and the things below – that is, that he was a physiologist or a natural philosopher. He denied at that trial that he had ever been interested in such things, but in the prison after his conviction, he admitted to friends that he had once been concerned with such things but then had embarked on a "second voyage." That is, as the Roman philosopher, Cicero, tells us, Socrates was the originator of political philosophy. That origination would then have taken place some time between that comic play by Aristophanes and the trial of Socrates.

Let us entertain the possibility that political philosophy was not only begun by Socrates, his pupil Plato, and Plato's pupil Aristotle but that, in fact, it was perfected by them. That possibility turns on the possibility that, after all, there is such a thing as human nature and so a nature of the political, and it turns also on the proposition that when we speak of nature, we speak of something that *is*, of being, and that "to be" means "to be always." If these things are true, then there has been no such thing as the "evolution" or "development" of political philosophy. What we have now is not a new and improved political philosophy but, at best, a political philosophy confronting new political circumstances or, at worst, a corruption of political philosophy. We suggested earlier that a critical moment in the history of political philosophy was its confrontation with revealed religion, transpolitical religion, the religion originating with Abraham and spread abroad largely by Christians and then by Christians and Muslims. If so, our seemingly far-fetched notion that classical political philosophy might be thought to have remained constant for nearly two thousand years would seem more plausible. Our examination of medieval political philosophy would then suggest that, rather than political philosophy changing, it, in fact, merely confronted that new circumstance, the new context of revealed religion. Political philosophers would then have had to adapt to or artfully evade the new circumstance. Would Thomas Aquinas appear then as an adaptation? Would Averroës appear as one who evades? Where would Maimonides fit? Is the adaptation by Thomas, which includes making it appear that "natural law" is what Aristotle meant by "natural right," a salutary adaptation of or a corruption of classical political philosophy? Does it simply put political philosophy "right with God," or does it introduce a discordant element into political philosophy?

Niccolò Machiavelli

Chapter Eight on Machiavelli was given the jarring title "A Kind of Betrayal." If medieval political philosophers adapted classical political philosophy to the new circumstances or evaded those circumstances, Machiavelli offers us an alternative to classical political philosophy. He brings about a political philosophy that sees the political questions from an altogether different point of view. It is not an evolution of but a straightforward change from classical political philosophy. To effect that change he has to undercut both classical political philosophy, which he regards as impracticable – which, of course, it consciously is – and biblical religion, particularly Christianity, which he regards as debilitating. We may state the character of that change compendiously as follows: Whereas Aristotle had regarded ethical questions as inseparable from political questions and Aquinas had separated them, Machiavelli perverts ethics in the service of politics. Instead of ethics and politics being reciprocal elements of the more general question of the nature of man and his perfection, a separated ethics becomes the handmaiden of political goals set in the absence of ethical considerations. This is something like what is meant when commentators say that, for Machiavelli, "the end justifies the means." The problem with that saying is that, of course, in truth ends do justify means, but the ends themselves are for Machiavelli liberated from any external standard of judgment. We all know that one does not get to the corner store simply because one has walked but rather that one walks to get to the corner store. The critical question is, should one go to the corner store? Why? Is it a good thing to do so?[1]

For Machiavelli, the horizon of politics is the political itself. Nothing stands above the political by which to judge the political. As for Christianity, he appears to teach that the Roman gods were good for the Romans because they were the creation of the Romans and they served the Roman purposes whereas for Machiavelli the Christian God is an impediment to the achievement of political purposes. Machiavelli is the first political philosopher to run on a campaign devoted to "change," but the nature of the change he offers has to be figured out by concentrated and prolonged study. In addition, for Machiavelli, classical political philosophy is an impediment because it raises as the standard the question of the best regime, the question of the right life for man, the question of human happiness and perfection, the question of justice, and the question of truth and its pursuit. The nature of man was seen by the ancients as appearing in man's completion or perfection. All the political questions followed from this. For Machiavelli, the nature of humans is seen in the lowest common denominator. Men are seen

---

[1] Since "supermarkets" were introduced in California in the 1930s, the "corner store" has almost disappeared from the American landscape.

as brutish, or at best clever, beings. The critical question becomes the question of the nature of the political order that accommodates itself to that fact. Socrates originated the activity known as political philosophy. Plato's writings disseminated the character of political philosophy to an audience wider than that allowed by the conversations Socrates held with his companions, but that dissemination was cautious, as can be understood by reflection on what we know as the "Seventh Letter" of Plato. The dissemination effected by Plato was widened by Aristotle, who, departing in his political conclusions only in small measure from the political conclusions of Plato, turned political philosophy into a teachable science. Similarly, Machiavelli's teaching waited for its wider dissemination and its acceptance upon the work of Thomas Hobbes, to which we now turn.

Thomas Hobbes

Hobbes (1558–1679) was graduated from Oxford at the age of nineteen and immediately became a tutor to the son of William Cavendish (later Earl of Devonshire). He was retained by the patronage of the Cavendish family for many years. He mastered Latin, Greek, Hebrew, and French. His first notable work was a translation in 1628 at the age of forty of the *History* (of the Peloponnesian War) by Thucydides. This was a translation by a great mind of a work by a great mind. It is a translation that is still a most worthwhile reading. At the age of fifty-two he produced *The Elements of Law Natural and Politic*. His masterwork was the *Leviathan*, written when he was sixty-three. His other works included *De Cive*, which translates into English as "Of the Citizen." It is in Latin and is rather like a companion to the *Leviathan*. A book that serves rather as a preface to *De Cive* is his *De Homine*, "Of Man." Hobbes tutored the young Charles (1630–85 [Charles II, 1661–85]) in the 1640s in France, where he had gone in 1641 and where he stayed until 1652 when it seemed safe to return to England. His writings were regarded, not without reason, as heretical, and his books were burned in bonfires at Oxford until as late as 1683.

The circumstances under which Hobbes pursued his philosophic endeavors are these: He was born in 1588 at the moment when the Spanish Armada was menacing England and subjecting its people to fear. We must remember that Spain was solidly Roman Catholic, that Martin Luther (1483–1546) and John Calvin (1509–64) had introduced Protestant reform into northern Europe, and that Henry VIII of England (1491–1547; reigned 1509–47) had broken from the Roman church in the 1530s perhaps not primarily on theological but rather on political grounds. That break opened a fissure in English life between those who followed Henry and those who remained devoted to the Church as it was centered in Rome. That fissure persisted from that point in the 1530s until nearly the end of the next century. During those 160 years Catholicism was suppressed in Britain and succession to the

Crown was under a dark cloud of fear that a monarch would succeed who had been reconverted surreptitiously to the Roman Church by what were seen as the seditious machinations of priests. To heighten this problem, several sects of Protestant faith were at odds with each other and sometimes at war with each other. Charles I was born in 1600 and was crowned king in 1625. His attempts to find a queen for himself in Spain or France were met by attempts there to restore him to Catholicism. Although he resisted his own reconversion, he entertained the possibility of allowing freedom again for Catholics in the realm and he similarly bargained for the support of the Scots by entertaining the temporary establishment of Presbyterianism in England. Civil War erupted in 1642 and, with interruptions, continued until 1651. In 1649 Charles was found guilty of treason by a Parliamentary commission, a remarkable event that foreshadowed the complete ascendancy of Parliament forty years later. Charles was beheaded. The period between 1649 and the restoration of the monarchy in 1660 is known as the "Interregnum." Oliver Cromwell (1599–1658), a member of Parliament, ascended to the position of Lord Protector in 1653 and held that place until 1658. During a particularly disorderly session of the House of Commons in which the several religious factions struggled with each other (each faction having at its beck and call its own army), Cromwell called for order in this unrelenting and unyielding conflict, it is said, by pleading, "By the bowels of Christ I beseech ye to consider it possible that you are mistaken." Hobbes, having taken refuge in France in 1641, stayed there until 1652. It was also these troubles from 1642 to 1660, however, that fostered an instability that opened the door for the unorthodox writings of Hobbes. Hobbes died in 1679, nine years short of the "Glorious Revolution" that, contrary to his arguments, ensured the supremacy of Parliament. Nonetheless it must be said that, on the whole, Hobbes won out.

Hobbes's *Leviathan* is a comprehensive teaching on politics. It consists of four parts divided into forty-seven chapters after which there is added a "Review and Conclusion." Part I is titled "Of Man." It has sixteen chapters of which the first eight, or perhaps the first twelve, may be described as his teaching on human psychology. The fact that the first chapter is titled "Of Sense" is a clue to the fact that Hobbes is a materialist. Aristotle had explained man as an animal endowed with *logos*, or reasoned speech. Man doesn't *invent* speech as a means to some predetermined end. He *has* speech. To begin an explanation of man with a statement on sense as Hobbes does intimates that the five bodily senses are the very definition of the nature of man, and in fact Hobbes says that there is, "no other act of man's mind that I can remember, naturally planted in him . . . but his five senses."(*Lev.* ch. 3, ¶ 11). Both Plato and Aristotle had understood intellection as conception distinct from perception. Hobbes says that "whatsoever . . . we conceive has been perceived first by sense" (*Lev.*, ch. 3, ¶ 12). This lays the groundwork for the view implicit in much of twentieth-century psychology that there is no such thing as the psyche about which to "*ologize*." To make a clumsy pun, there "ain't no such *anima* as the soul." Man is here understood as an extremely complex bundle of electromechanical signals surging about in the material substance of the brain. The mind *is* the brain. The present state of this view is reflected in the notion of "artificial intelligence," a notion that began after World War II as an accompaniment to the development of digital, as distinct from analog, computers. Its goal is to replicate the human brain mechanically. The ground for accepting this notion is fortified by the marvelous achievement in 2008 of a missile shooting down a dying, artificial satellite traveling in space at several thousand miles per hour. The relative success of shipboard gunnery firecontrolmen in shooting down an aircraft lumbering along at 250 to 300 miles per hour a few hundred feet above the surface of the sea during World War II does not even suggest such potential achievements as that in 2008, except perhaps to the most visionary mind. The ground for caution about the notion of artificial intelligence is supported by one or two calls to the bank to talk to the robot that answers about your account, or one or two calls to the airline to query that robot about your flight schedule.

Part II of the *Leviathan*, consisting of fifteen chapters, is titled "Of Commonwealth." Part III, with twelve chapters, is "Of a Christian Commonwealth." Part IV, with four chapters, is "Of the Kingdom of Darkness." Marsilius was a philosopher within Christendom who appears to us as possibly a Christian with a view of scripture at odds with the official view of the Church at Rome. It also appears possible that his fidelity to the philosophy of the pagans was a turn away from Christianity, a turn that had to be covert both in the interest of personal safety and in the interest of having his arguments listened to by the faithful. Similar choices present themselves in the case of Hobbes. Does the fact that he quotes scripture frequently and devotes twelve chapters to the character of a Christian commonwealth mean that he is, as some have said, a devout Christian? Does the fact that he writes at length of "the laws of nature" mean that he is a follower of the Christian natural law doctrine, or does the way in which he writes of it firmly distinguish him from the believers in the natural law tradition? The way in which one resolves these two questions will determine the degree of understanding reached respecting his whole teaching, his whole aim.

The student can reach a provisional understanding of the core political teaching of the *Leviathan* by a careful reading of Chapters 13 through 21, that is, the last four chapters of Part I, "Of Man," and the first five chapters of Part II, "Of Commonwealth." We shall confine our introductory remarks about the *Leviathan* to a compressed statement of his argument in these nine chapters, combined with a few illustrative examinations of some details in those chapters.

Chapter 13 is titled, "Of the Natural Condition of Mankind, As Concerning Their Felicity, and Misery." Hobbes makes it appear that he is writing of things of which others, particularly the ancients, have written, but he is most emphatically not doing that. He gives a new meaning to "nature." The reader needs to discern the character of that change and needs to keep in mind that the descriptions of things in this chapter and in the next two chapters, Chapters 14 and 15, are descriptions that apply not to man always but only to man as he is to be imagined in that natural condition. The first thing he asserts is that men are equal, equal in body. He supports this by saying that even the weakest "has strength enough to kill the strongest" under specified conditions, but does not the listing of the weakest and the strongest provide simple proof that men are not equal in body? Furthermore, is it not evident to the ordinary observer that men are not equal in body? They are not equally strong, equally swift, or equally beautiful. He then says that "as to the faculties of the mind … [he finds] yet a greater equality amongst men." Note the ellipsis in our quotation. What we have omitted, indicated by that ellipsis, is a long dependent clause, and that clause is itself modified by an inner clause. It is a kind of sleight of hand which can only be seen through by the reader who notes that the conditions Hobbes states in those dependent clauses are utterly beyond the possibility of empirical confirmation. Taking the sentence without those clauses, every sane adult can plainly see that men are not equally wise, equally prudent, or equally understanding. In other words, Hobbes imagines a nature of man in an imagined condition of nature. Not only is there no empirical evidence, there could not be, in the nature of things, any empirical evidence for either that man or that "condition of mere nature." Hobbes knows this and will shortly answer this objection. What is more, Hobbes says at the end of the introduction to the book that, although to know man is the hardest thing, he will teach us. Furthermore, he says that before he came along there had been no science except geometry (ch. 4, ¶ 12). That means that, contrary to the traditional view that Socrates had originated political philosophy, he, Hobbes, is truly the originator. Now Hobbes is a man of towering intelligence, and he clearly knows it. How can he, then, with a poker face, tell us that all men are equal? The answer to this is forthcoming. Hobbes gives us a clue in the paragraph proclaiming the equality of man's mental faculties. He says the proof is that all men are satisfied with their share, and there can be no greater proof of the equal distribution of something than that "every man is contented with his share." We have seen that Plato can make a small joke for us. Here we see that Hobbes, an otherwise sober writer, has made a joke on a par with that in the "Republic" where Polemarchus, after agreeing that the just man will harm no one, promised to harm those who disagree with the conclusions he and Socrates had come to. At least Plato was original. Hobbes is rather the Milton Berle of the seventeenth century. He stole his joke about equal distribution of mental capacity from René Descartes (1596–1650), who had made that same joke fifteen years earlier in the first paragraph of Part One of his *Discourse on Method*.

Because men are equal in the condition of mere nature, they are enemies when it comes to self-preservation and pleasures, so in that condition there is no way to dispraise force or wiles. That is, everything is permitted. In fact, "a man ought to be allowed to be master over many men." Is this not at first curious? It argues that because in nature we are equal, slavery is permitted, at least in nature. Furthermore, not only are we rivals, or enemies; we are not even naturally sociable. Thus, where Aristotle had called man a "political animal," Hobbes not only denies that man is political, he denies that man is social. He is not even sociable. There are "three causes of quarrel: competition, fear, and glory," and "without a common power to keep them all in awe" (i.e., in that condition of mere nature in which no such common power exists), there is a "war of every man against every man" wherein "life is solitary, poor, nasty, brutish, and short" (ch. 13, ¶¶ 3–9). Hobbes then answers the objection we made about empirical evidence. He acknowledges that it "may peradventure be thought, that there never was such a time nor condition of war as this." What he means is that such a condition exists in principle, at bottom, as can be seen when civil war breaks out.

Chapters 14 and 15 delineate some nineteen "laws of nature," the first two in Chapter 14 and the remainder in Chapter 15. The first sentence of Chapter 14 presents us with another instance of sleight of hand. His syntax makes it appear that he is simply continuing a long-held view about right, or law, or justice, but in fact what he presents is novel. He presents us with the very foundation of the modern notion of natural rights. First, it is well that we remind ourselves that the distinction between justice and a law or between justice and the law is a philosophical distinction, a philosophical examination of subphilosophic assumptions. The word for law, right, or justice in Greek is *diké*. In Latin, the word is *jus*. There is in Latin, of course, a word for a specific law, namely *lex*, but, *lex* denotes *a* law, and *jus* denotes *the* law, the law generally. The prephilosophic identity of law and justice continues to the present in common speech. In Italian the word is *giusto*, in French *droit*, in Spanish *derecho*, and in German *recht*. Hobbes begins Chapter 14 thus:

> The right of nature, which writers commonly call jus naturale, is the liberty each man has to use his power, as he will himself, for the preservation of his own nature, that is to say, of his own life, and consequently of doing anything which, in his own judgment and reason, he shall conceive to be the aptest means thereunto.

It is surely true that the right of nature is what the writers call the *jus naturale*, but to say that is no more than to say that the right of nature is what the writers call "the right of nature." What "the writers" never before had said was that that right was "the liberty each man has to use his own power" according to his own judgment, for the purpose of self-preservation. If Hobbes is, as he claims, the very founder of true political philosophy, then this is the first principle of the new, the true political philosophy. It is a radical departure from the past. It rests on the new moral outlook presented by Machiavelli. It codifies that new moral outlook, the outlook that severs ethics from politics thereby liberating politics from ethical consideration.

In Chapter 14 (¶ 4), Hobbes asserts that in that condition of mere nature which he has posited, "every man has a right to everything, even to one another's bodies." It is clear, however, to Hobbes as it should be to us, that if everyone has a right to everything, then nobody has a firm right, his own right, to anything. You cannot go to court to vindicate your right to your body, much less the right to your house, if every person on earth has an equal right to it. This really is the hell Hobbes has called the "condition of mere nature." Slavery is right if you are strong enough to inflict it on another. Might simply makes right. There is no right or wrong. As Hobbes flatly says in Chapter 13 (¶ 13), there is no just or unjust in nature. Furthermore, there is no propriety in nature, that is, nothing is proper to anyone, there is no property in nature. What I can take is mine for just so long as I can keep it. How better to explain the war of every man against every man where life is solitary, poor, nasty, brutish, and short?

What is to be done?

Hobbes makes the first fact of nature to be the fear of violent death. From this he deduces the first right of nature, the right of self-preservation. From the first right of nature he draws the first law of nature: Seek peace! The second law of nature follows from the first: The way to peace is for each of us to lay down our rights to establish civil society. This creates a sovereign with all of the power of all of us. In doing so it substitutes the fear of the sovereign for that fear that each of us had "in the condition of mere nature," the fear by each of us of every other. How many of our rights do we give up? All of them, except for the few that it would be self-contradictory to relinquish, and Hobbes does not hesitate to specify these. No one would, indeed no one could, relinquish his right to life for the purpose of preserving his right to his life. Similarly, it is by nature impossible for one to relinquish his right to his liberty, because without liberty one's right to life is not secure. Finally, if one has to beg his master – that is, his sovereign – for bread, he cannot be said to possess liberty. Thus, these are the rights that cannot be surrendered. The right to life is the ground of all life. Liberty is the fence around life. Property is the assurance of liberty. Every other imaginable right is signed over to the sovereign who by that very signing-over is created sovereign. A cluster of us in the condition of mere nature, each fearing every other, collectively signs over to one of us the sovereignty. It need not be according to merit that the sovereign is established. It could as well be by lot. The critical question of political philosophy is no longer "Who should rule?" The first order of business is simply that there should be rule, that someone or other should rule. This act of ceding one's rights to a sovereign, the act that moves us from the condition of mere nature to civil society, is called the "original contract" or the "social contract." Be alert: The usage of the second of these two expressions by careless speakers in the twenty-first century does not preserve the original meaning. In the original usage, the second expression was the simple equivalent of the first. The original contract is the social contract, the contract that creates civil society from the raw state of nature. It is a notion that is something of a parody of the biblical doctrine that God created the heavens and the earth from a condition of chaos. Whereas for Aristotle, the city "*is* by nature," but a given city *comes to be* by a specific human act, Hobbes conflates *being* and *coming into being*. For Hobbes, the city cannot be said *to be* by nature. The city is natural only in that it comes to be by way of a conscious and deliberate departure from nature, a departure demanded by the miserable condition of mere nature. Not in the *Leviathan* itself, but elsewhere in the works of Hobbes this is called the "state of nature," and it is called that by Locke, by Rousseau, and by us. The "state of nature" means, in its primary sense, the status or condition of nature, but over the three and a half centuries since Hobbes, the phrase has taken on something of a different shade of meaning.

Hobbes states clearly that one cannot lay down his rights to life or liberty (ch. 14, ¶ 8). He makes clear the right to property in Chapter 15 (¶ 3). Let us illustrate these unalienable rights by examining the second of them, the right to liberty. If one man enslaves another in nature, and let us suppose that the enslaved one takes an oath affirming his slavery, a sort of anticipation of what in civil society would be the signing away of something by means of a title deed, the slave makes his own liberty the possession of the other. That is, the slave "alienates" his liberty, which is to say, he "otherfies" it. Clearly the slave has lost his liberty thereby, but has he lost his right to liberty? It seems that Hobbes argues that the slave cannot do so. Any attempt by the slave to do so is negated by the very nature of the thing. If, in weakness, he gives up his liberty, he has a right of nature to recover it if he can.

In Chapter 15, Hobbes sets out the other seventeen laws of nature. The third law of nature is "that men perform their covenants made." Without this law, the others would have no substance. Hobbes offers several observations in these chapters on the nature of contracts, and the student needs to examine these comments to see the full character of Hobbes's argument and to speculate constructively on whether there are difficulties in it. We shall mention only two other things in Chapter 15. First, Hobbes tells us, "for the ninth law of nature, I put this *that every man acknowledge other for his equal by nature*" (ch. 15, ¶ 21). This explains how Hobbes can understand himself to be a superior human being and yet lay it down at the beginning of Chapter 13 that men are radically equal. It appears as a kind of salutary lie like the lie Plato makes Socrates suggest to his companions in the "Republic" that they must promulgate to those in the city in speech they have created. The problem Hobbes faces is that of the truly superior man. As Glaucon had argued to Socrates, many say that the truly manly man would never willingly submit to an agreement for justice, because such a man can take what he wants! There are such men, and Hobbes argues that justice, not existing in nature, can be established only in civil society and civil society itself cannot be established if men of a superior nature do not accept equality with the lesser men. In other words, as we shall state again later, it is not that the ancients were ignorant of the wonderful fact "discovered" by modernity, that "all men are created equal"; it is that the ancients and the moderns both appreciate that men are equal in some respects and unequal in others and, whereas the ancients regarded the *inequalities* as the politically decisive qualities, we moderns regard the *equalities* as the politically decisive qualities. In fact, the prefix "e" in equality is a negation of "quality." To speak of equality is to dismiss quality from consideration. For Hobbes, civil peace will never take the place of natural war if the strong and the clever do not acknowledge the equality of men in the politically crucial respects. Also, let it be remembered that the foundation of the modern doctrine of equality holds that men are equal only in this politically crucial respect. The modern doctrine of equality as understood by Hobbes and then by Locke and as enshrined in the Declaration of Independence never suggests what is evidently false, that men are equally beautiful, equally strong, or equally swift, nor does it suggest (except perhaps rather deviously) that men are equally wise or equally virtuous. Finally, the modern doctrine of the equality of men has to be transformed radically to make it mean that men are entitled to equal shares of good things. Anyone who wishes to make that transformation is obliged to present an argument on behalf of it that is as coherent and compelling as the argument Hobbes and Locke make for the original modern doctrine of equality. One's sentiment that men are entitled by nature or by law to equal shares of good things is not a substitute for such an argument. No one expressing such a sentiment has, may we say, a right to expect the one with whom he is arguing to accept that sentiment as argument nor should someone expect that stating such a sentiment with moral fervor transforms it into an argument.

In Chapter 15 (¶ 34), Hobbes admits that there might be other laws of nature, having to do with individuals, but he does not need to consider them in this book. In other words, ethics and politics are wholly sundered. One can devise a complete political science without the least consideration of ethics. Immanuel Kant (1724–1804) attempted to establish in his *Foundations of the Metaphysics of Morals* (1785) a comprehensive doctrine of ethics utterly divorced from means, and so, divorced from politics. Ten years later, in his only work that falls clearly in the category of political philosophy, "Perpetual Peace," he makes this assertion: "The problem of organizing a state, however hard it may seem, can be solved even for a race of devils, if only they are intelligent." (This quote appears in the First Supplement, about one page short of the end.) It is clear from what we have laid out here regarding Chapters Thirteen, Fourteen, and Fifteen of the *Leviathan* that, contrary to what an occasional historian, professor of political science, or professor of philosophy might say, Hobbes, rather than continuing the natural law tradition, is a conscious innovator. His innovation rests on a foundation laid by Machiavelli. Natural law, as it may have been spawned by the postclassical Stoics and as it was made firm by St. Thomas Aquinas, is quite distinct from the natural right understanding of the classical political philosophy of Plato and Aristotle. The modern natural rights doctrine that was founded by Hobbes and is the ground of the American political order is distinct from both natural right and natural law. The greatest problem many students have is the inability to read older things because of the astigmatism imposed on their understanding by the present spirit of the times. This is made more difficult because one of the present prejudices is that we are free of prejudice, free because of the Enlightenment of which Hobbes and Locke are great exemplars. In the fifth paragraph of the unnumbered chapter called "A Review and Conclusion" that follows Chapter 47, Hobbes, as though he had simply forgotten to mention it back in Chapter 15, adds a twentieth law of nature. That addition causes the reader to speculate that Hobbes may have separated the twentieth from the nineteenth law by a few hundred pages because the twentieth is inconsistent with the tenor of the first nineteen or perhaps because, being consistent with them, the whole scheme of Hobbes's natural law seems flawed. The gap between the nineteenth and the twentieth law of nature might just as easily be explained, however, by the mechanics of book production in the seventeenth century.

Chapter 16 is titled "Of Persons, Authors, and Things Personated." It can be treated summarily as follows: As paragraph 9 argues, inanimate things cannot be personated without civil government; and as paragraph 10 explains, there can be no dominion over persons without civil government. Thus, Christianity, being an inanimate thing, can only be personated by the Church, and that personation and its structure, clergy, and hierarchy cannot come to be but by the grace of the sovereign of civil government. The whole problem of the tension between faith and reason is shunted to one side by the act of Henry VIII that made the Church of England subordinate to himself. When Hobbes wrote the *Leviathan*, the Crown in England had already been for more than a hundred years both the chief political officer and the chief ecclesiastical officer. The principle of the First Amendment to the U.S. Constitution that is somewhat imperfectly called "the separation of church and state" is a variance from Hobbes's theme. The reasoning under King Henry's and then Hobbes's view of the superiority of state over church is that man cannot serve "two masters." Religious contests with the sovereign split the sovereignty. A split sovereignty is weak. A weak sovereignty invites the recurrence of that condition of war of everyman against everyman that characterizes the "condition of mere nature" and is the worst thing humanly possible.

Let us now glance at the opening chapters of Part II, "Of Common-wealth." Chapter 17, "Of the Causes, Generation, and Definition of a

Commonwealth," consists of fifteen paragraphs. Paragraph 13 allows that the sovereignty may be vested in either a single individual or in an assembly. Hobbes makes it plain that he regards monarchy as preferable, because a sovereignty made up of many parts is likely to be torn apart, but this question is secondary. The primary question is the fact of the establishment itself of sovereignty. Whereas both Plato's "Republic" and Aristotle's *Politics* may be said to be devoted, each in its entirety, to the analysis of various regimes and the identification and examination of the best regime, that whole inquiry is reduced to a small compass in the *Leviathan*. The same thing is true of Locke's *Second Treatise of Government*, which devotes about a half-page thematically to that inquiry. Hobbes does prefer monarchy and Locke does prefer some sort of parliamentary system, but for both of them the critical question is not the question of *which* regime but the question of the coming into being of *some* regime or other. Since Locke we customarily ask less whether a given regime is good than whether its origin vested it with legitimacy. Paragraph 13 of Chapter 17 goes on to call the Leviathan a "mortal god," which settles finally for him the rule of state over church canvassed in Chapter 16.

Paragraph 15 of Chapter 17 distinguishes between a commonwealth established by acquisition and a commonwealth established by institution. The former is a sovereignty imposed on a population by a strong man. The latter is a sovereignty created by the action of those over whom it is erected. Naturally, the reader pauses at this moment and wonders what the differences in the characters of the two are. Chapter 18 is titled "Of the Rights of Sovereigns by Institution," that is, the rights of a sovereignty originated by the action of the people. He lays down twelve rights of sovereigns by institution. The first four are as follows:

1. The covenant establishing the sovereignty having been made, no one may break it, and particularly there can be no covenant with God to break the political covenant.
2. There is no covenant between the ruled and the sovereign. There can be none because before the covenant there was no corporate body called the "people." There was only an inchoate mass of persons. When they make a covenant each with every other to vest the sovereignty, they vest it in whomsoever they please, but the covenant itself is made among the individuals and not between them and the sovereign, who does not exist as sovereign until the covenant creates him as such.
3. No one is exempt from the covenant. One may perhaps be free to pack up and leave, but if he is in the minority, even if it is a sizeable minority, he cannot stay and act the malcontent. If he is in he is in; if he is out he is out. Notice the rigorous rule of the majority and notice that the justification of majority rule is the absolute equality of the

members of the community in the crucial political respects. If all are "equal" – that is, if there are no better and no worse members – then the only way to decide things is by "weighing" the majority against the minority. It is clear that the greater "weight" is with the greater "mass." That element is politically right and the other is wrong. Hobbes does not say so explicitly but, given these facts, when Hobbes said that no one is exempt from the covenant, it can only mean that those in the minority fully accept as correct the choice of the majority or, one supposes, they must leave. If they leave, they are not "in" the covenant, but they are back in a state of war, each with each other and each with the now-established sovereignty.

4. The sovereign can do no wrong. Because nothing is just or unjust in nature and nothing firmly belongs to anyone, and because doing wrong means violating another's rights, no one can do wrong in nature. In the commonwealth, all the members have acknowledged certain rights to each other and all the other rights to the sovereign. The sovereign, however, has made no covenant with anyone; therefore, nothing belongs to anyone over against the sovereign. He can do many things an individual does not like, but he cannot wrong the individual because he has no obligation to any individual. The old English saying that "no writ may run against the crown" is the equivalent of saying that "the king can do wrong." The sovereign is above the law. There can be in England a case called *Rex v. Smith*, but there can be no case brought that is called *Smith v. Rex*. That is what it means to say "no writ may run against the crown," and that is what Hobbes means when he says that the sovereign can do no wrong.

These four "rights of the sovereign by institution," along with eight more illustrate Hobbes's preference for monarchy. The "mixed regime" which had been developing over the centuries in England, and which may be said to have settled finally with the Parliament Act of 1911, wherein the sovereign power appears to vest in the Crown, Lords, and Commons combined, presents a problem for Hobbes, and he argues plainly in paragraph 16 of Chapter 17 that sovereignty, properly understood, is indivisible. In paragraph 20, Hobbes answers anticipated objections to unmixed sovereignty in the hands of a monarch by arguing that no perceived burdens on the part of a people because of the existence of an absolute monarch can be nearly as bad as the condition of mere nature. In addition, he had already shown that every defect in the indivisibility of sovereignty is a clear cause of return to that state of nature, as witness the then ongoing civil war. These arguments are the prelude to his next chapter, to which we now turn.

It is always a good practice to think ahead a bit before turning the page. If Chapter 17 had distinguished between commonwealth by institution and commonwealth by acquisition, and Chapter 18 enumerated the "rights of sovereigns by institution," what will Chapter 19 be about? Will it be about "the rights of sovereigns by acquisition," and will those rights differ from the first set? Not quite. Chapter 19 is titled "Of the Several Kinds of Commonwealth by Institution and of Succession to the Sovereign Power." It appears that the sequel to Chapter 18 will have to come a bit later. Chapter 19 is a continuation of the examination of commonwealth by institution, and a continuation of the demonstration of the necessity of sovereign indivisibility. In paragraphs 1 and 2 of Chapter 19, Hobbes offers an alternative to Aristotle's *Politics* that reminds one of Machiavelli's burlesque in Chapter 15 of *The Prince* of the enumeration of the virtues in Aristotle's *Ethics*. Recall that in Book Three of the *Politics* Aristotle had shown that there were six possible regimes, rule of one, rule of a few, and rule of the many, one of each of these being good and one bad. Hobbes here says that there are only three possible regimes: monarchy, democracy, and aristocracy. "There be other names of government in the histories and books of policy (as *Tyranny* and *Oligarchy*). But they are not the names of other forms of government, but of the same forms misliked." To call the monarch a tyrant is sedition that leads back to the condition of mere nature which, as we have seen, Hobbes holds is worse than any kingship. One can speculate regarding the cause of this. Would the most lustful and intemperate monarch, being but one man, be capable of more than a small fraction of the discomforts – the rapes, murders, and thefts – we can each inflict on others in the absence of "a common power to keep us all in awe?" Paragraphs 11 and 12 of Chapter 19 show that an attempt to get around the problem by talking of constitutional monarchy fails, because there can be no such thing as an elective king or a limited king. Either a king is truly a king or he is not. If he is not, there is divided government which draws us back to that miserable estate, the condition of mere nature. Then, in paragraph 14, Hobbes shows that succession to the sovereignty in a perfect commonwealth must be with the sovereign himself. If such succession should be up to the parliament, the fissure would lead back toward the condition of mere nature. We add here the historical note that the birth of parliamentary supremacy occurred ten years after Hobbes's death in what is called the "Glorious Revolution" wherein William of Orange and Mary, by a bargain with the Lords and Commons, came to be joint monarchs (a strange self-contradiction) as successors to James II who had converted to Roman Catholicism and wakened the English fear that now came to be called the "Popish Plot." John Locke, in one of his few explicit differences from Hobbes, endorses constitutional monarchy and so the Glorious Revolution.

Well, now, have we reached the point where we might expect a chapter titled "Of the Rights of Sovereigns by Acquisition?" Almost! "A commonwealth by acquisition" are the first four words of Chapter 20, but the *title* of that chapter is "Of Dominion Paternal and Despotical." The Greek word of which the English "despot" is a cognate is δεσπότης (*despotēs*). It is translated as "master," both in the sense of master of a household and, more particularly, as master of a slave or of slaves. The Greek word that is the equivalent of the English word "slave" is δουλος (*doulos*). The English word "despotism" thus means rule over a political community that is like the rule of a master over a slave. Whatever might have been the earlier meaning of the word, the Greek word *despotēs* came sometimes to be used in antiquity as a term of reproach, which is the way the English word "despot" has perhaps always been understood. Hobbes straightforwardly uses the word in the title to Chapter 20. He uses the word "paternal" as it would be used in speaking of household rule but then he uses, as though it were something akin to paternal, the word "despotical." Apparently he wants us to understand that "commonwealth by acquisition" is rule like the rule of a master over his household and over his slaves, or simply as the rule of master over slave. He wants to be understood clearly. True monarchy is not constrained by anything on earth, but this is no cause for alarm because the sovereign is not foolish enough to destroy what is his own, his property. If he should use up some of his subjects because of lust or other appetite, or if he should destroy some of them because of anger or envy, again, he is only one man and he cannot possibly use or destroy very many, whereas the direct effect of war of every man against every man is many, many times worse than what we might call the "side effects" of indivisible and unrestrained monarchy, the sort of monarchy that those Hobbes treats as foolish people rail against and wrongly call "tyranny." Thus, the answer to the question as to how the rights of sovereigns by acquisition compare to the rights of sovereigns by institution is that they are exactly the same. This he says in so many words in paragraphs 3 and 14 of Chapter 20, and if anyone is inclined to cavil that a commonwealth by acquisition is made by a covenant that results from fear, so what? What is the difference between a covenant that establishes a sovereignty by institution, which results from the fear we have of each other, and a sovereignty by acquisition, which results from the fear we have of the strong man who imposes it on us? Fear is fear. If one responds that covenants from fear are invalid, citing the civil law, Hobbes flatly states that *covenants from fear are, in their nature, valid!* Even in civil society they are invalid not because of inherent invalidity, but because the positive law makes them invalid. It is proper for Hobbes to liken paternal rule to despotical rule because, contrary to Aristotle (who made a qualitative distinction between the community of the household and the community of the polis), for Hobbes the difference between family and civil society is merely quantitative. The latter is bigger.

If we are not persuaded by Hobbes, perhaps it is because we are too attached to traditional views that have somehow persisted despite Hobbes. His answer to that comes at the end of paragraph 19, the last paragraph, of Chapter 20. It includes the following two sentences:

For though in all places of the world men should lay the foundation of their houses on the sand, it could not thence be inferred, that so it ought to be. The skill of making and maintaining commonwealths consisteth in certain rules, as doth arithmetic and geometry, not (as tennis play) on practice only; which rules neither poor men have the leisure, nor men that have had the leisure have hitherto had the curiosity or the method to find out.

That is, Hobbes's predecessors did not have the "method," that is to say, the science. As we have already noted, Hobbes claims to be the true founder of political philosophy, of political science.

Perhaps you are still not persuaded by his argument. Stop. Does he not, in discussing commonwealth by institution (not to speak here of commonwealth by acquisition), establish the modern principle that legitimate commonwealths derive from the consent of the governed? In addition, if you are indignantly inclined to display bumper stickers about rights, is it not the case that the entire doctrine of natural rights, the doctrine at the core of all modern political science, has its origin in these teachings of Thomas Hobbes? Can you simply take the sweet without the bitter by an act of will, or must you not think the problem through?

Also are you fond of liberty? Chapter 21 of the *Leviathan* states clearly that liberty of the subject is only what the sovereign allows (¶ 6). Liberty depends on the silence of the law. Of course we are entitled to the liberties and the rights the law gives us, and in the American case these are undergirded by the Constitution. Can one demand "*natural* rights," however? Should we praise our courts for finding and "giving us" new rights beyond those granted by the laws and the Constitution? Did we not, in the condition of mere nature, possess every imaginable right, even the right to one another's bodies? How could a benevolent court hand out one more right on top of every conceivable right? Are judges gods? Does not the appeal to natural rights against the commonwealth present the specter of a return to nature, a return to that miserable estate of war of every man against every man where life is solitary, poor, nasty, brutish, and short? Must we not take note of the fact that, in the expression "American civil liberties," the words "American" and "civil" are an adverb and an adjective and that together they modify the word "liberties"? Does the American Civil Liberties Union, however good their intentions may be, believe that there is a natural right to be uncivil in civil society, and does that belief, by judicial fiat, translate into a civil right to be vindicated in the courts? "If every man should lay the foundation of his house on sand," should we take our toolboxes and head for the beach?

Summarizing some of the principal factors in Hobbes's teaching, we see first that he introduces the notion of the condition of mere nature, or, the "state of nature," a notion unknown to the ancients who conceived of natural right; second, he introduces the principle of radical equality in the politically crucial respects; third, he transforms the doctrine of natural right into the doctrine of natural rights; fourth, he introduces the notion of the original contract or covenant – that is, the social contract – and this introduces the firm doctrine that legitimate government rests on the consent of the governed; fifth, he insists on perfect sovereignty, absolute and indivisible sovereignty, as the surest way to keep sedition from casting civil society back into the state of nature. The whole scheme means that we move from a state of perfect but terrifyingly unsafe freedom to a state of near-perfect but safe and comfortable subjection. It is a subjection because we give up our rights so as to vest the sovereignty, but it is only a "near-perfect" subjection because there are some few – very few – natural rights that are incapable of being surrendered: These are the ones that our Declaration of Independence specifies as "inalienable." One *cannot* give them up.

Perhaps John Locke can help us out of such difficulties as are included in this catalogue. Let us now turn to him.

John Locke

In Hobbes's day, there were two universities in England, Oxford and Cambridge, both founded in the twelfth century. It would not be possible to sort them out as either public or private as is done in the case of American universities today. Setting aside the learned professions of law, medicine, and divinity, no one went to Oxford or Cambridge to prepare for a job or a career. It could almost be said that the whole curriculum was confined to various aspects of philosophy. The faculties were all clergy, Christian clergy, who until the sixteenth century were Catholic priests, but who, after the break with Rome by Henry VIII, and therefore, in Hobbes's day, were priests of the Church of England. Hobbes was a student in Magdalen Hall at Oxford, and it is said that he found the university intellectually stifling. In the *Leviathan* he asserts that the universities did not teach philosophy but simply "Aristotelity."

Locke (1632–1704) was at Oxford, too, in Christ Church College, but being more prudent and restrained (or perhaps simply more tentative in his views) than Hobbes had been, he contemplated entering into the life of a don (i.e., entering into an academic career). He fell back from that plan when he concluded that he could not bring himself to take holy orders (a precondition of such a career), so he went into medicine, a profession that he followed until, in 1666, when, having met and then become a friend and a literary and political ally of Lord Ashley, Chancellor of the Exchequer, medicine had to share Locke with those literary and political pursuits. (Anthony Ashley Cooper had been made Lord Ashley by Charles I. He later was elevated to the rank of first Earl of Shaftesbury.) Locke's medical skills saved Lord Ashley's life, and he took up residence with the Ashley family as Ashley's confidant and collaborator and as the family's physician. In 1683, the last book burning in English history took place at Oxford – some of the books burned were books by Hobbes – and Locke, seeing the *mene tekel* on the wall, went into exile, first in France, then in Holland, and, although he came back to England, he never again set foot on the grounds of Oxford University.[2]

The years of Locke's life were witness to the regicide, the interregnum, the Glorious Revolution, the Restoration, and the ascent of William and Mary to their shared rule. Some commentators have dismissed Locke as a mere supporter of the Glorious Revolution – that is, that his writing of the *Two Treatises of Government* was merely the literary extension of his partisan political opinion – but this presupposes that Locke was on a par intellectually with mere university professors. It notices two correlated things and leaps to the logical fallacy of assuming that, because Y and X occur together, X is the cause of Y. It is a double fallacy, because it assumes causation and it does not even entertain the possibility that Y was the cause of X – that Locke supported the Glorious Revolution because that revolution was consistent with his political thought and that he supported it only to the extent that it did so. The only sure way is to read carefully what he wrote and reflect open-mindedly on the soundness of what he wrote, rather than practicing psychiatry without a license. That easy dismissal of Locke is as little thought through as would be the dismissal of Plato because he was from a prosperous family or because it was assumed that he was no more than a reflection of Greek culture. It is kin to the view that arose in the nineteenth and twentieth centuries that we described earlier as holding that there are thoughts but no thinkers. That view is self-canceling. If Locke necessarily thought what he thought because of the times, then those who dismiss him do so only because of the thought of their times. Besides, it makes of Locke someone with the supernatural power to divine events of the future that these dismissive commentators know only because those events are in the past. How could Locke have known in the 1680s when he wrote the *Two Treatises* that the Glorious Revolution would take place successfully and that its success would never be reversed by subsequent political events? We need to remember that, for most of history, having wrong political (or theological) views meant severe penalties, sometimes including death. It is not without significance that Locke never openly admitted authorship of the *Two Treatises*, not even in a cryptic note to be found after his natural death. When he had occasion to refer back to the book, he always referred to it simply as "a book called *Two Treatises of Government.*"

The First Treatise is a refutation of a book by Sir Robert Filmer; the Second Treatise is a constructive argument that stands on the ground that had been cleared by the First. Filmer must have been born about the time Hobbes was born, or shortly thereafter. He was at Oxford in 1604 (Hobbes was at Oxford from 1603 to 1608). Filmer died in 1653. His book titled

[2] See Peter Laslett's introduction to his edition of John Locke, *Two Treatises of Government*, Cambridge, 1960, Cambridge University Press, pp. 18–25. For *mene tekel*, see *Dan.* 5:25–28.

Patriarcha, which may have been written about 1642, was published posthumously in about 1680, during the reign of Charles II, when such a book supporting absolute monarchy would have been safe in print. (During the Interregnum, Filmer's house was pillaged no less than ten times by supporters of the parliamentary party.)

Filmer's *Patriarcha* gave strong support for absolute monarchy and, in fact, for the doctrine of the divine right of kings. This doctrine was not understood by Filmer as it had been understood originally. The original understanding opposed kings to the pope. The new understanding, and that which is the understanding in present usage, opposes kings to peoples. Whether the new understanding was fostered by the likes of Filmer or had undergone a subtle change before him is not easily determined. John Neville Figgis (1863–1919) authored a book in 1907 titled *Political Thought from Gerson to Grotius, 1414 to 1625*, which explains the original meaning of the doctrine – that kings derived their installation directly from God and not mediately through the pope. Marsilius (1275–1342), Dante (1265–1321), and Petrarch (1304–74) had all opposed the powers of the pope identified with the papal claim of "plenitude of power." That opposition was the underpinning of the doctrine of the divine right of kings.

In the Preface to the First Treatise, Locke begins to dismember *Patriarcha*. He asserts firmly that consent of the people is the only lawful title to government. Then, as the text proper begins, he says that were it not for several things, including the applause the book had garnered, he would have taken it for a deliberate joke.[3] He briefly summarizes Filmer's conclusions in two phrases: first, "*That all Government is absolute Monarchy*," and second, "*That no Man is Born free*" [Tr. I,1,2]. In the third chapter, Locke presents Filmer's argument as holding that Adam had kingly dominion over his progeny by the natural right of fatherhood. In the fourth chapter, citing *Genesis* 1:28, he presents Filmer as arguing also that Adam had dominion – that is, political rule – by virtue of a direct donation by God. In the seventh chapter he explains that Filmer's argument rests on the unsupported acceptance of the proposition that inheritance is through primogeniture according to nature rather than through political choice, political choice dictated by the needs of aristocracy. Thomas I. Cook speaks of Locke's First Treatise as presenting a "contemptuous caricature" of Filmer's book.[4] Whether Locke's presentation is or is not a caricature, and therefore a falsification, he persuasively demonstrates that if Adam had had dominion naturally by fatherhood, positively by divine grant, or by both avenues, it would mean that then (in the seventeenth century, and so, now also in the twenty-first) there could

---

3 *Treatises*, I, Ch. 1, § 1. Subsequent citations will be in brackets in the text itself after this fashion: [Tr. I,1,1].

4 John Locke, *Two Treatises of Government*, with a supplement, *Patriarcha* by Robert Filmer, Thomas I. Cook, ed., New York, 1947, Hafner Press (Macmillan Publishing Co.), p. 309.

be only one king over the whole world and he shows that the possibility of establishing that inheritance of first son through first son from Adam forward to Noah and then from Noah's eldest (Would that be Shem, Ham, or Japheth? Shem is mentioned first [*Gen.* 6:10].) to the present. Because the Semites are held to be the progeny of Shem, then the governance of the whole world would have to be under the absolute rule of a single Jew, Arab, or other Semite. We might add that finding such a king would not only be a tall order but would clearly preclude any of those favored by Filmer – that is, anyone who had ever been king of England – and certainly it would then preclude Charles I, for example.

Whether some sort of posthumous petition for forgiveness of Locke is owed to Filmer, the argument of Locke's First Treatise sets a sound basis for the persuasive argument of the Second, which is titled "An Essay Concerning the True, Original, Extent, and End of Civil Government." If we take strictly the long title, that would oblige us to divide the analysis of it into three parts, origin, extent, and end. It is more convenient here to sort the nineteen chapters as follows: Chapters 1 through 4 are devoted to the origin of civil government; Chapter 5 is devoted to its principal end; Chapters 6 and 7 are devoted to the family and the household. Chapter 8 returns to the matter of origin, and Chapter 9 turns to the question of structure. Chapter 10, the shortest chapter, enumerates the different forms of civil government. Chapters 11 through 14 deal with the extent of, and so with the limits on, the elements within civil government. Chapters 15 through 19 deal with the pathologies of governments and with transitions from one sort to another, including the inherent right of a people to make such a transition.

This is an imperfect sorting of the chapters, but we shall do our best to cover the three matters expressly mentioned in the title, but in a manner that simply sketches Locke's treatment.

Chapter 1 has no title. It serves as an introduction. In it Locke asserts that his book will not be the cause of, but rather the cure for, "perpetual Disorder and Mischief, Tumult, Sedition, and Rebellion." He will achieve this cure by defining political power rightly and, as it turns out, demonstrating the true and only legitimate source of that power. Let us note that the term "power," which Hobbes had for the first time made the central question of politics, is an ambiguous term. We never know whether it means "may" or "can." For example, when Article II of the U.S. Constitution later states that "The President . . . shall have Power to" do several specified things, it means that it will not be unlawful for him to do so; it does not mean that he will surely be able to do so. Likewise, to speak of "legitimacy" is not to judge the goodness of a political order but only to examine its pedigree. In other words, both the word "power" and the principle of "legitimacy" take a step backward from the traditional and the most critical questions of politics. In this, Locke replicates the position taken by Hobbes. The one sure thing about the word "power" is that it always means not-yet-doing or not-yet-done.

The emphasis on power and on legitimacy backs away from the standards of appraisal employed by political philosophy for two thousand years.

Chapters 2 and 3, respectively, are titled "Of the State of Nature" and "Of the State of War." The state of nature is, he says, "a state of perfect freedom," and it is "a state also of equality." This, at first , seems identical with the argument of Hobbes, but with a "tut-tut" here and a "tsk-tsk" there he appears to separate himself from Hobbes by insisting that the state of nature and the state of war are two completely different things. Well, of course they are, just as "the ocean" and "blueness" are distinct from each other, but pretty nearly wherever there is ocean there is blue. Hobbes had shocked and angered set views. Locke means to win where Hobbes, whom Locke calls the "justly decried Hobbes," may be said to have lost. Locke insists that in the "state of nature" there is a "law of nature" and, in that state, every man is the executor of that law. Although this might calm the fears of those traditional readers who believe, if only indistinctly, in natural law, the careful reader will note that in Locke's explication the law of nature, because it has not been promulgated and because one must be a "studier" of it to figure it out (and who could be a "studier" of anything in that primitive state called the "state of nature?"), and because there is not a shred of evidence to show that many, or even any, denizens of the state of nature will be at all inclined to execute the law (for Locke, like Hobbes, holds that the first law of nature is self-preservation, not doing what is right), that law is altogether ineffective. It turns out that although the state of nature and the state of war are, indeed, distinct, wherever there is one there will surely be the other, and the last sentence of Chapter 2 along with the substance of Chapter 3 show that Locke wants the thoughtful reader to see that he agrees with Hobbes on the most fundamental questions. He simply writes in a way that is less likely to energize the pious ones who might be scandalized and, so, driven to vindictiveness.

A charming smoke screen is put in place in Chapter 3 to sedate the traditional reader. In instances in which one is offended in the state of nature, where there is no law and no power to which to appeal, Locke counsels an "appeal to heaven." This sounds like a wholesome, Christian call for submission and prayer. If we tally up the historical incidents drawn from scripture that Locke uses to illustrate an appeal to heaven, however, it turns out in each case to be an incident in which a commander who thought himself or his people wronged or endangered mustered his troops and led them into battle. "Appeal to heaven" is a convenient euphemism. The response to the inconveniencies of the state of nature is war, and what obviates that response is the contract that makes war no longer necessary because that contract obliterates the state of nature. It is, plainly, the original or social contract. This is just the way it is in Hobbes.

Chapter 4 is titled "Of Slavery." Let us start by reminding ourselves that until a certain point in time, every society, since time immemorial, had had slavery as an established institution. There was no ground upon which to oppose slavery. Generally, slavery had little to do with race; generally, it had to do with improved living and with households, not with production or with the acquisition of greater and greater wealth. It had to do with the generally accepted proposition that human beings are radically unequal in merit (particularly moral or intellectual merit) and, as Aristotle explains it, with the need to free the superior ones from household drudgery so that they might pursue higher callings, such as politics and philosophy. Slavery becomes wrong only in the light of that proposition of the Enlightenment – here, read Hobbes and Locke – that all men are equal in the decisive political respects. By Aristotle's standards, modern, racial, chattel slavery would have to be judged by asking the question whether it was natural or merely conventional. Judged by that standard, I have little doubt that it would fail the test, but that does not mean that every instance of slavery in the past would fail. Only by the new standard does every instance of slavery appear as a wrong. Just as Plato had Socrates show in the "Republic," we do, indeed, live in a cave, and our vision of things suffers from an intellectual astigmatism. We see the things of another time and another place through the distorting refraction of what "everybody" now knows. Because we know that slavery is wrong, simply wrong, we cannot see how anyone could ever have thought otherwise. This is proof that we are smarter than anyone else ever was, smarter and morally superior. I recall that in a fifth-grade class the teacher comfortingly assured us that "little boys now know more about medicine than doctors did a hundred years ago." By George, that made me feel wonderful. What progress! I prided myself on what an excellent fellow I was, and then, when I was about fourteen and in the tenth grade, I came across a few pages describing Galen and was confronted with the shattering revelation that Galen had known in the second century more about medicine than I would ever know, even if I lived on into the twenty-fifth. I mention the problem of intellectual astigmatism and the problem of moral and intellectual smugness only to come to a single proposition about Locke's Chapter 4. The careless reader will come to the conclusion that Locke approves of slavery and, ever so judgmentally, will dismiss him. The more careful reader will notice that Locke makes it plain that between the slave and his master there is no contract. They are therefore not in a civil state with each other, but in a state of nature, which is a state of war, and right is on the side of the slave as much as it is on the side of the master. The slave has a paramount right to reassert his right to his freedom. Now, here again, I feel good about myself. Locke seems right to me because he agrees with me, or is it the other way around? Do I agree with him because I am a modern man, a virtual storehouse of all the approved opinions established by Locke and the other great figures of the Enlightenment? Isn't it about time I woke up and got a new prescription for my mental eyeglasses? We are compelled, however, to notice that the arguments of Hobbes and Locke are never presented as mere assertions; they are arguments, and they are presented with inner consistency and with great persuasiveness.

Chapter 5 is titled "Of Property." It is one of the longer chapters and, in its serpentine way, it is fascinating. It can probably be regarded as the very foundation of modern economics, more fundamental even than the 1776 book by Adam Smith, *An Inquiry into the Nature and Causes of the Wealth of Nations.* Here is another place where reminding ourselves of ancient things helps our understanding. First, as we showed in Chapter 3 herein, the word "economics" is Greek and is formed of the words *oikon* for household and *nomos* for law (or custom, ways, system, or management). Thus, the primary meaning of economics is household management. Aristotle amply explained that the *polis*, or city, was one sort of community, the *oikon* or household another kind, and the household was subordinate to the city because the city aimed at the completion of human excellence whereas the household could, on its own, satisfy only the everyday, commonplace needs of humanity. Aristotle then discussed the several parts of household management – husband over wife, father over child, master over slave – and then, because the household needed material wealth, he asked whether the acquisition of that wealth was or was not a part of that science, the science of household management. He concluded that one sort of acquisition was, indeed, part of household management, or economics, was in accord with nature, and was limited – strictly limited – by the ends of the household. We used the example of a plow. The household needs a plow. It is probably a good idea to have a spare one, or perhaps a spare plowshare, but it would be proof of insanity if a householder devoted his life to acquiring more and more plows. Aristotle showed that there was another sort of acquisition, which was not a part of economics, was not natural, and was not limited, but he shut off further discussion of it because talk of such things was not proper for gentlemen. Throughout history, this genteel disdain for wealth, as such, was the mark of civilized life.

Christianity and its moral guidance of the West complemented Aristotle's view, and in fact reached beyond that genteel disdain. According to Christianity, the desire for more is not just ungentlemanly, it is sinful. The standard held up by Christianity is humility and poverty, a deliberate turning of oneself away from the goods of this world. Now, none of us was born yesterday. We know that gentlemen and even the Church often had wealth and sometimes lots of it, but the standard was nonetheless there – proper folks were to desire little and pious folks were to desire less. Both classical political philosophy and Christianity took this stand in the interest of the superiority of the soul over the body. It was in the context of this double restraint on acquisition that Locke undertook to liberate acquisitiveness. Hobbes had laid the groundwork by a science of the nature of man that put body over soul. The aim of life was not to be virtue for its own sake but self-preservation and, in fact, comfortable and prosperous self-preservation.

Locke approaches his liberating task rather gingerly. He starts by admitting the biblical proposition that the earth was given by God to men in common, but he shows that if a thing is held in common by mankind as a whole, it is of no use whatsoever to any individual. It just sits there. He then argues that if one develops something one makes it proper to oneself, makes a property in it. This is especially true of real property, land. An acre of possessed land, cultivated land, produces ten times the crop that open, untended, common land produces [Tr. II, v, 37]. Then Locke inches forward and allows that the difference is not ten to one, but a hundred to one [ibid.]. A moment later he suggests that the difference is the same as the difference between five pounds and a penny [ibid. II, v, 43]. If you know the English monetary system up until about 1989 – twelve pence to the shilling, twenty shillings to the pound – and do the math, you see that $12 \times 20 \times 5 = 1,200$, twelve hundred times the worth of an uncultivated field. Then Locke, to show how moderate and open-minded he is, backs off and says, well, would you believe a thousand to one [loc. cit.]? God, apparently, is parsimonious. Man, at least a man of the rational and industrious sort, is truly beneficent. Everyone profits from his acquisitiveness. There are a thousand times as many apples and a thousand times as many loaves of bread, not to mention some nice steaks, chocolate éclairs, and an occasional ice-cold martini garnished with a twist from the peel of an imported lemon. As Leo Strauss summarizes Locke on this point, "Unlimited appropriation without concern for the need of others is true charity."[5] Three more essential points: (1) Security of property under positive law is what activates industry; (2) the invention of money, which does not spoil as apples do, allows unlimited acquisition and so unlimited acquisitiveness; and (3) the utter freedom of acquisition that people had in nature, that is, in the state of nature, is fenced in by positive law within civil society.

   Although there is much more to be said about Locke and property, this is not a convenient place for such an examination. Let us turn to Chapters 6 and 7 simply to note that Locke offers radical innovation in his discussion of the family. It seems there is nothing natural about the family. Marriage exists simply as a contractual arrangement, and it is surely not, as the Church had held it to be, a sacrament. Most importantly, it need only last long enough to ensure that offspring reach a stage of maturity that allows independence. Because with human offspring a child arrives before that stage of independence is reached by the next senior child, that keeps husband and wife tied for quite a while but by no means for life. No such restraint binds other animals, because the first pup is on his own before the next litter arrives. Chapter 6 is titled "Of Paternal Power," but Locke quickly corrects this by reshuffling the letters of the word "paternal." Recurring to the question raised by the claims of Robert Filmer, Locke insists on the

5 Leo Strauss, *Natural Right and History*, Chicago, 1953, University of Chicago Press, p. 243.

equality of husband and wife in parental matters and he shows by a syllogism that, because father and mother are equal in their power over the children and mothers do not have legislative power over them, therefore fathers do not have such power, do not have dominion over their children. This settles the matter. There is no natural or divine foundation for kingship. The only legitimate source of rule is consent of the people.

Chapter 7 is titled "Of Political or Civil Society," but it begins with a further discussion of the family and gently makes a transition into the subject matter indicated by the chapter title. Chapter 8, "Of the Beginning of Political Societies," argues, as Hobbes had, that men are free, equal, and independent in the state of nature and are "put out of that estate" only by their consent. He lays the groundwork for departure from Hobbes by a heavy-handed emphasis on the weight of the people. In paragraphs 95 through 99, for example, he fairly bathes the reader's eyes in eleven usages of the word "majority" and eight uses of the word "body." Chapter 9 enumerates the shortcomings of the state of nature: there is no established law in it (Aha! There goes natural law!); there is no indifferent, that is, impartial, judge in it; and there is no power of execution in it. [Tr. II, 9, §§124–26] This list looks like the three "powers" allocated by the United States Constitution – but hold on! Some distinctions will have to be made in a moment. Hobbes had shown the necessity of giving up one's rights, all but the few unalienable ones, and all one's power to the sovereign to escape the evils of the state of nature. Locke shows that one gives up his legislative power and *wholly* gives up his executive power. He gives up also his perfect equality and his unfettered liberty of acquisition. These several things he gives into the hands of the legislative power established by the original compact, and he gives them up the better to preserve his liberty and his property. The difference in degree of surrender between his legislative and his executive power is the need for a residual retention of legislative power in case the whole system to which he has surrendered his powers may fail to preserve liberty and property. The end of government is, after all, "the preservation of property" [Tr. II, 9, ¶¶129–31, and see ch. 7, ¶94].

Perhaps the origin of political philosophy had been the need to protect philosophy from politics. The essence of political philosophy had been, from its beginning, the effort to identify the best regime. Plato's "Republic" and Aristotle's *Politics*, each in its own way, had compared all the imaginable regimes and had identified the best imaginable one. Each showed that the achievement in practice of the simply best regime was impossible or at least nearly impossible, so each of those books turned to the question as to which of the imperfect regimes was more or less better. Chapter 10 of Locke's Second Treatise, "Of the Forms of a Commonwealth," raises this question, but it consists of only one page in a tolerably long book. It is true that Hobbes had preferred indivisible monarchy and Locke prefers some sort of popular government, but, as we have suggested, this question is subordinated to the question of legitimacy, the question of the provenance of the regime, and on this question they are agreed: The consent of the people is the only rightful source of sovereignty and is, in fact, the foundational sovereignty. Thus, there is for both a primordial democracy out of which any regime is formed. For Hobbes, the state of civil society once formed by contract leaves no permissible questioning of the compact. A deal is a deal! This is because to leave the matter open is to open the door to dreadful bloodshed, civil war, and a return to that hellish state of nature. With respect to this matter, Locke parts company with Hobbes, but both Hobbes and Locke, each to keep true to his argument, allows for the possibility of the alternatives, monarchy or democracy. The problem with democracy had always been its instability and its partisan injustice. From Aristotle through to Machiavelli, all the philosophers had imagined, at best, an aristocracy and, failing that, some sort of mixed regime, a regime not of justice but of moderated injustice. Hobbes regarded a mixed regime as just a fancy name for divided sovereignty and as an invitation to horrors. Because of the principle of equality, the principle of consent, and the principle of the majority, Locke cannot opt straightforwardly for the mixed regime, but because of the same principles and because tyranny may lurk beneath the banner of sovereign indivisibility, he cannot follow Hobbes in a call for absolute kingship. What is more, aristocracy over the centuries in Europe had developed a sort of hardening of the political arteries. Locke does not fully develop but he does set out the elements of what becomes the modern alternative to the mixed regime, namely, the separation of powers. He does this in Chapters 11 through 15 to which we may now turn.

Chapter 11 is titled "Of the Extent of the Legislative Power." Locke sometimes means by the "legislative power" what he sometimes calls the "supreme power." It is the whole power of the people to make or, as it turns out, to remake the legislative power in the lesser sense. That lesser sense is the power vested by the supreme power in the legislative assembly that results from the contract that establishes the regime. To speak of the "extent" of that lesser power is to speak of the limits on it, but limits imply a counterforce or a separate power. The limits in force in the mixed regime are to be found in the mixture itself, the strength of the several "estates" holding each other in check. These are the aristocracy and the multitude, the somebodies and the nobodies, striking compromises between the two tyrannies either would impose or, as it developed in England after the Glorious Revolution, the Crown, the Lords, and the Commons, with an additional tension within the Lords between the Lords Spiritual and the Lords Temporal, the bishops and the earls. Locke cannot choose that. Neither can he quite choose what comes to be the separation of powers, because it is clear that the "legislative power" is in the Parliament which is, itself, composed of the three estates. There is no clearly separated "executive power," and, in fact, what the U.S. Constitution calls the "Judicial Power" is merely an aspect of, or the very gist of, what Locke calls the "executive power."

Locke sets out some four limits on the legislative power. The legislative power (1) does not extend to "absolute, arbitrary power;" (2) does not extend to "extemporary arbitrary decrees"; (3) cannot take property without consent; and (4) cannot subdelegate its powers – that is, it cannot pass its powers over to the executive [Tr. II, 11, ¶¶135, 136, 138, and 141]. Then he summarizes the four restraints [¶142], but in doing so he reverses the order of the first two, which makes one wonder which, if either, is the substantive restraint and which the formal or procedural restraint, so this rather looks like there are three, not four, restraints. Furthermore, he explains that consent for taking property does not mean consent of the individual from whom the property is taken. (One could easily see that such a restraint would negate the legislative power in favor of anarchy.) It means consent of the majority, and it takes only a moment to realize that that means the majority of the legislators, the delegates of the people [¶140]. The only one of the four that the summary leaves in its original state is the prohibition against subdelegation of legislative power. This throws two clouds over Locke's meaning. First, the clear meaning of the restraint itself is lost. Second, there is only the barest hint as to what and from where the restraint will be enforced. It turns out that the enforcement must lie somewhere within the legislative power itself. Let us see.

In the first listing of the four restraints, the first ("no absolute, arbitrary power") looks rather like a substantive restraint, that is, an establishment of the "what" of the matter. The second appears to be a formal or procedural restraint, that is, the "how" of the matter. With the reversal of the order of the first two rules, two things show themselves. First, the essence of the prohibition against "extemporary, arbitrary decrees" is simply promulgation: When the legislature passes a law, it passes a law. Second, in that reversal, what had appeared in the first formulation negatively as a denial of "absolute, arbitrary power" appears in the summary reformulation positively as the requirement that the legislative power only pass laws for the "good of the people." Fine, but is it not the majority within that legislature that decides and defines what is for the "good of the people?" How, then, is any of this a restraint on the legislative power? If Locke is here tacitly agreeing with Hobbes in disapproval of the mixed regime and if he does not quite choose as an alternative a clear separation of powers, we are at an impasse. It remained for the American founders to establish almost in so many words in the Constitution of the United States a clear separation of powers that completes what Locke had started, and firmly establishes what Hobbes had laid out, the principle that private appetite leads to public good, the principle that in modern economics is called the "invisible hand." Locke's solution rests in the legislature itself: The taking of property without consent is avoided if the legislative power is vested in a numerous body rather than in a single individual, if that numerous body is variable (i.e., subject to periodic elections) and if, having passed laws, the members of the legislative body are themselves subject to those laws. Because the preservation and enjoyment of property is what government is *for*, and because the legislative power is vested in a body of people who are themselves property holders, who could ask for anything more? We continue to live in a kind of fairyland today, a fairyland created with purpose by Locke. We actually think that there are substantive limits on the legislature. Maybe the sheer imagination of it leads to the partial achievement of it. I do not mean to suggest that there is not more to say in praise of the American founders, but this is not the place to say it. It is all we may do here to call attention to Article I, Section 8, of the U.S. Constitution and to Nos. 10 and 17 of the *Federalist Papers* by Hamilton, Madison, and Jay. One needs to pay close attention to Article I, Section 8, in comparison with *Federalist* 17 to get a view of the work of the founders and a basis for judgment of the degree of our adherence to what they achieved.

The title of Chapter 12 is altogether unsettling if we read it with any care rather than making the commonplace error of seeing there what we expected to see there. It does not enumerate "legislative, executive, and judicial powers" as the American Constitution does. The title of Chapter 12 is "Of the Legislative, Executive, and Federative Power of the Commonwealth." In reading the Constitution, we sensibly divide our understanding of "executive power" into the executive power over domestic affairs and the executive power over foreign affairs. Let us note that his powers in the case of foreign affairs are broadly stated whereas his powers over domestic affairs are limited to (1) making certain appointments by and with the advice and consent of the Senate, (2) giving advice to the Congress as to the state of the union, (3) recommending measures to the Congress for its consideration, and (4) vetoing acts of Congress subject to the veto being overridden. What we regard as the executive power in international affairs is what Locke calls the "Federative Power," the power to make treaties, to cooperate with other sovereignties, and to make peace, and, when those things do not work out, to make war, and so to take war seriously. There appears to be little of what we think of as the domestic side of executive power in Locke. It almost appears that what he calls the "executive power" is virtually confined to what we call the "judicial power." This becomes plainer fifty years after Locke when Montesquieu speaks of "la puissance législative, la puissance exécutrice qui dépendent du droit des gens, et la puissance exécutrice de celles qui dependent du droit civil" (the legislative power, the executive power dependent on the law of nations, and the executive power over things dependent on the civil, or domestic, law).[6] The moving party at the 1787 convention, for

---

[6] Montesquieu, *De l'Esprit des Lois*, Paris, n.d., Éditions Garnier Frères, vol. 1, bk. 11, ch. 6, beginning. The original of this work was published in 1748.

good and sufficient reasons, so mangled the meaning of "federal" that ever after it has been impossible to understand the word. To head the reader in the right direction it is enough to call attention to the fact that, despite our confident and repeated use of it, the very expression "federal government" is a contradiction in terms. Other than reminding ourselves that the Constitution never uses the word "federal," we must leave it at that.

Let us bring this part to a close by saying that the bulk of the Second Treatise to this point has agreed with Hobbes in fundamentals such as the state of nature and its relation to the state of war, markedly disagreed with his proposition that the state of nature is worse than tyranny, firmly preferred that the legislative power be vested in a numerous body (whereas Hobbes had preferred indivisible sovereignty), and focused on the preservation of property as the chief end of government. As was the case with Hobbes, Locke begins his argument with perfect freedom in the state of nature and ends it with near-complete subjection in civil society. As he explains, to be free is not to do "as one lists." Freedom is freedom to act within the limits of the law, and the law is that which is promulgated by the legislature, which in turn has its charter from the higher legislative power of the whole people. Chapters 16 through 19 profoundly add to Locke's departure from Hobbes. Whereas Hobbes had so feared recourse to the state of nature that he defined the sovereign power not only as indivisible but made any resistance to it, and even any criticism of it, impermissible – in fact, treason – Locke emphatically asserts that absolute monarchy is far worse than the state of nature, and he positively introduces the doctrine of the right, the natural right, to revolution. Hobbes had founded the modern principle of the consent of the governed. Locke is the founder of the modern principle of limited government, a principle unintelligible in ancient thought.

So much for modern, or enlightenment, or bourgeois political philosophy. Let us pause here to draw attention to a couple of the several differences between ancient and modern political philosophy, leaving the other contrasts to be set out in our next and last chapter. Ancient political philosophy drew a distinction between theory and practice. The gap between the two was bridged by the prudence of the statesman, and the statesman and the philosopher both knew that practice could never live up to theory. There was therefore built into political thought at both the philosophic and the political level a certain reserve, a certain moderation. The modern proposition that "politics is the art of the possible" is a partial acknowledgment of the ancient understanding. The modern academic alternative to the ancient distinction between theory and practice is the distinction between theory and application. For us moderns, a theory is to be *applied*, wholly and unreservedly. If it cannot be applied it deserves to be abandoned. The ancients spoke of cities that never were precisely because that was the only way to speak of the very best city, which was not an "ideal" toward which the statesman should strive – that would be utopian folly. The very best city provided simply a guiding light that enabled the prudent statesman to figure out what the best order of things the available material, human and circumstantial, allowed him to fashion. The statesman never once imagined that he could create on earth a replication of the city that existed only in the heavens. Machiavelli founded modern political philosophy by sneering at those "cities that never were" of the ancients. He sought to introduce, and succeeded in introducing, a more practical political philosophy, one that could be applied. He was so successful that whereas the only hope that the city in speech fashioned by Plato's Socrates might come into being in deed was the one-in-a-billion chance that philosophy and political power might accidentally coincide, Hobbes strove to create a political science as sure as geometry, and one must remember that in geometry there are axioms. Axioms cannot be proven. They are few and they are the very foundation of all that can be proven in geometry. You start with axioms and absolutely everything that follows follows as the night follows the day. Geometricians may make mistakes, but geometry cannot make a mistake. So practical is the vision of Hobbes that his "civil society" is not only possible; it is inevitable. Like the elementary school pupil over whom the present school system towers, we have, under the towering Machiavelli and the towering Hobbes, "achieved our goals" by lowering them. Machiavelli had made politics itself the horizon of politics. In place of those cities that never were imagined by the ancients we get a sure fire goal, a civil society that cannot help but come into being, but one that has nothing to look up to. Another way to see this contrast of goals is to see that where the ancients regarded the "good life" or the "noble life" the goal of politics, we, since Hobbes, regard self preservation – that is, mere life or, at best, comfortable life – as the goal.

Locke made politics just as certain as Hobbes did and ameliorated the resulting political order. To see how practical Hobbes and Locke were, let us look for a moment at the underlying principles of the American political order as those principles are enunciated in the second paragraph of the Declaration of Independence. (Notes follow immediately after the Declaration of Independence.)

We hold these truths to be self-evident,[A] that all men are created equal,[B] that they are endowed by their Creator with certain unalienable rights,[C] that among these are life, liberty, and the pursuit of happiness. That to secure these rights, governments are instituted among men,[D] deriving their just powers from the consent of the governed,[E] that whenever any form of government becomes destructive of these ends,[F] it is the right of the people to alter or abolish it and to institute new government,[G] laying its foundation on such principles and organizing its powers in such form as to them shall seem most likely to effect their safety and happiness.[H] Prudence, indeed, will dictate that governments long established should not be changed for light and transient causes.[I] ... But when a long train of abuses and usurpations ... evinces a design to reduce them under absolute despotism, it is their right, it is their duty, to throw off such government ... (etc., until there is posted a twenty-six-count indictment of the wrongdoings of George III, which we need not recount or evaluate here).

A. The expression "self-evident" is not the equivalent of "evident." Nor is a self-evident truth universally or easily evident. It does not mean "very, very evident." It means axiomatic. Like an axiom in geometry it needs no proof, in fact it can have no proof. It is the basis of any subsequent proof. A self-evident truth is evident in itself. Remember that Hobbes thought he had created a political science after the model of geometry.

B. Men are not created equal in all respects. They are not, by nature, equally strong, equally beautiful, equally swift, equally wise, or equally virtuous. In addition, certainly, they are not entitled in civil society to equal shares of good things. They are by nature equal simply in their natural possession of rights a certain few of which that cannot be alienated or ceded.

C. The term "unalienable right" is not the equivalent of the term "natural right." It signifies a subspecies of natural rights. Obviously, if some rights are singled out as "unalienable," that means that the others are alienable. That is just what both Hobbes and Locke had said.

D. The government does not create or give these rights. It acknowledges them and makes them secure. The Declaration of Independence gives three illustrations of unalienable rights and leaves it open whether there might be one or two more. Because they are like axioms in geometry, of which there are five, six, or seven (geometricians vary on the number), probably the number of unalienable rights is also very small – maybe only the three mentioned, maybe five, six, or seven. Certainly a citizen of a civil society does not have by nature an unalienable right to something simply because he really, really wants it. That would be the road back to the state of nature, a hellish place. Stop to think! How are governments instituted among men? Is it not by yielding all but the unalienable rights to a sovereignty so as to escape the state of nature?

E. How this consent is given is explained in note D, just above.

F. What are "these ends"? Are they not the security of the unalienable rights just mentioned? In addition, what does "pursuit of happiness" mean? Happiness, according to Aristotle, meant life lived in accordance with the virtues. Hobbes and Locke, however, redefine it, according to the materialism of Hobbes, as material happiness, which is why Locke defines the end of government as the preservation of property. That is why the Fifth and Fourteenth Amendments to the U.S. Constitution ensure the safety not of "life, liberty, and the pursuit of happiness," but of "life, liberty, and property." It is not because the authors of the Declaration of Independence were nice, liberal people and the authors of the Constitution were moneyed meanies. It is because the Constitution is, among other things, a law. It would be pretty difficult to go to court to vindicate your right to the pursuit of happiness, but an unlawful inroad into your property is a wrong that a court knows how to remedy.

G. This is a right of nature that, like the three that are specified, is unalienable. It is the right of revolution that Locke covered in Chapter 19 of the Second Treatise. By the way, notice that it is a trans-constitutional right, a right of nature. No constitution ever devised has contained a right to destroy it, a suicide clause. In addition, it is a right of the people, not the private right of every individual with a grievance. One cannot begin a campaign to bring down the Constitution and then, when apprehended, appeal to that Constitution as though one had a constitutional right to treason or sedition.

H. Notice that this leaves open the possibility that the people might want to establish a monarchy, although surely a constitutional monarchy, but it is just as likely that this clause is notice to George III and to the British Parliament that the Americans might wish to and by nature could establish a republican form.

I. Why not? Is it not clear that the government ought not to be abolished and the people thrown back into the hellish state of nature because potholes in the street are not repaired quickly enough?

So much for Hobbes, Locke, and their American progeny. We need to make only one more point before turning from modern political philosophy to what is called "postmodern" political thought. We had said a while back that classical political philosophy was so stable that, except for the modifications wrought by its confrontation with revealed religion, it remained amazingly constant from Socrates until Machiavelli, almost two thousand years. There is something about modern political thought, in contrast, that drives it to change. The American system, as illustrated by the Declaration of Independence and the Constitution, is the authentic heir of Hobbes and Locke. In fact, it is the Constitutional completion of the liberal philosophy of Hobbes and Locke. In his address at the cemetery at Gettysburg in 1863, Abraham Lincoln said that "our fathers" had "brought forth upon this continent a new nation conceived in liberty and dedicated to the proposition that all men are created equal." They had done so "four score and seven years" before. That moment of bringing forth the new nation was obviously calculated by Lincoln as the moment of the Declaration of Independence in 1776. By sheer coincidence (I guess), four score and seven years before the Declaration of Independence was 1689, the moment of the Glorious Revolution in England, and the approximate date of Locke's *Two Treatises*. That, in itself, shows some stability in modern political philosophy, but that is not the whole story. The principles of the French Revolution, which began just about the time of the installation of the new American government under its new Constitution, in 1789, differed in material respects from the principles of the American Revolution. The French revolution owed its underpinnings to the philosophy not of Hobbes and Locke but to that of Jean-Jacques Rousseau (1712–78), so, somewhere half or three-quarters of the way from the Glorious Revolution to the new American republic, there began a philosophical departure from the modern political thought of Hobbes and Locke, a departure that Strauss characterizes as the "first crisis" of modernity. It makes sense to turn now to postmodern thought and, aiming there, we turn first to Rousseau.

Postmodern Thought

"Postmodern" is a curious word. In fact we might ask whether it is a word at all. It appears to be a hyphenated expression from which the hyphen has been dropped, forgotten. What is more, accepting it as a word appears to us altogether fanciful. All our lives we have been told that modern things are the latest things. How could anything be later than the latest, and so the most modern? In contrast, if modern political thought means essentially the thought of the Enlightenment, and the Enlightenment is one way of thought (a way that follows on medieval thought, which, in turn, followed on classical thought), then three possible sequels logically suggest themselves: progress, decay, or restoration. These possibilities invite a reasoned confrontation of the alternatives: If there is something defective about modern political thought, is the correction of that defect to be found in the restoration of something older, or is it to be found in moving beyond to a corrected or refined modern thought? The notion of moving on rests on some notion of the defect being the consequence of the fact that the thought, like the thoughts that went before, is somehow a prisoner of its time. There must be found in a new time a sort of liberation from the old time, and, in fact, from times. A neat trick!

The word "postmodern" is of recent origin. It does not appear in the first edition of the *Oxford English Dictionary* in 1933, or in the first edition of the *Random House Dictionary of the English Language* in 1966, or in the *Encyclopedia of Philosophy* in 1967. The online (another new word) *Stanford Encyclopedia of Philosophy*, in an article dated September 30, 2005, attributes the origin of the term to Jean-François Lyotard in 1979, but the thing that is called "postmodern," that is, a certain sort of philosophy, or perhaps simply a certain sort of opinion, has its origins two hundred years earlier. A companion term, "deconstruction," was coined, according to the *Stanford Encyclopedia of Philosophy* article "Postmodernism," in 1967 by Jacques Derrida. Derrida (1930–2004) and Michel Foucault (1926–84), two Frenchmen, and Paul de

Man (1919–83), a Belgian, three of the twentieth-century figures identified with either (or both) postmodernism or deconstruction, were celebrated by academics in the United States, although there has been some dissent from that celebration.[7]

Although the two are closely related, "deconstruction" seems to have found a home in the twentieth century in literary criticism, whereas "postmodernism," whatever the provenance of the word itself, has an earlier origin. If Socrates, Plato, and Aristotle are the chief names in classical political philosophy, and al-Farabi, Averroës, Maimonides, Aquinas, and Marsilius are principal figures in medieval political philosophy, then it is easy to identify Machiavelli, Hobbes, and Locke as the great figures of modern political philosophy. Postmodernism is, perhaps because of its currency, not so easy to mark. Some of the more recent figures seem quite less in stature when listed alongside the eleven philosophers just mentioned, but for figures of philosophic first rank one might call Friedrich Nietzsche (1844–1900) the father of postmodernism and Jean-Jacques Rousseau (1712–1778) the founding ancestor of the movement. The key to postmodernism is the word "history," which we discussed at some length earlier but to which we must now return.

Jean-Jacques Rousseau

It may be that the origin of the notion that history is itself an entity to be studied, rather than simply being an account or a narrative of things, events, or occurrences, has its origin in the thought of Rousseau. Rousseau was born in Geneva. When he was nine, his father abandoned the family, and at the age of sixteen, Rousseau was off on his own, something of a vagabond. He encountered a Mme. de Warens, a woman several years his senior, who took him under her care. The strongest of possible attachments arose between them, and he stayed with her for nine years. Beginning in his early thirties, he fathered five children on a woman who was both his housekeeper and his mistress and, as we mentioned earlier, each in turn was committed to the Paris Foundling Home and quite forgotten, rather as a dog or cat might be dropped off at the pound. In his late thirties, his literary career began in earnest. The Academy at Dijon offered prizes for essays, and in 1750 he won the Academy's prize for his first Discourse in response to the question "if the reestablishment of the sciences and arts has contributed to the purification of *moeurs*." We preserve here the last word in the quoted question in the original French, because translating it into the rarefied, detached English word "morals" is misleading. The English word "morals" has a kind of preachifying character signifying an insistence as to how one ought to behave that is quite separate from an account of how

---

7 *See* David Lehman, *Signs of the Times*, New York, 1992 (1994), Poseidon Press.

one actually behaves. Allan Bloom translated *moeurs* as "manners/morals." The ancient Greek word *hoi nomoi* can be translated strictly as "the laws," but it has a broader reach that includes the laws and customs – the ways – of a people, something like what present Americans mean by speaking of the "culture" of a people. What the Academy asked was, in effect, Does the renaissance of arts and sciences make a people better? That is, does the restoration of the arts and sciences make more perfect human beings, better citizens, better followers of the "ways"?

Implied in the Academy's question is the possibility of a negative answer. In fact, implied is the possibility of a contrary proposition. Rousseau seizes on these possibilities. Perhaps it is possible for a philosopher to conceive of One Great Question and to spend his life reexamining it. Indeed, perhaps there *is* only one great question: What is the nature of nature? What are the natures of things? For the political philosopher the question is, What is the nature of man? It certainly appears that all of Rousseau's subsequent writings pursue the question asked by the Academy as he refashions it in his reply in the *First Discourse.*

Hark back now to the question of the tension between the political order and philosophy to which much of this book is devoted. Is it not plain that the Academy, quite without considering the alternative, asks its question from the point of view of the political order? Might the Academy not have asked instead, "Do our *moeurs* inhibit the improvement of the arts and sciences?" As the Preface to the *First Discourse* indicates, Rousseau appears to accept the Academy's question as raised but offers an answer that suggests the alternative. He argues that the arts and sciences will not improve *moeurs.* He flatters the Academy that it will understand him and he disdains to appeal to common opinion. In his Preface he says, "There will always be men destined to be subjugated by the opinions of their century, of their country . . . [but one] ought not to write for such readers when one wants to live beyond one's century." Thus, he consciously places himself as a philosopher as one who rises above the political order and the times. He will escape from what Plato had made Socrates describe as the "cave." The critical question we might ask, however, is whether his argument sustains that vaunted philosophic freedom. On the contrary, does Rousseau inadvertently begin a course of inquiry that eventually imprisons inquiry within the cave and throws away the key, that is, the key to the way out?

Over and over again, we have argued that old words lose their meaning and new words are coined ready-burdened with agenda. The word "lifestyle" coined or at least propagated in the 1960s is an example. Here, to raise a kindred problem, we must back up a few centuries. The expression "state of nature" comes into use with Hobbes and Locke in the seventeenth century. While Rousseau begins the process of undermining the political philosophy of Hobbes and Locke, he seems to accept its premises: The true nature of humans is to be found "back there" somewhere in a condition or state of nature. To be critical of the conclusions of Hobbes and Locke is to confront two possibilities: One may "go back" behind Hobbes and Locke – and so, behind Machiavelli – to classical political philosophy, or one may "move on," accepting the premises of Hobbes and Locke. Rousseau denies the conclusions of Hobbes and Locke, but he is compelled to offer different conclusions based on the same premises. Consequently, he cannot answer the question of the Academy by going back to Aristotle and asserting that man is a "political animal." If he had done that, his answer might have been that the restoration of classical sciences did indeed improve human beings. The core of that ancient science is tied to Aristotle's view of man as a political animal. The nature of man is perfected in and through the political community. There is no such thing as a "state of nature" in ancient thought, nothing even like it. Instead of going back to Aristotle, Rousseau goes back to nature, to nature conceived as a state of nature, or, as Hobbes had put it in the *Leviathan*, the "condition of mere nature."

Hobbes had preserved something of the ghost of Aristotle by asserting the necessity of fleeing the miserable estate of nature and finding surcease of those miseries in civil society, which is established by an original contract, a social contract. The nature of man is left behind in favor of a more salutary civil society created by invention or convention. Artificial man is more safe and more comfortable than natural man. To accept the premises but deny the conclusions, Rousseau must dispute the nature of the state of nature. Nature is not a war of every man against every man. The natural condition of man is stupid, but rather sweet. The sciences and arts make man artificial. Civil society, furthered by the arts and sciences, corrupts man. In fact the *moeurs*, concern for which moved the Academy to ask its question, corrupt man. The French of the eighteenth century are polite but insincere, inauthentic. (There was a Rousseau-flavored intellectual movement around about 1970 that thought of itself as the politics of "authenticity." One of its hallmarks was a display of impatience with old-fashioned manners.)

Rousseau, it at first appears, cannot go back to a historical state of nature any more than Hobbes or Locke could, so he goes back to Hobbes's imaginary "state of nature" and simply imagines it differently. Man is not, as Aristotle had asserted, a "rational" animal. His nature is found in sentiment, not thought. Rather than being at war with all of his fellows as Hobbes had seen him, he is driven by the consciousness of existence and the sentiment of compassion. Notice first and foremost: Compassion is a species of passion. Here Rousseau quite follows Hobbes. Man is defined not by reason but by the passions. As we suggested earlier, when people are asked today what they *think*, they answer by telling you what they *feel*. To mean well is to be right. To feel strongly is to be even more right. To be ardent is to be virtuous. Commitment becomes the most praiseworthy trait, which, if we think about it, would mark Adolf Hitler and Josef Stalin as the best of men. The shift from man as a rational animal to man as a feeling animal brings with it a great bundle of freight. If man is defined as a sentient being, what is to distinguish him from other sentient beings, namely all the other animals? Heaven only knows; perhaps we would have to ask what it is that distinguishes him even from plants! The beachhead of what follows from this is the curious, recent doctrine of animal rights. It does follow! In the early years of the twenty-first century, the argument was made that, because the DNA of the great apes matched more than 98 percent of the DNA of humans, they ought to have the same rights as humans. This is known as the Great Ape Project. Sure enough, the project made great strides toward statutory adoption by the Parliament of Spain in 2008. What is more, if the other animals are to be treated as people, are not people to be treated as the other animals? Will it not follow that the positive eugenics applied in breeding cattle will be applied in breeding humans? Sure enough! There are folks known now as "bioethicists" (another new word!), some of whom earnestly propose infanticide for infants who do not meet one's expectations and others of whom propose cloning humans to get better ones.[8] Curiously, something is lost in the progress of the doctrine that man is a simply a sentient being, a feeling being. The one thing missing in the quest for the perfection of the master race is feeling itself. Procreation pursues better chemistry, but it no longer follows the chemistry of love.

Something more is missing. As Walter Berns has shown, the problem with animal rights is that animals other than man are incapable of subscribing to a contract to respect each others' rights. Hobbes had, after all, a rational scheme. The state of nature is dreadful. Get out of it. To get out of it, form a social contract by yielding to a sovereign all of your natural rights except those the yielding of which would negate the purpose of that contract. These unalienable rights are the rights to life, liberty, and property. Some time after Hobbes, the expression "human rights" began to be used as though it were interchangeable with the expression "natural rights." This leapfrogs over the social contract. Without a conscious acknowledgment of the social contract, it becomes possible for earnest "activists" to demand within civil society rights inconsistent with civil society, rights that carry us back to that miserable state of nature. Here we have the progress of thought: From natural rights we progress to human rights, and from human rights we progress to the rights of primates. What is next? In my youth I was acquainted with an old lady who embraced a palm tree in her yard and burst into tears because a thoughtless gardener had pruned away the dead fronds on its trunk. The best that one could have said on that occasion would have been that at least the Supreme Court had not yet rested a decision on radical floraphilia.[9] We have made "progress" since Hobbes, and all

---

[8] *See* Wesley J. Smith, "Monkey Business," in *Weekly Standard*, vol. 13, no. 42, July 21, 2008, p. 15.

[9] If other people can coin neologisms, why can't we?

progress is beneficial, because the novel is the good, and to be an activist requires only commitment; that is its sole qualification.

Not able to go back to a recorded, historical state of nature, the best that Rousseau can do is to go back to ancient history, as though an older city were closer to nature than a modern nation is, except that we must keep remembering that, for Rousseau, nature is defined as a "state of nature." In his later and longer work *Of the Social Contract*, he amplifies a point raised in the *First Discourse*. He describes ancient Rome as superior to modern countries because the "citizens" of Rome were not the bourgeoisie or the proletariat of the city, but the gentlemen farmers of the countryside: strong, virtuous men of honor and valor, ready to die for their fellows. Modern men are not true citizens; they are just burgers, bourgeoisie, burg dwellers. Reading Rousseau is, as with reading any philosopher, rather difficult, however. His praise of the ancients is in language that dissembles. Like Machiavelli, Rousseau may not be as strong an advocate of ancient Rome as he appears to be.

A matter of style deserves mention. In answering the question of the Academy (and also in answering in the *Second Discourse* the Academy's question about the "Origin of Inequality among Men") and in *Of the Social Contract*, Rousseau writes in a somewhat aerated manner. He makes his argument in the rhetoric of uplift, of moral afflatus. This is in keeping with the elevation of feeling over thought, and from this we are able to form characterizations of the two prominent political parties to be found now in any western country: the prosaic party, the roots of which are in Locke, and the party of uplift, the roots of which are in Rousseau. To the partisans of the first part those of the second part seem flighty and unthinking; to the partisans of the second part those of the first seem mean and unfeeling.

A thorough canvass of Rousseau's two *Discourses* and his *Social Contract* would entail at least a semester's work, much of which would go into attempting to understand his doctrine of the "general will," but the purposes of this book confine us to touching on only one more topic respecting Rousseau, namely History with a capital *H*.

The *Second Discourse*, which is titled *On the Origin and the Foundations of Inequality among Men*, is preceded by an epistle dedicatory and a preface. Again, we need to take note that the question asked by the Academy as to the *origin* of inequality presupposes a prior equality. The question presupposes the truth of Hobbes's proposition that, in the condition of mere nature, men are equal, equal in both body and mind. Implied in that presupposition is the view that inequality is introduced by civil society. Therefore, supposing equality is somehow good, civil society is somehow at fault in the origin of inequality. Hobbes too had seen civil society as the foundation of inequality, but, because the state of nature is wretched, civil society is necessary and therefore good.

Some of Rousseau's works lack a dedicatory epistle; others are dedicated in a page or two and are, as is customary, addressed to some individual. The dedication of the *Second Discourse* is exceptionally long – from ten to sixteen pages, depending on the edition and the typeface – and is directed "To the Republic of Geneva" and addressed to "Magnificent, Most Honored, and Sovereign Lords." He begins by saying that he has been preparing himself for thirty years to present such a work to the city of his birth. That would mean that he set himself in this direction about the time he was ten years old, or just after his father had deserted the family. Such a beginning would be hard to credit were it not for the fact that Rousseau was, indeed, a remarkable man. Of the twenty-two paragraphs that make up the dedication, fourteen (the second through the fifteenth) are devoted to a sketch of a country that exists in his thoughts (something akin to a city in speech). He begins that sketch with the words, "If I had to choose my place of birth. . . . "

Describing that preferred commonwealth, Rousseau says (in the tenth paragraph) that he would have fled as ill-governed a republic where the people themselves ruled directly, and he goes on to say that such a government would be like those early ones that arose "immediately from the state of Nature." This is the first indication that he treats the state of nature not as something that exists only in principle, but as an actual epoch in history. For Aristotle, the *polis* had its *being* by nature, although the coming into being of any *polis* was a consequence of a specific act, a convention. He acknowledges that there must have been a first such event, but what existed before that first *polis* were other, lesser human associations. It would have been beyond fanciful to have conceived of individual men existing originally as solitary pieces in a game of draughts (or, to use a more American term, "checkers") on a board but not as teams of red or black checkers but each one as playing the game on its own, against all the others. To repeat, perhaps even more than is necessary, there is no such thing for the ancients as a state of nature – not even in principle, much less in history.

The first paragraph of the Preface that follows the Dedication contains the first suggestion of what comes to be called the science of anthropology. In addition, although that paragraph speaks of the nature of humans, something about his conception of that nature becomes clear in the opening sentence of the second paragraph where Rousseau speaks of "every progress of the human species" as moving it "ever farther from its primitive state." This suggests that what it is to be human, human nature, changes over time. This would mean, of course, that there is no such thing as the nature of humans; there is only the history of humans, or the career of humans. If one generation sees a certain conduct – cannibalism, say – as impermissible, our advice to that generation would have to be, "Get over it!" because who is to foreclose the possibility that mankind might "progress" to the point of finding cannibalism merely a matter of taste? In the seventeenth paragraph of Part One of the *Discourse*, Rousseau admits that men do differ from beasts, but the difference is only that men are, while beasts are not, perfectible. Here again we must see the difference between Aristotle and Rousseau. Aristotle held that *some* men could, given political life, achieve perfection of their nature, but the nature itself was all along there in their very being. Political life made possible the achievement of what was only potential in the absence of political life. For Rousseau, it appears that not only may a man come to be perfected, but mankind itself progresses toward perfection. Here again arises the contrast between the two parties in our time: the followers of Hobbes and Locke, such as the authors of the *Federalist Papers*, see human nature prosaically as a fixed thing. The business of politics is to accommodate itself to this fact. The followers of Rousseau, perhaps more poetically, believe wholeheartedly in progress, even progress in the nature of man. Karl Marx is a prime example, but, in a somewhat different fashion, so perhaps are those young people who imagine themselves the moral superiors of all their ancestors (and yet somehow imagine that that moral improvement will culminate in themselves). Herein lies the difficulty with progress, with History.

Near the end of the *Discourse*, in the fifty-seventh paragraph of Part Two, Rousseau says that it would be by "thus discovering and retracing the forgotten and lost roads that must have led man from the Natural state to the Civil state . . . [that] any attentive reader cannot fail to be struck by the immense distance that separates the two states." It is by this new science that Rousseau anticipates, the "science of man" that came to be called "anthropology," that the true nature of man will come to be understood. This new science is a historical science. History replaces philosophy. There is, then, no such thing as the nature of man, no such thing as to be human. Humanness has no nature; it has only a career. Here is the seed of the thought of the next century, the nineteenth. Also, here is the seed of the self-destruction of that thought, and here, perhaps it might be said, is the instrument of the assisted suicide of philosophy.[10]

Thinking about Rousseau and his researches into history, one cannot help but be reminded of a rather poor motion picture of 1940, *One Million B.C.*, starring Victor Mature and Carole Landis. An even worse remake of this, *One Million Years B.C.*, was made in 1966, starring Raquel Welch. A much better picture, *Quest for Fire*, was made in 1981 on a similar theme. All three movies, however, seem to accept as a given the proposition begun by Rousseau and pervasive in the subsequent science of anthropology, that somehow that very science of anthropology can dig up ruins and examine potsherds and can thereby figure out what the nature of humans *was* in the past and that therefore accepts the proposition put forward by Rousseau

---

[10] The translation used for the passages quoted in this section on Rousseau is that by Victor Gourevitch, *The First and Second Discourses and the Essay on the Origin of Languages*, New York, 1986, Harper and Row.

that what it is to be human changes over time, that the nature of man has no nature but has only a progress, a career, a history. If we do not like people, let us put our heads together and fix them. Let us create the new Soviet man without conscious reliance on Marx, Lenin, or Stalin.

We have not pretended here to give a full or proper account of Rousseau. The place to look for a compendious account is Allan Bloom's chapter on Rousseau in the Strauss and Cropsey *History of Political Philosophy* that we have mentioned several times herein. For a thumbnail sketch of how Rousseau fits into modern political philosophy, a good place to look would be the chapter "The Self" in what well may be the greatest piece, the masterpiece, of Bloom's life's work, *The Closing of the American Mind.*[11]

The book of philosophy closes the eighteenth century in the works of Immanuel Kant (1724–1804), who acknowledged his debt to Rousseau. A good way to look into Rousseau's notion of the "general will," which we have slighted here, might be to look backward to the general will from the vantage point of Kant's doctrine of the "categorical imperative." This doctrine is explained in a short book with a long title, *The Foundations of the Metaphysics of Morals* (1785). "There is, therefore, only one categorical imperative. It is: Act only according to that maxim by which you can at the same time will that it should become a universal law."[12] In his only work that falls clearly in the realm of political philosophy, an even shorter book, *Perpetual Peace* (1795), he shows his debt to Rousseau by calculating that perpetual peace will come as the consequence of the process of history. The full development of the doctrine of historical process comes with Hegel.

The Nineteenth Century

Georg Wilhelm Friedrich Hegel

Hegel (1770–1831) was born in Stuttgart. He studied theology at Tübingen, and, as his career developed, he taught at Jena, Heidelberg, and then Berlin. His writings include both theoretical philosophic works and practical political works. Except to remark on the connection between the two we shall ignore the practical writings and concentrate on the question of History as it appears in *The Philosophy of History* with some reference also to his *Philosophy of Right.* This concentration is necessary to keep within the confines of the general themes of this book, namely the origin and nature of philosophy and its relationship with politics.

In speaking of Rousseau, we suggested that his writings were somewhat aerated. Now all philosophic writing is more abstract than other prose. It cannot be otherwise. This is simply another way to speak of the distance of

---

[11] *The Closing of the American Mind*, New York, 1987, Simon and Schuster, pp. 173–79.
[12] Kant, *Foundations of the Metaphysics of Morals*, 1785, Lewis White Beck, tr., New York, 1959, Liberal Arts Press (later subsumed by Bobbs-Merrill, then by Macmillan), p. 39.

political philosophy from political thought in general. The character of that abstraction and its relation to the concrete varies however, as between, for example, Plato and Aristotle on the one hand and Hobbes, Rousseau, Kant, and Hegel on the other. In the case of the last four, the moderns, there is a progression, with the later ones accepting in important respects what the earlier ones had propounded. Thus, just as Rousseau appears to accept the reality of the "state of nature" that Hobbes had put forward, so Kant accepts the notion of the "general will" offered by Rousseau. As we noted, Kant's formulation, which appears to explain the general will, is what he calls the "categorical imperative." He notes that the highwayman cannot will the maxim underlying armed robbery as a universal maxim, for if everyone were a highwayman, the highwayman willing this as a universalized maxim would be beaten at his own game. The essence of highway robbery is that the highwayman wills a maxim for others from which he excepts himself. His criminality lies not in his maxim but in excepting himself from it.

Where Aristotle saw ethics and politics as two sides of the same question, Machiavelli began and Hobbes completed the perfect severing of the two. Kant's *Foundation of the Metaphysics of Morals* is the consummate attempt to create a priori a complete ethical system, an ethics wholly divorced from any concrete end. It appears almost as a burlesque of the classical notion that one develops the virtues not to get something for them but to have them. This is the meaning of the old saying that "virtue is its own reward." The common sense side of Kant's explanation of his scheme is that the adage "honesty is the best policy" is not about honesty but about policy. If a merchant gives his customer correct change he may keep himself out of jail or he may keep his customer coming back, but that proves only policy, not honesty. Still, one cannot help but think that, down the road, there is policy in being honest for the apparent sake of honesty itself. Would it not be the case that if the highwayman ceased to be a highwayman because he willed the maxim that no one, including himself, should be a highwayman, he would be doing to others simply what he preferred others do to him, or, put negatively, not doing to others what he preferred others not do to him? Would that be true honesty in Kant's sense or just good policy? One hesitates to find fault with the formulations of a mind as great as Kant's, but one is bound to wonder whether an ethereal ethics divorced from ends is possible.

It is true that Plato's doctrine of ideas is abstract to the ultimate degree, but in his distinction between being and becoming, between the conceivable and the tangible, he makes it clear that the tangible things can be understood only as reflections of the true things, the conceivable things, the ideas. In modern abstraction there is a progressive rarefaction from Rousseau to Kant to Hegel. Subject to a certain qualification, however, it is possible to regard Kant as plainspoken if contrasted with Hegel. The qualification, however, is that basing this measure of Hegel on his *Philosophy of History* does not give a fair reading, for that work is understood to be a compendium of Hegel's lecture notes edited in the light of two sets of notes taken by students, and those pesky creatures, students, are notorious for hearing not what was said but what they listened for.[13]

Subject to the cautionary remark just made, it seems fair nonetheless to explain Hegel's view of History in the following way. Understanding it requires appreciating his particular use of the words "reason," "dialectic," "spirit," and "mind."

"Reason" is understood by most people even today to be, as Plato and Aristotle had used the word, a faculty of the mind. It is that faculty by which one endeavors to understand or attempts to explain things – what they are and how they function. Human beings are endowed with this faculty to varying degrees. Some have more, some less. One cannot help but think of reason as itself a thing, something outside of us in which we participate. Hegel, however, seems to make it into truly a thing. He reifies it. It is not just that our intellects function by way of it. It does things. When we reason it is as though we are possessed by a *daimon*. It (reason) uses our intellection to achieve its goals. It achieves its goals over time through the historical process. It one over on mankind. Hegel goes so far as to call this the "cunning of reason."[14] Not to let ourselves get carried away in remarking this, maybe all that Hegel means is that reason functions through rules, that it is simply logic, and that logic has a driving force to it so that when we think of ourselves as "using" logic, in reality, it is using us. It works through us.

"Dialectic" is a form of the word "dialogue." The Greek roots of the word are *dia* and *logos, dia* meaning through, among, or between and *logos* meaning reason, speech, or reasoned speech. Plato's writings are called dialogues because they show a course of movement toward truth by a dialectical process of talking through or of one opinion talking up against another. These contradicting speeches progressively winnow out error, and the speakers, or at least some of them, thereby get nearer the truth. The dialectic constitutes an ascent from opinion, from ignorance, from prejudice. Note well: Only those involved in the dialogue make that ascent. Even the folks in the next room profit not a whit from the process, and surely CliffsNotes of one of Plato's dialogues gives nothing more than a false sense of assurance that one knows something or other. Hegel's use of the word "dialectic" does not quite mean what one finds in a dialogue written by Plato.

---

[13] See the Library of Liberal Arts edition of the Introduction to Hegel's *Philosophy of History* published under the title *Reason in History*, Robert S. Hartman, tr., New York, 1953, Liberal Arts Press, "Note on Text," p. xli.

[14] Hegel, *The Philosophy of History*, J. Sibree, tr., New York, 1956, Dover Publications, p. 33.

Plato indeed had meant by *nous*, or mind, something external to the particular minds of particular human beings. It was that toward which particular minds – or at least some of them – strove. That striving was by the dialectical process just mentioned. Plato and Aristotle were both fully aware that different countries had different "ways," or, to use the French word discussed earlier, different *moeurs*. These ways constituted, according to Plato's Socrates in the "Republic," a kind of box that imprisoned the individual minds. These boxes were dark caves instilling and enforcing established half-truths, a set of intellectual pieties. A small minority of a small minority of human beings, those deserving of the name "philosopher," carried on a lifelong struggle to escape from and remain free from their caves. The nonphilosophers in one cave regarded those in another as fools or villains, and those in all the caves where philosophers were present regarded those philosophers as both madmen and villains. Socrates spoke of an inner voice as a *daimon* that warned him against doing injustice. He claimed to be, as it were, possessed. To appreciate Hegel's understanding of "ways," a momentary excursion into the original meaning of the English word "genius" is useful. That original meaning is shown in nearly all of the twenty-five occurrences of the word "genius" in the *Federalist Papers* published in newspapers in 1787 and 1788 to support the ratification of the proposed, new constitution. As an illustration, look at what "Publius" (in this case, Alexander Hamilton) writes in the third paragraph of No. 60.

There is sufficient diversity in the state of property, in the genius, manners, and habits of the people of the different parts of the Union, to occasion a material diversity of disposition in their representatives towards the different ranks and conditions in society.[15]

The argument of Publius is in general a practical effort to show the virtues of the proposed constitution in the light of the raw material, the character, and the genius of the American people. A positive illustration of the diversity of disposition to which Hamilton refers is presented in *Federalist* No. 10, which argues for the control of factions, but a negative illustration of that diversity would be the difference between the views of the slave states and those of the free states. The two do not see slavery in the same way. What they see is what their ways, their genius, their manners and habits, their *moeurs* permit them to see. Only a superior intellect such as Hamilton's can see beyond those differences. Although the *Federalist* is, properly speaking, subphilosophic, it is surely a superior writing. It is still

[15] Alexander Hamilton, James Madison, and John Jay, *The Federalist*, Robert Scigliano, ed., New York, 2001, Modern Library, No. 60, third paragraph, p. 384. For a tabulation of the instances of use of the word "genius," see Thomas S. Engeman, Edward J. Erler, and Thomas B. Hofeller, eds., *The Federalist Concordance*, Chicago, 1980, University of Chicago Press, p. 319. Citations in the *Concordance* are to the Jacob E. Cooke edition, in this case, to p. 404.

the best book ever written on American politics. It is easy, by the way, to see in retrospect this accommodation of diverse views as a sellout, but to do this is to forget that the best a statesman can ever do is contained within the limits of the possible.

The *Federalist's* use of the word "genius" reminds one of the argument about the cave in the "Republic." There is a word in German, the cognate of the English "genius": It is *genie*. It meant in German in Hegel's and Hamilton's day what "genius" then meant in English. The two words in their respective languages are still cognates, but they now both convey the changed sense that time and use have wrought. The word that Hegel uses in most instances to convey what in English would be called "mind" or "spirit" (i.e., the state of mind or the *moeurs* or the underlying, overall view of things), however, is not *genie* but *Geist*. For Hegel, this spirit or mind is not only a reflection of a people, it is also a reflection of the time, the existing present. As the opening paragraph of the Introduction to *The Philosophy of History* shows, Hegel means to write a history of the world, a universal history. This intends a great feat. History had, at least until Dante, always been understood as particular, the history of this or that country or of the relations between this country and that. Hegel, however, sees the whole of human history as moving in a certain direction. The spirit of a new time, the *geist* of the new *zeit*, its *zeitgeist*, is in a state of conflict with that of the present time. This conflict, this contradiction, this universal history, moved by the cunning of reason, leads inevitably to a universal spirit, a world-spirit, a *weltgeist*. Hegel uses the word "dialectic" in a sense rather foreign to Plato's use. There is for Hegel a dialectical process in the conflict between one *zeitgeist* and another, and the seat of a spirit of the times is in some place, in some civilization. One cannot help but be reminded of the title of Samuel P. Huntington's 1996 book, *The Clash of Civilizations and the Remaking of World Order*. The Hegelian formulation for this world-historical process is to regard the present condition as the thesis, the rising condition as its antithesis, and the resolution of the dialectic between them as the synthesis. It appears that the contradictory antithesis is spawned by the thesis itself because, implied in every comprehensive view, is its contrary, its antithesis.

The movement of world history begins for Hegel with the zeitgeist of the Orient and proceeds through Greece, then Rome, and finally to the West. Specifically, the completion of the historical process, the culmination, the *weltgeist*, Hegel finds in the modern state, in particular, in the modern, German, Protestant, Christian state. This is where the cunning of reason leads the world. The West *is* the World, and Germany is the West. The culmination of the historical process, the self-realization of freedom, is found in the end of History, perfected in and by the constitutional monarchy of the German, Protestant state, the year of that perfection being A.D. 1806. Let us not forget one thing here. The implicit suggestion of historical progress that is in St. Augustine and then in Dante and is explicit in Hegel depends for its vitality on the belief in divine providence, specifically the Christian understanding of divine Providence, the fact and the substance of God's providing for us. History is itself a process, a movement, and God's hand is at its helm, but, stationed there by the cunning of reason, the process itself, the historical process, is in the engine room. This view is altered by Hegel's intellectual heirs.

Notice a couple of other things. First, for Plato, the dialectic took place between two or among a few more or less congenial associates whose limited views were pitted against each other. These associates generally shared a common *ethos* or moral structure. There was no reciprocal hatred based on ethnicity or religious doctrine, for example. The dialectical process led for one or more of the interlocutors to an improved view of whatever it was about which they conversed. Because Plato's dialogues were written down, it is possible for others, later, to re-create in their individual minds something of the movement the originals made toward the truth. At best, the truth was and could be again glimpsed as the fruit of that dialectical labor, but not even the originals, much less the later readers, could make the truth simply their possession – put it safely in their pockets. Also, certainly nobody else, nobody other than the participants – the original arguers or, at most, the later, studious, re-creators of that argument – could get anything at all from the dialectic. For Hegel, on the contrary, it is not live human beings but civilizations and their spirits, ideologies, ways, *moeurs*, or prejudices that conflict; first they profit, and then the whole world profits from that dialectic. This is another of the marks of the rarefaction of Hegel's thought, and it is the epitome of the modern notion of progress. We moderns praise progress and we praise and promote "change" because we take for granted that all change is change from the worse to the better. We look with a certain condescension on the whole course of history – world history, the career of mankind – as an inevitable preparation for the perfection that we, now, possess. Maybe Hegel was wrong that the end of things was captured in 1806 in the modern, German, Protestant, Christian, Constitutional monarchy, but surely, we believe, we are right that our perfection in the modern, secular, liberal democracy is the last stage of providence (not of divine Providence, but of providence with a lowercase *p* – with, that is, the inevitability of the historical process). At some point, the world-historical process, while maintaining its hold on the engine room, strode onto the bridge and took hold of the helm. We now see that all who went before us truly were fools or knaves. After a few stumbling blocks in the "less developed" civilizations are overcome, will we not be wonderful and lovable? What is more, the true millennium will come not, as Hegel thought, through the dialectic of wars, but through our lawyers dialoguing with their lawyers.

If there is indeed a historical inevitability, however, a process fueled by a reason understood not as a faculty of the human mind but as an entity that subsists of itself and is understood as cunning, that is, as willing a certain end that it foresees but that we can only see in retrospect, how could that dialectical process ever end? How could there be an end to history, whether it be in the Protestant German state or in anything else? Hegel's dialectic of history is what comes to be called "historicism," and, as that doctrine develops, it becomes clear that not only is an end to history possible, it is necessary if the dialectical process of history is not to show itself as an absurdity. If one does not accept, as Hegel posited, some sort of end to the otherwise endless progress of history, one is compelled to turn to nihilism, to the reduction of all history and all philosophy to nothing, to nothingness, to postmodernism. There is no world history, only a kind of aimless meandering that, as Shakespeare made Macbeth see it, is a "tale told by an idiot, full of sound and fury, signifying nothing."[16] To look for any meaning at all is absurd, thus absurdity becomes the very ground of some modern theater. That is to say, where once the word "absurdity" was a dismissal it becomes now an acceptance. Because all thought is absurd, let us be at peace with that fact. Why, however? Will that fact not cease to be in the course of history? Beginning with Hegel, every historicist view has been compelled to posit an absolute moment, an ahistorical moment, when we are able to see the ultimate historicity of every other moment, as though the clouds of the several zeitgeists momentarily clear and we see through the clear blue sky the truth itself. You will not deserve blame if, by chance, you see this as rather like cheating at solitaire, namely, coming to a satisfactory conclusion by hook or by crook.

Just as Rousseau was the principal critic of Hobbes and Locke, and so of the ground of modern understanding as a whole, and the ground, as it were, of the *zeitgeist* of postmodernity, historicism, so also the great critic of historicism is Nietzsche, to whom we must turn but not until we have said a few words about the partial, but crucial, disapproval of Hegel, by his intellectual heirs, Marx and Engels. Then we must say a word about a twentieth-century commentator on both Hegel and Marx, namely Alexandre Kojève.

Karl Marx and Friedrich Engels

Hegel's works influenced every corner of intellectual life, first in Germany and then beyond. Philosophers, near philosophers, academics, commentators, and critics lectured, wrote, and founded journals, some praising, some criticizing the new philosophy launched by Hegel. Ludwig Feuerbach (1804–72) began, as Hegel had begun, as a student of theology, but under

---

[16] Given the difficulty and rarefaction of Hegel's writing, the present author, diffident as he is regarding his own powers of analysis and understanding, has been aided in his conclusions by reading the excellent chapter on Hegel by Pierre Hassner (and translated from Hassner's French into English by Allan Bloom) in the Strauss and Cropsey *History of Political Philosophy* cited frequently herein.

the influence of Hegelian views he switched to the study of philosophy. He was, at first, a follower of Hegel, but then he turned into one of Hegel's critics. It looks as though his complaint was that Hegel, although appearing to be a materialist (and therefore an atheist, and so a thinker to be approved), in fact was driven by religion. Feuerbach lost his employment when the authorship of an antireligious work published anonymously was exposed as his.

Karl Marx (1818–83) studied law at Bonn and then philosophy and history at Berlin. He took his doctorate at Jena in 1841 on the basis of his thesis on Epicurus (342–271 B.C.) and Democritus (c. 460 B.C.). Early in his education he identified himself with the left wing of what were known as the "young Hegelians." His undisguised atheism made academic employment in Prussia impossible and, after a brief spell as editor of an economic journal, he went into exile, from which he never returned, to Brussels, Paris, then London. His first noteworthy publications were what are known as the *Economic and Philosophic Manuscripts of 1844*.[17] His lifelong partnership with Friedrich Engels (1820–95) soon began, and in 1845 they collaborated on *The German Ideology* (which it appears was not published until twenty years later, at which point it was, as their preface puts it, rescued from "the gnawing criticism of the mice").

The "theses on Feuerbach" at the opening of *The German Ideology* begin a pattern of merciless, biting, sarcastic dismissal of the Young Hegelians, a method of written works that continues through almost all of the writings of Marxians criticizing – no, one should say "crushing" – any intellectual from 1845 to the present who happens to oppose the one who is writing. In keeping with the modern attention to the practical as opposed to the theoretical, there is a blend of polemic and philosophy wherein polemic wins the day. The goal of philosophy turns from wishing to understand and to be understood, either by the few or by the many, to wishing to succeed as a political actor. Philosophy dissolves and reemerges as politics. An example of the philosophico-political polemic is V. I. Lenin (1870–1924), the founding father of the revolution of 1917 that led to the origin of the Soviet Union, who, in his *The State and Revolution* (1917), wrote polemic that is so biting it is almost delicious. He treated Karl Kautsky, a non-Marxian socialist, with such merciless derision in Chapter Six of that short book that it can be read over and over again with increasing amusement.[18]

---

[17] Comprehensive articles on Feuerbach and Marx can be found in *The Encyclopedia of Philosophy*, 8 vols., New York, 1967, Macmillan (Feuerbach in vol. 3; Marx in vol. 5), to which I am indebted for these details.

[18] Nearly forty years ago I counted up the instances in *The State and Revolution* where poor Kautsky is raked over the coals, but I can't find my note on that and this would not be a good time to interrupt my argument to count them up again. Someone who knows how to do a computer word count of a text might be able to manage this task quickly.

On the very first page after the Preface of *The German Ideology*, Marx and Engels refer to the dissolution by Hegel's critics of his positing of the "universal spirit." The Hegelian argument is dismissed as the "putrescence of the absolute spirit."[19] In other words, what Hegel had come up with, the notion of a *weltgeist*, was perishable and, like a tomato, that notion was bound to rot, to putrefy, and that is what happened to Hegel's "universal spirit" under the care of some of the followers of Hegel. Here we must again examine a word. The word is "ideology." We mean now by this word an attribute of what we call "culture." Ideology is to us rather like what Hegel conceived of as the "*zeitgeist*." That is, it is the moral and intellectual schematic of a culture. As Marx and Engels use the term in *The German Ideology*, they mean something like this, but they also mean something that puts this conception of it in a whole new light for us. To Marx, "ideology" means something like "idealism." Let us be careful, however. We often use the word "idealism" as a term of praise: An idealist is a good fellow who strives to achieve the ideal. In contrast, we sometimes use the word "ideology" in a neutral manner, that is, we mean by it the cluster of things we call our "values." This is contrary to common sense, however. We say that our values are simply our ways, and some time in the twentieth century the sophisticated sense in which "values" entered the language toward the end of the nineteenth century filtered down to ordinary people, even to people who had never read a book. The minute *our* values are seen as *just* ours, as just our *ways*, and we begin to talk of this in a sophisticated way, babble about diversity, and say that all "ways" are of equal dignity, then what we used to call "principles" or "morals" are seen as altogether arbitrary, as groundless. In consequence, if we want to be consistent, we are compelled to acknowledge that idealists are not such swell fellows. They are fools. We are too clever for the folly of idealism. We are realistic. We are above obeying the law. Worse, nothing anyone says can be taken seriously. We have reached the terminus, postmodernism, deconstruction. We can see that philosophy itself is a pipe dream, that is, a phantasm that floats up from an opium pipe. Surely we are too smart for philosophy. Have we not evolved? In contrast, we sometimes use the word not neutrally, but as a term of dispraise. We have the truth. Those other folks just have ideology. There is a problem with this, but maybe this notion is more wholesome. Maybe we behave better under this view (supposing that one thing is better than another).

---

[19] Marx and Engels, *The German Ideology*, R. Pascal, ed., New York, 1947, International Publishers, p. 3. It is not clear whether Pascal or someone else – perhaps the Institute of Marxism–Leninism of Moscow – is the translator. "Putrescence of the absolute spirit" is offered in both the Pascal edition and the C. J. Arthur edition (also published by International Publishers, 1970) as the English equivalent of *Verfaulungsprozess des absoluten Geistes* in the German, which seems altogether literal and correct. See Karl Marx, Friedrich Engels, *Werke, Band 3*, Dietz Verlag Berlin, 1969, *Die deutsche Ideologie*, p. 17. The citations herein are to the Pascal edition.

When Marx and Engels liken ideology to idealism, or treat the two words as interchangeable, this is not praise. It is simply equation. They mean that an ideology rests on ideas. Plato appeared to them foolish for prating about the ideas. For them ideas as conceived by Plato were fantasies. They were in fact like all philosophy, and so like religion and like poetry – just so much nonsense – phantasms of an intellect not rooted in concrete reality, and this is where Hegel and his followers had gone wrong. Marx and Engels write:

German criticism has, right up to its latest efforts, never quitted the realm of philosophy. Far from its general philosophic premises, the whole body of its inquiries has actually sprung from the soil of a definite philosophical system, that of Hegel. Not only in their answers but in their very questions there was a mystification.[20]

Whatever else may be said of Marx's views, to speak of Hegel's philosophy as "mystification" rings true. It is kindred to what we said earlier regarding aeration progressing from Rousseau through Kant to Hegel. Notice, however, that in the passage just quoted Marx characterizes philosophy itself as the wrong philosophy. To write sensibly, critics should have "quitted philosophy." If Machiavelli had been the first philosopher to betray philosophy in the service of politics, Marx was the first philosopher to deny the legitimacy or even the possibility of philosophy. Hegel had said that philosophy has been replaced by history. Marx sees the corpse of philosophy and gives it an indecent burial. There are indeed ideas, but they are not, as Plato had understood them, entities that subsist in themselves in a realm separate from the realm of perishable matter.

The production of ideas, of conceptions, of consciousness, is at first directly interwoven with the material activity and the material intercourse of men, the language of real life. Conceiving, thinking, the mental intercourse of men, appear as the direct efflux of their material behaviour. The same applies to mental production as applied in the language of the politics, laws, morality, religion, metaphysics of a people. Men are the producers of their conceptions, ideas, etc., – real, active men, as they are conditioned by a definite development of their productive forces, and of the intercourse corresponding to these, up to its furthest forms. Consciousness can never be anything else than conscious existence, and the existence of men is their actual life process.[21]

What Plato had called the "ideas" Hegel calls *geistes*, the spirits of the times, and he explains the historical process as a dialectic of these *zeitgeistes*. For Hegel, a *zeitgeist* had a substance of its own, rather as Plato had understood the ideas, but Hegel gives a modern twist to this in the following way. Aristotle had taught that the best practicable political order was in most cases some sort of "mixed regime." This was a mixture of oligarchy and democracy, both defective regimes, and in some cases that mixture might

---

[20] Ibid., p. 4.
[21] Ibid., pp. 13–14.

be enriched by an admixture of aristocracy, a better form of regime but one difficult to establish in itself. In the seventeenth century Hobbes modified Aristotle's teaching by making the passions rather than reason the basis of everything. To see appetite as ruling is to be a hedonist. There had been hedonists in ancient times, but they turned away from politics. Hobbes's hedonism is the foundation of the modern political doctrine which in economic terms is called the "invisible hand." He is, as Strauss calls him, the first political hedonist. He makes private selfishness and its conflicts the author of the common good. There is no common good as such. The common good is simply the mathematical consequence of the concatenation of conflicts of private appetites. Hegel follows in the train of Hobbes by seeing the dialectic of the *geistes* as a conflict, a historical struggle. Marx keeps the dialectic, the historical process, and the conflict, but he rejects the ethereal aspect of Hegel, the "mystification." Also, he seems to equate Hegel with the whole history of philosophy. All of it is nonsense. Instead of approaching a correction of Hegel by entertaining a reexamination of Plato, he rejects Hegel simply and he does this by bringing his particular form of materialism to bear. He keeps Hegelian historical process, Hegelian dialectic, and Hegelian conflict, and simply combines them with a certain version of materialism. Immediately following the text of *The German Ideology* just quoted, Marx and Engels say this:

If in all ideology men and their circumstances appear upside down as in a *camera obscura*, this phenomenon arises just as much from their historical life process as the inversion of objects on the retina does from their physical life process.

In direct contrast to German ideology which descends from heaven to earth, here we ascend from earth to heaven. That is to say, we do not set out from what men say, imagine, conceive, nor from men as narrated, thought of, imagined, conceived, in order to arrive at men in the flesh. We set out from real, active men, and on the basis of their real life-process we demonstrate the ideological reflexes and echoes of this life-process.... Morality, religion, metaphysics, all the rest of ideology and their corresponding forms of consciousness, thus no longer retain the semblance of independence.[22]

All ideology, that is idealism, that is all philosophy, has things upside down, with reality seen as a by-product of thought. The true case of things is that thought is heaped on the material process of history. It accrues because of what later Marxians dubbed "dialectical materialism." (Marx had never used this term, but its use by followers of Marx seems accurately to have captured what Marx argued.) Hegel and the Hegelians, like all philosophers before them, get everything wrong because instead of standing on their feet on solid ground they are standing on their heads on a cloud. As Marx and Engels put it in other writings, including *The Communist Manifesto* (1848),

[22] *Loc. cit.*

philosophy is a superstructure piled on top of whatever the material circumstances of the time are. "When reality is depicted, philosophy as an independent branch of activity loses its medium of existence. . . . Viewed apart from real history these abstractions have in themselves no value whatsoever."[23]

There is, of course, a great deal more to Marx and Engels and to the whole, bustling industry of Marxian scholarship, but it is sufficient to the limited purposes of this book to summarize by saying that Marx continues the historicism seeded by Rousseau and developed by Hegel. He does so by accepting the bulk of Hegel, excluding what Marx calls Hegel's "mystification," and putting in its place his particular version of materialism so that the historical dialectic leads to the end of history not as Hegel's Protestant, German state, but as the wonderful new world-to-come of absolute communism wherein marriage, private property, and the state itself wither away. We are back to Aristophanes' *Assembly of Women* but absent the saving grace of comedy.

The Twentieth Century

Those who called themselves "behavioralist social scientists" a hundred years after Marx, while not, as such, Marxists, were (and remain) in fundamental agreement with the Marxian[24] dismissal of philosophy. Marxian thought itself remains a vigorous intellectual ground throughout Western civilization as well as elsewhere in the world. Twentieth-century political science, for example, became liberated from political philosophy, and from philosophy itself; political philosophy became "political theory," and political theory became reducible to the history of political theory, that is, rather like this chapter, to a catalog of the excrescences on the historical dialectic. Finally it was found to be altogether superfluous by political science departments in some colleges and universities. "Theory" became mathematical calculations as to how to achieve certain political ends proposed by "values" which were – and are – seen as altogether divorced from "facts." Facts are what are; values are what-you-will. As Leo Strauss put it, this is "retail sanity and wholesale madness."

Such a science is instrumental and nothing but instrumental: it is born to be the handmaid of any powers or any interests that be. What Machiavelli did apparently, our social science would actually do if it did not prefer – only God knows why – generous liberalism to consistency: namely, to give advice with equal competence and alacrity to tyrants as well as to free peoples.[25]

"Only God knows why" because "generous liberalism" cannot be explained. It can only be asserted. If I am a follower of Stalin, Hitler, or

[23] Ibid., p. 15.
[24] A Marxist may be described as someone who actively pursues the political ends of Marx's doctrine. The word "Marxian" is an adjective that characterizes the study and favorable explanation of Marx's doctrines.
[25] Leo Strauss, *Natural Right and History*, Chicago, 1953, University of Chicago Press, p. 4.

a terrorist who murders numbers of civilians who have done nothing to offend me, you can dislike me, and you can make war against me, but you cannot argue with me, because my values and yours are equally free from facts, from any concrete reality. In matters of the greatest moment we are disarmed.

The "value-free social scientists," who prospered most in the 1940s and 1950s, were followed by a new breed of "New Left" social scientists and social activists. I think they can best be explained as having fully accepted the value-free social science of their teachers. Whereas the teachers had endeavored to liberate themselves from values in pursuit of their facts, the New Left turned its back on facts and embraced values. They quite consciously garnered mere facts in the service of their values, which means, of course, they cherry-picked their facts. In this they were the children, or at least the stepchildren, of Rousseau's substitution of sentiment for reason. Without the underpinning of what Strauss called "generous liberalism," philosophy has but a small step to take to join the oldest profession in offering its services for hire. Allan Bloom has called the New Left a curious mixture of Marx and Nietzsche. Having now again mentioned Nietzsche, it is time to turn to him.

Friedrich Nietzsche

Turning to Nietzsche (1844–1900), who ushered in the postmodernism of the twentieth century, we are compelled to pause and catch our intellectual breath. Strauss somewhere speaks of Socrates as the founder of the first youth movement. Machiavelli is second in this line and rather directly presents himself as such. Nietzsche is the founder of the third great youth movement, the one now in progress. Like all great thinkers, he does not care whether you remember his name or know that he is your founder, so long as the movement carries you along. If, as Strauss said, to read Maimonides is to find oneself in an enchanted forest, perhaps we could say that to read Nietzsche is to find oneself in an insane asylum where we are in constant danger of mistaking the inmates for the medical staff. What characterizes all philosophers and is carried to great length by Plato (or Plato's Socrates) and by Machiavelli is carried to the furthest extreme by Nietzsche. He is more mystical than Hegel; more indirect and obfuscating than Plato, al-Farabi, or Machiavelli; more poetic than Homer himself; more deliberately taunting than a whole theater full of stand-up comics; yet is often as blunt as Hobbes. We have had to exercise caution and experience fear in trying to understand the others we have dealt with so far, but trying to understand and explain Nietzsche is rather like standing on the edge of a precipice while the chorus, just to see what happens, shouts, "Jump!" A couple of things are clear. He is the founder of that youth movement that has captivated the twentieth and now the twenty-first century by bequeathing to us postmodernism. He self-consciously and declaringly accepts as inevitable the nihilism that he sees and we see as the consequence of the historicism of Hegel and Marx. He appears to do this to clear the philosophic decks so as to start anew. Those academic traditionalists who think that philosophy, and with it political philosophy, is an evolution or a progress which can be understood as "history" cannot confront the likes of a Plato, a Machiavelli, or a Nietzsche. We do not mean to treat these three as of equal rank; we only say that they all demand the greatest respect and they all require extreme care in reading because they all seem to get to the root of things, and each surely breaks or means to break new ground.

Born in 1844 in the village of Röcken bei Lützen, where his father, a Lutheran, was the town minister, he, with his mother, his grandmother, his two aunts, and his sister, moved to Naumburg in 1849 after his father's death. In 1864 he went to the university at Bonn to study theology but quickly turned his attention to philology, studying the Greek classical texts. In an action that would seem irregular to an American student, who is expected to acquire a lifelong attachment to his university, but an action that was customary for European students, Nietzsche left Bonn the next year to study with the philologist Friedrich Wilhelm Ritschl at the University of Leipzig. During a brief period of military service in 1867, he was badly injured attempting to leap-mount his horse. This was the beginning of what would be a lifelong struggle with various health problems. At the age of twenty-four, he began teaching at the University of Basel. He published his first book, *The Birth of Tragedy*, when he was twenty-seven. During the Franco-Prussian War of 1870–71 he served (because of his health) not as a horseman in a field artillery regiment, but as a hospital attendant. In 1879, because of health problems, he resigned his post at the University of Basel and spent the next ten years traveling about Europe and writing, among other works, *The Gay Science*, *Thus Spake Zarathustra*, *Beyond Good and Evil*, and *On the Genealogy of Morals*. In 1889 his mental health dissolved and he spent the last ten years of his life in the care of his mother and sister as his mental condition degenerated into insanity. One should perhaps not read his insanity backward and make it the retroactive cause of his sometimes seemingly mad writings. The character of his writings was, it seems, deliberately chosen by him as the proper vehicle for his views.

It would not be altogether wrong to say that he wrote just one book but that he wrote it, rewrote it, or embellished it over and over again. If, as Thomas Edison (1847–1931) said, genius is one percent inspiration and ninety-nine percent perspiration, it just may be the case that every great mind in philosophy had at an early age a lightning bolt of inspiration that opened his soul to all the great mysteries, and then spent his life thinking through the details. Among the parts of Nietzsche's thought were an understanding of mastery or nobility as the "will to power," the conception of a new breed of philosophers whom he characterized as "philosophers of the future" who would follow his lead in "overcoming" what it was to be human, and an acceptance as true the historicity of thought asserted by Hegel coupled with a revulsion at the dispiriting of all life that acknowledgment of that truth brought. Curiously, if philosophy had begun and had continued as the pursuit of truth, it ends as the spirited rejection of truth as deadly. The work of philosophy becomes not to seek truth, but to do something about it, something creative. God is dead but is needed. Philosophers must fill the need and, in the proper sense, will be rather as the new gods. They will be understood as the "creators." They will transcend humanity. They will become the "overmen." The acceptance of history and of the end of history brings revulsion because the end of history will mean the appearance of the "last men," the posthistorical men who will have nothing left to do that is grand – no worlds to conquer, no wars to win gloriously, no truths to seek – in a word, nothing that makes man man. Perhaps to escape from the rise of the last men, the solution to the end of history lies in some sort of recurrence of things, some kind of eternal recurrence. If the world is eternal – this one, not some fanciful world-to-come – then perhaps everything that can be remembered as happening has, in fact, happened over and over again countless times and will continue to happen, over and over.

Nietzsche completes devastatingly the critique of the modern that had been begun by Rousseau. He never writes the word "modern" without quotation marks or without curling his lip in contempt. He is particularly disgusted by democracy and equality, which he sees simply as the elevation of the "rabble," and he joins this contempt for the "modern" with his contempt for Christianity, which he sees as an indulgent celebration of death, a hatred of this world, a hatred of life, and a preference for an imagined afterlife. Alongside Nietzsche, Machiavelli's contempt for Christianity seems rather like the appearance of a minor Christian sect.

Beyond Good and Evil consists of a preface, nine parts, and, running consecutively through the nine parts, two hundred ninety-six numbered sections. The first words of the preface are "Supposing truth is a woman – what then?" Machiavelli, it will be remembered, had said that *fortuna* was a woman, and he had counseled the one who desired state to seize *fortuna* by the wrist and knock her around a bit, because that impetuosity and that manliness, that *virtù*, is what causes a woman to surrender. Elsewhere, Nietzsche speaks admiringly of Machiavelli, but he says that Germans do not know how to read him because Germans have no sense of humor. Here in Part One, "The Prejudices of Philosophers," at the beginning of Section 1, Nietzsche speaks of the "The Will to Truth." We are driven to wonder, what is "the will"? Is the "will to truth" the highest will, or even the right will? Certainly truth has not yielded to philosophers, he says. They have all been clumsy at courtship, and truth has never surrendered itself to them. What is to be done? Should one attend a sort of philosophical charm school? Should one approach truth with strength and directness, with impetuosity, the way a manly man would approach a woman? The first words of the third paragraph of Section 1 speak of "The problem of the value of truth." Perhaps truth is worth less than the philosophers had thought. Perhaps truth is not the proper goal of philosophy.[26] What, then, is?

Nietzsche asserts that all philosophy hitherto is reducible to some morality which was, in turn, merely an expression of "something ulterior" (I,6).[27] This seems to us the very seed of the current social scientific view that all values are without a grounding in reason. Anyone, he says, who, encountering a philosophic pronouncement, "hears nothing... except a 'will to truth'... does not have the best of ears" (I,10). In rare cases a will to truth may lead some metaphysician to "prefer... a handful of 'certainty' to a whole carload of beautiful possibilities; there may actually be puritanical fanatics of conscience who prefer even a certain nothing to an uncertain something to lie down on – and die. But this is nihilism" (Ibid.). This concern of Nietzsche is all the more interesting because nihilism is a good description of the views of postmodernists and deconstructionists of the present who, whether understandingly or not, are the heirs of Nietzsche. "Nihilism," a revolutionary and anarchist term coined in Russia in the early nineteenth century, shed its ties to its origin and came to mean either the view that moral standards "cannot be justified by rational argument" or the description of a state of "despair over the emptiness and triviality of human existence."[28] It may be that these two definitions point to two sides of the same coin.

Throughout *Beyond Good and Evil* Nietzsche continues his near denial of the possibility of philosophy and his condemnation of philosophers who preceded him. At the same time, he presents himself as the true philosopher and offers a prophecy of a new breed of philosophers, "philosophers of the future." Although it is difficult to conceive of him as a materialist, Nietzsche does in places dismiss the soul, referring to what he calls the "soul superstition" (Preface, the second paragraph). Nonetheless, having already faulted the science of physics, he turns his attention to psychology, which,

[26] The quotations of Nietzsche here are from the English translation of *Beyond Good and Evil* by Walter Kaufmann, New York, 1966, Vintage Books. The word that Kaufmann regularly translates as "value" is in the German *Wert* (plural: *Werthe*). This means "worth" or "value" in the sense in which Allan Bloom said that "values" were what he "got at Wal-Mart." Sometimes Nietzsche uses the word in this ordinary way, but sometimes he uses it in the sense of what came to be called "value judgments," that is, moral judgments, but he never defined "value" as he used the word. I believe it was Max Weber (1864–1920) who did that, thereby teaching social scientists the bifurcating distinction between "facts" and "values."

[27] The parenthetic citation "I,6" is shorthand for Part I, Section 6. Subsequent citations to *Beyond Good and Evil* will be made parenthetically in this fashion.

[28] See the entry for "Nihilism" in *The Encyclopedia of Philosophy*, 8 vols. (4 double vols.), Paul Edwards, ed., New York, 1967, Macmillan, vol. 5, pp. 514 ff.

in its original usage, meant the study of or science of the soul. Psychology, it turns out, is defective because it has not turned its attention to the will to power. Nietzsche himself is the first to do that (I,23). Therefore, as it turns out, the problem with that silliness about the will to truth is resolved by the centrality of the will to power. It is to this that philosophy must turn, and not just to understand it but to live it. We have come to the nether pole. Plato's Socrates had talked up a city in speech where the wise ruled with the devoted support of the nobles, the strong. Machiavelli had followed that alliance, but in an inverted way. Now Nietzsche tells us that nobility itself is defined by a consciousness of superiority the beacon of which is the will to power. Psychology, righted, "is now again the path to the fundamental problems" (Ibid.). The fashionable attachment to democracy and equality must be jettisoned. There are the weak and the strong, and the former rightly belong under the domination of the latter. Fifty years after Tocqueville had, from an aristocratic point of view, offered a tentative and partial approval of the modern democracy begun in America, Nietzsche comes out four-square for the recovery of aristocracy, but his identification of the natural aristocrats is not that they are wise, that they are formed by old families, or that they are virtuous, but simply that, knowing themselves to be masters and not deterred by any foolish sentimentality about equality and the alleviation of suffering, they are driven by the will to power to assert their mastery. At the beginning of Book Two of Plato's "Republic," Glaucon and Adeimantus ask Socrates to argue that Justice without rewards is preferable to injustice without punishments. In the course of presenting the problem, Glaucon says that "they" – some unnamed, strong people – dismiss justice as something the truly manly fellow would reject because he can take what he wants and does not have to make a bargain with the weak to get it. Remembering this, Nietzsche in his definition of the noble as those possessing the will to power, seems to be the very embodiment of those whom Glaucon called "they."

If the jurors who had condemned Socrates to death could have been resuscitated in 1886 and had compelled the philosopher Nietzsche to parade before them, they would have heaved a sigh of righteous self-satisfaction that they had indeed meted out justice in condemning to death the philosopher Socrates. Now it happens that there has always been a kernel of sense in the antipathy of the city to philosophy. In any case, the antipathy was always there. Thus, philosophers through the ages have always spoken a bit cloudily. Therefore, it is not surprising that, shortly after his firm assertion of the will to power, Nietzsche says, "I obviously do everything to be 'hard to understand' myself." To boast that one is attempting not to be understood is, however, to negate the attempt. It is as self-canceling as the promise of Strepsiades to Socrates in the *Clouds* that if Socrates would teach him how to cheat his creditors he would certainly pay Socrates for the teaching some time in the future.

Another contrast with Plato is appropriate here. Plato had made Socrates do two things in talking up the city in speech that we need to recall here. First, he had spoken of "vulgar virtue" and he spoke of it in the context of the recognition that peoples as peoples never live in accordance with truth but always in accordance with their attachment to the "shadows on the wall." That is, a people lives by its *mores*, the ways of its city, its morality, and its prejudices. Second, because what is wanted is therefore not to think that one can make the many become as only the few can become, but to give to the many wholesome prejudices in the place of the destructive ones they had imbibed from the poets. Granting these two things, philosophers should be kings. As kings they would be lawgivers. They would certainly not themselves find laws laid up in heaven, but would only find there a sort of "pattern," and, calculating what might be called the "genius" of the people of the city, they would lay down a web of morality, of law, of ways, which would be understood by the people as right, as just, and would be revered by them as such. Rather than possessing truth, the philosopher is a creature who spends his life in the unending pursuit of the truth. Nonphilosophers cannot bear to live that way. They need a sense of moral certainty to undergird their lives. The philosopher-king gives them that sense of certainty when he legislates the vulgar virtues. The city lives happily ever after, or at least for an appreciable time until it, like everything that has come into being, unravels.

Thus far, Nietzsche's scheme is not far afield from what we suggest is the argument of Plato's Socrates. The profound difference, however, is that Plato's philosopher king would establish the best regime, the one most in accord with what is by nature right that can be fashioned from the human beings at hand. The end of Nietzsche's regime is determined by its means, the will to power. The would-be ruler wants the power to rule not to rule well but simply to rule, to have the power. One cannot help at this point but close his or her eyes and imagine a ruler who starts a war just for the sport of it, for the hell of it. Surely the great tyrants of the twentieth century slaughtered millions in the pursuit of false ends, but if anything at all good can be said of them it can be said, rather weakly, that at least they had ends in view. They did not commit mass murder because of sheer boredom. Socrates, Plato, and Aristotle all saw mankind as having a nature, and that nature was understood to be fixed. There is a kernel in that nature, realizable in some humans, for true excellence, and, as for the others, most are capable of being formed into people with common decency and respect for the law. There is good in man, and sound politics can find and make the most of it. For Nietzsche, insofar as man has a nature at all, it is defined not by *eros*, but by will, specifically the will to power. Those who have it in high degree are truly noble and are fit to rule. Those who lack it or who have it to a lesser extent deserve to be ruled. All of the latter would appear to fit Aristotle's definition of the natural slave. In another sense, man is for Nietzsche almost infinitely malleable. It almost seems that for

Nietzsche, in the train of Rousseau and then of Hegel, man has not so much a nature as a career. What it is to be human changes with the times, yet that would contradict Nietzsche's doctrine of the "eternal return" and would make impossible the creativity of the new philosophers, moved as they would be by the will to power. Also, we are disinclined to suspect patent self-contradiction on the part of a genius like Nietzsche, unless we can find some ulterior purpose in it. Despite a healthy contempt for democracy and equality, something that seems to go along with those things, the idea of progress, comes to mind as a near attribute of Nietzsche's thought. If such is there, it presents a problem for him, the problem of history.

Nietzsche foresees a new sort of philosopher in the future and a new sort of philosophy (II,42). These philosophers in the future will, apparently, not seek or have truth: Each will have his own truth. "One must shed the bad taste of wanting to agree with many" (II,43). These new philosophers will be genuine free spirits, not like those in Nietzsche's day who herald themselves as such but who "belong, briefly and sadly, among the *levelers*... being eloquent and prolifically scribbling slaves of the democratic taste and its 'modern ideas'... they are unfree and ridiculously superficial.... What they would like to strive for... is the universal green-pasture happiness of the herd, with security, lack of danger, comfort, and an easier life for everyone.... [What] they repeat most often are 'equality of rights' and 'sympathy for all that suffers' – and suffering itself they take for something that must be *abolished*" (II,44). Life is not for truth. It is for living, and if untruth suits living better than truth, so be it (I,1–2).

Part Three is titled "Das Religiöse Wesen," which Kaufmann translates as "What Is Religious." Nietzsche begins Section 45 thus: "The human soul and its limits... is the predestined hunting ground for a born psychologist and lover of the 'great hunt.' But how often he has to say to himself in despair: 'One hunter! Alas, only a single one! And look at this huge forest, this primeval forest!' And then he wishes he had a few hundred helpers and good, well-trained hounds that he could drive into the history of the human soul and round up his game" (III,45). Nietzsche knows that, like Moses and Machiavelli, he will not live to see the promised land. He cannot do the job of the new philosophy alone. He needs followers, a few hundred, maybe those future philosophers of whom he spoke a moment before. The first task for this cadre is to enquire into the history of the soul of the religious man. We soon see that Nietzsche's ultimate meaning of the phrase "das religiöse Wesen" is not "what is religious" but "the religious neurosis" (III,47). Religion, and especially Christianity, is a sickness. The progress of humanity must involve a cure. Nietzsche warmly praises the Old Testament, but gluing the New Testament to it and calling the combination "the Bible" is the "greatest audacity and sin against the spirit" that literary Europe has on its conscience" (III,52). He notes the rise of atheism. God is dead. This produces, we see, a kind of religious enthusiasm without the bother of a

God (III,53). To adapt a term from beer marketing, it is religion "lite." As a self-respecting atheist, Nietzsche finds this contemptible. The truth of Nietzsche's observation is seen in what the newspapers now, meaning some sort of compliment, call an "activist." There are no qualifications for being an activist. One appoints himself as such. With a morality engendered suddenly by popular sentiment, a morality not of principles but of "values" that lacks either a foundation in rationality or a foundation in fear of God, one has a "commitment" characterized by moral certainty. If it is not what Nietzsche had labeled "the will to power," it is at least a kind of willfulness, a willfulness that demands followers and castigates the hesitant as sinners.

There is, Nietzsche tells us, "a great ladder of religious cruelty," the three chief rungs of which are human sacrifice, particularly of one's first born, then sacrifice of one's own very nature, and finally sacrifice of God himself (III,55). It appears, however, that a new vista opens.

[W]hoever has . . . looked . . . down into the most world-denying of all possible ways of thinking – beyond good and evil and no longer . . . under the spell and delusion of morality – may just thereby, without really meaning to do so, have opened his eyes to the opposite ideal: the ideal of the most high-spirited, alive, and world-affirming human being who has not only come to terms and learned to get along with whatever was and is, but who wants to have what was and is repeated into all eternity.[29]

Entering that new ground opened to us by the new vista, "The philosopher as *we* understand him, we free spirits – as the man of the most comprehensive responsibility who has the conscience for the over-all development of man – this philosopher will make use of religions for his project of cultivation" (III,61). This is the "philosopher of the future," one who will have learned from Nietzsche, and let us notice his task: "the over-all development of man." According to the biblical text, God made man after His own image,

---

[29] Kaufmann, in a footnote here, directs us to Sections 10 and 11 of the next-to-last chapter of *Thus Spake Zarathustra*, which, he suggests, are a focal point of Nietzsche's doctrine of the "eternal return." The chapters in *Zarathustra* are not numbered. This chapter is titled "The Drunken Song," and, indeed, its text reminds one of someone who is so drunk that he has to hold on to the grass to keep from falling off the world. The doctrine of the eternal return seems to me to be reminiscent of an argument presented by "the Stranger" in Plato's *Statesman* that things have come into being, degenerated, and then recurred over and over numberless times. This argument is consistent with a general proposition held in philosophy. To appreciate that position, it is best to start with its opposite, the finitude of things in consequence of the biblical view of a specific time "when God began to" fashion the earth and all things in it. What follows from this finitude is the inevitable end of that world to be wrought by that very God. Philosophy, commonly, views the world as eternal. If it is eternal – if it has no beginning and will have no end – then it makes perfect sense to suppose that "there is nothing new under the sun," that whatever happens most likely has happened numberless times before or, as some wit has put it, "It's déjà vu all over again." As we shall see when we speak again of Hegel and Marx as we must shortly do, finitude in the Hegelian or the Marxian sense presents problems to which the only comforting answer might well be Nietzsche's doctrine of the eternal return.

but it seems that a pupil of Nietzsche must do the job over, and this time do it right. Hegel had seen that "development of man" as the consequence of the historical process, and he had seen that process as having come to an end. Nietzsche sees that change as the forthcoming consequence of the creative act of the new philosopher, an act of supreme playfulness, an act fueled by the will to power. Also, one must suppose, that remaking will by no means be the last remaking. If transpolitical religion had, as we suggested earlier, seemed to take away the reason for philosophy as the search for truth, so the new philosophy, the philosophy of the philosopher of the future, will find employment for philosophers, and it will be employment with assured employment security. The job is endless, but the work will rest not on a rea-soning regarding the needs of man but on the will of the philosopher. The philosopher, strengthened by an inner sense of his superiority, his mastery, will accept his responsibility gracefully. If in some cases this is not to be, however, some sort of sect or cult might properly develop.

If a few individuals of such noble descent are inclined through lofty spirituality to prefer a more withdrawn and contemplative life and reserve for themselves only the most subtle type of rule (over selected disciples or brothers in some order), then religion can even be used as a means for obtaining peace from the noise and exertion of *cruder* forms of government and purity from the *necessary* dirt of all politics. . . . Asceticism and puritanism are almost indispensable means for educating and ennobling a race that wishes to become master over its origins among the rabble and that works its way up toward future rule. (Ibid.)

Let us not lose our way here. The mention in the just-noted passage of "selected disciples or brothers in some order" must not allow us to drift into imagining that Nietzsche has had second thoughts and has reverted to nice, German, Protestant, Christian religiosity. God is dead. The "disciples" and the "brothers" will, indeed, be in something akin to a monastery, but their lives will not be devoted to religious piety and, as near as one can tell, not to the philosophic pursuit of the truth, either. What else can drive them but the "will to power"? If they prefer to lord it over each other rather than over "the rabble," will it not perhaps be due solely to some sort of timidity or to mere laziness? At the lowest level of analogy, Nietzsche here reminds us of the explanation Plato's Socrates gives to Glaucon and Adeimantus of the lives of the silver class in the city in speech devised there in the "Republic." In describing the community of wives and children – the "second wave" of argument – Socrates borrows the notions of "marriage" and "hymns" from the lives of ordinary people to sanctify a scheme of positive eugenics learned from the breeding of dogs and horses. Here, as we shall see, the analogy of Nietzsche with Plato trails away.

Part Four is titled "Epigrams and Interludes" and consists of Sections 63 through 185. The sections are, largely, as the part title promises, one-liners. We shall, for the sake of economy, skip all of the 123 sections.

Part Five is titled *Zur Naturgeschichte der Moral*, that is, "On the Natural History of Morals." Nietzsche opens the first section of the part by outlining what a description of morals from place to place and from time to time would be, and his approval of this mode implicitly disapproves of any effort scientifically to establish a prescription of morality. We remind ourselves that Aristotle began with descriptive and out of that developed by reasoning a prescriptive ethics. It may be with this in mind that Nietzsche says that all of the philosophers so far "wanted to supply a rational foundation for morality" (V,186). This dismissal of reason as the basis for morality is, as we have already suggested, the ground of what comes to be heralded as the fact–value distinction of twentieth-century social science, a science that aspired to but never achieved a lofty stance "beyond good and evil."

Part Six, "We Scholars," provides a keen insight into the death of philosophy. "The [scientific man's] declaration of independence, his emancipation from philosophy, is one of the more refined effects of the democratic order – or disorder." German culture had become "an elevation and divinatory subtlety of the *historical sense*. . . . [I]t may have been . . . the wretchedness of the most recent philosophy itself that most thoroughly damaged respect for philosophy and opened the gates to the instinct of the rabble. . . . Philosophy reduced to 'theory of knowledge' . . . a philosophy that never gets beyond the threshold . . . is philosophy in its last throes. . . . How could such a philosophy – *dominate*" (VI,204). Here we see that not only does Nietzsche subordinate philosophy to power, to the will to power, but the transformed philosophy, the philosophy of the future the seeds of which he plants, is a philosophy that *can* dominate and that *wishes to* dominate. This is rather a burlesque of the Platonic conception of a philosopher king who would rule only to avoid being ruled by lesser men. The Platonic philosopher is the only one fit to rule because he is the only one who despises politics. In Nietzsche's "philosopher of the future" we have finally resolved the millennia-old tension between philosophy and the *polis* by the dissolution of philosophy in the fluid of politics. That toward which Machiavelli nodded, the subjection of the wise to the powerful, is here perfected: The wise become the powerful, but they do so not reluctantly to save philosophy but because philosophy is, and always has been, truly defined as the will to power. The movement from the Platonic resolution of the tension between philosophy and politics to the Nietzschean scheme is a movement from philosophy's reluctant acceptance of rule to an altogether transformed philosophy's willful seizure of rule. Plato knew perfectly well how unrealistic the proposal for a philosopher king was. It is not clear that Nietzsche understands how unrealistic his scheme is, or that he understands that its success would gratuitously drive a stake through the heart of an already dead philosophy. Despite Nietzsche's refreshing contempt for the "rabble," "we" philosophers have become no better than those we contemn. We rule not because we are fit to rule but only to satisfy the itch to lord it over the ruled. Our guide in legislating a new vulgar morality is neither wisdom nor piety. We do it because we can and because, you know, we really want to. We do it just for the hell of it.

For an ordinary college professor to presume to be this critical of a genius such as Nietzsche must surely call to mind the effort of the Lilliputians to tie Gulliver down. Fifty years ago, William Prosser, a noted law professor, wrote a mock "Obituary" of "Grover Cleveland Boggs, first and heretofore only Dean of Suggs Hall, the Law School of Pottawatamie University." In a moment of self-reflection on my presumption in criticizing Nietzsche, I remembered that obituary. In it, Prosser pretended to struggle to find something good to say about "Dean Boggs." In one instance he wrote, "His most notable contribution to legal scholarship – if one excepts his unfavorable review of the second edition of *Wigmore on Evidence* – was the outlines he prepared for his courses."[30] We shall come momentarily to proper appreciation of Nietzsche, but first we must set down a few more lines of criticism. Nietzsche writes:

More and more it seems to me that the philosopher, being of *necessity* a man of tomorrow and the day after tomorrow, has always found himself, and *had* to find himself, in contradiction to his today: his enemy was ever the ideal of today.... By applying the knife vivisectionally to the chest of the very *virtues of their time*, they betrayed what was their own secret: to know of a new greatness of man, of a new untrodden way to his enhancement.... Every time they said: "We must get there, that way, where *you* today are least at home." (VI,212)

With apologies for my rudeness, this is poppycock. First, he intimates that all philosophers had always been what he had predicted might come along as his disciples, namely, "philosophers of the future." Second, Plato did not find himself "in contradiction to his today." He found himself in contradiction to what had always been and would always be. Third, leaving aside the anachronism of attributing some notion of an ideal to Plato, Aristotle, Cicero, al-Farabi, Maimonides, or Machiavelli, is there a scintilla of evidence that any of them sought the enhancement of man? None had ever heard of "History" as a process. None supposed that "man" was a work in progress. None, with the possible exception of Machiavelli, were politicians or sought mastery. None supposed that the many could be greatly improved. In short, none of them had heard of Rousseau, Kant, Hegel, or Marx, and all would have been disappointed to learn that these and, yes, Nietzsche himself, would be part of "their tomorrow." Finally, although they all were critical of the existing moralities, none, not even Machiavelli, longed for a political order "beyond good and evil."

Throughout *Beyond Good and Evil* Nietzsche casts sharp lances of criticism and ridicule at European, and especially German, culture and scholars of the nineteenth century. One of the focal points of this litany of dismissal is

---

[30] William L. Prosser, "Obituary," *Journal of Legal Education*, vol. 12, no. 4 (1960), p. 559.

the problem of history. A biting reference to history occurs in part seven, "Our Virtues." There Nietzsche writes:

The *historical sense* (or the capacity for quickly guessing the order of rank of the valuations according to which a people, a society, a human being has lived: the "divinatory instinct" for the relations of these valuations, for the relation of the authority of values to the authority of actual forces) – this historical sense to which we Europeans lay claim as our specialty has come to us in the wake of that enchanting and mad *semi-barbarism* into which Europe had been plunged by the democratic mingling of classes and races: only the nineteenth century knows this sense, as its sixth sense. (VII,224)

Hegel and Marx were, as we noted, principal figures in the seizure by the new conception of History of the high ground previously held by Philosophy. Allan Bloom regarded Alexandre Kojève's *Introduction to the Reading of Hegel* as the best exposition of Hegel's thought. Hegel, as we noted earlier, regarded the historical dialectic as having come to completion. History had come to an end. Kojève (1902–68), a Russian-born Frenchman, was a Marxist thinker, and Marxian doctrine held that Hegel was in error. Hegel, we must remember, had philosophy standing on its head according to Marx. Looked at through the lens of materialist-based dialectics, Marx found history not quite finished. It would be complete in that happy day to come when the whole world had been communized under the dictatorship of the proletariat and the state had subsequently withered away, or so Lenin explained Marx. For some time, Kojève followed Marx on this matter, but later in life he rethought things and came to the view that Hegel had been right all along: History had come to an end in 1806. To those of us who are not initiated into the mysteries, it is difficult to understand how anyone could say either that history is over or that history – absent divine, apocalyptic intervention – might be over at some predictable time in the future. Either way, the "end of history" presents a difficult problem for us and an especially difficult problem for Nietzsche. For us, the uninitiated, the way to understanding appears to be to grasp and accept the view of history as a process rather than seeing it either as a sequence of events or as an ordered account of that sequence. Nietzsche is attuned to this matter, so he sees the rationale for the doctrine of a culmination, an end of history. He foresees dreadful consequences, however.

The End of History

It seems that Nietzsche, being a philosopher, and therefore fixed on "tomorrow and the day after tomorrow," quite naturally finds himself in contradiction to what we may call "his today." A principal impediment put before him by his "today" is the historical sense. The problem itself may be stated as the opposition of history to life. After history ends, the sun will still rise in the East and, daily, and on time. People will still rise and retire;

be born and die; and eat, sleep, work, play, couple, and reproduce. The difference will be that History, defined as a process of the interaction of successive "world-historical" "moments," will come to an end when that process works itself out to perfect completion by reaching a preordained state of affairs. There is a Christian air of divine providence in Hegel's view of *zeitgeistes* contradicting until an ultimate, uncontradictable, *weltgeist* results. For Marx, the engine of History is rather the dialectic of class struggles. The end result, as Kojève understood it, will be a universal, homogeneous state. He considered the routes that might be taken to that end. Nietzsche had favored the consolidation of Europe into one political entity, something he thought would be a good in itself. As James Nichols explains, Kojève favored for a time the development of a "Latin Empire" of the European states and their North African colonies that together surround the Mediterranean Sea, not for its own sake, as an end in itself, but as a way station en route to the universal homogeneous state. He also reflected on the competition between the Soviet Union and the United States and, as between the two, he came to regard them as pretty much alike but saw the United States as the likely victor and also as a truer embodiment of Marxism. This view he apparently based on Henry Ford's having, early in the twentieth century, raised the wages of his employees without having been forced to do so.[31]

A striking thing about Kojève's understanding, if we consider him in his Marxian stance that history had not yet come to an end, is the view that it is the duty of philosophers to work actively for those intermediate political achievements that will facilitate the progress of history toward its destiny. Philosophers become not philosophers but political actors. Needless to say, involvement will cancel the detachment that is essential to philosophic inquiry. Philosophers become revolutionaries. Will they take sword in hand and kill? Will they, with a view to that final historical state of affairs, commit treason against their country? Several American citizens were Soviet spies – a lot of them not for pay, but for the ultimate historical good as they conceived it – for the chance to take an active part in the glorious completion of historical inevitability. Was Kojève a Soviet spy in France?[32] If, however, the happy end of the historical process is inevitable, why need one help it along?

[31] We are at a quaternary stage of analysis here which calls for caution by the reader. I am relying on James H. Nichols, *Alexandre Kojève: Wisdom at the End of History*, Lanham, MD, 2007, Rowman and Littlefield. Nichols, in turn, is explaining Kojève, who, in his turn, is interpreting Hegel. What ties this all to the present state of mind of the ordinary reader is this passage by Nichols: "The strange thesis about the end of history, while accepted by almost no one, does none the less give voice to a powerful strand in the thinking of many people for the last two centuries. One can see this point most simply by reflecting on the fact that most people believe, one way or another, in progress. They believe one historical epoch is essentially different from another, that fundamental change takes place in the world, and that historical change is overall for the better" (as cited, p. 3).
[32] For an inquiry into this possibility, *see* Nichols, *op. cit.*, Epilogue.

What led Hegel to the conclusion that history had ended in 1806 may have been the victory of Napoleon over the Prussians in the battle of Jena in that year, a victory that promised to usher in a universal acceptance of the French Revolution's doctrine of human rights. Hegel had also, in philosophical introspection, concluded that he, himself, had achieved absolute wisdom. Thus, he was the culmination of philosophy. If philosophy is understood as the *pursuit of* truth, it is no longer needed, at least not in its original guise. Nichols gives us a summary description of Kojève's shift from the Marxian view that history still needs a revolutionary push to Hegel's earlier view that history is over, that no more world-historical events will happen. Here is a portion of that summary:

[Nichols offers some] concluding reflections on this shift in Kojève's understanding regarding the meaning of the end of history. In a way, one can state the difference easily enough. For the earlier Kojève, the standard Marxist . . . stance applies: the end of history is somehow basically known but actually achieving it lies in the future as our project, our task, our goal, the success in achieving which is contingent since the human future cannot be known. For the later Kojève: Hegel was right in the first place; history ended in 1806; what happens now is the working out of details of implementation that are of less than world-historical significance. We are therefore no longer called to heroics, for instance revolutionary action with risk of life in bloody battle; philosophy (or, now, philosophy that has in the decisive respects become wisdom) no longer exhorts us to pursue a project of world-historical import, but rather shows us to see our true situation and have the wisdom to accept our fate.[33]

This very summation points to the problem of the condition of posthistorical man. Kojève, when reminded of Nietzsche's view of the end of history, attempted to offer some reassurances that all would be well. Let us go back to Nietzsche to get an understanding of the problem. In a work titled "The Use and Abuse of History," Nietzsche writes:

We do need history, but quite differently from the jaded idlers in the garden of knowledge, however grandly they may look down on our rude and picturesque requirements. In other words, we need it for life and action, not as a convenient way to avoid life and action, or to excuse a selfish life and a cowardly or base action . . . but most people will tell me that it is a perverted, unnatural, horrible, and altogether unlawful feeling to have, and that I show myself unworthy of the great historical movement which is especially strong among the German people for the last two generations.[34]

---

[33] Nichols, *op. cit.*, p. 95.

[34] "The Use and Abuse of History" is part of a collection titled *Thoughts out of Season* (p. 3). The title has also been translated "On the Advantage and Disadvantage of History for Life." These two alternative translations of the title seem equally right to me. Perhaps from habit, I prefer the translation of the text by Adrian Collins. It bears the title, "The Use and Abuse of History." It was published in a series called "The Library of Liberal Arts" which was founded by Oskar Piest, who for many years ran it as virtually a one-man publishing house. In due course the Library of Liberal Arts series was subsumed by the Bobbs-Merrill

In "The Use and Abuse of History," (1873? 1876?) rather than recruiting a few hundred disciples as he suggests in *Beyond Good and Evil* (1886), Nietzsche had envisioned a smaller group:

Suppose one should believe that no more than a hundred men, brought up in the new spirit, efficient and productive, were needed to give the deathblow to the present fashion of education in Germany; he will gather strength from the remembrance that the culture of the Renaissance was raised on the shoulders of such another band of a hundred men (p. 14).

[Having sorted history into three types, Nietzsche writes of one of those types]: Monumental history lives by false analogy; it entices the brave to rashness, and the enthusiastic to fanaticism by its tempting comparisons. Imagine this history in the hands – and the head – of a gifted egoist or an inspired scoundrel (p. 16).

He goes on to call attention to the probable consequences of this history in the hands or head of such an egoist or such a scoundrel, but we must not take this as though he means to discourage such. See what Nietzsche proposes here! If his hundred disciples infiltrate the educational system, those he has elsewhere called the "rabble" can be moved to utterly destroying the moral and political system. A new generation can be fashioned who hold the present and its antecedents in contempt and who, beyond the good and evil of their today are taught a new ethic of their tomorrow, and why not? "Every past is worth condemning . . . everything that is born is *worthy* of being destroyed" (p. 21).

Nietzsche regards the historical sense as having surfeited, drowned, and suffocated modern men. History is true. The end of history has seemingly come, but these are truths that are deadly. What matters is life. As we saw in *Beyond Good and Evil*, philosophic pursuit of truth is ill-considered. Sometimes untruth is what is needed. The claim of the scholars to objectivity is mistaken.

No, be honest at any rate! Do not pretend to the artist's strength, that is the real objectivity; do not try to be just if you are not born to that dread vocation. As if it were the task of every time to be just to everything before it! . . . Who compels you to judge? . . . Some birds are blinded that they may sing better; I do not think men sing today better than their grandfathers, though I am sure they are blinded early. But light, too clear, too sudden and dazzling, is the infamous means used to blind them. The young man is kicked through all the centuries; boys who know nothing of war, diplomacy, or commerce are considered fit to be introduced to political history. We moderns also run through art galleries and hear concerts in the same way as the young man runs through history (pp. 40, 44–45).

Company, which in turn was swallowed by the Macmillan company. Page citations herein will be to the Collins translation, which may by now have migrated to yet another publishing house.

The deadly effect of the end of history is the meaninglessness of life. Posthistorical man is the "last man." These dispirited men are treated in *Thus Spake Zarathustra* (1883–85). Zarathustra speaks thus:

What do [the people] call that which makes them proud? Education they call it; it distinguishes them from goatherds. That is why they do not like to hear the word "contempt" applied to them.... Let me speak to them of what is most contemptible: but that is the *last man*.... Alas, the time is coming when man will no longer shoot the arrow of his longing beyond man, and the string of his bow will have forgotten how to whir!... Alas, the time of the most despicable man is coming, he that is no longer able to despise himself. Behold, I show you the *last man*. "What is love? What is creation? What is longing? What is a star?" thus asks the last man, and he blinks. His race is as ineradicable as the flea-beetle; the last man lives longest.... [A]t this point [Zarathustra] was interrupted by the clamor and delight of the crowd. "Give us this last man, O Zarathustra," they shouted. "Turn us into these last men! Then we shall make you a gift of the overman!" And all the people jubilated and clucked with their tongues.[35]

The last men are truly the living dead. The rabble, the people, the many, always contemptible, have at the end of history lost any possibility of redemption. Unable any longer to despise themselves, they laugh at Zarathustra's sermon. ("Sermon" is the right word, because the whole of *Thus Spake Zarathustra* is a deliberate burlesque of scripture.) If the "last man" is the symbol of the end of history, bring it on! Who cares? We are quite content to live meaningless lives. We are quite content to let Zarathustra, Nietzsche, the philosopher, whoever, become the "overman" who will create our new values for us and who will herd us like the goats we are, as long as we are comfortable, as long as we are fed.

Let us turn to a last look at "The Use and Abuse of History":

Historical culture is really a kind of inherited grayness, and those who have borne its mark from childhood must believe instinctively in *the old age of mankind*.... Does not this paralyzing belief in a fast fading humanity cover the misunderstanding of a theological idea, inherited from the Middle Ages, that the end of the world is approaching and we are waiting anxiously for the judgment...the origin of historical culture, and of its absolutely radical antagonism to the spirit of a new time and a "modern consciousness" must itself be known by a historical process. History must solve the problem of history. Science must turn its sting against itself.... I believe there has been no dangerous turning point in the progress of German culture in this century that has not been made more dangerous by the enormous and still living influence of this Hegelian philosophy (pp. 48, 50, 51).

It is devilishly difficult to put all the pieces of Nietzsche together in one's mind and to make overall sense of the sum of it. I make no pretense of having done so. What stands out is that he has captured the essence of

35 *Thus Spake Zarathustra*, the First Part, in *The Portable Nietzsche*, New York, 1954, Viking Press, selections from Nietzsche translated by Walter Kaufmann, at pp. 128–30.

modernity, that is, of Enlightenment thought, and of its unsolved problems as it seems to crash within the nihilism proffered by the historical sense in the nineteenth century. His heirs, the postmodernists of the twentieth and the twenty-first centuries, who have dotted some i's and crossed some t's, have not furthered his thought in any substantive way or to any significant degree. It would be a treat if Nietzsche could examine those heirs for us after the manner of his examination of the German thinkers of the nineteenth century and of their historical sense. A question comes to mind: If the "rabble" are as contemptible as Nietzsche thinks, why does he expend so much energy showing his contempt? Did he want something from them that he ought to have known was not there? Plato, by contrast, never had any unrealistic expectations of the many and so did not need to lose his temper over their shortcomings. The philosophic solution of the problem of the many is as old as Plato: It lies not in the many itself but in the few. Nietzsche understands this, thus the doctrine of the overman. This still does not explain the need for such a pitch of annoyance. Why is there not present in Nietzsche that sedate acceptance of the facts of life that one finds in Plato?

10

Ancients and Moderns

In the fifteenth chapter of "The Prince," Machiavelli states unequivocally that he means to depart from the ancients who talked of "cities that never were" and to teach rather "the effectual truth." He makes it plain throughout the *Discourses on Livy* that he means to introduce "new modes and orders." In that fifteenth chapter of "The Prince," he indicates those new modes and orders by writing a burlesque of Aristotle's *Ethics*. In the *Ethics*, Aristotle taught that virtue is a mean between two extremes, one of excess and the other of defect. Machiavelli, in a way, also treats virtue as a mean, but instead of presenting several triads of which the middle in each case is a virtue, as Aristotle had done, Machiavelli's mean is an alternation between the praised thing and the blamed thing, depending on circumstances. In other words, virtue in Machiavelli's sense is knowing when to do what ordinary people call "virtuous," knowing when to do what those ordinary people call "vicious," and doing what needs to be done, no matter what those old fools in ancient times taught. This is the "more effectual truth" about politics.

As Leo Strauss put the matter, Machiavelli, like Moses, never reached the Promised Land. Certainly, however, the cadre of young men he sought followed him and succeeded in an intellectual revolution that most importantly gave us all a new moral outlook. It is almost true to say that we are all Machiavellians. Being reminded that St. Augustine had opposed those Romans who, keeping true to their devotion to the pagan gods of earlier Rome, blamed Roman Christians and Christianity itself for the weakness of Rome that allowed Alaric and the Visigoths to sack the city in 410, we note, as was mentioned earlier, that Machiavelli re-echoes the praise of pagan religion over Christianity. He must, of course, do so deviously. Again relying on Strauss, the whole of the *Discourses* seems to call Christianity to account before the wisdom of Livy, then seems to debunk Livy by the evidence of Roman history, and then, finally, seems to undercut the authority of Rome itself. He does this, however, by suggesting in "The Prince" that Christianity is an effeminate religion, what with its turn-the-other-cheek demands, and that what the Italian states needed was the manliness – the *virtù* – of the ancient Roman religion, infused as it is with satisfyingly bloody sacrifices to its gods, to fight off the incursions of the *ultramontanes*, the French in particular. This illustrates well the lesson of Chapter 15 of "The Prince" that the old morality needs to be replaced by "the more effectual truth." To see a more brazen dismissal of Roman history, however, one needs to read his play, the *Mandragola* (*The Mandrake*). Besides the portrayal of the Church, in the person of Brother Timothy, as utterly corrupt, venal, and hypocritical, Machiavelli's telling of the seduction by Callimaco Guadagno of the hitherto chaste wife, Lucrezia, is a deliberate show of contempt for the most sacred moment in Roman history, as Livy tells the story, namely the rape of Lucretia that is presented as the impetus for the overthrow of the Tarquinian tyranny and the establishment in 509 B.C. of the Roman Republic. One might as well write a play that portrays George Washington as a founding member of the Liars' Club, in a play that is a kind of "If I Did It" version of the chopping down of that blasted cherry tree.

As successful as Machiavelli's "new modes and orders" have been, either "effeminate" Christianity won out over the new definition of virtue, or Rousseau's redefinition of human nature as essentially "sentient" rather than rational, or Kant's formulation of the ethics of intention, or perhaps some other cause, aborted the seeded rebirth of the manly religion and the manly virtues that Machiavelli sought.

It was once the case – perhaps sixty or seventy years ago – that one could not get all the way through the eighth grade of a decent, public school in America without learning to recite the cardinal virtues – prudence, courage, moderation, and justice. My experience shows me that it is possible now to ask a college class of forty or more students if anyone can state the cardinal virtues and to get a blank stare from all, or perhaps a blank stare from most and a cautious recitation by one or two, who happened to be from a churchgoing family, of not the cardinal virtues, but the Christian virtues – faith, hope, and charity. For the most part, however, mentioning virtues in a college class puts everyone on guard. It sounds preachy, almost, forgive me for saying it, "judgmental."

What do we praise on campus now? Good intentions. Sensitivity. Men showing their "feminine side." Openness. Being nonjudgmental. These are pretty close to what Allan Bloom called the "softer" virtues, the "feminine" virtues, as he lamented the disappearance of interest in the manly virtues of justice, courage, and moderation. As far as sexual morality is concerned, every form of sexual activity that can be conjured up by the most fevered imagination is all right as long as it is not "unprotected." The words "protected" and "unprotected" are usually pronounced with near-churchly primness, as though one proved human excellence, near sanctity, by choosing the better of these two. The expression "have sex" is no doubt meant to be a gentler, more polite euphemism that enables us to talk easily of things of which, in polite company, we did not talk at all. Euphemism although it may be, the use of it to countenance all sorts of things that once were at least subject to questioning, makes it sound dirtier than the good, old-fashioned, Anglo-Saxon four-letter word.

Finally, one needs to mention another word, one which triggers gushing tears and hushed expressions of praise, a word describing a quality than which nothing is more praiseworthy. If one listens to the shallow talk of those who give or sell advice to those who have or seek a "relationship," one hears the word piously mouthed or sees it soberly written every day. Paid dating services promise to find for the anxious maiden (Wait! Have I lost my mind? Is there any longer any such thing?) the fulfillment of her dreams – a man who is "not afraid of commitment." Commitment is good. If you fail at it you are nonetheless praised for meaning well. It does not matter if you never think of what used to be called the "sacrament" of marriage. What matters is that if you bring a partner to bed you are committed to staying in that bed at least until the week is out. You do not have to shoulder any responsibilities. You just have to show that you mean well. Even if you marry, the hackneyed old vows grounded in scripture need not be uttered. Some time in the 1960s or 1970s a secondary actress on *The Mary Tyler Moore Show* spun off into her own television show. Some time after it began, she and a character in the show were, in the show, married. They certainly did not bother with those old vows. They wrote their own vows. How authentic! How sweet! As I remember the vows, they added up to something like "I promise to love, honor, and cherish you as long as I love, honor, and cherish you." Who could ask for anything more? In praising commitment, one forgets that the most committed man of the twentieth century was Adolf Hitler. He really wanted what he wanted and he gave every ounce of his being to the effort to get it.

Every college campus abounds in posters urging the students to "get involved." Should one not first get informed? College seems now to be less about improving one's understanding than about heightening one's zest for pursuing one's commitments, commitments that are the product less of thought than of praiseworthy sentiments. Are you "concerned" about the "environment"? Should we mount an armed offensive into the Sudan because we are "concerned" about the genocide in Darfur? Should we, in contrast, be morally outraged that we did mount a military offensive in Iraq or in Afghanistan? Which of all these things should lead us to "demonstrate"? Should we demand an end to "global warming"? Where can we best "make a difference"? These are the questions on campus. We ask why should we demonstrate but we must never ask what it is to demonstrate, what it is that we do when we "demonstrate." Do we demonstrate our "concern" or do we demonstrate our weight – that is, do we threaten force to get our way against whatever the results of democratic politics may be?

All of these slogans, these manifestations of the "bumperstickerfication" of moral and political discourse, are peripheral to – that is, they dance around – the moral and political questions that were once raised by the discussion of the virtues and the vices. We dismiss as judgmental or preachy all the old talk of virtues and vices but we preach in the most sonorous tones as of the pulpit about commitment, sensitivity, concern, and recycling. This amounts to a burlesque of Machiavelli's burlesque of Aristotle's *Ethics.* What brought us to this pass? Was it one of the things mentioned earlier – Christianity, Rousseau, or Kant? All of these things deserve to be kept in conversation, but I think we need also to consider Thomas Hobbes. Quite properly, we discussed Hobbes in the previous chapter. We need here mention only that he is the originator of the modern notion of "natural rights." He effects that origination in the course of arguing that "in the condition of mere nature" all men are equal, and then he goes on to show that the very fact of that equality makes the condition of mere nature a condition of war of every man against every man. This is, simply stated, hellish. Life in that condition is "solitary, poor, nasty, brutish, and short," and Hobbes spells out these grievous things. Where Plato had shown that wisdom must rule, Machiavelli had shown that wisdom ought to have a place in rule, and each of them had conceived of the solution as some sort of alliance of wisdom and the characteristics of the gentlemen, Hobbes, who was surely one of the most brilliant minds ever to confront political questions, does two critical things. First of all, he follows Machiavelli in severing ethics from politics in contradistinction to both Plato and Aristotle, who saw them as inseparable aspects of one science. Second, Hobbes dismisses even the gentlemen. The political community – what Hobbes calls "civil society" – is, he argues, a "contract." In other words, it is not simply natural. Aristotle, following Plato in distinguishing between "to be" and "to come into being," asserts that the *polis* simply *is* by nature, although he also explains that any given *polis* "comes to be" through the activity of someone who founds it. For Aristotle, the coming into being of a *polis* is a process of growth. First, there are lesser communities, and the first of these that is sufficient to supply everyday recurring needs is the household. Clusters of households then appear as a village, a community of kindred households. At some point, it may be that a thoughtful founder persuades two or more villages to combine so that more than ephemeral needs can be satisfied. The product of this combining is the *polis,* the highest, most complete, and most comprehensive community, the community toward which the fulfillment of what it is to be human points. Man is, by nature, a political animal. Unlike the other animals, man is that animal whose potentiality can only be realized in and through the political community. Hobbes, having invented the notion of a prepolitical "state of nature," seems to regard civil society as natural only in that man's condition in nature naturally forces him to flee nature by means of a contract – what in later writers came to be called the "social contract," that is, the contract that precedes and makes possible all other contracts.

Gentlemen are the sort who keep contracts because they are too haughty to seem to need to break their word. This is the hallmark of the nobles. They are, and they see themselves as, men of honor. Seeing themselves as such, they do not hesitate to demonstrate the self-knowledge of their superiority. That is to say, they are inclined to "lord it over" the others. Hobbes, however, asserts that such noble haughtiness is "a generosity too rare" to be counted on as the foundation of civil society. The foundation of civil society is that which assures that both the original, or social contract and all the lesser contracts, the contracts whose legitimacy is itself dependent on the greater, the original, contract are enforceable. Because the honor of the nobles is too weak (because too rare) to ensure the keeping of contracts, what is needed is a sure thing. That sure thing is fear – fear of violent death that authors the social contract and fear of severe punishment that keeps us faithful to that contract. Nobody is without that. Given our fear, each of every other, in nature, the only solution is the creation by contract of a sovereign power, a "power above us all to keep us all in awe." We live in peace in civil society because our fear of the sovereign frees us from the fear of each other. This is a large part of what Hobbes means by saying what on its face is nonsense, namely, that in nature all men are equal.

Just as it is not the case that "everyone" thought the world was flat until Columbus discovered otherwise, so it is not the case that the ancients had no inkling of human equality and that we moderns "discovered" it. The more sensible formulation is that both ancients and moderns see that men are equal in some respects and unequal in others but that the ancients regarded the inequalities as the politically decisive attributes – wisdom, courage, moderation, and justice – so we moderns have come to regard the equalities as the decisive foundations of civil society. Machiavelli had lowered the political horizon to the merely political, and this was the very foundation of modern political understanding. Hobbes completes the process by grounding civil society not in the heights of humanity but in the common denominator of human nature. As the ancients knew, courage is not the absence of fear, it is the overcoming of fear. Human excellence, achievable by only a minority, comes about through habituation to the virtues, and the chief of the virtues are virile. Hobbes invents for us the doctrine of natural rights or human rights, rights that exist not because of some legislative dispensation or because of the grace of God, but just because of our nature. As he explains in the fourth paragraph of Chapter XIV of the *Leviathan*, in the condition of mere nature "every man has a right to everything, even to one another's body." This is what makes the condition of mere nature a war of each against all and so what makes necessary a contract that brings peace in the form of an overpowering fear that liberates us from the fear of each other. Even Hobbes sees, and Locke sees also, and the Declaration of Independence reduces to the level of a battle cry, that although nearly all of the rights of nature have to be surrendered to the sovereign so that he can guarantee us peace, and so prosperity, there are some rights that it would be self-contradictory to surrender because it is to secure them that we give up all the others. These are the rights to life itself, to liberty, and to property. The right to life is the irreducible right, the very foundation of civil society. Liberty is the fence around, the necessary condition of, life. To have what is one's own – propriety, property – is the necessary condition of liberty. It is not needless to say that Locke makes plain that liberty is not the same as license. Liberty is the liberty to do what the legislative power – which is what Locke calls that which Hobbes had called the "sovereign" – allows. It is not liberty to do as one pleases, the law be damned. This is the case because if we had not surrendered all our surrenderable rights, if we had not alienated them, that is, signed them over, to the sovereign or the legislative power, governance would not have the capacity to protect us from each other, to liberate us from that condition of mere nature, which is a condition of war of every man against every man where life is solitary, poor, nasty, brutish, and short. It is almost a digression but it is needed to dot each *i* and cross each *t* of this explanation for us to say here that the silliest corruption of the modern doctrine of natural rights is the equation of the expression "unalienable rights" with the expression "natural rights." It makes no sense whatsoever to speak of unalienable rights unless to distinguish them from alienable ones. The Declaration of Independence leaves open the possibility that there might be a fourth or even a fifth right that inquiry might disclose as belonging in the list with life, liberty, and property as unalienable, but the notion that the list is infinite is the complete destruction of the modern foundation of civil society. The second most silly thing is the notion that a noble, courageous Supreme Court can discover new rights willfully left unacknowledged by the legislative power. We surrendered all of our rights, except the unalienable ones, to the legislative power to bring peace, to free us from fear. By nature, we had every imaginable right, even the right to any use we might think to make of each other's bodies. If we have a government that rests on our radical equality, then no doubt it is up to us if we want to withhold a fourth or a fifth or some more rights – to refuse, that is, to alienate them. Such additional rights are not to be understood as the gift of a kindly gaggle of judges. There are some that we could not have surrendered. It was by our judgment at the moment of contract that we might have withheld one or more others. Our safety depends on effective government, and unless at the moment of contract we withheld a right we might have surrendered, we must be supposed to have surrendered it. We cannot eat our political cake and have it. We cannot at one and the same time have the license of the condition of mere nature and with it the security of civil society. To put it another way, if we had every imaginable right, how can there be every imaginable right plus one right, or two? We may have the right to amend our Constitution to secure, perhaps at our peril, additional rights. The judicial power, however, does not include the power or the duty to act as though it could be equated with *our* power.

This drift in popular opinion away from the clear understanding of this matter by Hobbes and Locke that is also the foundation of our political order is merely illustrative of a general principle of modern political thought – drift itself. Perhaps some drift is the inevitable consequence of the inherent frailties of modern thought, but that does not mean that every whimsical change is the inevitable consequence. We had suggested earlier that there was a certain stability of ancient political philosophy. We said that except for two things – admittedly two big things, revealed, transpolitical religion and openness to the nation or the empire as the proper object, along with the *polis*, of political inquiry – the character and content of political philosophy remained constant from its inception in the person of Socrates until its overthrow in the person of Machiavelli. Modern political philosophy, on the contrary, seems to have inherent in its character and content a certain inevitability of movement, a fate to be played out in the course of time.

These last-mentioned sillinesses, the equation of "right" with "unalienable right" and the notion that an ever-so-kindly corps of judges thankfully adds some rights to an infinity of rights, are only an illustration of the proclivity of the political philosophic thought of modernity to skitter, drift, and plummet to what might even be called a "reductio ad absurdum." Despite Machiavelli's apparent wish for a tough, new religion that would stiffen the spines of statesmen, the radical egalitarianism that is the offspring of Hobbes's foundation means not necessarily a new, Machiavelli-approved religion, but at least a new, popular morality that is consistent with the moral reduction to the smallest common denominator of mankind. No longer are the virtues that require patient development and habituation in that minority of men whose finished development is the very purpose of the *polis*, even at the expense perhaps of the satisfactions of the appetites of the many, the virtues we expect and the virtues we foster. We bet on a sure thing. We look for, and as a community praise, those qualities that can easily be demanded of everyone (or, perhaps of everyone except the few with indomitable spirits who hanker after exception and even after tyrannical power), namely the soft, easy qualities to which we now attach the name we used to attach to the strong things, the virtues. We call commitment, sensitivity, and such things "virtues" whenever we dare to use that word, a word that is "so yesterday." The new, softer, fashionable virtues do not much rock the boat. The new virtues enable us to get along. Who knows? Perhaps in our quest for ever more "rights" and ever more license, we have made ourselves so agreeable that we open ourselves and the door to tyranny itself.[1]

---

[1] See Paul H. Rahe, *Soft Despotism: Democracy's Drift*, New Haven, CT, 2009, Yale University Press.

Let us finish our task by summarizing some contrasts between ancient and modern thought and between ancient and modern politics.

First, to the extent that political philosophy can be observed less from the standpoint of its cause, which may be described as the defense of philosophy from the envy and hatred of the many, and more from the object or end of political philosophy, which is the search for the best political order, it may be said that that object can be redefined as the search for natural right, for what is by the nature of things, simply right. That object, natural right, pursued by unassisted human reason, is altered somewhat by the notion of natural law, which, despite Stoic forays in early postclassical times, is largely the work of Christian thinkers. This may be one of the smaller consequences of the connection and the difference between classical and medieval philosophy, but it is certainly a difference that must be kept in mind when trying to understand either. The great change in this matter comes with Thomas Hobbes who, grounded in his straightforward egalitarian doctrine, a doctrine consequent to or identical with the individualism, materialism, and so the attendant atheism that are aspects of the lowering of the horizon of politics, introduces the doctrine of natural rights. The difference between the singular "right" and the plural "rights" is earthshaking. The change from what is by nature right to what by nature are my rights is far from being merely an incremental "evolution" of the classical natural right doctrine. It is a complete about-face. Hobbes is not just another old fogey natural law or natural right teacher. He tells us in the thirteenth paragraph of Chapter XIII of the *Leviathan* that a consequence of the condition of mere nature that he describes is that "nothing can be unjust. The notions of right and wrong, justice and injustice, have there no place." In addition to this, "[j]ustice and injustice are none of the faculties neither of the body nor mind." Nor is there any "propriety," any mine or thine, in nature. The existence of natural rights in each of us is not the proof of – but the stark denial that – there is anything in nature that is right or wrong.

Second, the ancients understood ethics and politics to be two chapters of the same book, as it were. Thus, the human consequences of moral things were the perfections of the political things. In that regard, the virtues were *for* something. The consequence of the virtues was happiness. This, however, did not mean individual, external rewards to individual human beings. The aim of man was understood to be "happiness," but happiness was understood to be a life lived in accordance with the virtues, and such a life was understood to be dependent on or identical with political life. The essence of the saying that "virtue is its own reward" is that virtue is never rewarded; it needs no reward, for to have the virtues is itself to be rewarded. Biblical religion, religion that is a consequence of Abraham's unquestioning obedience to the will of God, changes this. St. Augustine is quite critical of the pagan virtues. They are self-congratulatory. True virtue is obedience to the revealed Word of God, and the chief consequence of that obedience, held in the sight of the believer, is reward in the life to come: "pie in the sky by and by," as the Marxian ridicule puts it. Liberal, Enlightenment, or bourgeois virtue is exercised to be rewarded here and now. One is moderate not to be moderate and so to be satisfied with oneself, as Augustine would characterize it, but to have a better figure or a higher paying job. Now, for the ancients, ethics and politics are parts of the same science, in fact are the same science seen from two different perspectives. They have to be separated, or, rather, one needs to be abstracted from the other for each to be better seen. Repeatedly, in the "Republic," the *Phaedo*, and the *Phaedrus*, for example, Plato abstracts the soul from the body or the political from the economic to get a better look at the one or the other. Nobody has ever seen a disembodied soul or a political community without households, that is, politics without economics, the public without the private. Such abstraction, as we have already argued, falsifies while it focuses on the one thing abstracted from the other. Full appreciation of the thing or things studied depends on our putting them back together and getting a less clear but more comprehensive view while remembering the clearer but partial view afforded by the abstraction. The separation of ethics and politics, the supposition that each is a science standing on its own feet, is, however, a different sort of thing from the abstraction, which is a mere matter of focus. The complete cutting off of the one from the other makes possible a kind of tough-guy politics unconcerned with moral questions and, at the same time, a kind of rarified ethics that tries to examine moral questions as though they were independent of questions of political completion. The greatest exponent of such rarified ethics was Immanuel Kant, who, in his *Foundations of the Metaphysics of Morals* (1785), criticized the ancient view of ethics because it did not separate moral conduct from ends – not at all. His attempt to show in that book an ethics properly grounded – that is, grounded in itself – culminates in the notion of a "categorical imperative," an imperative that rests on nothing outside of itself: "So act such that the maxim of your action can be universalized." Thus, the essence of criminality is not simply that it breaks the law but that the criminal makes an exception of himself. The bank robber could not possibly will that everyone rob banks. He is in favor of the law against bank robbery. Only if everyone else is law-abiding is bank robbery enriching for the bank robber. Kant's severance of ethics from ends could just as well be a condemnation of Christian ethical doctrine as it is a condemnation of what he sees as classical ethical doctrine. In addition to being a figure in the Enlightenment, he is, following Rousseau, to whom he acknowledges some intellectual debt, one of the critics of the Enlightenment. In the course of arguing against what he conceives to be classical ethics, he makes an argument that would come nicely from the pen of someone who, in a genuine restoration of classical ethics, might also criticize bourgeois ethics. Kant argues that the maxim "honesty is the best policy" is false ethics, for if one is honest because it is sound policy to be honest, he is not, in fact, honest. He is politic.

So much, then, for a statement of how the view of natural right has changed and how the view of virtue has changed. Let us finally contrast general principles of ancient politics with those of modern politics. We shall have to do this twice. First, we must see all the principles of antiquity together and see how they are related then see all the principles of modernity together and see their interrelationship. Second, we shall have to list all the ancient principles in terse statements on one side of a page and oppose to them on the other side of the page terse statements of the modern principles. In this way, we can see three things.

First, we can see in our contrast how each individual element of the modern scheme is a direct and polar opposite of its counterpart in the ancient scheme. Second, we can see how the whole of the modern scheme is profoundly different from the whole of the ancient. Third, we can see in the contrast the inner consistency of each of the two sets. To do this is to justify, condone, explain, or understand the whole ancient scheme and then to justify, condone, explain, or understand the whole modern scheme. This would allow us to have an emphatic preference for either the ancient or the modern while saving us from thoughtless or narrow-minded rejection of the other. Our best guide in making a choice or perhaps in weighing the two open-mindedly is the example of Aristotle in Books Three and Four of the *Politics* where he gives us a statement of the different polities and a statement of a complete political science and he does so with gentle and empirical moderation.

To begin with, we need to remind ourselves of the underpinning of modern political philosophy and to understand that underpinning as a profound and deliberate departure from the underpinning of ancient political philosophy. The modern underpinning aims at a more practicable political order. So successful is the modern project in this regard that the order conceived is one that cannot fail to be realized. There is a subtle contrast in thought processes that helps to explain this. The ancients fully understood the superiority of speech over deed. Obviously, what one speaks of can be infinitely better than what one can establish. To understand this, we have to remind ourselves of the fact that we must never understand the spoken thing as what can be called an "ideal." Most emphatically, we must never speak of the ancients as having conjured up an "ideal state." Let us, again, work backward on this problem. The word "state" means, to begin with, status or condition. The change in usage that turns the word "state" into an ambiguity such that we now speak on the one hand of the state of a thing and on the other hand we are able to reify *the* state and speak of it as itself a thing seems to have begun in the sixteenth century. The state, or the nation-state, is a modern phenomenon. The word "state," and the equivocating expression "nation-state" are imperfect attempts to translate

the Greek word and so the Greek conception of the *polis*. The word "ideal,"
in contrast, means in the strictest sense, as an adjective as a dictionary might
define it, "of or pertaining to an idea." Reading the book we call Plato's
"Republic," we find that – even leaving aside the fact that there is no word
"state" in his language – there is no warrant for translating Plato's language
into "ideal *polis*." The closest we can come is the instance where Plato has
Socrates speak of the idea of the man and its likeness in the city.[2] This,
however, far from encouraging the expression "ideal city," "ideal state," or
even "ideal *polis*," forbids us to use such an expression. The second aspect
of the problem is that when we now speak of an "ideal" we mean something that is beyond reach but for which we should anyhow strive. There
is a passage in the "Republic" that speaks of a distant target and suggests
in such a case aiming one's arrow higher than would appear correct. It is
a mistake to read this as though the text means that we should come as
close as we can to establishing in deed a city characterized by a communism of material goods and all other things because such a communism for
the gold and silver classes is established and is absolutely established in the
city in speech talked up by Socrates and his interlocutors. A more sensible
construction would be to suggest that we see that the communism of the
city in speech is a consequence of, as well as a contributing factor to, the
justice, and especially to that kind of justice Aristotle calls "distributive justice," that is the apparent aim of the city in speech. We must remember,
however, that the first goal of the city in speech appears in what Socrates
calls the "third wave of argument." It is the unrestrained, unencumbered,
absolute rule of wisdom itself. The constant chatter we now hear of "social
justice" or of "comparable worth" warms the cockles of our hearts, but, upon
examination we see that the aim of "social justice," that is, of redistribution
of wealth, in modern times, has behind it no examination of the character
of or need for wisdom in ruling. So far is it from being based on the rule of
wisdom that it is in fact based on the envy and the prejudices of the many,
and the many are those who, as al-Farabi taught us in the tenth century,
cannot follow rational argument and so must be led by "similitudes," that
is, wholesome stories, salutary lies. Because, as is amply shown by the text,
the city in speech will never come into being in deed, the approach to a
practicable approximation of the justice sought and the rule of wisdom
sought will have to be by means altogether different from those pursued in
speech in the case of the city in speech that Socrates and his interlocutors
talk up. The "three waves of argument" through which the city in speech
is completed in speech are equality of the sexes, communism of the gold
and silver classes, and the rule of philosophers (made possible through the
enforcement of it by the silver class). The silver class, which itself exists only
in speech, is the counterpart in speech of the class of nobles or gentlemen

[2] *Republic*, Bloom translation, 369a.

that may in deed exist in actual cities. The office of the statesman is to find practicable political means that are different from the means – the crazy, impossible means – through which the city in speech reaches its ends to reach practicable ends that are a decent reflection of the ends of the city in speech. Even here it is easy for me to be misunderstood. Let me, therefore, say it again: Equality of the sexes and communism are not the *end* of that city in speech; they are means to that end. To reach a politically decent end that is practicable does not in any way suggest clutching to one's breast the means used to pursue the end of the city in speech. The clearest way to see this is to read Book Two of the *Politics* where, among other things, Aristotle poker-facedly misrepresents Plato's "Republic" and deftly debunks the whole scheme, only to make the common sense observation that ends will not be achieved by means inconsistent with them.

The clue to the ancient understanding, following the appreciation that speech is higher than deed, lies in appreciation of the ancient view of "theory and practice." The enormous gap between what one can say and what one can do is, as well as may be, bridged by the wisdom (i.e., the practical wisdom, the prudence) of the statesman and – as unpleasant as it is for us to contemplate – the selection of political leaders on the basis of their appeal to the envy and prejudices of the many is not the way to wise rule. For this reason, setting the city in speech as our "ideal goal" would be doubly in error and would be sure to achieve the opposite of our intentions, however so generous and altruistic those intentions might be.

In the place of the ancient connection between "theory and practice" we moderns have substituted the notion of "theory and application." To us, if a theory cannot be directly (i.e., without mediation) applied then the theory must be abandoned and we must go back to the drawing board. However defective this idea is, it is more so if we read it back into the understanding of the ancients. Such an anachronistic attribution divides us into two camps: those of us who are woolly-minded enough to attempt something as near as possible to the city Plato's Socrates talks up and, in contrast, those who, like thousands upon thousands of modern students (and far too many modern professors), petulantly ask, "Well, if Plato didn't *mean it*, why did he write it?" It would be better to see that Plato did mean it but that he did not mean it as we would mean it. We need to learn from the ancients what they knew so well that they did not even need to express it, namely, that speech is better than deeds. To learn this from the ancients is not to countenance the spinning of political fairy tales. It is, in fact, to enable us to protect ourselves from such fairy tales by appreciating that what can be described is not necessarily what can be effected.

What we have said on this point so far needs sharpening by making the straightforward assertion that modern political science means to be altogether practicable. Curiously, modern political scientists are probably taken less seriously by statesmen than the ancient political philosophers were by the statesmen of their day. It cannot be said, however, that it started so with modern thinkers, else it would have been the case that thinkers like Machiavelli and Hobbes would have been forgotten before they laid down their pens. In fact, Machiavelli expresses the first part of the modern dispensation when he says, as we quoted him in the two preceding chapters:

[S]ince it is my intention to write a useful thing for him who understands, it seemed to me more profitable to go behind to the effectual truth of the thing, than to the imagination thereof. And many have imagined republics and principates that have never been seen or known to be in truth.[3]

Approximately 135 years later, Hobbes completes the modern founding by setting out a doctrine that is (1) materialistic; (2) as a companion to that materialism, simply egalitarian; and (3) despite Hobbes's conclusion favoring absolute monarchy, anchored in the radical democracy that is the very face of radical equality.

It is almost surely the case that when Machiavelli speaks of those who imagined political orders he had Plato in mind but when he says that "many" have done so, it is hard to think that he excludes Aristotle from those he summarily dismisses, although Aristotle's *Politics* is far more practical and practicable than Plato's "Republic." In fact, his analysis of the political community is, as his first sentence promises, drawn directly from observation. Relying on Aristotle, we may now enumerate the principles of ancient politics.

1. The *polis* is by nature.
2. The *polis* is complete.
3. The aim of the *polis* is the good life.
4. The good *politeia* rests on the inequality of men.
5. The stability of the *polis* is grounded in friendship.
6. The viable *polis* is relatively small.
7. The best *politeia* is kingship.

1. Aristotle's assertion that the *polis* is by nature rests on his understanding, an understanding that he shares with Plato, that there is a distinction between being and coming into being. Whereas the *polis* is by nature, the coming into being of a specific *polis* is the product of a specific human act at a specific time. The *polis* is by nature – that is, natural – because man is by nature a political animal, an animal the completion or fulfillment of whose nature requires the coming into being of the *polis*. Man is such a being because he is possessed of *logos*, reasoned speech, speech that argues about the good and the bad, the noble and the base, and the just and the unjust. Many lesser animals communicate, but they do not argue. Even parrots, which imitate speech, do not speak.

---

[3] Machiavelli, "The Prince," the first paragraph of Ch. 15 (de Alvarez translation).

2. The *polis* is complete in two senses. First, it must be large enough to have that complex division of labor that enables it to satisfy all the needs of man, all the needs man has for the fulfillment of his nature. The *polis* is built on preexisting villages that, in turn, are clusters of households, but households and even villages are sufficient only for the satisfaction of daily recurring needs, mainly the needs of the body. Second, the *polis* is complete in the sense – and it is best to express this in a double negative – that there is nothing of human concern that can be said to be not of political concern, not the concern of the *polis* to resolve. The *polis* is, without exceptions or reservations, comprehensive. If we start from the individualism of the present and view the comprehensiveness of the ancient *polis*, we commit the anachronism of mistakenly calling the ancient *polis* "totalitarian."

3. The aim, end, or purpose of the *polis* is the good life. It aims not just at providing the occasion or the circumstance that allows the good life. The good *polis*, the *polis* that deserves the name, is fashioned to develop and actualize the good life. The good life is not understood as the good of the life of the body, however. The good of the body is readily achieved by the household and by the village and, surely, the coming into being of the *polis* does not negate this, but the good life sought and developed by the *polis* is life lived in accordance with the virtues. The *polis* means to habituate men to virtuous conduct and, for this reason, a critical function of the *polis* is that habituation, and so, education. Education is not about making a living, about self-expression, or about self-esteem. It is about virtue, and that includes both the moral virtues and the intellectual virtues. This enables the successful student to be a good householder and also to take part in ruling the *polis* and in being ruled in turn – in being a virtuous and law-abiding subject of the political community. For these reasons Aristotle sometimes speaks of the "good life" and sometimes of the "noble life." The good life is, in the fullest sense, the noble life, the life of true human excellence.

4. Men are unequal in their capacity to develop the virtues that, taken together, define human excellence. The sound *polis* rests on an acknowledgment of this fact and it nonetheless purposefully aims at the development of the good life. Thus, although it does not stifle or harm lesser men, it does not form itself with a view to their development or with a view to the fulfillment of their commonplace appetites. This sounds harsh to modern ears. It sounds elitist. Well, it should not be seen as harsh, but it must be recognized as elitist or we do not understand it. The good *polis* aims at the perfection of the most perfectible men, and men are, with a view to perfectibility, radically unequal. That means that the less perfectible men serve the political community in a way that contributes to the success of the *polis* in fostering the perfection of the more perfectible ones. This is difficult for us moderns to swallow, so it is difficult for us to see and to believe. It is true, however, that not everyone who is *in* the *polis* is *of* it. Not all the denizens of the city are citizens of it, for a citizen is, according to Aristotle, one who

takes part in ruling and being ruled in turn, and even we modern democrats agree that we do not really want to be ruled by men who do not have the moral and intellectual virtues. It is for this reason that we have elections rather than follow the ancient democratic principle of choice by lot.

5. Because it would not be a happy city in which the laws were obeyed only because of fear of punishment, the higher reason for law-abidingness other than the habituation of those who are citizens to morally fine conduct is mutual trust. One may go further and speak of mutual affection and concern. Mutual concern has as its prerequisite close knowledge of one's fellow citizens, the kind of knowledge that precludes even the thought of political campaigns. If the city is too large, it loses that mutual knowledge. It loses that friendship which is its natural aspect, that friendship which makes possible mutual trust and mutual care. Where people are friends and so care for each other, there is no need for a welfare state, its bureaucracy, and the coldness of both. Where the mutual concern and the friendship are gone, unity is gone. Where there is no unity there is not a genuine community.

6. Therefore, the *polis*, although big enough to provide a comprehensive division of labor, is relatively small. The larger city is no longer a true city. It is cold. The citizens are strangers to each other. Strangers do not care for each other.

7. Aristotle teaches that the truly good *politeia* is kingship. A viable kingship, in the truest sense, requires two things: the presence of one man who is so superior to all the others in the city that he is "like a god among men," and the presence of a population so tame and sensible that it submits to the absolute rule of such a superior man. Such a man is exceedingly rare and so also is such a population. If we multiply one rarity by the other the geometric consequence is an infinitesimal rarity. It is possible but unlikely. Aristotle then suggests that aristocracy is a *politeia* that is somewhat more likely to come into being but perhaps only in some fortunate places. The only other good *politeia* is, strangely enough at first, what Aristotle calls "Politeia." It is, it turns out, a mixture of two bad *politeias*, democracy and oligarchy. It is not nearly as good as aristocracy, but it is measurably better than either of the components from which it is formed. Also, it is quite possible. It is the best that one can hope for most of the time for most cities.

Now let us see the elements of the modern, democratic understanding:

1. Civil society is conventional.
2. Government is limited.
3. The ground and the end of civil society is self-preservation.
4. The politically decisive factor of human nature is equality.
5. Civil society is held together by respect for individual rights.
6. A civil society is, it appears, not limited in size.
7. A complicated democracy achieves political moderation.

1. Because the ground of everything is matter there is no distinction between being and coming into being. What is is simply what comes to be. It is evident that there is no civil society until a civil society comes to be. Thus, one cannot find the nature of man by looking for his perfection or completion. One finds the nature of man by imagining man in a condition of mere nature. Where Aristotle might have explained the nature of an acorn by calling attention to the perfected acorn, the oak, Hobbes would explain the nature of an oak by calling attention to the acorn. The nature of a thing is "back there" in its beginnings. An incident of this is that it is now more difficult to say that someone has "not turned out well." Properly speaking, man has no nature. What you see is what you get. To say otherwise is to commit the sin of being judgmental. The only way to turn out ill is to turn out judgmental. Because the condition of mere nature is a condition of war of every man against every man, life in that condition is "solitary, poor, nasty, brutish, and short." The only sense in which we can say that civil society is "natural" is by saying that nature is so harsh that we naturally ought to get out of it. One gets out of it not by completion of that which is immanent in man but simply by getting out of it. One gets out of nature by a contractual arrangement that brings civil society into being. In nature, "man has a right to everything, even to one another's body." Thus, everyone has a right to everything, but nobody has a right that can be vindicated. Nothing is, in nature, proper to man: not property, not a nature, not a proper development, not justice, nothing. The contract that ends the miserable condition of nature is the mutual rendering up to a sovereign of all one's rights except for the few the surrender of which would be inconsistent with the very reason we surrender any rights at all. It would be self-contradictory. In the words of the Declaration of Independence, to secure the few unalienable rights we alienate, we sign over all the alienable ones to the sovereign we establish. If the sovereign pleases, he can give back some rights. These are properly called "civil rights." What the sovereign gives he can take. The few natural rights that are unalienable are, according to Hobbes, life, liberty, and property. Also, the Declaration of Independence says that the possession of these rights and their unalienability are among the truths that we hold to be "self-evident" – that is, they are like axioms in geometry. They are evident in themselves. One need not because one cannot seek for something beneath or behind them from which we can by a calculation prove them. They cannot be proved. When their self-evidence is called to one's attention, he cannot deny them. They are in politics what axioms are in geometry. They are the things that you do not need to prove with anterior evidence because merely to state them is to prove them. By saying that equality and rights are among the self-evident truths, the Declaration of Independence suggests that there might be one or two more, perhaps, but just as in geometry there are only about five axioms – maybe as many as seven – so in politics there are three, or perhaps one or two

more than three. Finally, to clear up a problem that might arise, because we moderns do not mean by "happiness" what the ancients meant, namely life lived in accordance with the virtues, to speak of the "pursuit of happiness" is, it seems, nothing more than a right to pursue the material conditions of happiness as we now understand it, namely, the right to accumulate material property.

2. Civil society is incomplete. We speak of "limited government." It is limited, essentially, to the preservation of life. How you turn out is not the government's business. If someone with great human potential chooses not to bring that potential to fulfillment but to squander it in trivialities or in what, in earlier times, would be called sin, that is not the government's concern. The government does not have a right to habituate us to the virtues.

3. The most profound mark of limited government is this: It cannot aim at human excellence. The development of human excellence is a private matter. Civil society is fundamentally limited to assuring physical safety. The aim of society is the bottom line of our several aims, self-preservation. This is because:

4. All men are created equal, equal in the decisive political respects, and because men are manifestly unequal in the capacity to perfect the moral and intellectual virtues, the perfection of the human potential for moral and intellectual virtues cannot be the purpose of government for, if that were the purpose, the whole reason for being of the government would focus upon a minority, perhaps a small minority. It misunderstands Hobbes, Locke, the Declaration of Independence, or the U.S. Constitution to suppose that the equality of men of which they severally speak means that there is something wrong, unjust, obscene, or unfair in the fact that some chief executive officer of a large corporation has a great deal more wealth than, say, a college professor, a violinist, an unwed mother, or someone who is aged. Indeed, it would be easier by far to find a basis for redistribution of wealth, to speak of distributive justice, or to suggest (as the Athenian Stranger does in Plato's *Laws*) limiting the wealth of the wealthiest households to four times the wealth of the lesser households if we turn away from modern principles with their emphasis on equality and look instead to the principles of antiquity. We do not mean to suggest that there is a ghost of a chance of returning to ancient principles but only that we can best understand the Declaration of Independence by interpolating two words that are not in the text, thus: "We hold these truths to be self-evident that all men are created equal [in that] they are endowed by their creator with certain unalienable rights, among which are life, liberty, and the pursuit of happiness."

5. The connectivity of the modern, liberal democracy is an almost religious mutual respect for rights. This is true even if it happens that common reflection on rights seldom distinguishes civil rights from natural rights; or, in the case of civil rights, constitutional rights from statutory rights; or,

strangely, rights from the mere objects of appetite. We are all amateur constitutional lawyers and solemn pronouncers of moral principles – with an
emphasis on the word "amateur."

6. The fundamental aim of government is understood not to be "soul-
craft," as columnist George Will phrases it, but mere preservation, mere
protection of life, with all else (until the advent of the welfare state brought
into clear focus the comfortable preservation or bounteous life that is the
aim of civil society as Hobbes and Locke explain it) being regarded as strictly
private matters. The hallmark of modern politics is limited government.
Because that means that the whole character and demeanor of government
is thinner than the government of the ancient *polis*, it follows that it can
be spread further, much further. Medieval political philosophy, given its
interconnection with revealed religion, had already suggested that nations
and even associations of nations could be the objects of political inquiry
as well as could the *polis* itself, but it is not clear on the surface whether
that turn of philosophic attention is merely an accommodation forced on
philosophy by the advent perhaps of Christianity and certainly of Islam. The
suggestion of such a turn by al-Farabi and other Muslims differs markedly
from the Christian Augustine's talk of the "city of God." That city described
by Augustine covers the whole globe, but it is not a city characterized by
political rule. It is rather a community of service to God through fellowship
in Christ that subsists in addition to the temporal rulerships, and it tolerates
the existence of the many cities of this world despite their purposes which
are different from and even antagonistic to Christianity. Lest we drift too
far away, let us repeat with emphasis that limited government, government
limited in its ends precisely because it is grounded in equality despite the
fact that men are radically unequal in their capacity to reach the highest
ends, can be stretched over a greater territory and a greater population.
This, along with the companion principle of security of rights, means that
the intimate knowledge of and mutual concern for one's fellow citizens no
longer needs to be, indeed, no longer *can* be the connective tissue of political life. Indeed, patriotism itself comes into question and comes to be seen
as an impediment to a dreamed-of single governance of the entire human
population. What one finds in Immanuel Kant's *Perpetual Peace* in 1795
and, in its train, the League of Nations, then the United Nations, and then
the strange notion that the United Nations is some sort of a government
and can and may legislate for the whole human race is not comparable to
Dante's *De Monarchia* (about 1317 or shortly after). When Dante discusses
"world government," he means first of all the world composed of the Roman
Empire or its political ghost. The argument of *De Monarchia* is reducible to
the proposition that that world would be governed better by the emperor
than by the temporal pretensions of the pope. Hobbes taught that the life
of men in a condition of mere nature was the pure hell of war of every man
against every man and that the solution was the establishment of peace by

the creation of a sovereignty. He went on to note that the war of every state against every state would continue even after peace was established within states, and he said that the war of states was much easier to bear than the war of men. It is not at all surprising that people of intelligence infinitely inferior to the intelligence of Hobbes would attempt to solve that which he left unsolved simply by applying to states in a condition of mere nature the same solution that Hobbes had applied to men in that state. The end result is a pious wish for a single governance of the whole human race, the sort of thing anticipated by Kojève's "universal, homogeneous state." That leaves the question of perpetual peace at the level of a pious pronouncement and leaves the question of whether such a government would be good government of the whole human race in the realm of pious hope. Such hopefulness, which can be seen as one of the softer virtues discussed earlier, does not examine the question of whether the world would be able to back away from such comprehensive power if, after its coming to be, it were the vilest and most crushing tyranny in the whole history of the human race. The pious hope for world government generally puts off the question of good government until later. There remains a standoff between rational skepticism and pious hope.

7. It would not be much of an overstatement to say that every page, every word, of Plato's "Republic" and likewise every page and every word of Aristotle's *Politics*, is a comparison of the several alternative *politeias* and a concentrated effort to identify which one is best and which others rank next, and then next, and so on. Plato's resolution appears to culminate in the rule of a philosopher king, although he plainly shows the near-impossibility of such a result and he covertly intimates the possibility that democracy might be the second best solution. Aristotle, after showing that kingship is the best, grades aristocracy as second best and then shows that what he calls "Politeia" is the best *politeia* that can be hoped for for most *poleis*, that is, most cities. *Politeia* is not really a separate, identifiable regime. It is a mixture of elements of democracy and oligarchy. The remarkable thing about Hobbes and Locke is that it is not much of an oversimplification to say that each of them spends but half a page on the question of the several regimes. Hobbes does prefer absolute monarchy and Locke does prefer some sort of popular government, but for each of them the question as to which kind of government is to be desired is a secondary question. The primary question is the question of some sort of government coming into being in the place of that miserable condition of mere nature. Hobbes establishes equality as the ground of politics. His argument was so harsh and so evidently destructive of existing pieties that it waited on the more indirect rhetoric – one may say the "smooth talk" – of Locke for its success. With Locke, the principle of equality is fortified into a movement toward popular government as the only acceptable regime. The evident problem, a problem that Alexis de Tocqueville saw clearly in the middle of the nineteenth century, is that,

given the grounding in equality, the possibility of a mixed regime after the fashion of Aristotle's *politeia* – or, indeed, after the fashion of the English constitution – becomes much more problematic. How then can one hope that the government of all men might be moderate? The many are, by their nature, immoderate, fickle, and impassioned. Some substitute for the mixed regime must be found. The *Federalist Papers* answers the question by saying that in a "wholly republican republic" – that is, in a wholly unmixed regime that rests on the principle of radical equality (which, by definition, makes it plain that there is nothing to mix) – the only solution must be mechanisms, forms. The single most notable of the forms in the American Constitution is the separation of powers, but there are others. America puts its trust in the form of the Constitution rather than in the substance of human excellence. It has worked pretty well for more than two hundred years, and the founders deserve our thanks. As with climate, however, a mere two hundred years of political life means that the whole matter of the American political order must still be regarded as an experiment. Just as there can be a so-called virus in a computer that eats away its innermost parts, so equality as the greatest of the inward springs of modern politics may yet make self-destruction inevitable. Patriotism does not permit us to turn a blind eye to this matter. The continued search for the best *politeia* is not, "like, so yesterday."

Let us repeat something here. Just as there are many people, some with advanced degrees, who imagine that "everyone" thought the world was flat until Columbus proved otherwise, so there are many people, some who teach history, philosophy, or political science, who think that the poor, benighted folk of antiquity did not "know" that all men are created equal and who think that equality was "discovered" in modern times and is true and that the simple truth of it shows that the political conclusions of antiquity do not even deserve to be remembered or taught. Like many things that we "know," that is not true. As we have suggested herein, both the ancients and the moderns know that there are some aspects wherein men are equal and some wherein they are not equal. The ancients regarded the inequalities as the politically decisive aspects of human nature. We regard the equalities – which, in reality, are reducible to the single proposition that we are equal in our possession by nature of certain rights, some few of which are unalienable – as the politically decisive things. If we look again at the contrasting principles of the ancients and the moderns, we see that it is possible to list inequality and equality as the center of ancient and modern political thought, respectively. In each case, everything coheres. All the principles of the one "hang together," and all the principles of the other do likewise. Also, if it is an overstatement, it is not much of an overstatement, to say that all the principles of antiquity are consequent to inequality (and that inequality is a brute fact of human nature) and that all of the principles of modernity are consequent to equality (and that equality, properly understood, is a brute fact of nature). Let us now, in graphic form, state the old and the new principles so that we can see them next to each other.

The *polis* is by nature.	1. *Civil society is conventional.*
The *polis* is complete in two senses.	2. *Government is limited.*
The end of the *polis* is the good or noble life.	3. *The end of civil society is life, pleasant life.*
Men are unequal.	4. *Men are equal.*
Friendship enables the *polis* to cohere.	5. *Respect for rights makes society cohere.*
The *polis* is rather small.	6. *Civil society may be large.*
The mixed regime promises moderation.	7. *Separating powers, and so forth, promises moderation.*

To begin well the study of political philosophy we need to consider both of these sets of principles thoroughly and dispassionately and we need to reflect on the aims of the philosophers and the problems they confronted. We need to reflect on the nature of political philosophy so that we are not distracted by mere approximations to it. We need constantly to keep in mind the connections between theory and practice. We need to take seriously questions as to the origin of philosophy and of political philosophy. In our studies we need to be open-minded, but we must not be shallow or infirm. There is nothing that counts so much in our lives as deep and unhindered reflection on these matters. We need to read the primary books by the political philosophers themselves and the best of the commentaries on them.

In his "Fireside Chat" in March 1937, President Franklin D. Roosevelt told his radio listeners that he hoped they had read the United States Constitution recently. "Like the Bible," he said, "it ought to be read over and over again." The primary texts and the best commentaries in political philosophy are like that. Most are more subtle than the American Constitution. They need to be read with extreme care and again and again and again.

Finally, let us quote a saying current in antiquity. "Well begun, half done."

Epilogue

"A man's got to know his limitations."
　　　"Harry Callahan" in *Magnum Force* (1973)

This is a book about philosophy by a nonphilosopher addressed to non-philosophers. Whether it is possible to make such a book work is questionable. In the Prologue, I tried to explain why I was attempting to do so. That explanation is continued here by way of a somewhat less brief autobiographical sketch. Certainly I am not a philosopher and will never be one. For the past sixty years, as "Harry Callahan" admonished, I have been trying to find my limitations, to overcome them as much as may be, and to make the most of what is within them. Shortly before my sixteenth birthday, I quit school and got a job grinding spectacle lenses. I joined the Navy at the age of seventeen in late 1943 and served aboard the aircraft carrier *Intrepid* in combat in the Pacific until the end of the war. In 1948 I went back on active duty and served in a shore billet for four and a half years. In 1949 I began taking classes in off-duty hours at Los Angeles City College. I soon realized that I had found my calling, but the beginning of the Korean War delayed the pursuit of it.

In three years of part-time study at Los Angeles City College, I took courses in psychology, sociology, anthropology, and history, but no courses in political science. I began to question my initial acceptance of the social sciences when, in one of my psychology classes, the professor confidently asserted that philosophy would no longer be necessary because "scientific" psychology had taken its place. Over time those doubts have multiplied. In the meantime, I figured out that I wanted to study political science.

By the time I was ready to leave the Navy, my wife and I had had our first child, so I knew I would have to go to a university in a big city where I would be sure to find work to support the three of us. New York and Chicago were the two big cities that first came to mind. I wrote to Columbia University in New York and to the University of Chicago. Columbia sent me a form to fill out and a catalog. Carl Wennerstrom, in the University of Chicago admissions office, himself a student in the university's Divinity School, sent me a three-page letter that answered all my questions and told me that, because I was older than twenty-five and a veteran, I could skip the bachelor's degree and apply for admission to the university's "Three Year Master's Program." I applied, and Chicago sent to Los Angeles City College an eleven-hour general education examination that the university had itself devised. It took City College two days to administer the test to me. It was a difficult test. I passed it and entered graduate school in political science with two and a half years of high school and one and a half years of college and without ever having seen the inside of a political science book. While traveling to Chicago (by way of San Juan), I encountered a University of Chicago professor who asked me what field within political science interested me. I answered, "Political philosophy." "Then," he said, "you will want to study under Leo Strauss." I had never heard of him. In 1955, having finished the required course work for the master's degree and having determined to continue in academic life, I began to study with Leo Strauss. Over the next six quarters I took seven courses under him.

Some people have no luck. Some can go through sixteen or even more years of schooling and never have a memorable teacher. I was lucky. I had several, including a sixth-grade English teacher, Mrs. Geffken; a tenth-grade geometry teacher, Mrs. Middendorf; an undergraduate psychology professor named Patterson; and a civil procedure professor, Benjamin Kaplan, during the year I was a fellow at Harvard Law School. They were all inspiring and excellent, as were Herman Finer, Herman Pritchett, and Leonard D. White at Chicago. Leo Strauss outshone all of them put together. He had the keenest mind and was the most meticulous scholar of anyone I have ever encountered and, with little help from the rest of the profession, made great strides in rescuing political philosophy, and even philosophy as a whole, from the desuetude into which it had fallen. Moreover, he was a compelling classroom teacher. There was not a shred of pomposity or of obscurantism. He saw his job to be making as intelligible as possible the greatest minds in history so that they, the greatest teachers, had direct access to our minds. Although I was never one of his best, I was from the first his devoted student.

After twelve years of teaching, which included positions at Santa Clara University and the University of Washington, I accepted a tenured position in a Canadian university. Giving up that tenure after four years, I tried my hand at some other things, and, in 1981, just as I was finishing another two years of active duty with the Navy, I got out of the blue a call from Georgetown University inviting me to spend a year there as a visiting professor. I gladly accepted, and the year stretched into four. I thanked in the Acknowledgments heading this book, and thank here once more, the three professors at Georgetown who made those four years the most satisfying in my career as a teacher. Thanking them here cannot adequately indicate their unfailing hospitality and their provision of sound counsel.

I taught at Georgetown a section of the undergraduate course Elements of Political Theory. Over the four years there I taught it several times. I had a great many excellent students, and all had sound backgrounds in customary patterns of schooling. I came to appreciate that many who enjoyed that advantage were only a little better prepared than I had been. Perhaps the greatest failing they displayed was the fancy that once having been assigned a text it could be dismissed on the grounds that "I've already had that." Although I had published books and articles in the fields of constitutional law and political theory, I had never attempted a textbook. I began to see a need for something in addition to the primary texts and the first-rate commentaries that a student who, either from the zero base whence I had begun or from the mistaken notion that once-over-lightly counted, might find helpful in coming to or back to the primary texts with an open mind. During the twenty-five years since my stay at Georgetown, years during which I have continued to teach and write, the thought of this book came back to me constantly, and at last I could no longer put it off.

For the past fifty years I have been making up for the lack of a sound, liberal education. I am still far from caught up. One does not make oneself out of whole cloth into a "gentleman" in the older sense of that word and, anyhow, the democratic imperatives of our times disallow the aristocratic notion of "gentleman." Perhaps I have become a fair to middling second-class brain (as al-Farabi would put it). This book is addressed to kindred souls. It may or may not have turned out well. Even if it has succeeded in its aims, it cannot pretend to be a substitute for a good teacher in a genuine liberal arts program in a university that remembers its mission – a rare enough thing at any time, as Hobbes has shown, and a thing in peril in the present day.

If this book has found its way with you, you will want to go on to the "big leagues." When such a quest is begun it is like falling in love. Love never lets go. This means that you will not want to go on to a school because it has a winning football team or because *Newsweek* magazine says it is at the top of its list. If you want to study political philosophy, it is possible that you will want not a philosophy department, as many of them are now constituted, but a political science department, and then only one of the fairly small minority of political science departments that take political philosophy, in its original sense, seriously. If you find a place that has one excellent teacher you are in clover. If you find a place with two such excellent teachers you will have found a home in the intellectual counterpart of the Garden of Eden. Fine teachers sometimes retire, sometimes move to a more congenial intellectual environment, and sometimes are so inconsiderate as to die. If I mentioned six or seven good places, what I would say might be true this year but false the next. Make some provisional guesses. Go online and find likely universities, then study the syllabi for political philosophy courses that can sometimes be found there and make a nuisance of yourself: Ask everyone you know whose judgment you respect to advise you and talk things through with you.

Be warned: Great teachers are not plentiful. There are some, but you have to know how to find them so that you can learn from them. Maybe this book will help you to stop short and rethink your school and course choices. Maybe if you have found a good teacher, this book will help you to be taught. In either case, it will have done its job and I will have done mine.

We began with my defining political philosophy as the "free and radical pursuit by unassisted human reason of the truth about political things." As I drew close to finishing this book, I was falling asleep one night and a thought began to cross my mind. You may recognize what comes next as an experience that you, yourself, have had. The completion of my thought came to me in a dream. It is this: Standing by my original definition of political philosophy, I nonetheless saw an alternative, although incomplete, way to express it. Political philosophy is not so much a basket full of demonstrations as it is a long, subtle, surprising, never-ending dialogue, a dialogue with others and, sometimes with oneself, that brings one ever closer to the truth. When this pursuit truly takes hold of you, nothing else will seem a likely alternative. As I said, it is a little like falling in love.

Index